P9-APO-489

real estate investment by objective

judith creedy
norbert f. wall

real estate investment by objective

mcgraw-hill book company

new york   st. louis   san francisco   auckland   bogotá   düsseldorf
johannesburg   london   madrid   mexico   montreal   new delhi
panama   paris   são paulo   singapore   sydney   tokyo   toronto

Library of Congress Cataloging in Publication Data

Creedy, Judith.
Real estate investment by objective.

Includes index.
1. Real estate investment. I. Wall, Norbert F., joint
author. II. Title.
HD1375.C663   332.6′324   79-14085
ISBN 0-07-013495-2

Copyright © 1979 by Judith Creedy and Norbert F. Wall. All
rights reserved. Printed in the United States of America. No part
of this publication may be reproduced, stored in a retrieval
system, or transmitted, in any form or by any means, electronic,
mechanical, photocopying, recording, or otherwise, without the
prior written permission of the publisher.

1 2 3 4 5 6 7 8 9 0   BPBP   7 8 6 5 4 3 2 1 0 9

The editor for this book was W. Hodson Mogan, the designer was
Elliot Epstein, and the production supervisor was Sally Fliess. It
was set in Electra by Offset Composition Services.

Printed and bound by The Book Press.

TO
ESTELLE VIRGINIA WILBERT
AND
PETER F. McINERNEY

JAC

TO
MY WIFE
AND
MOTHER AND DAD

NFW

contents

Preface   xv

Introduction: Why Consider an Investment in Real Estate?   1

SECTION ONE: THE WHICH

1   Which Kind of Investor Am I?   13

The Dozen Parameters of an Investment Profile, 17
Income, 17
Net Worth, 19
Level of Liquidity, 21
Sensitivity to Loss, 22
Capital Available, 23
Security, 24
Risk/Yield Requirement, 26
Term, 29
Participation, 31
Experience, 32
Management Role, 33
Control, 34

2   Which Goals of Mine Can Real Estate Investment Satisfy?   43

Objective: Income, 49

Objective: Tax Shelter, 58
Interest, 58
Depreciation, 59
Capital Gains, 62

Objective: Capital Turnover, 64

Objective: Capital Appreciation, 68

Changing Objectives, 83

3   Which Kind of Real Estate Can Best Satisfy My Goals?   87

Residential, 97
Size, 97
Lease Provisions, 100

Quality and Durability of Income, 101
Location, 102
Management Requirements, 102
Financing, 103
Liquidity, 103

Retail, 104

Size, 104
Lease Provisions, 105
Quality and Durability of Income, 105
Location, 106
Management Requirements, 106
Financing, 107
Liquidity, 107

Office, 107

Size, 108
Lease Provisions, 108
Quality and Durability of Income, 108
Location, 108
Management Requirements, 109
Financing, 110
Liquidity, 110

Industrial, 110

Size, 110
Lease Provisions, 111
Quality and Durability of Income, 111
Location, 111
Management Requirements, 112
Financing, 112
Liquidity, 113

Land, 113

Size, 114
Lease Provisions, 114
Quality and Durability of Income, 115
Location, 115
Management Requirements, 116
Financing, 116
Liquidity, 116

Special Purpose Real Estate, 116

Size, 117
Lease Provisions, 117
Quality and Durability of Income, 117
Location, 117
Management Requirements, 118
Financing, 118
Liquidity, 118

4   Which Ownership Vehicle Can Best Serve My Goals?   **121**

Sole Proprietorship, 122

Partnership, 124

Corporation, 129

5   Which Advisors Will I Need?   **135**

Accountant, 140

Appraiser, 141

Architect and Engineer, 143

Broker, 143

Insurance Broker, 145

Lawyer, 145

SECTION TWO: THE WHAT

6   What Is Real Estate?   **153**

Trends, 153

Principles, 163
Supply and Demand, 164
Substitution, 172
Change, 175
Conformity, 176
Highest and Best Use, 177
Future Benefits, 182

The Bundle of Rights, 183

7   What Makes Real Estate Investment Different?   **191**

Case Study I: Employment Center Moves In, 199

Case Study II: Retail Chain Goes Bankrupt, 203

Case Study III: Highway Realignment Opens Real
                Estate Opportunities, 205

8   What Is Value? What Is Price?   **211**

Market Value, 211

Price, 214

The Appraiser's Approaches to Value, 218
The Cost Approach, 218
The Income Approach, 221
The Market Data Approach, 228

9 What fuels Real Estate?   **231**

The Delights of Leverage, 231

The Lender's Position, 234

Loan Terms, 246
Downpayment, 247
Constant, 248

The Danger of Leverage, 255

Kinds of financing, 257
Balloon, 257
Interest-Only, 258
Purchase Money, 258
Juniors, 260
Wraparound, 262
Leasehold, 264

SECTION THREE: THE HOW

10 How Are Buyers or Tenants Captured?   **273**

Layering of Objectives: Investment versus Use, 273

Owner-Occupiers, 275

Mixed Motives, 278

Tenants, 283

Developing a User Profile, 284

11 How Is a Market Analyzed?   **287**

Activity Identification, 288
Market Area Delineation, 291
Demographic Description, 293
Demand Analysis, 296
Supply Analysis, 297

Residential, 299

Retail, 302

12 How Is financial feasibility Established?   **309**

Apartment Building Analysis, 312
Property Description, 312
Market Analysis Summary, 312
Leases, 312
Income Analysis, 314
Vacancy and Collection Losses, 314

Expense Analysis, 314
Net Income, 315
Capitalization Rate Development, 317
Value of Property, 318
Debt Service, 318
Cash Flow, 318
Real Estate Taxable Income or Loss, 318

Shopping Center Analysis, 320
Property Description, 320
Market Analysis Summary, 320
Leases, 321
Income Analysis, 323
Vacancy and Collection Losses, 323
Expense Analysis, 325
Net Income, 325
Capitalization Rate Development, 326
Value of Property, 330
Debt Service, 330
Cash Flow, 331
Real Estate Taxable Income or Loss, 331

13 How Are Leases Developed?   **339**
Date of Lease and Parties, 344
Description of Property, 344
Construction, 345
Alterations, Additions and Improvements, 345
Term, 346
Rent, 348
Recordkeeping, 350
Options, 350
Assignments and Subletting, 351
Type of Business, 352
Use of Premises, 353
Utilities, 353
Insurance, 354
Maintenance and Repairs, 354
Signs, 355
Association, 356
Eminent Domain, 357
Destruction of Property, 357
Notice, 357
Access, 358
Subordination, 358
Remedies for Default, 358
Surrender, 359
Security Deposit, 359
Miscellaneous, 359

14 How Do I Put It All Together?   363

Real Estate Terminology   373

Appendix: Examples of Selected Depreciation Methods   391

Index   395

list of tables, illustrations and worksheets

TABLES

1   Key Investment Comparisons, 7

2   Effects of a Change in Expense Level, 53

3   Effects of a Change in Tenant Credit, 82

4   Effects of Different Purchase Prices, 217

5   Effects of Leverage, 233

6   Application of a Constant, 250

7   Variable: Downpayment, 252

8   Variable: Interest Rate, 253

9   Variable: Term of Loan, 254

10   Reverse Leverage, 256

11   A Second Mortgage Loan versus Refinancing, 261

12   A Wraparound Comparison, 264

13   Level Constant Payment Plans, 269

ILLUSTRATIONS

1   Giant Johns-Manville Firm Moving to Denver, 199

2   Work Begins on $43 Million J-M 'Quarters, 200

3   Fleeing Cities, a Company Finds Suburbs Encroaching, 200

4   Grant Will Close Nine WNY Stores, 203

5   Gautieri Buys Former Grant Store, 204

6   **Fight down the Road to Improve Illinois 53,** 205

7   **Shopping Center Planned,** 208

8   **Note,** 238

9   **Mortgage,** 242

WORKSHEETS

1   **Cash Flow Statement,** 18

2   **Net Worth Statement,** 20

3   **The Dozen Parameters of a Conservative Profile,** 38

4   **The Dozen Parameters of a Venturous Profile,** 39

5   **The Dozen Parameters of a Moderate Profile,** 40

6   **The Dozen Parameters of Your Investment Profile,** 41

7   **Objective Selection,** 85

8   **Selection of Real Estate Type,** 119

9   **Ownership Choices,** 132

10 **Advisors,** 148

11 **Apartment Building Income Analysis,** 313

12 **Apartment Building Expense Analysis,** 315

13 **Apartment Building Pro Forma Analysis,** 316

14 **Shopping Center Income Analysis,** 324

15 **Shopping Center Expense Analysis,** 326

16 **Shopping Center Pro Forma Analysis,** 327

17 **Income Analysis,** 334

18 **Expense Analysis,** 335

19 **Pro Forma Analysis,** 336

preface

Just as an investment in real estate is unique, so too is this book. It has been constructed as a series of building blocks with you as the foundation, so that you can gain control of the process of investing in real estate. Where you now find yourself both financially and psychologically will determine your objectives. Your understanding of your personal objectives will then enable you to design a strategy to obtain what you most want. Any investment strategy which is not designed to meet your objectives will not serve you well.

We recognize that you do not have expertise in the field of real estate investment or you would not be likely to buy this book. But you do have the interest to pick it up: That is the essential. It will be your interest which fuels your gains in knowledge and provides you with the power to apply yourself. If you have never invested in real estate, you can use your interest to effect an entry. If you have already started, you can use your interest to widen your investment horizons.

While successful real estate investment is difficult, we can testify that it is not impossible. It does not take genius. It does take interest (which you are at this moment exhibiting), knowledge, perseverance and creativity. This book will attempt to capitalize on your interest, increase your knowledge and structure what you learn in a way that will be most immediately useful to you. It will also help you to reap the many rewards of perseverance and creativity.

We do not pretend that real estate investment is easy. It is much like a sedimentary rock, a cementing of complex pieces and separate fragments. The rock that results forms a whole. It is only when the rock is formed that we can see whether it would be most suitable to leave it where it is or use it in a garden or a roadbed.

In the same way, this book brings together the elements of real estate investment to form a coherent whole. Each chapter builds on the previous chapters. Only after you have read all the chapters will you be able to determine the shape of real estate and make your decisions regarding it.

Learning sequentially as real estate investing is presented in this book parallels the way a professional investor in real estate actually operates. The real estate investor who is successful is the one who can put the elements into the proper sequence. Real estate investment works by examining what you want to accomplish first, collecting the necessary information second, finding a property and analyzing it third, acquiring it or a better one fourth, and operating the property acquired to your advantage fifth.

Real estate investment is emphatically not for everyone. People who want to make a million dollars in a few minutes should look elsewhere. The only people who get rich quick in real estate are those who write the get-rich-quick books.

Real estate investment is the best way we know to create and protect wealth. But it does not reward those who will not take the trouble to match their objectives with a particular real estate investment that can best help them meet their goals. It is also not for people who allow the prospect of what may seem like a great sum of money and number of tax write-offs to overwhelm their judgement. Moreover, real estate is not generally for people who prefer in-and-out trading or who wake up every morning wanting to plunge into a new activity.

To help you determine whether real estate is for you, the book has been organized into three sections. Section I involves the decisions you must make before you can start investing in real estate. The five chapters in Section I will help you define yourself as an investor, choose your primary objective, select a type of real estate that best meets your objective and that most interests you, decide upon a legal structure that might best meet your needs, and determine how many and what kind of advisors you will want to involve in order to pursue an investment in real estate.

Section II presents the general information you need to know in order to understand the world in which a real estate investment operates. This section includes discussions of what real estate really is and the distinctive mode of thinking that is required for real estate investment, a mode of thinking which can be built on your interest. A major concern will be the difference between price and value, which will be developed so that you can utilize your understanding of both for profit. This section will also explore how real estate financing works.

Section III will focus on the process of investing in a particular property. It describes the selection process step by step: (1) reaching an understanding of the motives of the buyers or tenants who will provide you with the sale price or income you seek; (2) identifying a market, analyzing it, and using the information developed from a market analysis to select a property to investigate and (3) establishing a property's ability to satisfy your financial objective. In addition, a chapter will focus on what can be a major determinant of financial success, lease development.

The last chapter in Section III will cover ways to acquire a property with little or no capital. It will also include a discussion of how to safeguard yourself against impulses which can cause you to forfeit your goal.

Once you have reached that point in the book, you will have simulated the exact steps an experienced investor in real estate takes and in the sequence which makes the process work. It takes knowledge and experience to move from the freshman team to becoming a professional in any activity. We are attempting here to provide the basic knowledge you must have. We have attempted to relate our real estate experience to you in order to give you a broad foundation upon which you can build your own experience.

That is another reason why you will have to read the entire book to benefit from it. The professional in real estate understands the entire process and thus knows the different ways in which he or she can profit from it. At each point in the process there are different opportunities for profit.

Each building block in this book will elevate you to a new view. Each new elevation will increase your understanding of the relationships among what has gone before and what will come after until the real estate investment process forms a coherent whole for you.

Moreover, each new view that you command may cause you to

re-evaluate previous decisions you have tentatively made along the way. After all, you may not see the hill you want to climb until you reach the third, ninth, or even twelfth course of building blocks. For that reason, we suggest that you review your decisions when you reach the end of the book to take into account your elevation in knowledge of and exposure to real estate experiences.

Some of the terms you encounter in this book may be unfamiliar to you even if you have already invested in real estate. We will define them as we go. But we are also including after the text a comprehensive glossary for your continued use. Real estate investment, like any specialized field, has its own jargon and kinds of expertise. An ability to understand and use its special terms will both enlarge your opportunities and increase your chances of achieving your objectives.

acknowledgements

The world of employment being what it has been, a woman of my age has not, of course, had mentors. I have, however, been blessed with editors and colleagues whom I hold in great respect and with whom it has been a singular pleasure to work. I would especially like to single out Gerard C. Ekedal, Stanley Ferguson, Alena Wels and the late Arthur Krahmer of The Journal of Commerce, Marshall Loeb of Time Magazine, and Kiril Sokoloff of McGraw-Hill. I am delighted to have this opportunity to thank them warmly for their generous support. In addition, I could not have written this book or survived its gestation period without the wise counsel and sustaining vision of Lynn Eyerman.

Judith Creedy

It is extremely difficult to ponder the contribution of the many people who have contributed to my experience in real estate over the years. Although many of my peers are not named, I wish to acknowledge their contribution in helping build my store of knowledge.

One of the people who encouraged my growth in my formative years is John W. Kleinke, Senior Vice President of Talman Federal Savings and Loan Association. James C. Downs, former Chairman of the Board of Real Estate Research Corporation, a subsidiary of the First National Bank of Chicago, was one of my most influential mentors and I owe a great deal of thanks to him for his direction and patience. Of special importance to me in my professional development was Harold F. Yegge, former Vice President of Real Estate Research Corporation.

To all the other people who have assisted me in my career and who have enabled me to write this book, I say "Thank you."

Norbert F. Wall

Special thanks go to Paul S. Kempner of The Kempner Corporation of New York City for his patience in reviewing the manuscript. We also want very much to thank John A. Creedy, Marion Weil, Mildred Lenhardt and Maura Fitzgerald for their generous support services. Laura Jerabek deserves special thanks for her excellent preparation of the manuscript.

Judith Creedy
Norbert F. Wall

Real estate is a unique investment for a diversity of reasons. It can supplement or replace your other sources of income. It now offers more tax shelter opportunities than any other investment. Making a change in it can create value where little or none was evident before. And real estate's capital appreciation potential is excellent. But these agents of the creation of wealth form only a part of real estate's enduring appeal to investors.

Real estate has proved to be the best protection against inflation yet devised. Properly selected, real estate positively thrives on inflation for three reasons: First, as a tangible asset, its value increases as a direct result of inflation. Thus, the value of your investment rises to keep you at least even in purchasing power and often ahead as the demand for tangible assets increases in tandem with inflation.

Second, unlike other tangible assets, real estate investments can produce income and most frequently are structured to do so. You have unusual opportunities to maintain purchasing power through a variety of protections, such as the level of tenant quality you choose and different lease safeguards.

Third, a real estate investment is usually financed through a long-term mortgage loan. In the debtor role, the property pays back the mortgage principal with fixed, cheaper dollars. The longer inflation continues or the greater its rate, the cheaper the dollars paid back. If you were an investor in bonds or money market instruments, you would be in the creditor position and thus be paid back in cheaper dollars. Moreover, you can, as part of a strategy in real estate, increase the supply of dollars you receive from your tenants at the same time cheaper dollars are paid back to a lender. With fixed-income investments, you do not have the same protection.

But, today it is not sufficient for an investment to be an excellent inflation hedge. An investment strategy must encompass deflationary periods as well. Properly selected real estate is also unusual in its ability to resist deflation. It can accomplish this in part because it has intrinsic utility.

Beyond that, real estate is often a primary necessity. It may form one angle of survival's triangle: Food, clothing and shelter. In actuality, all three are real estate. The basis of food is the real estate upon which it is grown. Cotton and wool are produced from the land, as are the petrochemical products which make up much of our clothing today. The places where food and clothing are purchased are also real estate. As a result, real estate frequently adjusts as flexibly to deflation as it does to inflation.

Real estate is unique in yet another way. Alert investors, who have chosen and structured their real estate investments carefully, most often have plenty of time to react profitably to economic, social, technological and financial change. Certainly, there are none of the sudden, violent swings in value too often seen on the ticker tapes or at auction houses. But, all these benefits pale beside the ultimate singularity of investments in real estate.

Real estate's true distinction, and to many investors its greatest appeal, lies in the kinds and amount of control an investor can establish. You can create and maintain value in real estate investment to a far greater degree than you could with investments of other kinds. You can build a property, change its use, renew it, switch tenants, manage it, maintain it, increase or revalue its income, decrease the expense ratio and obtain better financing for it. The choices you or your working partners make regarding these opportunities to affect the value of your real estate investment will enable you to control in considerable measure the outcome of your investment.

A real estate investment is unique because it is amenable to individual control. It is essentially an individualistic activity. It contrasts with investments where, as an individual investor, you cannot establish direct control over a rise or fall in investment value.

Financial investments certainly offer no such control. As an investor in financial instruments, you might undertake to purchase a General Motors car, boost your consumption of grains and pork bellies (in the form of bacon) or take out a personal loan. Such actions, however, so indirectly affect the value of a GM share, commodity futures contract, an interest-sensitive bond or a money market instrument that individual control cannot be said to exist.

In real estate, you or your working partner can stimulate demand through all the actions we listed above as well as through advertising and adjustments in leases. There is a whole host of actions you can take to maintain and even increase the value of your investment. Something as simple as a change in the color of paint on the exterior of an apartment building can make all the difference.

Unlike the case in real estate, you can do nothing to affect the level or timing of income from non-real estate income-producing investments, such as those that provide dividends or interest payments. Dividend amounts are typically fixed for long periods of time or raised by the management of the company issuing the stock in response to the company's performance and the broad economic conditions in which it operates. Your actions as an individual investor do not affect the dividend rate or its timing. If you can personally affect a stock's value and/or its income, you are probably forbidden to profit therefrom by virtue of your corporate position and the insider rules of the Securities and Exchange Commission.

Interest payments on bonds and money market instruments are fixed. The rate on a particular investment is set not by your individual activity but by broad market conditions. Completely out of your personal control are interest rates, foreign exchange rates, oil prices, resource availability, overall business and consumer confidence, and other aspects of the national or world economy which can daily buffet the financial markets. In contrast, you can take many actions to affect not only the amount of income you receive from a real estate investment but also its timing.

Non-real estate tangible investments do not offer you control either. The value of gold fluctuates between fears of inflation and deflation, art with current fashions and so on. Even worse, the value of some of the tangible assets in which you might invest is set by virtual monopolies far from any influence you can exert. For example, diamonds are largely controlled by De Beers.

Your unique ability to control an investment in real estate to a greater degree than you can any other investment can give you an unexpected benefit. While this is an intangible reward, there is great personal satisfaction in being able to point with pride to real estate in which you have invested. Something about its degree of permanence and its quality of being real and productive as a result of your involvement causes an intense pleasure. Without sentimentality, making a property work financially and usefully is a profound source of joy. The more the property is a result of your ideas and work, the more such satisfaction can reward you.

Other investments permit only limited activity. Typically, you can investigate them and decide to buy, hold or sell. Even these actions may be turned over to analysts; stock, bond or art brokers; or personal financial advisors as may suit your investment needs.

Real estate offers the opportunity, for those investors who want it, of much more active participation, including the chance to collect a fee for management of the property. And if you choose to be a passive investor in real estate, one who contributes capital to make the property work, you can profit from your active partner's many opportunities to affect value positively, structure tax shelter beneficially and change the property's income stream or other features to reward you.

However, we do not mean to suggest, as too many others have done, that real estate investment is a universal panacea. No investment is perfect and any statement to the contrary is both unrealistic and insulting to your intelligence. Certain trade-offs are required to obtain the multiple rewards of a real estate investment.

Certainly, an improvement suffers from wear and tear. Its tendency to deteriorate over time will require you or an active partner to care for it under a regular maintenance program. Otherwise, repair expenses will rise unnecessarily, thereby cutting into income. Poor maintenance will also cause value to decrease.

Other trade-offs involve liquidity, a potentially longer term and higher carrying charges. A direct real estate investment's relative degree of illiquidity stems primarily from the local nature of the real estate market. Real estate, in most cases, can not be transported elsewhere. That lack of portability cuts into the potential market, but it can be a blessing in disguise, as it insulates each local market from short-term national and international fiscal and monetary upheavals.

Except for the very largest and highest quality projects in real estate, there is no national market. No centralized exchange exists as it does for financial investments or for some other tangible assets, such as art which is sold at auction.

The market for financial instruments is obviously the deepest and broadest. Financial instruments are the easiest to own. There is a more limited number of people who can, and should, invest in real estate, as it is not suitable for everyone. This also serves to limit the market. But the market for real estate is by no means as shallow as the market for non-real estate tangible investments. Furthermore, there is much you, as an individual investor, can do to affect the quality of your investment in real estate and, thus, its relative liquidity.

Even the highest quality real estate investment tends to take more time to dispose of than does a financial instrument. Even assuming a buyer is immediately found for your investment, negotiations and certain legal requirements for transfer, such as a title search and contract drafting, will consume some time, typically several weeks. Of course, there are investments in real estate which are highly liquid, such as certain partnership interests and the stock of real estate–related companies.

Carrying charges are higher. On undeveloped property, holding expenses include property taxes, insurance and interest on any mortgage debt. As there is usually no or inadequate income to cover these expenses, the selling price and the time frame involved for sale of an undeveloped property must be calculated so as to compensate you adequately for the carrying costs incurred.

On improved property, expenses typically increase. Taxes, insurance and interest are included, as are charges to cover maintenance and repairs, water and sewer service, utilities, heat and employees, if any. But improved property generates an income stream which should be designed to cover the higher expenses and give you a profit in addition.

The costs of acquiring and selling real estate also tend to be higher. In addition to commissions, legal, accounting, inspection and valuation fees are frequently required. Choosing to change a property from one state to another is likely to involve additional fees for professional help as well as capital costs to accomplish the change. To make it simpler to compare different kinds of investments, this and the other important investment considerations have been summarized in Table 1.

Useful as a summary of key investment considerations can be, a decision to invest in real estate does not rest solely on information like that in Table 1. It must be based on your needs and desires and your understanding of how real estate can meet them.

We have designed this book to help you make a decision to invest or expand your present investment in real estate. If, after acquiring a feel for what is involved, you decide to undertake a real estate investment program, our book can then assist you further. It will help you identify your kind of real estate, the best legal structure for you, what advisors you will need and what you need to know about real estate in general. It will also help you select and analyze a particular property.

You will benefit from our book mainly because it will enable you to base your decisions solidly on your own needs and desires, not on abstractions. It is the ultimate fit between yourself and a particular investment that is most conducive to successful investing.

TABLE 1
Key Investment Comparisons

	Financial Investments*	Non-Real Estate Tangible Investments†	Real Estate
1. Income Potential	Fixed dividends on stock, fixed interest from bonds and money market instruments.	None.	Rental income which can be adjusted to meet your needs.
2. Capital Appreciation Potential	Yes for stocks and commodity futures; no for bonds and money market instruments if held to maturity, yes if traded.	Yes.	Yes. In addition to appreciation from inflation, you can create value through your own actions.
3. Tax Shelter	Limited to capital gain shift; also possibility for interest deduction if debt involved (except for municipal bond involvement).	Limited to capital gain shift; interest if debt involved.	Capital gain shift; interest *and* depreciation.
4. Inflation Hedge	Paper investments: Less likely to maintain purchasing power than tangibles; interest and dividend income fixed; in creditor position as bond or money	Tangibles, so value tends to increase; however, no income; can take debtor position.	Tangible so value tends to increase with inflation; income can be adjusted to maintain purchasing power; debtor position.

TABLE 1 (Continued)
Key Investment Comparisons

	Financial Investments*	Non-Real Estate Tangible Investments†	Real Estate
	market instrument holder; can also assume debtor position, except for municipals.		
5. Deflation Hedge	No intrinsic utility, not necessities. Those in creditor position may collect more valuable dollars; those in debtor position less likely to be able to adjust debt as seizure of asset involves little effort.	Utility but not necessities; debt less likely to be adjusted as seizure of property by creditor involves little effort.	Intrinsic utility and often necessity; income and expenses may be adjusted; debt potentially adjustable as creditors not in good position to run property after seizure.
6. Sources of Investment Value	Largely external to individual investor; influenced by national and international economic developments.	Largely external to individual investor; influenced by national and international developments; in some cases, controlled by monopoly.	To some degree result of actions external to individual investor; to greater degree result of individual investor's actions.
7. Opportunities for Control of Value	Decisions to buy, hold or sell.	Decisions to buy, hold or sell.	Decisions to buy, hold or sell; to change through re-

8. Reaction Time Available	Frequently short; as result, control may pass to broker, fund manager or trader within broad guidelines.	Somewhat longer but may be very short, particularly if monopoly is involved.	Longer, as real estate is relatively well insulated from short-term economic gyrations; there is also more an investor can do to react to all changes.	newal, building, refinancing, use, operations management. Requirement for active control can be fulfilled by you or through your active partner.
9. Depth and Breadth of Market (Liquidity 1)	Deepest and broadest.	Shallowest.	Moderate; depends on local market conditions and quality and size of investment.	
10. Disposition Time Frame (Liquidity 2)	Shortest.	Short or long, depends on market.	Longest, depends on market and legal transfer requirements.	
11. Care of Property Required	Storage of paper in personal safe, bank or broker's office; bookkeeping.	Storage or other protection for gold, art, stamps, etc.; deterioration over time of antiques, art, cars, etc. requires maintenance, also insurance.	Deterioration over time requires maintenance program to keep value up; also insurance.	

TABLE 1 (Continued)
Key Investment Comparisons

	Financial Investments*	Non-Real Estate Tangible Investments†	Real Estate
12. Carrying Costs	None unless there is a fund manager's fee or a bookkeeping charge; interest if debt involved.	Storage and insurance fees; interest if debt involved.	Minimum of taxes, insurance and interest; if improved property, also operating expenses; legal and accounting fees.
13. Acquisition/Disposition Costs	Commission costs for execution of trades; possible fees to financial and tax advisors.	Commissions and possible fees to financial and tax advisors; possible fees for expert inspection.	Commissions, legal, accounting and inspection fees, title search fees.

*Financial investments include stocks, bonds, money market instruments, commodity futures contracts.
†Non-real estate tangible investments include art, gold, stamps, antique furniture, etc.

section one: the which

Consideration of your individual traits, capabilities and desires is the essential starting point for developing a successful real estate investment strategy. You must be the pivot. Without you squarely in the center, any investment you undertake is likely to be seriously flawed. Certainly, it will be unnecessarily hazardous.

Developing a successful strategy requires taking stock of yourself as a potential or actual investor in real estate. What you learn about yourself will make it possible for you to discard in advance investment alternatives which are unsuitable or unrealistic. This process of evaluation and elimination will enable you to find real estate investments with characteristics and capabilities that mesh well with yours and thereby can assist you in achieving your objectives.

Knowing what you want and what you can get is the key to any investment strategy. Investors who know what they are doing and why, in regard to both themselves and the property in which they invest, greatly enhance their chances for success.

There are an even dozen investment parameters that will delineate your own investor's profile:

1. Level of income from sources other than real estate investment

2. Net worth level

3. Level of liquidity

4. Sensitivity to loss

5. Capital available

6. Need for security

7. Risk/yield preference

8. Term preference

9. Participation

10. Experience

11. Management role

12. Control

These dozen, when combined with your choice of investment objective in Chapter 2, will form the base for your subsequent investment choices.

Each of the parameters ranges along a continuous and changing spectrum, as indeed do the choices available in the next four chapters. Thus, the choices within each parameter are relative. You may have a great deal of experience you can apply to your first investment or you may have very little. You may consider that you have a high level of net worth or a moderate or low level. How you rank yourself will depend on how you perceive your position in relation to what you choose to accomplish at first. As you continue to invest, your position may change in order to reflect such things as changes in income, net worth and experience, but again in relation to where you then are heading.

In some cases, you may discover that your preference or requirement is so overwhelmingly high or low that you can not yet describe yourself as an investor. For example, your need for security may be so high that it is an absolute. If you will not accept any degree of risk, then you have discovered that you are not properly an investor.

All investments, including real estate, involve degrees of security and risk, from the most secure such as short-term United States government securities, to the most risky, the gambler's table. Your discovery of an absolute need for security may occur despite the fact that not investing also involves a risk, the risk of continual erosion of capital as a result of the operation of inflation.

As another example, you may discover that your level of personal liquidity is nil. In that case, perhaps you should wait to invest in real estate until you develop some liquidity. Investments in real property, by their very nature, tend to be somewhat less able to generate instant liquidity for an investor than some other investments can. However, you may decide, based on your relative lack of liquidity, to invest in those real estate investments which can be liquidated quickly, such as the stocks of companies in businesses related to real estate.

The ranges of choice relate to what makes you feel personally most comfortable. It is much like establishing how much money will carry you comfortably through the day. Some people, as was apparently the case with a famous Congressman who later became President, do just fine with five dollars in their pockets. Others are uneasy unless they tote a packed wallet, bulging with cash and credit cards to cover every possible contingency.

But there is another consideration. None of the choices exists in a vacuum. External factors will require modifications of your decisions. For example, carrying only five dollars would limit you to small purchases. It would certainly prevent you from undertaking a long trip requiring the purchase of an airline ticket or payment for transportation to and from the airport.

Similarly, a choice of yield might be unrealistic if the investor fails to consider what is available in the market place. If your choice of yield were extremely high, it is likely to limit you to investing in properties of the most marginal safety. Properties may not even exist which produce that high a yield.

Just as your preferences and requirements do not operate in a vacuum, neither do they operate completely in isolation from one another. For example, the choice of an extremely high yield may prevent you from realizing other aspects of your investor profile, such as a moderate desire for security.

Some relationships among the parameters are more obvious than others, such as the correlation of participation, experience, management and control. The more you actively participate, the more experience you gain and the more effectively you can manage your investment. The more you manage, the more you will be able to control the events which ensue. These four parameters form a definite learning curve, which starts with participation in order to gain experience and the ability to manage. Then, the additional capabilities you gain will enable you to control your investment program.

Similarly, the amount of income you make, your net worth, liquidity level and sensitivity to capital loss are all linked to the capital sum you can make available for investment. Your need for security and your risk/yield requirement are partially a function of the previous parameters. But they are also connected to the time frame in which you prefer to operate.

A more subtle relationship is based on the difference between desire and ability. You may have the ability to undertake a particular task, such as bookkeeping or repairs to a property, but you may not have the desire. Conversely, you may want to manage some aspect of the investment, such as leasing, but not yet have the ability to match your desire. Again, you may now have a certain degree of liquidity, but desire more. Fortunately, real estate investments are flexible enough to accommodate an extremely wide spectrum of desires and abilities.

As you can see, it will not be sufficient to fix your current position within these parameters. You must constantly attend to where you presently are and where you want to be in the future. Not only will the act of investing itself cause relative changes within each parameter, such as a potential increase in your net worth or income. But, more important, your knowledge of the direction you want to take over time can serve to bring together your desires and your abilities. You will then see more clearly the strategy you must follow if you are to increase or change your capabilities to achieve your desires.

Moreover, the direction in which you desire to move will bear most heavily upon subsequent choices you make, such as the objective for which you aim, the type of property in which you invest, how you structure ownership, and even the kind and quality of advisors you will need.

As we discuss the dozen parameters, keep in mind what choice along the spectrum best describes you now and how you would like to describe yourself five or ten years hence. At the end of the chapter, you will find several worksheets. Some are already filled in as samples. One, however, has been left blank so that you may construct your own real estate investment self-portrait. We have attempted, in the following discussion, to break out the 12 parameters in as critical a path as possible to facilitate your choices.

THE DOZEN PARAMETERS OF AN INVESTMENT PROFILE

1. Income If you are not already familiar with personal financial analysis, you may need some forms with which to work and perhaps consultation with an accountant or a financial planner. We have included some forms for you to fill out to make the job easier. For example, the best instrument you can use to establish how much income you have to spend and invest after you meet your obligations is a cash flow statement, such as the one illustrated in Worksheet 1.

Such a statement involves dividing your expected sources of income for this year and for each of the next five years or more into fixed and variable categories. You can then match up your fixed expenses with your fixed income. For example, your mortgage payments should be correlated with your most reliable sources of income, as the payments themselves are fixed. You should perhaps consider all expenses which strongly determine the standard of living you prefer as fixed, even if such expenses are partially discretionary. Your variable income, such as bonuses, can then be matched against those expenses you consider luxuries you could easily forego.

Once you have completed a cash flow statement, your next step is to determine the relationship between your income and your standard of living. If there is no gap between your present income and the standard of living you have adopted or desire to adopt, then you could rank your income as more than adequate or high. Conversely, if there is a wide gap between your present income and the lifestyle you want to achieve, you would rank your income as inadequate or low. If your income is adequate in relation to your desired lifestyle, your choice on the worksheet at the end of the chapter would be moderate.

Looking ahead perhaps five or ten years, you should estimate the standard of living you want to achieve or maintain at that point. If it is the same as your present lifestyle and you estimate that your income will grow sufficiently to maintain it, you would characterize the income level desired with the choice of same. However, you may want to achieve a higher standard of living and you may not expect your present sources of income to allow you to fulfill that

WORKSHEET 1
Cash Flow Statement

	Fixed	Variable	

INCOME:

1. Earned:
   Salary _____ _____
   Commissions _____ _____
   Other sources of
   income such as
   director's fees,
   freelance activities _____ _____

2. Investment:
   Interest _____ _____
   Dividends _____ _____
   Capital gains _____ _____

3. Other: _____ _____

   Total: _____ + _____ = _____

EXPENSES:

1. Household:
   Mortgage loans _____ _____
   Property taxes _____ _____
   Insurance _____ _____
   Utilities _____ _____
   Maintenance _____ _____
   Repairs _____ _____
   Other _____ _____

2. Personal:
   Food _____ _____
   Clothing _____ _____
   Medical and dental _____ _____
   Non-property insurance _____ _____
   Sundries _____ _____
   Entertainment _____ _____
   Other _____ _____

3. Education:
   Children   _____   _____
   Self   _____   _____

4. Transportation: _____   _____

5. Other taxes:
   Local   _____   _____
   State   _____   _____
   Federal   _____   _____

6. Investments:
   Storage   _____   _____
   Management fees   _____   _____
   Insurance   _____   _____
   Debt service   _____   _____
   Advisors' fees   _____   _____
   Other   _____   _____

7. Other expenses: _____   _____
   Total: _____ + _____ = _____
   Coverage ratio of fixed income to fixed expenses: _____

---

desire. Then you would jot down next to your present level-of-income ranking a desire to achieve more income.

2. Net Worth At the same time, you should create a net worth statement to establish the status of your wealth. A statement such as that in Worksheet 2 lists the value of all your assets, such as your home, stocks, bonds, cars, personal property and insurance, whatever you own. After subtracting your liabilities, perhaps the mortgage balance outstanding on your home, car payments not yet made, margin debt and so forth, your net worth in dollar terms can be determined.

For the purposes of Worksheet 6 at the end of this chapter, you

WORKSHEET 2
Net Worth Statement

ASSETS:

    CASH:
        Savings accounts $ _____
        Checking accounts   _____
        On hand   _____

    SECURITIES (Market Value):
        Governments   _____
        Publicly traded corporate stock   _____
        Publicly traded corporate bonds   _____
        Mutual fund shares   _____
        Privately held stock or bonds   _____
        Stock options (less exercise cost)   _____

    LIFE INSURANCE (Face Value):
        Individual   _____
        Group   _____

    REAL ESTATE OWNED (Market Value):
        Primary residence   _____
        Vacation home   _____
        Investment   _____

    RETIREMENT INTERESTS:
        Profit sharing   _____
        Vested pension contributions   _____
        Pension and profit-sharing death benefits   _____

    DEFERRED COMPENSATION   _____

    PERSONAL PROPERTY   _____

    OTHER ASSETS   _____

                                  Total Assets: $ _____

LIABILITIES:
Mortgage debt $ _____
Notes to banks   _____
Notes to others   _____
Debt owed to brokers   _____
Debt owed to insurance companies   _____
Taxes owed   _____
Charge accounts payable   _____
Contingent liabilities   _____
Other liabilities   _____

Total Liabilities: $ _____

NET WORTH (Assets less Liabilities): $ _____

have a high net worth level if the excess of assets over liabilities is what you perceive as large. You have a low net worth level if you consider the excess small; in between and you would rank yourself at the moderate level.

In addition to helping you make the next series of choices in Chapter 2, your net worth statement will enable you to see how any investment you undertake will affect your net worth or wealth. And, by looking ahead five or ten or more years, you can estimate how much growth in net worth you want to accomplish. Jot down next to your current net worth rank what you want to achieve in the future.

3. Level of Liquidity It is not enough to evaluate only your income and net worth. You should also analyze both to see how liquid your assets are. That will help you determine how well you can handle financial emergencies. If an emergency occurs, will you have to raise cash quickly? And can you?

This question is especially relevant when you are considering a real estate investment. Even the best of real estate investments generally takes a few months to sell in order to raise cash. The lag is due largely to the mostly local nature of the real estate market and the size of capital that is sometimes, but, as we will show, by no means always, required.

Unless you invest in real estate through the stock market or you have the right to cash in a limited partnership interest quickly, you will find that a real estate investment is most unlikely to meet a potential need for instant cash. Even if you were to slash the price of a direct "brick and mortar" investment sharply in order to attract a buyer more quickly, you would still have to satisfy all the legal requirements for transfer of ownership. These requirements generally take a few weeks to accomplish.

As a result, you will, in most cases, have to look to your other assets to give you sufficient liquidity, particularly to how well you are insured against major risks. After examining your financial position carefully, you may find that you consider yourself well able to cope with financial emergencies. That would match a high personal liquidity level. If you have some resources immediately available, you probably fit into the moderate column of Worksheet 6. If you would find it hard to raise cash quickly in an emergency, you have a rather low liquidity level.

An extremely low level of liquidity may dictate either building it up before you start investing or choosing to invest only in ways that will give you a fair measure of liquidity. You should also consider where you want to be in terms of liquidity in the future and jot that down next to your current ranking.

4. Sensitivity to Loss   Another aspect of your financial condition is your sensitivity to investment loss. How much can you afford to lose before your lifestyle is threatened? No one advocates that you invest with money needed to put food on the table or a television set in each bedroom if that is the lifestyle you prefer. Nor is anyone advocating investing all the money you need to provide for protection against financial emergencies.

You should, however, consider how long it is likely to take you to replace any money you might invest. If it would take you a long time to amass an amount of capital with equivalent purchasing power, you might want to reconsider the level of risk you are willing to bear. In other words, you might have to settle for a lower level of risk than you would choose if the money involved were more readily replaceable.

But the final measure is primarily psychological. You may determine how sensitive to loss you are by imagining what would happen to your income, net worth or lifestyle if you lost your investment capital.

If you are fairly comfortable with the possibility of loss, then your sensitivity to loss is relatively low and the risks you are willing to take may be correspondingly high. If you react very negatively to the idea of losing money, your sensitivity to loss is relatively high. An in-between reaction would be moderate.

In noting where you want to be in the future in regard to this parameter, it may also prove useful to imagine how you might feel about not achieving your objective and instead having to reduce your income and net worth estimates for your five year planning horizon. Investors tend to become more sensitive to loss over time, particularly as assets grow, but this is not always the case. For example, some millionaires positively like to gamble, while others take the opposite tack.

5. Capital Available   At this point, do not worry about the properties a particular sum of capital will command. Real estate investments range in size from a single ten dollar stock purchase to multimillion dollar equities. In some cases, no capital at all is required. In any case, we definitely advocate starting small in order to gain experience. In that way, you increase the likelihood of success with larger projects because you can rely on your own firmly based knowledge.

Instead of concentrating on what a particular sum will allow you to accomplish, take your cash flow analysis and determine how much excess income, if any, you have left after meeting the expenses most directly related to your standard of living. If you want to build up additional cash liquidity, you might subtract an amount for savings. The remaining sum is what you could make available for investment.

As we have indicated, how much is enough is a purely relative question. An investment amount on the order of 10 to 20 percent of your gross income would come to $3,000 to $6,000 if your gross income were $30,000. The same percentages would produce $10,000 to $20,000 if the gross income involved were $100,000. Certainly, $3,000 would be enough to enable you to participate in many publicly offered limited partnerships as well as in real estate stocks; it would even provide the downpayment for a small home that may have been foreclosed upon.

If the amount you determine you can use for investments is relatively large, perhaps $25,000 or more, rank yourself as high in capital on Worksheet 6. If the sum is relatively small, perhaps $5,000 or under, rank it as rather low. If it is in between, it may fit the moderate ranking best. You should also indicate next to the rank you have chosen the capital sum you would like to make available in the future.

How much you have to invest affects to some extent the risks you may be willing to undertake, but it is not as direct a relationship as you may think at first glance. Thus, if you have a small amount to invest, you may choose a high risk in an attempt to make your capital grow faster. On the other hand, you may be a fairly conservative investor and therefore prefer to conserve the small amount of capital you have by choosing a less risky investment.

Investors whose capital grows to greater size or is already at a high level seem to have a tendency to become more interested in safety and risk reduction over time, or a preservation-of-wealth objective. Alternative strategies to achieve that objective might indicate the purchase of a series of smaller properties for diversification or a larger property than the one with which an individual investor started.

However, it is not always that straightforward. You may find that you want to take advantage of a higher potential yield on one property involving somewhat more risk, while at the same time you protect the bulk of your capital by investing in properties that are considerably less risky.

6. Security   Your level of financial security obviously affects your need for security. If you have achieved a comfortable level of income relative to the financial demands of your chosen lifestyle and a high level of net worth and liquidity, you may feel relatively secure in terms of your financial position. That relative security may mean you want most to protect your wealth or it could mean you can afford, both financially and psychologically, to take more risks.

On the other hand, if you have yet to achieve that level of financial security or if inflation and financial emergencies continue to interrupt your financial progress, you may feel relatively insecure financially. That could mean you prefer to play it safe, taking very few risks. Alternatively, it could mean you would like to make more risky investments with the potential of achieving a sudden jump in financial security.

Your personal make-up is likely to be the deciding factor. Particularly important may be how you have reacted to experiences to which you or your family have been exposed.

Thus, your most vivid memories may be of the Great Depression, which often capriciously destroyed lives and financial standings. You may have been much affected by financial reverses suffered more recently by your own family or by others you know. You may feel that lifestyles and values are changing today in ways that make it harder for you to protect your own lifestyle from a steady or sudden decline.

If you find, upon examination, that you worry a lot about how you are going to protect your family, your lifestyle and your position in the community, your need for security is relatively high. This may be true regardless of your current financial position. Fortunately, the level of protection you can achieve through investing in real estate remains high. The same forces are operating today which have caused properly selected properties to hold and increase in value relative to other investments in the past.

At the other end of the spectrum, you may feel a relatively low personal need for security. You and your family may not have gone through bad times or you may be confident that you can make it back in even better shape if you get knocked down. Perhaps you have already suffered a body blow and promptly landed back on your feet. You may feel that most things in life rest squarely on your personal ability to create or recognize an opportunity for financial progress. Using your own capabilities to take advantage of an opportunity may provide you with a sufficient sense of security. Certain real estate investments are unusual among investments in that they offer you exceptional opportunities to apply your capabilities to the creation of value.

You may fit neither of these descriptions. You may have responsibilities you worry about meeting as well as the feeling that you can meet most of them through your own personal actions. You may want to provide security for yourself or your family without picturing yourself as either conservative or adventurous, descriptions implied by the intensities at either end of this parameter's spectrum.

As a result, you might describe yourself as moderate in your need for security, perhaps with a bias more toward one end of the spectrum than the other. That would give you a greater number of potential real estate investment opportunities. You have not placed as many limits on your choices as have those selecting the outer limits of the spectrum.

7. Risk/Yield Requirement If one side of a coin represents the need for security, the other denotes your willingness to undertake risks and the level of reward that will induce you to take a certain risk. All investment risks, including those in real estate, are considered in comparative terms. Each real estate investment is at least potentially comparable through its yield to every alternative investment in the market place.

Investors, who make up the markets, rate risks from low to high in the following order:*

> United States government securities, backed by the full faith and credit of the federal government (in reality by the United States government's ability to create money if the worst were to come to pass)

---

* This order is, of course, subject to changes in market judgement.

Corporate bonds, backed by a corporation's assets

Municipal bonds, backed by a municipality's taxing authority

Common stock, backed by the market's assessment of a corporation's value

Moral obligation bonds, backed only by the willingness of a legislature to pay off in the event of trouble

A personal loan made to an individual with a poor capability of meeting the payments

This by no means exhausts the list of investment possibilities. But it is clear that risks are rated by the market in terms of the credit or backing available to the investment. The investor's question is: How will I get paid back the amount I invested plus a profit on the loan I have made of my capital, or, to put it in exact terms, how will I get a return of and on my capital?

The answer lies in the credit of the user of your investment, whether it is the credit of a company issuing bonds or the credit of a tenant on a lease. The more secure the credit involved, the less risk there is and thus the lower the yield requirement. And the reverse, of course, is also true: The less secure the credit, the higher the yield an investor would require as compensation for the greater risk to his or her capital.

Yield is a function not only of risk but also a function of the liquidity of the investment, its management or supervision requirements and its size. Yield requirements tend to rise if an investment is relatively less liquid and requires relatively more supervision or work than others. Yield requirements fall if the converse is true. Yield requirements also rise as the size of the investment increases. The number of people who can afford an investment diminishes as the size grows.

Thus, investments in real property, which tend to take somewhat longer to sell than paper investments and which, in real estate, require more supervision, tend to command somewhat higher yields than do other comparably secure investments of the same size. However, investments in real estate can be structured to provide more liquidity and involve less management through such devices as net leases and some limited partnership interests, as we will discuss in Chapters 2 and 4.

Two kinds of security are provided by real estate. One involves the credit of a tenant who pays for the use or loan of a space. The higher the likelihood that the tenant will meet the rent payment, the lower the risk the landlord faces.

The other security lies in the property itself. The property can come back to you at the end of its use by others or be sold, depending on your objective. The better the opportunities for reuse or sale, the less overall return may be required during a lease itself. If you are investing for long-term appreciation, this aspect may appeal to you. In addition, of course, the property itself may appreciate in value, which would increase your capital.

Other considerations can change the usual relationship of secure credit—low risk—low yield and its opposite. A determination of the yield required also involves the term of the investment. A loan for three months is theoretically less risky than one for 20 years. Less that could be detrimental to your capital is considered likely to happen in three months than might occur over 20 years. For example, interest rates are not likely to change as much in three months as they might change repeatedly over a 20-year period. Also, a property is not likely to deteriorate as much physically, economically or functionally in three months as it might over a long time period.

However, time is inextricably linked to considerations of credit. Thus, a three-month lease to an unstable poor credit tenant would be considered more risky than a 20-year lease to a top credit like IBM. Most real estate investments, those where the investment is directly in the physical property itself, involve a somewhat longer term than other investments. But, the yield requirement depends both on the credit involved and the term over which it will be involved. Thus, the yield is not necessarily always higher on a longer term than on a shorter term investment.

Properties undergoing change to a new state deserve special mention. Where development is taking place, such as the improvement of undeveloped land or a change in zoning or the renovation of an older building, risks are higher than they are for established properties. Neither the ultimate credit nor the term is yet known for sure in most cases. Liquidity is generally poor until the change is completed and potential purchasers know better what they are getting. Management requirements are high and demanding because change is involved. As a result, the yields required to induce an investor to invest are naturally high.

Right now, we are concerned with the level of risk you are willing to undertake. There is generally an inverse relationship between the security you need and the degree of risk you are willing to assume. For example, if your need is for secure investments that are as solidly contained against adverse occurrences as is humanly possible, your willingness to undertake risk and the yield you can expect are both relatively low. On the other hand, you may like the idea of investing in potentialities for a higher risk/reward ratio. Finally, you may feel most comfortable with a moderate risk and its concomitant moderate yield: One not quite so low as that of an investor who needs more security nor quite as high as that of a venturous investor.

You should also take a look at what you want to achieve financially in the future. If you are starting with relatively small financial resources and your goal is relatively high, you may have to make a choice. You could reach that goal by increasing the amount of risk you are willing to take now. Then, if you reach a certain financial level, you may no longer need high risks and high yields and can thus reduce them. Or, if you find higher risks unacceptable, you may have to reduce somewhat what you want to achieve financially. For the description of yourself in the future, you should note what kind of risk/yield level you expect to find acceptable then.

8. Term The time period over which you want to invest is also an important consideration. For example, you may want to achieve a specific goal, such as an increase in your income to a certain amount within five years, a relatively short (or low as on the worksheet) period. You may then be able to provide comfortably for your children's education. Alternatively, you may have in mind a very long time frame for investing. Perhaps you want to create wealth for your retirement or your children or grandchildren. You may also consider yourself a very impatient or patient individual, or you may fall somewhere in between.

Certainly, as we have mentioned, investing directly in real estate does tend to require somewhat longer time frames than do certain other investments. But there are ways to make short-term investments in real estate. Moreover, there can be a positive trade-off between the somewhat longer term generally required of real estate investments and your opportunities to affect risk, as we shall see in Chapter 2.

There is yet another cluster of related attributes: Participation, experience, management and control. Investing in real estate can provide unusual opportunities for involvement. Indeed, a real estate investment can become a source of intense enjoyment beyond the financial rewards sought from all investments.

At its most extreme, when you have had an idea that you think will produce a profit, and you have made the analysis, physically designed a project and built it, you are rewarded with a substantial thrill. Once you catch the real estate fever to this extent, real estate becomes part of your lifestyle. You eat it, sleep it, play it or anything which can be done in or on real estate. The personal satisfaction that comes from creating a project that works or from building or fixing a property is intense.

It is much like starting your own business, where so many of your capabilities are required. That may also be the only other investment which allows you, through a multitude of actions you can take, to maintain and create value in your investment.

Certainly, the value of other investments is largely a result of factors beyond a single investor's control, as we have mentioned. Thus, what makes a stock rise or fall, a bond's yield change, or the price of gold gyrate is largely external to the activities of any particular individual. Unless you are in a highly unusual position in our society, able to effect a change in the value of the dollar or of bank rates, your actions will not contribute to the value of the investment you hold.

Moreover, your experience can only have an impact on what to buy and when to buy or sell. Your participation is effectively limited to buying and selling. In contrast, while forces external to your actions certainly affect value in real estate, your own actions can be a major or the major force involved. We will discuss a variety of actions you can take to affect value in Chapter 2 and also in Section III of this book.

9. Participation You should determine the level of participation that makes you feel most comfortable. Here the difference between desire and ability comes most clearly into focus. For example, you may have a certain amount of capital to invest but decide that you do not want to be a full participant in that investment.

You may have experience, management capability and the ability to control an investment, but want none of it. Involvement on a day-to-day basis may not be what you enjoy. Moreover, your life may be filled with other activities which interest you more.

However, we recommend an active stance initially. The old story of the janitor illustrates why. He started out taking care of one building owned by someone else. By applying the experience and skills he acquired, he wound up owning ten buildings himself. These buildings proved to be highly profitable because he knew and understood his investments backward and forward, and from top to bottom.

Our recommendation goes hand in hand with starting small. If you start small and actively participate in your investment, you gain valuable experience. You can trade up in size and complexity most efficiently. When you reach your goal, perhaps 500 apartment units in ten years, you will be on top of the design and packaging of the investment from the most sophisticated stance achievable, that of the investor who has done it herself or himself.

Moreover, if you still want to be an active investor at that point, you will be in the perfect position to oversee the professional management needed for the larger properties. If you want to become a passive investor down the line, you will be in a superior position to select the best passive investment going. You will have been exposed to the skills necessary to conduct a proper and thorough evaluation of the investment offered you.

Your abilities, your temperament and the time you have available will, of course, determine your level of activity. We hope you will select an investment in which you are able to participate initially. In that case, you would rank yourself high in participation desired. Your rank is moderate if you want to participate in some phases but not in others. For example, you might leave leasing to a leasing agent. But, if you want to be a passive investor in all aspects except the initial investigation and decision to invest, a role we believe should not be delegated completely to others, mark yourself low in participation desired.

You should also take two further steps regarding participation. As we continue through the last three parameters and the rest of the book, mark down the specific activities in which you are interested in participating. In addition, you should also note any differences between your capabilities and what you want to participate in now or in the future. That will help you determine the real estate investing skills you most need to concentrate on developing personally. It will also help you figure out what real estate roles you will need to hire someone else to undertake.

10. Experience Stop and think about all the experiences you have already had with real estate. Think about your own home in terms of comfort and space planning. Ask yourself why certain stores attract you and others seem repellent. Consider the adequacy or inadequacy of specific office layouts you have encountered, or, if you are involved in manufacturing, take a critical view of the way a plant functions.

You are as much a consumer of real estate as anyone else. Ask yourself how you would do things differently and why. Question yourself and friends as to what makes one property desirable and another not. Consider why you would or would not rent a particular office. Think about why some locations are better than others.

If you have been making your own repairs, renovated parts of your house, added on rooms or attended to the hundred and one details that go with owning your home, you have expertise you can apply directly to any property you purchase as an investment. What you know about your community and whom you know can also be turned to good account. As we continue to discuss the skills required to put together a real estate investment, keep your eyes open for whatever expertise you have, for experience you can apply.

If you have special expertise, perhaps as a lawyer or an accountant, you have a special opportunity. You can invest more quickly through using your skills. Perhaps you could take part of your fee for handling real estate investments for others in the form of an equity interest in the property involved.

If you are already capable of taking charge of a property, from selection and analysis to operating it, rate your experience level as high. If you are a novice, rate it low. But, don't count yourself out. There are ways to invest in real estate without specific real estate investment experience. If you are experienced in some areas but not others, jot down what you can do and rate your experience level as moderate.

As you gain experience, you will also increase your knowledge and understanding of the real estate investment process. As a result, you will be able to expand your horizons and go on to tackle both roles and investments that you may not even know exist now.

11. Management Role The kind of experience you possess will affect the management role you foresee for yourself. Real estate management of existing properties consists of a rental, maintenance and financial program. You may have some experience in leasing, collecting rents, taking care of a property physically, making repairs, paying bills and preparing financial statements, or you may feel you could quickly learn on a small property.

In that case, you may decide that part of your compensation for investing should come from becoming the property's manager. Further, you may decide that you want to substitute your own time and effort for that of hired employees, or you may choose to apply your experience in managing office personnel to managing real estate employees.

A real estate manager typically collects a fee of four percent to five percent of rentals for the expertise he or she brings to running a property and for coordinating the functions involved in management. Management of a property under development tends to take much more experience and expertise in such areas as construction management and initial rent-up. Because it requires more management, the compensation is generally higher.

If you desire to and can fulfill the role of property manager, rank yourself as high in terms of the role you desire to undertake. If you can assume portions of the management role, rank yourself as moderate.

Even if you are unskilled and thus rate yourself low, it is highly unlikely that you would not be able to manage some aspect or quickly learn how. Just the process of living and working in properties will have equipped you with some capabilities that you can exploit in a real estate investment. For example, you may enjoy painting walls or organizing financial matters.

It is much more likely that you have skills employable in real estate management than that you have had experiences applicable to commodity straddles or bond funds before becoming involved as an investor. And, certainly, if and as you become more involved in management, you will be able to expand into more properties, different properties and more complex properties, as the janitor in the story did.

The less your initial management capability, however, the more careful you should be to select real estate with which you are most familiar. For example, you might acquire a single family house to rent to a tenant. If you already own your own home, you could accomplish most, if not all, of the management functions connected with that property.

Owner-managed property is almost always more productive and better maintained. Of course, once a property reaches a certain size, an individual owner will personally be able to do less and less of the management. But, generally speaking, an owner-manager has a greater natural interest in seeing to it that everything is done well. And the more productive the property and the more it is kept up, the more valuable it typically becomes.

12. Control The amount of control you can exert is an outgrowth of your participation, experience and management choices. There are various kinds of control. Thus, you have complete ownership control if you own the real estate yourself: You can acquire a property, sell it, fix it, give it away, use it in a divorce settlement or anything you like within the limits of the law, the market and any lender's requirements. You may even decide you want to control your property's surroundings by buying additional real estate adjacent to it, as Citicorp in New York and Walt Disney World in Orlando, Florida, have done in order to eliminate objectionable behavior around their operations.

If you take in partners, you lose some control. You can retain day-to-day operational control, but you may not be able to buy or sell the property without consultation and approval. Thus, management control can be separated from ownership control. If you choose to become a passive investor, your control is even more limited. It lies only in choosing the right working partner and the right property in which to invest.

The more participation you have, the more experience you can apply, and the larger the management role you can undertake, the more control you can possess. Real estate investments are highly unusual in the number of controls they allow you to establish. Moreover, an unusual amount of control over the value of your investment is possible. Besides buying and selling, you can improve the income, decrease expenses, renovate to attract certain tenants and obtain better financing. Security also comes into play here. The more you are able to control the investment, the more secure you may consider it.

If you feel capable of exerting a great deal of control and want to do so, you should indicate this on Worksheet 6 under high. If you feel you can assume little control, show this in the column headed low. Anything in between should be reflected in the column marked moderate. It is particularly important here to consider where you want to be in terms of control in the future. You may want to aim for management or ownership control. In that case, you will then be able to concentrate on those capabilities and experiences you need to develop.

In sum, investing in real estate can be distinctly different from investing in its alternatives. You can participate in more aspects; you can bring your total experience to bear on more aspects; you can manage and you can control more aspects.

You may have noticed that certain patterns developed as we

discussed the ranges within the dozen parameters. One of these can be described as a conservative profile: If it fits you, your need for security is probably high, your willingness to take risks is correspondingly low, and thus the yield you require is also fairly low. Related to this is your low willingness to absorb losses: Whatever you have, you want to keep and protect.

You also want a fairly high level of personal liquidity because you do not want to cash in assets disadvantageously. You probably tend to think in terms of the medium- to long-term: The need you feel to protect your assets is not apt to depart. You are also somewhat more likely to have a high income and net worth to protect, although you may be of a conservative bent without yet having achieved a substantial financial position. Whether you want to participate extensively, apply your experience or gain some, take on a management role, and assume control is up to you; such decisions tend to be highly individualistic.

By way of contrast, you may find that you have taken what we call a venturer's position. You assume you can make up for any losses you incur, so you are more willing to take higher risks for their higher reward when they come through. You are also more impatient. You want to see the results of what you do in a relatively short time frame. Most important to you may be opportunities to apply your experience and management expertise. Participation and control may be musts. You may want to be the doer and the activator. If you do want an active role here, you are likely to take on the developer's role.

If neither of these profiles fits you, consider the moderate position. It is largely a matter of gradations: You may be more likely than the venturer to have low to moderate experience or to want moderate to high security. Compared to the conservative, your income and net worth are not as likely to be high; or, to put it another way, there may be more you currently want to achieve financially.

The risks you are thus willing to take to get where you want to go may be a little higher than a conservative might like but a lot lower than the venturer's preference. The risk you are most comfortable with fits right in with your moderate need for security.

How you put your moderate profile together in terms of participation, experience, management and control is solely up to you in terms of your abilities and proclivities within each parameter.

For all their innate diversity, investment strategies do tend to fall into these three basic groups: Conservative, moderate and venturous. But each can and should be cut to your own measure to reflect your individuality. Your ability to shape a strategy to mirror and express many personal facets is an especially appealing aspect of investing in real estate.

Worksheets 3, 4 and 5, which follow, reflect conservative, moderate and venturous profiles, respectively. You will note that only where there is one mark next to a parameter do we consider the choice within a parameter fixed. Where there are two, for example, a moderate mark and a high or low mark, it might mean that there is a tendency toward conservatism or venturism or that such an investor has a choice. Where all three columns have marks, it indicates that the parameter is essentially variable for that particular group of investors. One investor in that group might be described best through one of the marks, another with an entirely different mark.

Worksheet 6 gives you an opportunity to fill in a current description of your own investor profile. To make clear the direction you want to take, note also what you want to achieve at a certain point in the future. For example, you may want to achieve a higher net worth level than the one you presently possess. Such a choice will have considerable impact on the alternatives you select to round out your strategy in the next four chapters. In fact, within the perimeter of what is available to an investor, the next series of choices will ultimately depend on the investor profile you now establish.

WORKSHEET 3
The Dozen Parameters of a Conservative Investment Profile

	High	Moderate	Low
1. Income From Other Sources	X	X	X
2. Net Worth Level	X	X	X
3. Liquidity Level	X	X	
4. Loss Sensitivity	X		
5. Capital Sum Available	X	X	X
6. Security Desired	X		
7. Risk/Yield Level		X	X
8. Term Horizon	X	X	X
9. Participation Desired	X	X	X
10. Experience Level	X	X	X
11. Management Role	X	X	X
12. Control Needed	X	X	X

WORKSHEET 4
The Dozen Parameters of a Venturous Investment Profile*

	High	Moderate	Low
1. Income From Other Sources	X	X	X
2. Net Worth Level	X	X	X
3. Liquidity Level	X	X	X
4. Loss Sensitivity		X	X
5. Capital Sum Available	X	X	X
6. Security Desired		X	X
7. Risk/Yield Level	X		
8. Term Horizon		X	X
9. Participation Desired	X		
10. Experience Level	X	X	
11. Management Role	X		
12. Control Needed	X		

* Active role assumed here. If investor seeks passive role, then parameters 9–12 could be low.

WORKSHEET 5
The Dozen Parameters of a Moderate Investment Profile

	High	Moderate	Low
1. Income From Other Sources		X	X
2. Net Worth Level		X	X
3. Liquidity Level	X	X	X
4. Loss Sensitivity	X	X	X
5. Capital Sum Available	X	X	X
6. Security Desired	X	X	
7. Risk/Yield Level		X	
8. Term Horizon	X	X	X
9. Participation Desired	X	X	X
10. Experience Level	X	X	X
11. Management Role	X	X	X
12. Control Needed	X	X	X

WORKSHEET 6
The Dozen Parameters of Your Investment Profile

	Current			Future
	High	Moderate	Low	(Indicate Time Frame) More/Same/Less
1. Income From Other Sources				
2. Net Worth Level				
3. Liquidity Level				
4. Loss Sensitivity				
5. Capital Sum Available				
6. Security Desired				
7. Risk/Yield Level				
8. Term Horizon				
9. Participation Desired				
10. Experience Level				
11. Management Role				
12. Control Needed				

Once you have explored the personal qualities which will have an impact on your decision to invest in real estate or make you most comfortable with certain kinds of real estate, you should examine what you want to accomplish for yourself or for your family. What is the single most important objective you want an investment in real estate to meet for you? You can select from the four basic real estate investment objectives:

1. Income   3. Capital turnover
2. Tax shelter   4. Capital appreciation

All real estate investment goals have as their basis the creation and protection of wealth. But each of the four objectives involves a different emphasis, a different method of creating and protecting wealth.

Investing in real estate is somewhat like taking a trip to New York. You have different goals and desires which can be satisfied by using different methods of transportation. Thus, if you must get to New York in just a few hours for an unexpected business meeting and you live or work at a considerable distance, you are limited to flying. Your overriding objective could be defined as getting to New York quickly.

However, if your reason for going to New York is pleasure or a combination of business and pleasure, you may decide to take several days to make the trip. If you have several days, your choices may widen to take in a train, a bus, or an automobile trip along an interstate highway or on secondary roads. If you add in your preference for enjoying the scenery along the way, you may then restrict your choices to taking a train or driving on byroads. Your preference for exploring the countryside at your leisure might then dictate the choice of driving along the secondary roads.

Just as getting to New York is the point of the trip described, so is creating and preserving wealth the point of investing in real estate. However, in order to accomplish that, you might most need to supplement the income you receive. That would limit your choice to properties that best produce income. Alternatively, your income may already put you in such a high tax bracket that you most require tax shelter to protect your income. Then, other properties might be more appropriate.

On the other hand, you may decide to increase your capital position through the process of developmental change; therefore capital turnover might be the objective for you. Or you may most desire to increase and protect your capital through a capital appreciation strategy. Your definition of an objective to reflect your personal needs and preferences should channel you into those types of real estate and specific properties within each type that can best achieve your goals.

Typically, investors in real estate move from one goal to another, usually starting with income and ending with capital appreciation. There is no reason why you can't and every reason you should change your objective as your investor profile changes. After all, when you outgrew your high school clothes, you went out and acquired a more appropriate wardrobe for the next stage in your life.

However, to be successful in real estate investment, you should select one objective, the one that best fits your present stage of life, and make it your overriding goal at any one time. As the other real estate investment objectives are interrelated, you should then rank the other goals behind the primary one you have selected. Chasing after all four objectives equally will only dissipate your energies and resources.

Your singleness of purpose will put you in the catbird seat, in control of yourself and able to take control of the process of investing in real estate. Most important, you will always have a clear-cut objective against which to measure the myriad real estate investment opportunities available, with their variegated physical, financial and legal structures.

Once a major goal is the effective reference point around which your real estate universe swings, you will find that choosing types of real estate in which to invest, deciding how to structure your purchases, and conducting analyses of specific properties will all be easier to undertake. Furthermore, you will discover that the clearer your purpose and the more defined your investor profile, the more efficiently your broker, accountant, lawyer and other advisors can serve you.

Without a primary goal, real estate investing often seems excessively confusing. Each category of real estate (residential, office, industrial, retail, land and special-purpose) and each specific property can and will send you a multiplicity of signals about the goals attainable through it. It helps to be able to separate the apples from the oranges in terms of your own interests.

For example, let us consider the acquisition of a shopping center or an apartment building. They look and feel as different as an apple's skin and an orange's rind. Each kind of improvement serves different human activities just as apples and oranges serve different nutritional needs. Each is affected differently by market forces, locational influences and financial structuring, to mention but a few factors, just as an apple grows in one climate and an orange in another.

But all these differentiating characteristics are secondary, as necessary as it will be to analyze them. The shopping center and the apartment building can both serve the primary goal of income, just as the apple and the orange are both primarily fruit. Their income streams, however, are as different as the taste of an apple and the taste of an orange. Thus, the important question becomes which income stream is most compatible with your goal ranking and your investor profile.

When you understand the four goals of real estate investment, you can sort through all the varieties of opportunities more quickly. From that perspective, industrial parks, mobile home parks, apartment buildings and shopping centers only look confusingly different on the surface, not in their essence as income-producing real estate. Such a perspective may even open up more investment opportunities for you. Without the ability to categorize real estate by the objective it best serves, you might not realize that a particular property can meet your goal.

More often than not, one and the same property may help you

achieve different goals, a point those selling it will not be slow to emphasize. For example, a property may generate both immediate income to supplement your other sources of income and also create a tax shelter. However, it is unlikely that a property will meet different goals with equal efficiency.

We will illustrate this point with a property which throws off considerable amounts of income and which also has a large amount of tax shelter in the form of interest deductions and depreciation. The greater the income the property generates, the more the tax shelter will be used up. Not much, if any, tax shelter will be left over to protect your other income from the effects of taxation.

There could also be another problem with this property. You may pay too much for it. Because of its ability to shelter income, you could pay a premium for the right to the tax shelter and also for the right to income you may not want. If you had analyzed the property in terms òf a tax savings goal, you could then have met that goal at less cost by buying a property that produced proportionately less income and more tax shelter or by buying only that portion or slice which consists of tax shelter.

To equip yourself properly to categorize real estate and to weigh one property against another in terms of your overriding goal, you will have to learn some of the jargon real estate professionals fling about with such abandon. The jargon, onerous as it may seem, does serve a purpose. It enables all investors, experienced or neophyte, to communicate with some precision exactly what can be accomplished through each property.

We use the phrase "some precision" deliberately. Real estate terminology varies slightly from region to region. Even professionals sometimes get into difficulties by not taking into account semantic variance. It is best in each case to obtain a precise definition at the outset of what the other parties to a transaction really mean when they use a particular term. Understanding the correct terminology applicable to each goal and each kind of real estate is another way of making sure you are comparing apples with apples, or oranges with oranges, if the latter is what you prefer.

Thus, we have used the word property throughout the last few pages to convey a specific meaning, namely, the totality of what you can acquire. Property in this sense does not mean just the land, nor does it exclusively mean the structural improvements on the land, such as an apartment building, a parking lot, a tennis court or anything constructed.

Property means the rights or interests you can acquire. In many cases that will include the land and any improvement on it, but in others it may be just the land or just the building if you are not interested in acquiring the land underneath the building. It can also mean the right to tax shelter, the right to occupy the premises as a leaseholder, a fractional interest you may inherit, or the right to receive payments on a mortgage loan in conjunction with the right to take the property if the payments are not made. We will discuss the various real estate interests and rights further in Section II.

Property can also mean something which is owned, particularly land or real estate that is owned. More commonly, property is used to denote a specific parcel of land or real estate.

At the same time, we have carefully avoided using the terms investment and equity until we could define them properly, as many people tend to confuse their meanings. An investment, for example, means the total value of a property.

Your investment, however, can and generally does mean something different and is commonly called equity to distinguish it. The equity in a property is the value of the property less any debt on the property. For example, you may buy a property worth $100,000. If you obtained a mortgage loan of $80,000, you would have to invest $20,000 to meet the difference between the value of the property and the debt.

Five years later, you might have paid down the mortgage balance to $70,000 and the value of the property might have increased to $130,000. At that time, the amount of equity would be the difference between $130,000 and $70,000. Your equity of $60,000 would then be a composite of your original cash equity ($20,000), debt reduction ($10,000) and inflation ($30,000).

In another example, one that would not be an everyday occurrence, you might acquire a property at a price of $100,000. You may have obtained a real buy because the seller had to move quickly. The property may then be appraised at a value of $175,000. You may be able to obtain a mortgage loan for about 70 percent of the property's appraised value. The mortgage loan would then come to $120,000. Your equity in the property would be $55,000, or the difference between the value of the property and the debt.

There are several varieties of equity. Generally, you put up cash to acquire a property. The difference between the value of the property and the mortgage loan you obtain to finance the rest of the purchase would then be called cash equity. But you might, as we have just seen, be able to obtain a mortgage loan for a greater amount than the price of the property. The difference between the value and the debt would then be another kind of equity, one you can pocket a portion of in cash.

Another variety of equity occurs as a result of paying off the mortgage loan. As you make principal repayments to the lender, you are increasing the amount of equity you possess. As you amortize the loan in this way, the difference between the value of the property and the debt may grow, and so will your equity, through what is called equity build up. The property may also increase in value because of inflation. You would then have developed an inflation equity. Or, you may undertake to change the property in a way that enhances its value above what it cost you to make the change. That would be called a developer's equity.

The real test of any investment is the measurement of the return or potential return on your original cash equity. The other varieties of equity are somewhat outside your control, in terms of your ability to use them in competing investment opportunities. Only when you sell the property can you assemble all the equities involved and establish your total return. In some instances, you may be able to refinance and take out some of these combinations of equity for your own use.

The value of your equity will be reflected on your statement of net worth. Any increase in your equity will at the same time increase your net worth and thus your wealth. To help you select your primary goal, we will examine how each of the four objectives creates and protects wealth.

OBJECTIVE: INCOME

In your analysis of your financial posture, you may have discovered a gap between the amount of income you receive and the amount you would like to receive. An income-producing property may help you fill that gap.

It could be that you want more income now to achieve the lifestyle you would prefer or simply to develop the ability to pay off bills more easily. Or you could want more income to maintain your lifestyle after you retire. You may want to retire early and thus need supplemental income to make up for the customary decrease in income that occurs as a result of early retirement.

You may not need more income now but expect to need it in the future. Unlike most other investments, real estate investments possess the advantage of allowing you to develop a strategy for receiving income when you want it. For example, you might acquire a property and design the lease on it so that the income stream starts flowing several years hence. Alternatively, you might invest in building an apartment complex that would take two years to complete. Only upon completion would income production start. Or, you may be able to structure your rentals to increase at set times when you expect to need additional income.

Income has many different meanings in the world of real estate. The term income is used in five different ways: Gross income, effective gross income, net income, cash flow, and real estate taxable income or loss.

Gross income is really your rent roll, the amount of rent you could collect for the use of a property if it were fully rented. Frequently, however, that is not the amount you actually collect. For instance, you may have an apartment that is vacant for a period or you may give a new retail tenant free rent for a few months in return for the store operator using his or her own capital to make alterations. The effective gross income, thus, is the actual rent you collect for any given period.

Once effective gross income has been determined, actual operating expenses, such as heat, taxes and insurance but not debt service or depreciation, must be subtracted to establish net income. Net income is the difference between your effective gross income and your operating expenses.

Net income is not necessarily your profit, as it is in manufacturing concerns. If there is any debt on the property, you must next subtract the payments due or debt service. The debt service consists of both interest and amortization or principal repayments. Only after allowing for debt service will you reach the cash flow figure. Cash flow equals the amount of money you can put in your pocket.

You must also take another step, that of applying interest deductions and depreciation write-offs, before you can establish real estate taxable income or loss. On the surface, the cash flow of a particular investment may look inadequate; but upon further analysis, you may discover that the tax advantage makes the property an attractive investment. We will discuss how to establish and analyze gross income, effective gross income, operating expenses, net income, debt service, cash flow and real estate taxable income or loss in Section III of this book.

The term income stream refers to the dollars as they are delivered to you. You may, for example, be paid net income once a year, either at the beginning or end of the year, or you may receive monthly rent payments from apartment dwellers or the operators of a series of small stores. We shall generally be discussing income streams in this chapter.

Income streams range across a wide spectrum of risk. Incomes are rated by the market primarily on their quality and durability. The higher the quality and durability, the lower the yield required because the risk perceived by investors is smaller, and vice versa.

The income's quality and durability rating is related directly to the quality and durability of the tenant as the source of and backing for the income. Thus, you should look first to the credit standing of the immediate source of income, the tenant. As an example, we will consider two sources of income you might have: the Caterpillar Tractor Company and a local bowling alley.

We have all learned that size of assets is not an iron-clad guarantee. The bankruptcies of Penn Central and W. T. Grant, billion-dollar corporations that they were, should have driven home the lesson that a company's quality of assets and management is what counts. Nonetheless, it is immediately obvious that Caterpillar is more likely to provide a higher quality income stream than is a firm that runs one bowling alley.

Similarly, a shopping center with a major tenant such as R. H. Macy would tend to give you a higher quality income stream than would a small office building with several small tenants. R. H. Macy is a highly rated credit and has substantial net worth, both of which are measures of quality. In comparison, the tenant of a small office would have a lower credit rating and lower net worth, reflecting its relative insecurity.

Examining the immediate source of income is important. But so, too, is a look at the ultimate source of your income. If your tenant's business is based solidly on necessities, you are on firmer ground than if it is based on fads or luxury goods. Thus, R. H. Macy and Caterpillar, respectively, sell widely affordable clothing and tools for development, both likely to be strong sources of future income.

A solid family-run drugstore may have three aspects of quality going for it: Its business is based on what have come to be perceived as necessities, it may have a relatively high net worth and also business expertise. Certainly, its quality would not be rated as high as that of a Triple A rated company, but its rating is not likely to be as low as a newly established bowling alley.

This is not to say that sources of income ultimately based on the provision of pleasure can not provide reliable sources of income for a period of time. It does, however, involve a recognition that activities that fulfill the need for pleasure tend to change more rapidly than do items that are staple, such as basic foods, clothing and shelter. Finally, tenants whose businesses cater solely to the luxury market may be disproportionately hurt by economic curtailments.

You should view a prospective or actual tenant the way a financial lender would, as a credit risk. You will, after all, be lending the use of your property to someone else. The question then becomes one of relative likelihood that a particular tenant will meet the payments on your loan.

Your decision will also be affected by the length of time you can expect to receive the income. Thus, a 30-year lease to a tenant like Caterpillar is more likely to be a durable source of income than is a 30-year lease (if you can get one that long) to a tennis court operator. The chances that Caterpillar will be around that long are better than those of the tennis court operator, if only because Caterpillar is organized as a business to endure while the tennis court operator is unlikely to have resolved the problem of business continuity.

The income's durability can also be affected by changes that take place over time near your property. If neighboring real estate begins to decay, a large, creditworthy firm is more likely to have a positive impact on that process. A small operator is less likely to be able to take any action that could help reverse the tide and may even go out of business as a result of the change.

The property involved can also affect the durability of the income. The functional utility of any property changes over time. For example, a decade ago a store was more functional if it was 120 feet deep. Today, it is more functional, at least in a shopping center, if it is 90 feet deep. Developments in technology also cause changes in utility that may not be anticipated. In order to compete, tenants involved in such changes may have to move to more suitable properties. The problems of functional obsolescence are most serious in any special-purpose real estate.

Real estate designed for use as shopping centers, office or industrial space tends to be more adaptable to the uses of many different tenants than properties designed for a single-purpose use. Skating rinks are not likely to make good squash courts, and vice versa. But, a dress shop might make an excellent shoe store with little trouble or expense required to effect the change. As a result, your income stream from such real estate is less likely to suffer lengthy interruption.

How vulnerable your income stream will be to expense increases also affects its quality and durability. After all, if your expenses rise and you are not able to increase the rent roll or pass the increases on to your tenants, your net income will inevitably decline.

You can see the effect of a relatively small change in expense level from the example in Table 2. We assumed an apartment property worth $500,000 with a mortgage loan of $400,000 for 25 years at a 9.5 percent interest rate. Debt service would then be $42,000 a year. The equity investment in the example is $100,000. The expense increase of $6,000, as can be seen, would cut both your cash flow and your first-year yield on equity by more than half.

There are several kinds of protection against the risk that expenses will rise and eat into your income. All require prior planning, particularly as they relate to lease preparation, in order to maximize their effectiveness. In apartment properties, your best protection may come from your ability to raise the rent frequently as short leases come due. It is not customary and in some areas may be illegal to charge apartment tenants separately for increases in property taxes, insurance, heat and other operating expenses.

You can, however, pass such increases on directly to commercial or industrial tenants because of escalation clauses written into their

TABLE 2
Effects of a Change in Expense Level

	Before Expense Increase	After Expense Increase
Gross Income	$100,000	$100,000
Vacancy and Collections Allowance	−5,000	−5,000
Effective Gross Income	95,000	95,000
Expenses	−42,000	−48,000
Net Income	53,000	47,000
Debt Service	−42,000	−42,000
Cash Flow	$ 11,000	$ 5,000
First Year Return on Equity	11%*	5%*

*For purposes of illustration, we have not considered any equity build up.

leases. Office, retail or industrial tenants with such clauses in their leases are obligated to pay any increases in the operating expenses which you were able to negotiate with them. These escalator payments would be above and beyond the base rent the tenants owe you. Of course, if you have a poor quality tenant, the escalation clause may be unenforceable.

You may also be able to pass on more expenses to your tenants by making certain capital improvements. Whether or not that makes economic sense will require careful evaluation of the yield you can obtain as a result of your capital investment. The most typical improvement involves the conversion of an apartment, office or retail building from a mass-metered electrical system to individually metered electricity. On the first, you pay the electrical bills for the whole property; on the second system, the tenants each pay their share directly to the utility company. Another improvement might involve converting the present water or heating system to a directly charged system. This is not likely to be allowed in apartment buildings, where you are obligated to provide such service as part of the overall rent.

Another kind of protection comes from a net lease, one carefully and specifically designed to lay off all or most of the expenses on the tenant, not on you, the landlord. Thus, a tenant with a net lease is generally responsible for paying property taxes, water and sewer charges, the cost of utilities, maintenance and structural repairs, and all other operating expenses.

A net lease which requires a tenant to pay absolutely all expenses and be responsible for all increases is known as a bond net lease to emphasize its similarity to a bond investment's most desirable features. However, a net lease of any kind is worth only as much as the credit of the tenant involved. The higher the quality of the tenant, the more protection you are afforded.

It is also important that net lease clauses be drafted with great skill so that your income is actually net. One of the problems is the definition of a net lease, which can vary across the country. The issue is the net income you will receive. Any increases in expenses which are not passed on to the tenant will decrease your net income and thus reduce your yield.

Net leases require little management involvement as the tenant is mainly or solely responsible for care of the property. All that is required on your part may be receipt of a check from the tenant and sending in payments of any debt service and insurance premiums, as well as some inspection of the property to make sure the lease provisions are being observed.

Inflation poses yet another risk to income. Net income of $10,000 today probably will not be worth as much in purchasing power ten years from now. You can attempt to keep whole by periodically raising rents if you have short leases or by providing for periodic increases in longer leases.

On commercial and industrial leases, you can also attempt to write in a cost-of-living clause. The rent would then increase as the government's cost-of-living index rises. Many tenants naturally resist such clauses. That may give you an opportunity to be creative in thinking up a clause a tenant will accept. One broker was able to persuade a tenant to accept a cost-of-Pepsi clause. Whenever the cost of Pepsi goes up, so will the income, on the assumption that the price of Pepsi incorporates some measure of inflationary adjustment.

Your ability to participate in a retail tenant's gross revenues can also serve to protect your income stream from inflationary erosion. The theory is that the gross sales should reflect increases for inflation as a retailer raises prices on the goods sold. If you can insert a percentage clause in the lease and if the sales exceed a certain amount, you will obtain the right to a percentage of the retailer's gross. Of course, the tenant will try to set the trigger amount extremely high. Extra payments of this nature are known as overages, because they are over the base rent.

If you are not able to write in such clauses or receive their benefit or raise the income in another way, you may still be compensated for inflationary erosion of income. Inflation itself may be increasing the value of your property. This may merit a switch from an income objective to a capital appreciation objective.

The market's assessment of the quality and durability of an income stream determines its judgement of risk and thus of the yield required to make it worthwhile to invest in order to receive that income. An income stream that stems from tenants with low credit ratings would be judged more risky and thus would require a higher yield. An income stream of high quality and durability would bring down the risk and thus the yield. The yield you require on your equity depends both on what is available in the market and what you find acceptable in quality and durability or risk level.

The actual yield on any investment can not be determined until a property is disposed of. You should receive not only a return *on* your equity but also a return *of* your equity. Until a property is disposed of, the assembled equities, such as cash equity, built up equity, and inflation equity, can not be determined and thus your total rate of return on and of your investment can not be determined. This point is a source of massive confusion. Therefore we will repeat: *The actual yield on any investment can not be determined until a property is disposed of.*

An interim yield can be calculated, however, and certain assumptions can be made in order to estimate the return of the investment. For those who enjoy "numbers," we anticipate here later chapters which will explain the process in detail. Calculating an interim yield's adequacy depends on how an investment compares with alternatives in the market place in terms of its risk, size, management requirements and liquidity.

Generally, the less risky the investment is perceived to be, the lower the yield will be. Similarly, the less management and capital required, and the more liquid or easily sold the investment is, generally the lower the yield will be.

For example, a major shopping center tenant with high net worth may sign a net lease requiring little investment supervision. The yield requirement might then be only 9.3 percent or even lower. In contrast, a tennis court operator with low net worth, a low credit rating, and a somewhat higher management requirement in terms of collecting the income and protecting the investment might mean a yield requirement of 15 percent or more.

If it seems hard to give up 15 percent for only 9.3 percent, you can be well compensated for doing so as part of your investment strategy. Not only are you more likely to receive the income steadily, but the lower, more secure yield will be one factor in the calculation of an increased value for your property and, thus, for your equity.

To show the effect of different levels of yield, we will take as an example a neighborhood shopping center with six tenants. The tenants might include a drugstore, a bakery, a dress shop, a hardware store, a stationery store and a delicatessen. Each tenant owns only a single store operation and, while each has adequate net worth, none is a top credit. The six pay a total of $50,000 a year in rent. After subtracting your expenses, you are left with $35,000 a year in net income. (We will also assume for the moment that there is no mortgage on the property.)

Now an opportunity occurs to rent three of the stores to a large, top credit bank on a long-term net lease. The bank wants to put in a neighborhood branch. After the bank moves in, you still receive $50,000 in gross income and $35,000 as net income each year.

The amount of your net income has not changed as a result of substituting the bank as a tenant. But the quality and durability of that net income has changed dramatically, because the income from the bank is of higher quality and durability. Moreover, you will need to supervise the bank tenant less than the remaining three small tenants. Before the bank moved in, you might have expected a yield of 13 percent to reflect the risk, size, management requirements and liquidity of your investment in a property with six small tenants.

After the bank moved in, your expected yield might have dropped to 10.5 percent, reflecting the improvement. The yield requirement on the bank's half might be only eight percent. Averaged with the 13 percent still required on the other half, the new yield would be 10.5 percent.

In effect, you have traded off a lower yield for a more valuable property. We will use a capitalization method to show what the value of the property might have been before and after the bank moved in. Establishing a capitalization rate, which processes net income and yield into value, is a highly technical procedure which we will discuss fully in Section II. We will assume here a capitalization rate of 15 percent before and 12.5 percent after the bank occupied the premises. Using these figures, the property would be valued at around $230,000 before and $280,000 after, a difference of $50,000. The more secure tenant would have caused your equity to jump by that $50,000.

OBJECTIVE: TAX SHELTER

Keeping more income for your personal use, rather than the government's use, can be achieved by sheltering income from taxation. In reality, it is a different way to increase spendable income for personal use or investment purposes.

Thus, an individual whose income is relatively low might want to increase it by establishing another source of income through investing, as discussed in the preceding section of this chapter. However, someone already at a high level of income who adds yet another source of income might discover, under our graduated income tax system, that a higher percentage of all income is going to the government. Such an investor might find it more advantageous to protect some of his or her present income from taxes and in that way increase personal spending power.

Tax shelter is really tax deferral, as more investors are coming to realize. At some point, the taxes which have been deferred will have to be paid. Until that time, you can benefit from the use of dollars that would otherwise have gone to the government. Due to inflation, a dollar in the hand today is worth more than a dollar that has to be paid out in taxes tomorrow. In fact, the present worth of having a dollar to spend today is going to be much higher the longer the payment of taxes can be deferred. Moreover, you have the benefit of being able to use the dollars saved from current taxation without having to pay any interest for your use of them.

While other investment tax shelters have been significantly curtailed in recent years, real estate still generates hefty tax savings. Investing in real estate can provide you with tax shelter in three different ways through: (1) Interest deductions, (2) Depreciation and (3) A shift from paying current high ordinary income taxes to paying a lower capital gains tax in the future.

Interest If you borrow, interest is what you are charged for the use of the money borrowed, or the cost of money. Formerly, taxpayers were allowed to prepay interest for several years. This bunching of interest payments into one year substantially raised the amount of interest that could be deducted to reduce taxable income. However, changes in the tax laws now disallow any prepaid interest if such a prepayment would materially distort income. And since that distortion of income was precisely the point, most prepayments will be disallowed.

However, interest owed during the early years of a mortgage loan is naturally larger, as the loan has yet to be repaid significantly. The larger deductions that result can provide effective tax shelter during the early years of the loan.

For example, we will assume that the interest on a mortgage loan you obtain to finance a property comes to $5,000 the first year. That $5,000 can be used to shelter income, thereby lowering the amount of taxable income you report by $5,000. The difference between what you would have paid in taxes had you not invested in real estate and what you actually pay after you invest is your profit, known as tax savings.

If you are in the 40 percent bracket, not being taxed on $5,000 is worth $2,000 in tax savings to you. If you are in the 60 percent bracket, not being taxed on $5,000 is worth $3,000 to you in tax savings. The higher the tax bracket, the more tax shelter is worth. In the second year, the amount of interest you can deduct will decline slightly as some of the mortgage loan principal will have been paid back and you are charged for the use of less money.

Investors wishing to take advantage of the interest tax shelter generally invest in improved property. Lenders are more willing to make mortgage loans with a high loan-to-value ratio and thus higher interest payments on improved property than they are on land, if they are willing to lend on unimproved land at all. Lenders view improved property as less risky because there is an established income stream that will provide them with a source of repayment for the money lent.

Depreciation Investors who own improvements on land can write off the cost of the improvements over certain time periods in recognition of the wasting away nature of improved property which tends to deteriorate. Land can not be depreciated because, by its nature, it does not waste away over time. For this reason, tax shelter investors often participate in ventures where the land underneath an improvement is sold to another group of investors who want income from a ground lease. Then the tax shelter investors, who own only the improvement, can depreciate the total cost of their venture.

The basic approach is to write off the same amount of improvement cost each year over a life set by the government. Under such a system, called straight-line depreciation, a building estimated to have a 40-year life with a cost of $100,000 when you acquired it would produce depreciation write-offs of $2,500 each year for 40 years. However, there are two ways to increase the amount of depreciation you can take and thus further reduce your taxable income. The first accelerates the write-offs allowed during the early years of ownership through various formulas; the second involves using shorter lives to achieve the same result.

While the same total amount of depreciation is involved, the accelerated methods allow you, in effect, to pull part of the write-off allowed in later years into the earlier years of ownership so that your immediate write-offs are increased. There are various methods of accomplishing this, such as sum-of-the-years digits and 200% declining balance. Under the latter, for example, you would be allowed to take 200% of the straight-line write-off for the first year. Thus, generally as in the example above, your first year depreciation write-off would be $5,000. Each year, the amount you could take would decline until it was actually lower than the amount the straight-line depreciation method would have allowed you.

Sum-of-the-years digits, 200% declining balance and 150% declining balance methods are allowed only on new residential buildings, in line with the government's desire to reward most those who increase the country's multi-family housing stock. Owners of older apartment buildings and new or old retail, office or industrial structures are not allowed any acceleration, although certain non-housing renovations now qualify for investment credits.

However, older structures can produce attractive tax shelter. For one thing, the land value is often only 10 to 20 percent of the total acquisition price, thereby giving you a higher ratio of improvement allocation. Thus, more of the cost of the property can be depreciated. Second, older structures have shorter lives. An improvement worth $100,000 with a 20-year life remaining would provide you with $5,000 worth of depreciation annually under the straight-line method.

There are special situations or problems the government wants to solve by manipulating the tax laws. These can also produce more rapid write-offs than straight-line. One involves the extensive rehabilitation or new construction of housing for low and moderate income families under government guidelines. However, such investments involve highly restricted income streams and profit ceilings. Another is the renovation of buildings designated as historic landmarks. Both investments will allow accelerated depreciation and renovation may also allow the use of shorter lives to boost the amount of depreciation allowable in the early years of the investment.

Accelerated depreciation has two drawbacks. At some point in the investment, generally seven to fifteen years after a property is acquired, the depreciation you are allowed drops below the amount you could have taken if you had chosen the straight-line method. At that point, depreciation stops being a productive tax shelter. Most investors sell when that point is reached.

However, that sale generally triggers the second problem connected with the use of accelerated depreciation. Ordinarily, the difference between what the property cost you and the amount for which you sell it would be considered capital gain, which is taxed at a relatively low rate. However, the use of accelerated depreciation will cause some of that profit to be taxed at ordinary income rates, which are generally much higher. This problem is known as depreciation recapture, as the government tries to recapture the benefits you have received from the additional write-offs you have taken through acceleration. Only an investment in low to moderate income government housing now allows you to escape recapture by holding a property over a long term.

Depreciation recapture can be avoided through the use of component depreciation. It involves using shorter economic lives for many of the parts or components of an improvement and applying straight-line depreciation to each part. If a building is composed of a high proportion of components with significantly shorter lives, such as electrical wiring, elevators and so on, than the life of the entire building, the amount of depreciation you can take can be boosted appreciably over the length of the shorter lives. But, because you use straight-line on each component, you will not face depreciation recapture if you sell the property.

You will, however, still have the problem of crossover. At some point, the amount of depreciation you can take will decline below the amount you could have taken if you had used straight-line on the entire improvement.

Capital Gains   The capital gains tax shelter involves shifting from a high tax rate, that on ordinary or earned income, to a lower tax rate, that on a capital gain. The difference in tax rates can produce substantial savings and thereby increase your spendable income or preserve your capital.

At present, ordinary income, such as income from rents, dividends and interest paid to you on a loan you make, is taxed at up to 70 percent. Earned income can be taxed at up to 50 percent. In contrast, the nominal capital gains tax rate ranges up to 28 percent. Up until this 1978 tax law change, the interplay of the minimum income tax and preference item treatment could cause the effective capital gains tax rate to reach a maximum of 49 1/8 percent. These are recent changes and illustrate how the tax laws are being altered.

To at least some degree, on the basis of your own knowledge, you will be able to penetrate the professional thickets otherwise involved in real estate investment. It is like being able to splint a broken arm for long enough to get someone to a hospital. But, tax shelter expertise is more like what is involved in open heart surgery. No one without extensive, specialized training should even attempt such an undertaking. Moreover, tax shelters can look deceptively easy to get into, but a skilled team of surgeon-equivalents may be required to get you out of trouble if a mistake is made as a result of an earlier misunderstanding.

You will need expert help in handling tax shelter, unless you are yourself a lawyer or accountant who specializes in real estate tax shelters. Expert planning can eliminate or mitigate many of the problems involved with both income and estate taxation. The tax laws, which create the tax benefits, are purposely designed to be difficult to use.

Certainly, that is one of the risks involved in investing for the purpose of tax shelter. Compared to the other objectives, the tax shelter aim makes you most dependent on expert legal and accounting advice, the kinds of expertise it is most difficult for a layperson to understand and therefore control.

Investing for tax shelter is easily the riskiest real estate objective you can select. It is the one aspect of real estate over which you can have no control, and not only because you are not likely to be an expert real estate tax lawyer or accountant. The tax laws themselves, which create the opportunities for tax savings, arise from complex legislative trade-offs over which it is difficult, if not impossible, for an individual taxpayer to exert leverage.

Moreover, what is the law today may change tomorrow as a result of legislative decisions not only at the federal level, but also at state and local levels of government. In addition, changing interpretations of what is permissible fly thick and fast from both the taxing authorities and the courts.

The basic risk, however, lies in swimming against the historical tide. From the imposition of Magna Carta on King John in 1215 to the latest "tax reform" acts, the trend has been toward a diminution of special privileges for those more well off than the general level of society. In any society based on equal opportunity under the law but not on equal ability, there will always be more people with an interest in eliminating privilege than there are people who want to uphold special rights. It is the same problem faced by landlords under our political and economic system: There will always be more tenants upholding their interests than there are landlords defending theirs.

While tax deferral is at present a legitimate aim of certain high-income investors, it requires a careful examination of the underlying economic soundness of the property acquired. For one thing, the tax laws may change and wipe out the tax shelter for which you invested. If that happens, the underlying property which produced the tax shelter will be all that is left of your investment. The better it is, the more it can benefit you in other ways.

For another, the acquisition of a property which produces very little income so that you can obtain an appreciable amount of tax shelter may be considerably more risky than you might think. If expenses go up or the gross income declines even moderately, you could find yourself with a property you have to subsidize for a time.

Frankly, investing in real estate for the objective of tax shelter is an expression of the larceny in all our hearts. And sometimes we get carried away by the prospect of not paying the tax collector for a time. A much more realistic approach is to consider tax shelter the cream on top of the milk. Then any tax shelter you receive is a welcome by-product of your investment, but the economic soundness of the property is the underlying asset.

OBJECTIVE: CAPITAL TURNOVER

Large sums of money can be achieved over a relatively short time period through a capital turnover investment. Because change is involved, the risks are high, but so too are the potential rewards.

To seek capital turnover, you must be a risk taker, an investor who wants to take more of a flyer for a higher profit than others do. If you become an active turnover investor, your role as developer will be to put all the pieces together. You spot the opportunities and then turn them into realities. You are the catalyst for change, an entrepreneur who creates a return out of time, effort, and the risks you take.

Typically a property is acquired, some change in it is made to make it more useful and it is then sold as rapidly as possible to capitalize on the change. You must be able to envision what a property can become, not limit yourself to what it currently is. Capital turnover is the imaginative realization of potential.

Becoming an entrepreneur need not involve much investment capital. For example, one way to make a profit is to spot an opportunity for changing the zoning on a parcel of land from residential to the more valuable industrial designation. You may be able to option the land for only a few thousand dollars and then obtain the zoning change. Once the new zoning is approved, you can then take up the option to acquire the land and resell it at a large profit to an industrial buyer you have located. You will have added value to the site by making it more immediately useful to the buyer. And you will have saved the buyer trouble and risk.

Often, however, capital turnover does involve large sums of working capital. You may become the passive investor who puts up capital to fulfill a property's promise. Major corporations frequently join in partnership with a developer to provide the capital necessary for the largest developments. On a smaller scale, individual private investors may put up the capital necessary.

Professionals whose services are needed by the developer may also form a joint venture to participate in the opportunity for profit. Perhaps a lawyer who is an expert in zoning matters, an accountant or another professional might take an interest in lieu of a fee or part of the fee. That could help cut down to size any working capital needed to make the venture come together.

The classic kind of change involves making physical improvements to land. For example, putting in roads or sewer and water connections increases the utility of land to a residential subdivision builder. At each stage in the process of developing unimproved land there are separate opportunities for a capital turnover investor. Such an investor may even undertake the whole job from optioning the land, changing the zoning, acquiring the land and putting in the infrastructure such as streets to building the homes, office buildings, retail stores, industrial plants or whatever encompasses the final use of the land.

Buying one piece of land and joining others to it to create what is called an assemblage also adds value. The larger parcel of real estate is generally of greater utility. Land, however, is not the only type of real estate available for capital turnover investments.

There are as many varieties as can be imagined. For example, a capital turnover investor may become involved in changing an improvement from one use to another, as has happened with the new use of older factory space for residences, offices or retail stores.

Many railroad stations have been turned from their original use into restaurants or offices.

A building might also be renovated to attract better tenants in order to improve the quality of its income stream. A property might be acquired and a large new mortgage loan obtained. All these changes would enhance the value of the property in the eyes of an investor interested primarily in the property's income stream, tax shelter or appreciation potential.

It is much like what the manufacturer of lamps accomplishes. A lamp is more valuable put together than it is when it is in pieces. Thus, the company which melds together the design, wiring, base and shade stands to make more than the manufacturers of the components. Anything that has more utility when you finish with it has an added value above the value of the parts that went into making up the product. The whole purpose is to maximize the value realized.

Like the lamp manufacturer, you do not want to benefit over the long term from the added value which you have created. You want to sell the improved product as soon as you can make the profit you want. In that way, you can realize its maximized value in a lump sum. You will then have the opportunity to turn your increased capital over once again.

Taking on the developer's role can require a larger time commitment than does active involvement in real estate investments for other purposes. It may even turn into a full-time job, as it would if you were to go into the construction of condominiums or other types of improvements or if you chose to assemble large plots of land for building sites. As any kind of developer, however, you must be available to make the decisions necessary.

Development is also a sophisticated business, as it involves the putting together of potentialities. It requires enough experience in real estate to spot opportunities for change and profitable resale and sufficient expertise or access to expertise to turn an opportunity into a reality. The development role gives you the greatest opportunity in real estate to apply your experience to the creation of value and to exert control over the process. It is your decisions that are most likely to make or break a project.

Generally, there is a greater need for working capital in turnover investments. For one thing, because of the very nature of turnover projects, all the risks and costs involved usually occur at the front end of the investment instead of being spread out more evenly.

For another, the real estate acquired tends to be less financeable. Unimproved land, for example, is not as financeable as improved real estate because of questionable provisions for debt service. A mismanaged property with a current poor quality income stream will also be less financeable than one with a high quality income stream. The loan-to-value ratio on a mortgage loan of this type would not be as high because the source of repayment is relatively so insecure.

In addition, any type of real estate you acquire for capital turnover purposes is less likely to generate sufficient income to pay property taxes and other holding expenses while it is in the process of change. Moreover, your overhead expenses are likely to be relatively high compared with those for the other real estate investment choices.

Fees to lawyers, architects, land planners, soil analysts and a host of others, depending on the real estate and the change involved, must be paid. The services you require from them are apt to be more extensive, which will raise their fees. The cost of physical improvements may also be incurred.

Short-term construction loans may cover most of these costs, but at a very high price. Interest rates on construction loans are high, reflecting the risk involved, and the interest charged must be paid currently. A financial analysis must be undertaken to estimate if and when a financial return will occur. Both hard costs and soft costs, such as fees and interest, are recaptured from the proceeds of sale. It is important to determine when that sale is most likely to take place. What is left after sale of the property less your operating expenses is your profit or entrepreneurial return.

A number of risks are characteristic of capital turnover investments. Delays are endemic due to zoning approval and environmental permit processes. Interest rates may go up on construction loans. Construction cost overruns are more than likely. Holding periods may turn out to be longer than anticipated because market conditions have changed. Because of the higher risks involved and the time and effort required, turnover investments must be designed to throw off higher profit margins than other investment vehicles.

Investors attempt to keep the term of capital turnover projects relatively short in order to reduce some of the risks. Less is likely to go wrong over a shorter time period. In addition, if the project is relatively large, such as a residential subdivision or a shopping center, the acquisition of land, construction and sales may be staged. Thus, the developer might acquire only as much land and construct only as many homes as he or she anticipates can be sold in any one year. The remainder of the land might be optioned. Lot sales may be phased or renovation may be carried out only a portion at a time.

These management techniques reduce the working capital tied up at any one time, and the sales produce more working capital for the next stage. Pre-leasing, or leasing to tenants at any stage before a property is ready for occupancy, may also help cut the capital required provided you can use the tenants' deposits. Pre-leasing will also help significantly in obtaining financing, as a lender can then see how a loan will be repaid.

A relatively high degree of liquidity or capital reserves is necessary to reduce risk. The larger the reserves available, the more the developer can weather unexpected but inevitable delays, such as those due to additional zoning hearings, weather, material or labor shortages, increased costs or slow market absorption. Basically, however, it is the developer's skillful application of experience and capability which will most reduce risks to manageable proportions.

OBJECTIVE: CAPITAL APPRECIATION

If you are most interested in preserving and increasing your net worth or wealth, then capital appreciation is the goal that will best serve you. You may want to use the appreciation to protect and increase your capital position in order to create a life estate to sustain you, perhaps when you retire. Or you may want to protect the wealth you now possess and create more wealth so that you can then pass it on to your children or grandchildren.

As a capital appreciation investor, you acquire real estate to act as a hedge against inflation, which destroys wealth through erosion of value. Carefully selected real estate has thus far proved to be an excellent hedge against loss in value and has also proved capable of increasing in value during inflationary periods.

There are two interrelated reasons for this: A greater number of dollars or other monetary units is required to acquire real property as inflation continues and the value of a dollar diminishes. Thus, inflation acts to keep your purchasing power even as the value of the real property goes up in dollar terms. Furthermore, the dollars you pay back on any loan you take out to acquire real estate are declining in value as a result of inflation. When you obtain the dollars by taking out a loan, they have a higher purchasing power than when you pay them back, a tactic which still has a counter-inflationary effect.

However, inflation does more. The number of dollars you might receive if you were to sell the property tends to be greater than a strict accounting for purchasing power would require, because people perceive real property to have greater value than dollars or paper investments representing dollars.

That perception of greater value comes from the recognition that real property, such as furniture and art, but especially real estate, has an intrinsic value. Dollars and paper investments have no value in and of themselves. Their value lies only in their role as a medium of exchange or as a representation of value that lies elsewhere, perhaps in a company which produces a commodity in demand, such as bread.

All real property has some utility to people. It may lie in the pleasure art can provide. Or it may lie in shelter for living, working or recreational pursuits, which is what real estate provides.

Even in deflationary periods, real property tends to hold its value better than paper investments. During economic declines, people still need to purchase food, clothing and shelter. Well selected real estate with tenants who retain the power to purchase what they need will not drop in value as rapidly as will paper investments. The latter, having no intrinsic value, will reflect declines in purchasing power relatively quickly as people are increasingly forced to concentrate on buying necessities.

Thus, in the Great Depression of the thirties, the value of stocks plummeted for three full years. In contrast, real estate properties with strong tenants declined in value much more slowly than even the stocks of the strongest companies.

But there is an additional major reason why real estate holds and increases its value better than other forms of real property: Real estate properties most frequently produce income, as art, gold and other real properties do not. In inflationary periods, rental income tends to rise or, if it is an amount fixed by long-term leases, can be protected from erosion through such devices as a cost-of-living clause.

Even in deflationary periods, income property with strong tenants does relatively well. This is partially a function of any long leases involved, which are not immediately renegotiated to reflect worsening economic conditions. Even real estate with less strong tenants and shorter leases is able to protect income flow to some extent by reducing rents in proportion to reductions in expenses.

Expenses relating to employees and services, such as privately obtained trash removal, may drop rather quickly in such an economic setting. Fixed contractual obligations, such as insurance premiums and mortgage loan payments, may also be renegotiated. Insurance premiums may decline within a year when the premium payment becomes due. Mortgage loan payments may decline in amount if it is a question of the lender having to take back a property, a task for which lenders are ill-equipped. Principal repayments may be postponed and even interest costs may drop, although not as quickly, as lenders pay less for the money they use for loans. Charges paid to municipalities for property taxes and water use and to publicly regulated utilities are much slower to decline.

As you can judge, real estate with poor quality tenants, perhaps tenants who have to close their doors for lack of business, would suffer disproportionately in a recession or depression. These tenants may even be forced out of business if the squeeze between their income and expenses becomes too severe. As a result, such real estate tends to lose value more quickly. Land also tends to lose value relatively rapidly as the demand for development dries up to reflect economic conditions. Real estate with residential tenants would tend to hold up better in value as a result of governmental subsidy of personal incomes.

Nonetheless, carefully selected real estate tends to have the most power to protect wealth and increase in value. That is because there are more ways to protect what creates value in real estate than in other forms of real property. Art or gold or any of the other forms of real property do not, as we have noted, produce income, a form of protection, nor are they available for new uses, as real estate can be.

As you can see from these descriptions of the capital appreciation process, you will not be the major force that protects or enhances the value of your equity. While you and the capital turnover investor both want an increase in wealth over time, you also want to protect your equity as much as you can. Thus, the method and usually the time frame involved will differ radically.

The protection of and increase in value will occur as a result of the operation of inflation and/or someone else's activity. For example, your equity may suddenly increase because a road has been built near your land by a subdivision developer or because an interstate highway exit is to be placed near your land by a state highway department.

What happens to property when a subway is constructed is a highly visible example. Before the city of Toronto built its subway, rank after rank of small buildings marched as far as the eye could see toward the outskirts of the city, with taller buildings generally confined to the downtown area and to land adjoining expressways. Once the subway was in progress, tall buildings began to go up at appropriately zoned and serviced sites near subway entrances and exits. The concentrated flow of people moving past these sites on their way to and from the subway created the conditions necessary to make some taller edifices worth building. People naturally wanted to work or live near the transportation they would use.

As a result, some land near subway entrances and exits in Toronto, particularly parcels where such municipal services as sewers were expanded at the same time, became more valuable as a more valuable use could be made of it. The owners of these sites, however, had not done anything to bring about the increase in value.

Similar effects have occurred as a result of actions undertaken by state and federal pollution control agencies. For example, when the number of parking spaces in certain downtown areas was frozen to reduce air pollution from automobiles, a number of existing parking garages suddenly became more valuable. These garages then had a virtual monopoly. They will face no effective competition for a long time as it takes a long time to develop the mass transit commutation alternatives proposed by the agencies.

Your most important role as a capital appreciation investor will lie in identifying opportunities resulting from external change. You will need to understand what has worked in the past and how that may be changed by technological, economic and social trends currently under way. Then you can apply your observations to make a profit from the appreciation that occurs as a result of change.

Think back, for example, to the construction of the interstate highway system, a major transportation change. Each time a new section of the highway was planned, real estate that would be accessible from the highway shot up in value. Investors who were foresighted enough to acquire real estate near the exits of the highway system, that is, land which could benefit from new uses, reaped the great increase in value that occurred.

If you should hear that a new factory is to be built in your town or become aware that there is some growing need, you might begin to dream of how this could change real estate uses around you. In many ways, it will be your imaginative foresight that will enable you to reach your goal of appreciation.

Your big risk is time. Weighing the future probability of developments not yet visible is a difficult task. Not all real estate benefits from speculative increases in value: If a highway is built in one place, it will not be built in another.

Nor will all real estate benefit from increases in value due to inflation. Some may become obsolete before your equity has appreciated enough to have made it worth your while to acquire and pay the holding costs. For example, the land use allowed by a zoning authority may change from the more valuable commercial to the less valuable residential.

An example of change occurred along Route 1 because of the construction of the interstate system. Route 1 had been a favorite road for vacationers to take. As a result, hotels, motels, restaurants and recreational facilities had grown up alongside it. Then the interstate was built, and its higher technology made driving easier. As a result, traffic flowed away from Route 1 onto the interstate. The technological obsolescence of Route 1 caused the travel facilities to become economically obsolete. Their value went down as the value of real estate near interstate exits went up.

One way to reduce your risk is to become a speculator who operates over the short term. Typically, a speculator might buy real estate, such as land in the immediate path of development, and sell it within a short time for more money. A speculator does not usually change the real estate in any but the most minor ways. He or she is simply the owner who holds it until the coming development actually attracts buyers who are willing to pay more than the speculator did. The short term the real estate is held holds down the risk that something detrimental to its value will occur while it is being held.

More typically, however, investors pursuing capital appreciation are interested in the long term, perhaps until retirement or beyond to an heir's enjoyment of the real estate's value. And that longer term usually requires the utmost in protective techniques to reduce risk.

One way to increase the odds in your favor is to select real estate that is most likely to increase in value at rates higher than other real estate. For example, mid-Manhattan real estate is relatively more likely to grow in value at a higher rate than real estate in the outer boroughs of New York City. Certain economic activities that are likeliest to increase in the city require high density and quick access to the face-to-face business interchange that mid-Manhattan provides. In contrast, real estate bought in an area that is still declining, perhaps an old factory row now used only by small, unstable firms, may eventually increase in value as land uses change, but that is less likely and may take longer.

Another way to protect the value of real estate and potential increases in value is to select real estate that will have more than one shot at value increases in the future. The more kinds of uses to which real estate can be put, or the fewer restrictions on it, the better the chance that it will appreciate.

Thus, real estate bought in the town of Madison, Wisconsin, has three major uses for which it might be in demand. For one thing, there is a university in Madison, which creates student and faculty demand for places in which to live, eat and otherwise occupy themselves. It is also the seat of the state government which, if it can not use the real estate itself, may create a demand for it through its employment of a wide range of personnel. Madison also has a diverse economic base, both agricultural and industrial, which again widens the uses to which real estate might be put. In addition, there is a high concentration of research and development firms located advantageously near the university. As a result, Madison can be characterized as an area with relatively high incomes, which means certain properties can command relatively high rents.

Real estate in general is likelier to appreciate in Madison than it is in a town without such diverse and strong demand. But real estate may appreciate even more rapidly in Memphis, Tennessee. It is not only a university town with a strong agricultural and industrial base but, in addition, has ready access to the interstate highway system and the major river transportation system. In Memphis, therefore, there are additional sources of demand from firms needing a superior transportation network. Thus, real estate values may increase even more rapidly.

By way of contrast, we might look at the relative desirability of investing in a single industry town. Detroit, for example, has never developed beyond its reliance on the automobile industry. But the automobile industry has changed since its early days and now finds it more advantageous to locate new plants around the country. As a result, Detroit has only a single major use source for the real estate located there; furthermore, that source is declining as the use spreads over the countryside.

Washington, D.C., is also a single industry town, its industry being the national government. However, even when a policy of decentralization was established, there was a limit to the amount of possible dispersion. Too much capital had been spent on government buildings, highways and airports in order to facilitate the necessary interaction among government employees. Moreover, the symbolic and historic value of Washington is such that it will endure as a government town.

Real estate with restricted use potential is less likely to increase in value as rapidly as real estate with fewer restrictions placed on it. For example, zoning may prohibit industrial development in the middle of a developed residential area. It is not likely that such zoning can now be changed, as a change would result in highly incompatible neighboring uses. Thus, real estate in that area may never appreciate as greatly as real estate elsewhere that has the potential for commercial or industrial use, both more valuable uses than is purely residential.

It is important to look to the land potential when you size up real estate for the purpose of accomplishing capital appreciation. Buildings typically do not last much beyond 40 years at full economic use. If the time frame is long enough, the land is what will be left after the building has become physically, functionally or economically obsolete. Thus, over a time period as long as or longer than a building's span of useful life, it is the residual value of the land that will be the ultimate source of potential appreciation as the land is put to new uses.

If you plan to hold real estate for more than a few years, the holding costs, such as property taxes, will eat up your capital. The appreciation you then may realize may not be sufficient to pay you back what you invested as well as increase your capital. Because of this, most long-term capital appreciation investors seek out real estate with the additional protection of an income stream.

If there will be a relatively short holding period before you expect appreciation to occur as a result of external development, you may want to put up a one or two story building in the interim. Such a building is known as a taxpayer because it usually generates just enough income to pay your major holding cost, property taxes. (Of course, very old taxpayers betray where an owner's hopes for future development went astray.) Or you may want to establish other interim uses, such as a parking lot.

The further out you expect the time period to extend, however, the more likely you will be to seek out real estate that can protect your capital better, namely real estate with top credit tenants and strongly protective leases.

What happened to Penn Central should serve as a cautionary

tale: The former New York Central owned the land on both sides of Park Avenue in New York, land that became building sites for the most desirable office space in the world after World War II. That would normally have acted to enhance the land's value, and it did in the short run.

However, in some instances the New York Central wrote long-term ground leases that allowed for limited increases in rent as time went on. Thus, the leases did not adequately protect the railroad's income stream from the effects of inflationary erosion of income. By the time the late 1960s rolled around, the railroad, then the Penn Central, needed cash to run its railroad operations, which had been hard hit by inflation, among other problems. Unfortunately, the income from the ground leases was not going up at rates commensurate with inflation. As a result of having tied up the land in long-term leases with steadily declining returns, the New York Central's interest in the land became less valuable as inflation increased.

Failing to safeguard an interest adequately can cause someone else's interest to rise in value. For example, we will assume that company A, the owner of a plot of land, has leased the land to company B for 40 years. At the time the lease was written 20 years ago, the ground was worth one million dollars and the rent charged was four percent of the land's value, or $40,000 in annual rent. At that time, a four percent yield was the going market rental rate. Company A failed to provide for increasing the rent.

Now it is 20 years later and comparable land is worth ten million dollars on the market. Rents for comparable land today are set at ten percent of value, not four percent. Company B still pays just $40,000, because, under the lease, company A can not raise the rent to reflect the land's higher value or the current market rent.

Company B, however, can sublease the land to company C for ten percent of the ten million dollar value. The rent payable to company B would be over one million dollars, which could make it well worth company B's while to move elsewhere. Company B can pocket the difference between its rent and the rent it gets paid, or $960,000. Obviously, its interest in the property has become more valuable than company A's interest due to the way the lease was written. Of course, as the lease nears its end, company A's interest will grow in value because it will soon be able to write a better lease; company B's interest will diminish in value as it approaches loss of the lease and thus loses the right to sublet that space.

Hindsight is, of course, a great teacher. Moreover, significant changes in leasing and financial techniques have developed over the past 30 years. In the future, there will be equally significant changes, both in terms of outside forces and ways to deal with them. Investors who make money will be the ones who are forward enough to think about how such changes will impact on value and how best to deal with them. It helps to have tenants with the strongest credits and also to have leases as full of contingent safeguards as your lawyers can devise.

In our discussion of capital appreciation, you may think it odd that we have not once mentioned capital gains or the lower tax rates that apply to capital gains. Most United States investors tend to think in terms of capital gains as a result of the way the tax code is written. Many United States investors plan their real estate investment strategy around holding for long-term capital gains and then selling the property to realize the gain at a low tax rate.

A minor reason we have not defined long-term appreciation in terms of the tax benefits of capital gains is that the benefits were much reduced by the Tax Reform Act of 1976. Before TRA 1976 was passed, the top tax on the sale of a capital asset held long term was 35 percent, significantly less than the top tax of 50 percent on earned income or the maximum of 70 percent on unearned income, such as rents, interest and dividends. After TRA 1976 was enacted, the top tax on capital gains could go as high as 49 1/8 percent, too close to the top tax on earned income to make capital gains the efficient tax shelter it once was. After the 1978 tax law, the top capital gains tax rate fell to 28 percent.

Moreover, a capital gains tax at death was enacted in 1976 so it would become less easy to pass wealth on intact to one's heirs. Such a tax may have its effective date postponed, but its imposition in the first place does not tend to make a capital gains strategy more attractive. What has happened once is more likely to happen again. Proper long-term planning is necessary to take care of these tax problems.

Appreciation is a much more important concept. It involves a shift in investment strategy that has just begun to be appreciated here in the United States. Certainly, even investment strategies will change in emphasis over time. Keeping a watchful eye out for such changes is as important, if not more so, as keeping up with population shifts and lifestyle changes that can affect your investment for good or ill. This change in appreciation strategy is a prime example.

European investors are far ahead of all but the most sophisticated and wealthiest United States real estate investors in using long-term capital appreciation as their prime method of preserving and increasing wealth, not to pay less in taxes on the sale of an asset. European investors may emphasize this aspect of long-term capital appreciation because Europeans have had much more experience than have United States investors with the interrelated effects of wars, unstable or ineffective governments and inflation. All three act to destroy security and wealth.

The concept of using the long-term appreciation potential of a real estate investment to protect and enhance wealth is not new to all United States investors. Relatively old money in the United States also values this strategy above all. An illustrative case involves the original United States fortune.

John Jacob Astor may have made his vast sums in the trading of fur, but once he had his fortune, he put much of it into real estate in Manhattan, Switzerland and in what was then the territory of Wisconsin. When Astor died in 1848, his will, among other things, directed that his substantial real estate holdings be held for the lifetimes of his immediate heirs. No real estate was to be sold by his trustees except to provide funds to improve the remaining real estate and as necessary to found a public library. All of Astor's real estate could be leased to provide income for his heirs while it could also be appreciating in value.

The large United States fortunes tend to take refuge in real estate investments, once the money has been accumulated through industrial and merchandising activities. And this money typically chooses as its prime objective, in some cases capital turnover, but particularly capital appreciation. It now tends to prefer capital appreciation with the most secure and protected income streams capturable and devisable.

Such a strategy assumes great importance when inflation becomes a permanent feature of the economic landscape, as it seems to have become in the United States. Of course, United States inflation is not usually as severe as it is in other parts of the world. Nonetheless, any amount of inflation makes it vital to become more conscious of an investment strategy which can repair inflation's ravages and take advantage of it to create additional wealth. Such a strategy requires major adjustments in the way you approach long-term investments in real estate.

For one thing, changes in tax laws will have little impact. The tax aspect is simply not an important feature if you hold real estate for long periods of time. Moreover, there are ways to realize the wealth without triggering a taxable event.

For another, the shift in yield requirements, part of the change required by this strategy, can pay you important dividends. In the past, United States investors have had a strong tendency to seek a higher yield so that they would receive higher current income or cash flow. As a consequence, many United States investors have concentrated more on the short-term potential in real estate and on real estate involving somewhat more risk. The average holding period on income-producing real estate has been between seven and ten years.

By way of contrast, European investors have long been willing to accept a lower yield over a much longer time period in return for a more secure investment. What they give up in yield and immediate income or cash flow, they more than get back from an increase in security and a greater potential for preserving and increasing capital through appreciation in value.

We will take as an example of this the neighborhood shopping center introduced in this chapter in our discussion of income. As you will remember, the center originally had six tenants and generated $50,000 in gross income and $35,000 in net income a year. Each of the tenants had a rather low net worth; we judged the yield required to reflect this to be 13 percent. Once the branch of the bank that was a top credit moved in to take the place of three of the tenants, the value of the property took a jump. The net income remained the same, $35,000, but the yield dropped to 10.5 percent.

In order to establish the property's value, we capitalized the net income, one method of valuing a property. Before the bank occupied half the premises, the property's value was $230,000; afterward, it was $280,000, an increase of $50,000 in equity. The income stream's increased security also meant additional protection for the equity or wealth.

As either net income increases or the capitalization rate, which includes the yield, decreases, real estate will increase in value. Changes in either of these two factors can impact positively or negatively on value. Provided leases are properly planned and drafted, inflation, by its nature, will produce higher incomes. That, in turn, will raise the real estate's value.

On the other hand, the capitalization rate is far less likely to fluctuate, as it incorporates a major function for the financing of the property. Because of the character of real estate financing, which is fixed over a long term, capitalization rates will not vary significantly over the life of an investment. Thus, the higher net incomes will tend to translate into a more valuable parcel of real estate.

Inflation may also cause a direct increase in a property's value, as it would cost more dollars to acquire it the longer inflation continues. Your equity in a property is also building up as the mortgage loan is paid down. As your equity increases, so too does your net worth. In addition to these three ways your equity can increase, you are also getting a yield on your investment in the form of current income.

This changed concept of the appreciation strategy also involves reappreciating what you can do to reap equity increases. Most United States investors, as we have mentioned, think of realizing their appreciated equity only through a sale. That results in an immediate source of cash which can then be used to pay current or future living expenses. However, if the proceeds are used for expenses, your net worth will decline.

If you choose to reinvest the sale proceeds, you will be faced with the problem of finding another investment opportunity that will do as well for you as the property you just sold. You will also have to pay the sale and purchase costs of shifting from one investment to another, which can result in a diminution of net worth.

An entirely different approach involves the realization of the increase in equity through borrowing. You can use the money obtained through borrowing as part of your retirement strategy or for any other purpose. What happens to your net worth depends on what you choose to do with the money you have taken out of the property. If you choose to spend it on current consumption, your net worth will decline. If, instead, you save or invest the money borrowed, your overall net worth will not be affected. The increase in liability as a result of financing will be offset by an equal asset.

Moreover, your remaining equity may continue to grow in the fashion discussed above. Of course, you will have to give up some of your current income from the property to pay for increased debt service. In effect, you have traded off some of the current income for a lump sum.

It is enlightening to consider what would happen if you refinanced the neighborhood shopping center we have discussed. Before the top credit tenant moved in, a lender would probably have made a loan for 66 2/3 percent of the property's value, or about $150,000. After the security of the income stream improved, a lender would probably increase the loan-to-value ratio to 70 percent of the higher value of the property, or $195,000, a difference in loan amount of $45,000. We will assume as in Table 3 that both loans were for 25-year periods, both had an interest rate of 9.5 percent and that the first loan did not have a prepayment penalty clause.

For sacrificing less than $5,000 per year in periodic income, you have increased your net worth by $50,000, obtained a lump sum of $45,000 in cash, and raised your first year yield from 24.1 to 41.6 percent.

You may want to use that borrowed money to invest in additional real estate with the potential of long-term capital appreciation. You would then have two or more properties with capital appreciation potential where before you had only one.

TABLE 3
Effects of a Change in Tenant Credit

	Before Top Credit Tenant Moved In		After Top Credit Tenant Moved In and Property Was Refinanced
Value of property:	$230,000		$280,000
Loan-to-value ratio:	66.6%		70%
Loan:	$150,000		$195,000
Net income:	$ 35,000		$35,000
Debt service:	− 15,735		− 20,455
Cash flow:	$ 19,265		$ 14,545
Original cash equity:	$ 80,000	Adjusted cash equity:	$ 35,000
First year return on cash equity:	24.1%	First year return on adjusted cash equity:	41.6%
Equity in property:	$ 80,000		$ 85,000
Cash from refinancing:	-------		+ 45,000
Total net worth:	$ 80,000		$130,000

CHANGING OBJECTIVES

In isolation, each of the four objectives we have discussed can work for you. However, in reality, each property is likely to exhibit a combination of reasons to invest or objectives that can be achieved through that property. You, too, may have a combination of reasons to invest.

Given the multiplicity of satisfactions you can enjoy from any one property, your ability to select a property that will reward you the most depends upon your selection of a primary goal, with all other goals ranked behind it. Once you have selected your primary goal, you will find it far easier to get on with the business of locating a property that will best achieve it.

Your goal is likely to change over time, just as you changed clothes when your graduation outfit was no longer appropriate. So, too, will your personal needs and desires change. As a result, you should constantly appraise where you are presently and where you want to be in the future. For example, you may now select the goal of higher current income. As a result, you may in the future reach a point where protecting the increased net worth you may also enjoy becomes predominant. As you continue to invest, you may want to acquire some real estate that is best at achieving one objective and other real estate that is best at achieving a different goal. This will give you a means of diversifying and provide you with more protection.

Your investor profile is also likely to change over time. Such changes may cause you to select a different primary objective. For example, your financial ability to carry properties may improve to the point where you want to consider capital turnover projects. Or, you may gain enough experience as you progress to want to tackle taking charge of a particular real estate task. The most compelling reward of real estate investment lies precisely in this: that you and your investments can grow and change together over time.

We have included Worksheet 7 at the end of this chapter for you to rank yourself as high, low or moderate in terms of each objective. Under each objective is a list of what can be achieved. If you want to achieve higher current income, you would rank that goal high and perhaps increased net worth as relatively low at this stage. Worksheet 7 will allow you first to round out your investor profile on a current basis; its second column can then be used to describe your objective choice at a point you select in the future in comparison with your current goal selections. Again, the direction you choose will have a profound impact on the shape of your investment strategy.

WORKSHEET 7
Objective Selection

	Current Choice			Future Choice (Relative to Current Choice)		
Need or desire for:	High	Moderate	Low	More	Same	Less
1. SUPPLEMENTARY INCOME						
Current:	——	——	——	——	——	——
Future:	——	——	——	——	——	——
2. TAX SHELTER						
Shelter other income (interest and depreciation):	——	——	——	——	——	——
Preserve wealth (capital gains shift):	——	——	——	——	——	——
3. CAPITAL TURNOVER						
Use of experience:	——	——	——	——	——	——
Income from value created:	——	——	——	——	——	——
Creation of wealth in form of large current sum:	——	——	——	——	——	——
4. CAPITAL APPRECIATION						
Retirement:	——	——	——	——	——	——
Creation of wealth over time:	——	——	——	——	——	——
Retention of wealth:	——	——	——	——	——	——
Transfer of wealth:	——	——	——	——	——	——

RANK YOUR OBJECTIVE CHOICES:

Most important current objective: 1. _____

2. _____

3. _____

Least important current objective: 4. _____

By developing an investor profile and ordering objectives, you have imposed certain restrictions on your next decision. Your selection of a type or types of real estate in which to invest will reflect your capabilities, your needs and also your reaction to the real estate available in the market place.

We have elected to discuss the six basic types of real estate investment opportunities: residential, retail, office, industrial, land and special purpose, such as a tennis court. These are the types of real estate with which you are most likely to become involved, either through seeking them out yourself or through being approached to invest in them. Each type is a special field in itself, because each serves a different purpose and operates in a different real estate market.

As we observed in Chapter 1, the investment markets consider investments comparable in terms of risk, denomination of size, management requirements and liquidity. Investors also consider types of real estate in these terms as well as others, such as location and financing capability. So should you as an actual or potential investor in real estate.

Experience has shown that the quality and yield of high grade residential real estate compared to those of mediocre residential real estate vary more than a high grade residential differs from a high grade retail or other type of real estate. Thus, a high quality income stream from a shopping center with top credit department store tenants, an office building with a top credit firm as a tenant, a plant with a top credit manufacturing tenant and land subject to a ground lease with a top credit tenant are rated as equivalent risks with equivalent yields.

A major high quality residential complex may exhibit an even lower risk/yield rating, even though the individual tenants do not have the net worth capacity of the top retail, office and industrial tenants. The desirability of a residential property stems from the size of the market. There are many more residential users than there are business users in the nation. Thus, the source of demand for this supply of product is potentially much greater.

Moreover, incomes of individuals are more likely now to exhibit stability, given the extensive network of governmental and private income supplements that balance out individual losses of salaries and wages. Various income supplements for individuals have now become the norm, whether they are called unemployment insurance, union supplements, Social Security or welfare. Direct income supports for businesses are rarer, as the Lockheed controversy illustrated. In general, residential use is also more of a necessity than is any other kind of use. Vacation homes, of course, represent a major exception to this rule.

At the other extreme lies special purpose real estate. Even a special purpose property with a top credit tenant is considered inherently less secure. By a wide margin, fewer tenants are available for and tenants are less easy to substitute in a property designed for a special use. For example, only a limited number of sports teams are available to occupy a stadium complex as compared with the number of businesses needing office or retail space.

Conversely, stores, offices or a factory filled with unstable tenants which are small in size and net worth would receive comparable high risk ratings from the investment market. Investors would require higher yields to justify investments in such properties. Residential real estate with a poor quality income stream might be considered slightly less risky than the above examples due to income supplementation and potentially greater tenant substitution.

Special purpose real estate with a shaky source of income and land with an inadequate source of interim income would be rated as even less secure. What will be done with them if an income stream dries up is less likely to be clear to potential investors or lenders than what can be done with residential, commercial, office or industrial real estate.

If your objective is immediate income, the highest quality and durability and the greatest amount tend to come from intensively used established properties. For residential, this may mean an apartment building located where an increase in population boosts demand. It also tends to mean an apartment complex which caters to the middle class, the broadest market, particularly those segments such as young and older adults who are likely to prefer apartment life.

Stores in an already developed area will also tend to be capable of capturing more trade and thus can pay higher, more stable rents. In addition, more store operators are likely to want to establish stores in a developed area to take advantage of the higher density.

The most secure industrial source of income is tantamount to an annuity. Large-scale operating or distributing plants net leased to a firm like General Motors produce annuity-like income streams. So too does land net leased to an office property occupied by a top credit tenant. In such cases, also, there is usually no management obligation.

Just as all types of real estate can be structured to produce income, so too can all types be considered in terms of their potential for capital appreciation. The market, again, would rank similarly all types with like potential for long-term capital gain.

There is more potential for future capital appreciation in real estate that has not yet reached its most intensive use. Thus, a shopping center located in a cornfield has more room to appreciate as development grows up around it than does a shopping center with established high densities. There is a great deal of potential in change. Areas experiencing a renaissance in the inner city are likely to appreciate faster than areas not undergoing such change. The same phenomenon can occur in the suburbs, although the lower overall densities involved and the wider variety of locations available for intensified development tend to restrict high levels of appreciation.

However, not all real estate within each type will be suitable candidates for capital appreciation. For example, real estate subject to highly restricted uses is less likely to appreciate than if it were not so subject. Future land use potential is of particular importance in any long-term capital appreciation strategy. The land is what will be returned to the investor as time goes by.

All types of real estate are also suitable for capital turnover purposes. Again, however, only certain ones within each type will merit the attention of an investor seeking capital turnover. Undeveloped or partially developed land lying directly in the path of development is the most obvious example. But any real estate with high appreciation potential from projected future demand which you can change the property to meet would be attractive. Thus, any improved real estate ripe for profitable change, whether it is residential, retail, office, industrial or special purpose, would make a good candidate.

For the tax shelter investor, all types of real estate have the potential for capital gain, although only those exhibiting a high potential for capital appreciation are likely to turn the potentiality into actual gain. However, not all types can produce high depreciation write-offs and interest deductions.

As we have discussed previously, land can not be depreciated at all, nor is there likely to be as much interest to deduct, as land is not as financeable as is developed real estate. Special purpose real estate may also be viewed by lenders as less financeable than other types of real estate because it, like undeveloped land, involves more risk. Real estate involving high risk tenants is also less financeable and thus produces less interest to deduct.

Depreciation write-offs are most rapid on new residential improvements. However, depreciation can also be rapid if you become involved in government-subsidized housing programs or landmark rehabilitation of any kind of improved real estate. Tax credits are available for certain non-housing renovations.

All types of real estate, except for land itself, involve either new or older structures. Different kinds of risks and rewards are involved in each. For example, buildings under construction can more easily be investigated for physical soundness by an architect or engineer whose services you have engaged. The physical condition of an improvement that is in a completed state is harder to determine, as much that is important to the structure's integrity is hidden from view behind walls, ceilings and floors.

Existing structures, however, have the merit of proven economic track records. Getting at the proof, of course, can be something else again, as most sellers are reluctant to divulge complete operating details. Nonetheless, you are in a better position to investigate and estimate the economics of an older structure that has been in use than that of a new one. In the latter case, unless tenants who will take care of all expenses have been signed up in advance, you are effectively purchasing unprovable estimates. Your hope is that the economics of the property will prove similar to that of comparable properties in the area.

Income may also be realized immediately from an existing income-producing property. Typically, a new property takes a considerable time to rent up to full capacity. And, even if tenants have been signed up in advance of actual occupancy, they are not usually obligated to pay full rent until the premises have been delivered to them suitable for full use, a condition that may take some time to accomplish. In a property that is being upgraded, tenants may receive a rent concession for a period while either the landlord or the tenant completes the renovation.

Existing structures require close examination for functional obsolescence. New buildings are the criteria by which older buildings are judged in terms of functional utility. New building designs usually incorporate the latest demands for efficiency and amenities on the part of users. An older building must, therefore, meet certain minimal competitive standards of utility for present and future needs. For example, an older office building with completely inadequate space for modern office equipment would be judged considerably less competitive and attract fewer tenants than a new building designed with such space in mind or an older one that could be inexpensively renovated to provide adequate space.

Some older buildings provide a considerably higher grade of space and amenities than newer ones do. High ceilings, attractive detail and commodious space are increasingly in demand for residential, office and retail use by users in revolt against some aspects of modern architecture. However, the operating expenses of such structures must be carefully evaluated, as older structures were not designed to be the efficient energy and labor savers the newest structures are.

The location of older properties can also be an important competitive consideration. Often, such structures sit astride attractive traffic flows which can benefit you in two ways. First, a high density of traffic can pull in or help you retain tenants. And, second, an older, relatively low rise structure built when the land underneath was relatively inexpensive may be due for redevelopment to a higher rise structure if the land has become more valuable. This occurs as a result of intensification of surrounding land uses.

There can be other advantages besides space, amenities and location to holding an older structure which is competitive with newer buildings. Such a building is likely to have a competitive edge over the newer ones in terms of rents. As inflation continues, your competitive advantage would tend to grow provided no technological or social change renders your property obsolete in a way that can not be economically or physically corrected.

As a result of material and labor increases, each wave of new buildings is likely to cost more to construct. That, in turn, will require more debt capital, which will raise money costs. The higher cost will also mean higher property taxes and insurance premiums. As a result, rents in newer structures are likely to continue to increase. That will tend to narrow the new structure's market, while expanding the market for older structures. As demand for the older structures increases, rents can be pushed upward to produce a larger income stream. At that point, the cycle repeats itself and more new buildings are produced. In your evaluation of older and newer structures, the emphasis should be on comparative yields and returns on specific investment opportunities.

Older structures which have deteriorated in some way can be good candidates for capital turnover projects. Such candidates are usually easy to spot. They display symptoms of poor management, perhaps high continuing vacancies, indifferent maintenance or poor financing arrangements. Such symptoms in older, still functional properties can be highly visible signals that an opportunity exists for you to create more value through change than the change will cost you.

Ultimately your choice of a type of real estate turns on your personal interest. You may find that your initial objective could be achieved by investment in a neighborhood shopping center, a moderate-sized apartment building or a professional office building, either new or older. All three may be equivalent in risk and, thus, yield. Let us also assume that all three require an equivalent investment and produce equivalent incomes, tax shelter and capital appreciation. However, the shopping center and the office building may both meet your additional requirement for less management involvement. Your actual choice of the shopping center may be determined by your greater knowledge of retail and by its greater personal appeal.

It is important to attend to what most interests you. Familiarizing yourself with each type's specialized jargon, management requirements, locational influences and market behavior can prove an insuperable task if attempted all at one time. Overburdening yourself in this way may even prevent you from recognizing unusual opportunities within a type, a recognition that depends on depth of knowledge as well as breadth. Letting your preferences restrict your initial choice to one or two types of real estate will measurably improve your chances of success.

We have also taken the approach that it is best to start small and work up. Acquiring real estate involving top credit tenants or an interest in them has obvious advantages: High security and long term. Such properties are also usually larger physically. Thus, they have the potential to make the market, which would also increase security.

Certainly, a 10,000 home subdivision, a planned unit development with a large number of homes plus schools and some jobs, a new town which serves all its residents' needs or a huge apartment complex can dominate the local residential market. So, too, can a large-scale office or industrial park or a regional shopping center. Real estate of this magnitude tends to set the standards against which nearby real estate of the same type is measured. Moreover, if such an improvement is attractive both in design and maintenance, it may attract compatible new structures or new uses of existing surrounding ones, change transportation patterns to favor it, and so on. All this would tend to increase its value. Smaller sized real estate is undeniably more dependent on the general market.

A large-scale property may also enable you to spread your costs over more units of production, thus bringing down expenses and thereby rents or sales prices. A larger market would then result. The largest sizes risk, however, overwhelming the available market. They also tend to involve government more heavily. For one example, the pollution produced by huge industrial plants or through the traffic generated by shopping centers, office, residential or recreational complexes may involve environmental impact statements, delays due to the governmental decision process and increased expenses to meet pollution standards.

Large-scale top-quality real estate usually involves substantial sums of equity capital. It is the kind that big money, such as pension funds, insurance companies and individuals of substantial net worth, seeks out. But, even if you have sufficient capital to acquire an investment in real estate on such a large scale, we have reservations about doing so for your initial entry into real estate.

We recognize that the quality of such real estate makes it highly marketable and thus to some degree more liquid. However, the market for such real estate is a shallow one. Just as there are relatively few individuals able to afford a home worth $250,000 or a diamond ring worth six million dollars, so too are there few investors available to acquire large-scale interests in real estate investments.

Top-quality tenants also pay far less for their floor space than do other tenants because the risks and, thus, the yields required are low. As a consequence, the incomes available are relatively low. The highest grade of tenant knows that it makes or breaks the project for you in terms of drawing in shoppers, for example. Such a tenant also knows that you can not obtain financing for the project unless it is already on the lease.

As a result, you are lucky to break even on the space you rent to such tenants in a shopping center or an office building. They might pay four dollars a square foot compared to the ten dollars or more you might obtain from the lower quality tenants. Single users of industrial properties, such as General Motors, also know that your prime reward lies in the security of the income they pay. You earn less as a consequence. If you seek to build income, top quality real estate will not help you build it as rapidly as other properties of somewhat less quality.

There is a more fundamental reason for our position. We feel that success in real estate investment comes from following a learning curve. By starting with relatively small properties and a small investment, you will be exposed to real estate investment at its most basic, in a way that will enable you to learn the most.

Certainly, top quality real estate is the most complex, involving teams of professionals who have worked up to that eminence. It takes experienced nationwide leasing agents to capture the interest and commitment of a Macy's, a Caterpillar or an IBM. It takes the best of skilled planners, financial feasibility experts, promotional agents, mechanical systems managers, ad infinitum.

Starting small will put you in these positions. You will be exposed to the problems and the opportunities involved in managing real estate to increase income and value. By learning the skills involved, you can translate your experience gains into the satisfaction of knowing what you are doing. That, in turn, will enable you to move up to more substantial investment opportunities. Moreover, your learning on smaller real estate involving smaller capital sums will be accomplished at less risk to your investment strategy.

Typically, an investor starting in real estate needs more income, so he or she buys a duplex or a fourplex, fixes it up and obtains extra income. Then the investor may sell that one and buy two. As this process continues, the need may change from immediate periodic income to lump sums of capital. Then the investor may switch some of her or his energies to capital turnover projects. And that, in turn, may necessitate investing in tax shelter opportunities as well. Finally, the investor may become interested in long-term capital appreciation, preserving and increasing the wealth that has been accumulated.

This wealth curve is immensely facilitated by a corresponding experience curve. Thus, even if you want and can now afford to acquire 1,000 apartment units, you might be better off starting with a 100- or 150-unit building. That would give you a feel for what such an investment is about. Not having such a feel or the intuitive understanding that personal experience can bring will put you at the mercy of the promoters of the 1,000-unit venture and of your advisors.

Becoming to some degree involved will also tend to increase the kinds of real estate which appeal to you. As an investor, you will naturally associate with other investors. One of these may be involved in marinas, which may capture your interest at some stage in your development. As you build adequate financial reserves and experience, you will be able to capitalize on such opportunities.

In fact, we suggest you join a local branch of the main organization of owner/operators involved in the type of real estate you select. One such organization is the Building Owners and Managers Association International (BOMA), 1221 Massachusetts Avenue NW, Washington, D.C. 20005. This organization may help to direct you either to its own local chapters or to organizations appropriate to the size and type of real estate you have chosen. (BOMA tends to represent the larger scale owners, but its surveys of operating ratios are invaluable to all owners.) An organization for apartment owner-managers is the National Apartment Association, Suite 604, 1825 K Street NW, Washington, D.C. 20006. Another, for people involved in new construction and remodeling, is the National Association of Home Builders, 15th and M Streets NW, Washington, D.C. 20005. Not only will you learn a great deal of management information you should in any case acquire, but by attending meetings of the local group associated with the national organization, you will also be exposed to more opportunities.

Even if you intend to become a passive investor, you should require discussions about the physical constraints on the real estate in which you are acquiring an interest, its management, its market and other details in the reports your working partner sends you. Starting small will help here, too. The group you join will be small enough for you to insist at the outset on such reports. You can then bring what you learn to bear on your next passive investment.

In our discussion of each type of real estate, we will concentrate on the smaller ends of the scale, both in terms of physical scale and capital needed for acquisition. We have again provided a worksheet at the end of the chapter for you to note your preliminary choices.

RESIDENTIAL

You may be most comfortable starting with residential real estate. After all, you are most likely to be familiar with this type of real estate as a consequence of having lived in housing all your life. You can start by thinking about the information you already possess in terms of what you consider would make a particular home attractive or unattractive to a buyer or renter.

Size The spaces in which people choose to live range all the way from single rooms to spacious triplex apartments and mansions. The differences reflect what are really distinctions in ability to afford a space as well as distinctions in its appropriateness and acceptability.

There is a relationship between the size of a space and the affluence of its consumer, although this is not an absolute. The argument in Congress over banning large cars because they use more gasoline illustrates the relationship well: Many in Congress assumed that large cars served no functional purpose, that such cars were simply symbols of affluence. But, as individuals with large families pointed out, large cars can also be necessities.

Given general equality of condition, the larger the space, the more expensive it can be to purchase or rent. And, also generally speaking, the larger the space, the smaller the market for it. Relatively few people can afford the most expensive housing products. Thus, the most affordable housing tends to be small in scale and low in price compared to the largest, most expensive kinds.

Appropriateness and acceptability also play a role in what makes people choose the kind of housing they do. For example, most people feel that owning a single family home is the most appropriate and acceptable form of housing for the purpose of raising a family.

But, not all families can afford today's high-priced freestanding houses. Thus, other forms of housing have sprung up which try to approximate the ownership and use aspects of the detached house. For example, townhouses, using party walls, small yards and perhaps such devices as a blanket insurance policy, make individual units more affordable. The clustering together of freestanding homes is another device used to try to bring the home price down.

Yet another expedient is the mobile home, which is relatively inexpensive because of the manufacturing process involved. Also along the continuum is the apartment owned by the family occupying it. Such apartments are known as cooperatives if each family owns a share in the property with the right to occupy a particular space or as condominiums if the family owns the apartment outright and shares in the ownership of common areas such as halls, roofs and even recreational facilities. Such forms of ownership share reduced maintenance with the apartment form of housing.

Housing choices form a continuum, with a great deal of movement back and forth among the choices, particularly as a result of changes in age and family formation. Thus, one form of housing is often highly substitutable for another. In effect, any one form is competing with all the other forms.

However, more sharply than do other types of real estate, residential real estate divides into those properties most suitable for sale to those who will be living there and those most suitable for renting. In the types of real estate occupied by businesses, very few people are likely to know whether a business owns or rents the real estate it uses. Even fewer will care. In residential real estate, everyone tends to know and care. Thus, any particular local residential area is likely to be dominated by either real estate individuals own or real estate individuals rent. This is an important consideration as you can only defy what the local market considers most appropriate for residential real estate for a short time.

Thus, in most areas, single family detached homes are considered appropriate for ownership, particularly by families. Some areas do consist of homes for rent, but not many. You can acquire and rent a single family home in an area dominated by homeownership for a while. But you have to be careful to rent to a family who will keep it up as well as the neighbors do or you will have to give it the care you would give your own home. Otherwise, it will deteriorate by comparison with proximate homes, and you are likely to have trouble reselling it at the price for which you hoped.

Duplexes, triplexes and fourplexes can go either way. Thus, they can be wholly owned by the occupants, partially occupied by an owner and the remainder rented or wholly rented. Larger buildings more typically are wholly rented, although there is a growing trend toward cooperative or condominium ownership. In many areas, you can convert a rental building into an ownership building and sell each unit for more than it cost you to buy it and upgrade it to attract owner-occupiers. However, in some areas you are likely to run into political resistance organized on behalf of tenants who might be evicted in the process.

Investors interested in long-term income and tax shelter potential generally stick to real estate designed for and used by tenants. Single family houses do not usually generate rental income beyond the break-even point, if that, and they are limited in the amount of tax shelter they produce. Such homes are best considered an interim income source to be held for capital appreciation in rapidly developing areas.

Small-scale rental housing might include the duplex, triplex, fourplex, the urban rowhouse or even a 10- to 12-unit apartment building if your financial resources and experience are a little greater. You will run a somewhat higher risk of vacancies with small-scale real estate. One vacancy in duplex can wipe out 50 percent of your income, in a fourplex 25 percent of your income, whereas one in a 50-unit apartment building constitutes only two percent of income.

However, smaller scale residential real estate enables you to substitute time and effort if money is in short supply. It also places you in the best position to make an inexpensive arrangement with a tenant or another building's superintendent to handle repairs, trash removal, snow removal and other comparable jobs. Smaller scale residential real estate also restricts the possibility that rent controls may interfere with your operation of it. Such rent controls as have been applied generally exempt real estate with very few tenants.

As you gain more experience and perhaps greater financial capability, you can move up in size to the middle range, such as the 10- to 12-unit building or the 50- to 100-unit building. Such buildings may be slightly more likely to have commercial tenants on the ground floor, giving you an opportunity to diversify the type of tenant as well as your experience.

Lease Provisions Residential leases generally fall into two short-term categories: (1) One-year, two-year or three-year terms or (2) Month-to-month leases. One type usually predominates in an area or for a particular level of tenants. The advantage of short-term leases is that they enable you to react more quickly to economic conditions than you can with the generally longer term leases on other types of real estate. Thus, with residential leases you have more frequent opportunities to keep up with expense increases and with inflation. Of course, you must also be involved in a more or less continual leasing program.

In most cases, apartment tenants can not be charged escalators or other separate charges for necessary services such as hot and cold water, heat and janitorial services. Moreover, rents generally can not be increased within the term of the lease unless a capital improvement, such as wiring for air conditioning, is made. Separate fees can be charged for the replacement of lost keys or more frequent painting than is the norm or may be required by the locality.

Most residential leases in an area will be standardized by the local real estate board. There will, thus, be less need for negotiating particular terms in this largely take-it-or-leave-it situation. However, you can generally add clauses requiring security deposits in different amounts, such as one month's or two months' rent and, in some areas of the country, cleaning deposits. These clauses protect you in the event that damage beyond ordinary wear and tear should occur; they also cover any unusual cleaning costs before the apartment unit can be re-leased.

You may also decide to insert clauses forbidding pets or allowing pets only by written permission subject to their causing no damage. In some cases, in order to cover the potentially greater damage, owners require larger security deposits from tenants with children.

In markets where there is an overabundance of space, you may have to offer rent concessions to tenants to get them to sign your leases. Concessions can include forgiveness of rent for a month or two at some point during the lease, extra decorating services or free utilities. When you examine income streams on nearby comparable properties it is important to consider whether rent concessions are being offered, as concessions reduce income.

Quality and Durability of Income   The quality and durability of the income you receive depends partly on your competition and partly on the level of tenant to whom you rent. Thus, you may risk rapid turnover if you acquire rental real estate in an area where tenants would prefer to be owner-occupiers of single family homes. If their choice of apartment living is dictated by affordability you may be particularly vulnerable if the government institutes new programs that subsidize homeownership beyond the current tax deductions allowed and insured mortgages offered. New production techniques in housing may also lower the cost of detached housing and increase your competition.

Concentrating on the apartment markets which seem to prefer apartment living, such as young and older adults, may help. Of course, if you aim at singles, particularly young adults, who make up the most mobile segment of the market, you may also have rapid turnover. This will increase your renting costs, as you will have to redecorate apartments for new tenants more frequently and you may suffer from more vacancies. Of course, singles can be charged relatively higher rents because they tend to have fewer financial responsibilities.

Renting to the middle class tends to give you the broadest market in many areas, although this market is the one most vulnerable to the lure of homeownership. Choosing to rent to people in the upper income category may leave you most vulnerable to downturns in the economy as supplemental income programs rarely come to but a small fraction of any incomes lost at this level.

Not only should you consider the amount prospective tenants can now pay in rent, but also what they may be able to pay at lease renewal time. Thus, individuals showing a steady increase in income as they move up a career path or gain seniority are more likely to be able to afford the increases you may need to charge. Tenants who do not seem likely to be able to afford increases will negate the chief appeal of the short-term apartment lease: Your ability in moderate to strong rental markets to raise rents relatively frequently to make up for expense increases and for inflation.

Location Implicit in our discussion of the quality and durability of income is the effect of the building's location. The most desirable residential real estate is in areas restricted to residences. Such areas are free of noxious influences. Thus, residential real estate on a main avenue or next to a service station would be less desirably located than a property on a side street with little traffic. How sensitive your potential tenants will be to incompatible uses depends to some degree on the state of shortage existing in your area. Market shortages, of course, usually correct themselves given enough time, which could leave a building in a less desirable location vulnerable to excessive vacancies.

Residential real estate is also considered to be well located if it is relatively near employment suitable to those living in the building and near shopping, schools and community facilities. Thus, generally, a suburban area within 30 minutes of a white-collar employment center is more likely to produce steady income than is one where employment is 60 minutes away.

People tend to prefer to live conveniently near jobs, schools, shopping and other community facilities used frequently. Real estate where such conveniences are not yet available but will be developed may well exhibit a higher potential for capital appreciation than for immediate income. Conversely, real estate located near rapid transport in a city, the most intensive transportation developed, would tend to command the highest rents.

Generally speaking, the more desirable the location, the better the quality of tenant you can attract. You can also attract more tenants, and they are likely to stay for longer periods.

Management Requirements Residential rental real estate tends to require more operational management than other types. This may be because tenants feel their space is home, which has many more emotional overtones than does workspace or recreational facility.

People also come in all temperaments. And in their own homes, they may be less likely to subject their feelings to discipline. The opportunities for misunderstandings, resentment and downright rancor are correspondingly great. Experience has shown that individual standards of cleanliness, care for property and control of children range all over the lot, with little or no regard to income level.

A management approach which does not take this into account will compound the difficulties inherent in taking such actions as raising the rent and making repairs. As a rule, the better the management and the more positive it is, within economic reason, the better the chance of collecting rent on time and of recovering the real estate in good shape at the end of a lease. Adequate reserves for normal wear and tear and even for some degree of deliberate vandalism may have to be factored into your rents.

Adequate tenant education will certainly help to mitigate some of the problems. A diligent effort to rent to people with high quality references can also help. You should also give due regard to your own temperament. A negative approach to tenants is likely to help cause negative behavior. Patience is also necessary. If you are not a patient person, perhaps you should start practicing; if you are already patient, you will have to guard against being taken advantage of.

Financing Single family homes are most favored by institutional lenders because the market is generally so broad and because people will, as a rule, go to greater lengths to keep a home they own. Apartment houses also tend to be considered good loans because the income streams of such properties are somewhat less subject to fluctuation. Furthermore, many lenders are restricted to investing mainly in residential real estate, which can increase the sources of debt financing available to you.

Liquidity Single family houses also tend to be the most liquid real estate investments, again because of the depth and breadth of the market. For the same reason, the most liquid apartment buildings would be those serving the middle class. The size of the investment required also affects liquidity, just as it does appreciation potential.

Thus, a home selling for $200,000 is not only limited in the number of buyers who can afford it but, for that reason, may have approached the outside limit on its appreciation. A medium-priced house costing $75,000, in a market of comparable houses ranging from $60,000 to $120,000, is both more liquid and has more room to move up in value.

A medium-sized apartment building, such as a 50-unit structure, also tends to be fairly liquid. There are relatively more buyers for it than there would be for larger scale real estate, although relatively fewer than for smaller scale real estate. However, the reduced management requirement that comes from having real estate capable of supporting at least a superintendent can make this size of real estate a more desirable acquisition for a broader range of investor. Real estate in the more desirable locations also tends to display increased liquidity.

RETAIL

You may also find commercial real estate a good type with which to start. There are many more commercial tenants than there are industrial or special purpose tenants. You can start by thinking through what attracts you in a store and what tends to deter you from shopping in some stores.

Size The largest shopping centers, the regionals, are distinguished by the number of major department stores that anchor them. They provide the pull needed to move shoppers into the smaller specialty stores. The next largest may include a junior department store and/or a large supermarket as anchors in combination with specialty stores. Neighborhood centers are usually occupied by a supermarket plus a number of smaller stores with services needed in the neighborhood. These might include a drugstore, a liquor store, a stationery store and so on. Smaller still are stores on, perhaps, a main street which concentrate mainly on services such as shoe repair.

Each size draws on a smaller and smaller trade area. In fact, the trouble with many older, smaller marketing areas in smaller communities is that the trade area no longer supports them. With the coming of the automobile, larger trading areas became possible, which allowed for larger stores offering goods at more competitive prices.

However, if population densities are growing in such towns, particularly if apartment units are constructed within walking distance, such bypassed trading units may be revitalized. This can provide a good opportunity for a capital turnover investor to renovate the stores to make them attractive again.

Lease Provisions In almost all cases, retail store operators lease their premises. Stores differ, however, in how rentals are calculated. Thus, a uniform square foot rental figure might be quoted for a store selling such necessities as food. By having the most essential food items in the rear of the store space, the layout encourages shoppers to make purchases throughout the store.

In contrast, most of the business in more fashion-oriented stores, such as clothing boutiques, is focused in the front of the store. Thus, the less deep the store, the more desirable it might be. Square foot rentals are likely to be higher for the front portion of the store than for the rear part. In fact, if the stores are very deep, it might make sense to chop off the rear portions to increase the space available for parking.

Leases on retail facilities tend to provide for escalators to cover increases in expenses and perhaps a cost-of-living increase to combat inflation. They may also provide for overages, or a percentage participation in the store operators' gross sales.

Quality and Durability of Income Quality and durability of income is highly variable. It ranges from the credit rated tenants in the regionals to small, new firms. Many people, in the effort to achieve the dream of running their own businesses, open shops that are poorly capitalized and poorly operated. The individualistic sort of person who is likely to start a business tends not to take advantage of courses and other help designed to improve the entrepreneur's chances of staying in business. In most cases, new businesses of every type fail because of management difficulties. Thus, the most critical factor in your evaluation of a business tenant may be your judgement of how well that tenant handles management functions.

To minimize the risks, you might want to set up minimum tenant selection criteria for the smaller scale entrepreneurs. Thus, you might insist that each of the store operators has engaged in business before, that each has the necessary capitalization to stay in business at least six months or a year and/or that the store be adequately stocked. Finding out a prospective tenant's plans can only help, as can listening to what a tenant thinks your store will do for his or her business. The more thoughtful the answers you receive, the better your chances of achieving a reliable income stream.

Location The best locations for commercial real estate are those which have high accessibility and high visibility. If shoppers can not see a store and can not get into it, they will not go shopping there. In all areas except those dependent on public transport, there must be space for adequate parking facilities, and drivers must easily be able to turn off well traveled streets into these parking areas. Even in downtown locations, there must be adequate parking space for delivery trucks and for shoppers who do use their cars.

Good store locations exhibit characteristics that are somewhat opposite to those needed for many residential developments. Thus, it is not good for a store to be located on a quiet side street. A certain amount of automobile or pedestrian traffic must pass by if the store owner is to intercept some of it for customers. For successful interception, the store must appeal to the income level and needs of the people who live or work nearby.

Management Requirements Small commercial operations require somewhat less management than does residential real estate. For example, some services you must provide to apartment tenants, such as trash removal, sidewalk cleaning and interior decorating, may not be required. Commercial tenants usually handle these items themselves. However, you may become involved in enforcing these lease provisions and others, such as proper signage. Leasing requirements are heavier. You are likely to need more services from your lawyer in drawing up leases and from a leasing agent in helping you negotiate leases.

You may also find, particularly with small operators, that it will pay you to learn something about their businesses. Then you may be able to make suggestions for improving their sales through better displays. You may also want to develop cooperative advertising among several retailers to boost business for them all.

Financing Small commercial operations generally are less able to attract financing from an institutional source. Such lenders generally require a less favorable loan-to-value ratio and might also charge a higher interest rate. A second loan from a seller may be necessary. Of course, a tenant with the quality of a bank will help you obtain better terms. It may also help if you acquire real estate with apartments over the stores. That combination will provide you with an additional source of income, which may be more secure.

Liquidity Commercial real estate is only as liquid as the size of the property, solidity of the tenants and the desirability of the location allow. The better these are, the more liquidity there will be.

OFFICE

Office buildings can also make an appealing first choice. You are apt to be able to bring to bear at least your own experiences of working in an office and visiting the offices of other people. Moreover, you may be involved in leasing your own office space.

Companies which own their own headquarters buildings tend to do so for reasons of prestige. Such buildings are often uneconomic from an investor's point of view, as the company may have spent more on the building than can be recaptured in rent. Most office users, however, rent.

Size Office real estate ranges in size from skyscrapers to suburban low rise office buildings to buildings with offices over retail establishments. In some cases, single users occupy the whole building; in others, the building is cut up into separate, smaller, medium-size offices with some tenants taking whole floors.

Lease Provisions Office leasing is a specialized field, one with which you may need help at first from a leasing agent. Typically, leases are quoted on the basis of cost per square foot of usable space excluding hallways and other common spaces. However, if a lessee has the entire floor, the per square foot rental can be figured on a gross basis and will include all areas on the floor.

You may be able to negotiate tax, insurance and labor expense escalators with your office tenants. You may also be able to obtain a cost-of-living increase clause. However, percentage rentals are not typical.

Quality and Durability of Income The stability of your income stream will depend partly on the demand for your lessee's business and partly on his or her business acumen. Newly established services tend to be a problem. Thus, the current oversupply of young lawyers may reduce the chances for success of any one lawyer just now setting up his or her office. Buildings occupied by older, more established firms will provide a more stable source of income.

Some thought should also be given to the degree of vulnerability certain tenants have in economic downturns. Doctors and dentists may suffer little negative effect. However, architects, particularly those serving the market for individual homes, may suffer disproportionately from recessions.

Location Office space usually follows residential space for two reasons: There must be lessees and employees from the surrounding area to fill up the office space; and many office operators gear their services, particularly professional services, to the surrounding population. Office space can be highly compatible with residential use, as office lessees do not produce noxious influences. Even the traffic congestion produced is relatively minimal because people do not tend to travel to offices in the numbers they do to stores. Truck traffic tends to be limited to that involving office supplies and equipment repair services.

The best locations for office buildings are those with easy accessibility both in terms of traffic flow and parking, particularly in areas geared primarily to automobile travel. Certain kinds of tenants are best located only in certain areas. Thus, dentists may locate near almost any residential area, but orthodontists and legal service firms tend to be utilized mostly by upper-income families.

This may change. The increasing use of third-party payments for these services may cause them to spread out to reach more of the population. Also, the lifting of the ban on professional advertisements may mean that such offices can be located in relatively less visible space. Prestige, however, is likely to continue to be a factor. Thus, in a small town, legal offices are more likely to locate over a bank than over a grocery store.

Management Requirements   Small office buildings typically require some personal management. In many cases, owners are expected to provide maintenance services for the common areas and for the exterior, even though lessees may contract for the cleaning of their own offices. Owners of office buildings are also more likely than those of retail space to provide for redecorating or repartitioning as space needs expand and contract.

Some kinds of offices, such as a doctor's or a lawyer's, may need extensive partitioning to ensure a high degree of privacy. Other offices are more open and thus less expensive to provide. Doctors and dentists tend to require more extensive plumbing facilities. Doctors also require elevator services if they are located above the ground floor.

You are not likely to become involved in your tenants' businesses. However, you may want to insist that signs on and in the building meet your standards. The more attractive the signing, the more people will be attracted to the building.

Financing Office buildings may attract relatively more financing from institutional lenders, particularly if the tenants are well established. Specialty office uses, such as a medical building or a legal building, tend to be somewhat more attractive to a lender. There is often a positive reason for certain office tenants to locate in such a property as the services they and their clients need are attracted to the buildings. For example, a pharmacy might locate in a medical building and a typing firm specializing in legal secretarial services in a legal building.

Liquidity Office real estate is only as liquid as the quality and durability of the income stream and the property's location and size allow. It may attract more buyers because it involves somewhat less volatile tenants than comparable retail real estate. In many cases, office tenants have had to undergo extensive training in order to offer their services and are thus somewhat less likely to change work directions. Buyers may also be more attracted because there is generally less management involvement in small-scale office properties than in either retail or residential real estate.

INDUSTRIAL

Industrial real estate is somewhat harder to start with. Most such operations involve relatively large spaces for the use of machinery in plants or storage in warehouses. You may also be less familiar with the needs of such users.

The larger space requirements tend to require investments on a larger scale. You might need to form a partnership or join one. Industrial real estate is also somewhat more complex, partly as a result of a need for increased health and safety protection. This may require you or your working partner to have more experience.

Size Large industrial real estate includes the industrial park, which might encompass several hundred acres and include compatible office buildings and a hotel, the large assembly plant of several million square feet and the warehouse designed for national distribution of goods. Next in line in terms of size are the medium-sized industrial plant and regional warehouse facility. Smaller opportunities may lie in the more locally oriented plant and the warehouse designed to serve local needs. In cities where streets and utilities are already in place, it might be possible to construct a small plant on suitable vacant land.

Lease Provisions   Most industrial real estate is net leased. Thus, the user is responsible for all operating expenses and care and maintenance of the property. As a consequence of that, rentals tend to be somewhat low on a per-square-foot basis. However, the main determinant of the quantity of rent is the credit of the tenant. A low credit tenant should produce more rent than a high credit one.

Quality and Durability of Income   Industrial real estate's quality and durability of income depends on the credit of the tenant involved. The Triple A credits provide annuity-type incomes as a function of their high degree of security.

Location   More than any other use, industrial real estate depends on excellent transportation facilities. Raw materials must be moved in by truck, rail or barge. Employees must have good access by car in the suburbs or by mass transit or foot in the city. Manufactured goods must move out to the next stage of production or consumption by truck, rail, water and, increasingly, by air.

Thus, while residences can be served by secondary and tertiary access roads and an office or retail complex by a main street or highway, the industrial facility must usually be located with rapid access to the most developed forms of transportation, that is, to the interstate highway and the airport.

Industrial users may also require copious quantities of water of a certain quality, special sewage arrangements and utility services. Particularly important are energy sources, as industrial users tend to consume the most energy. Industries which compete over wide geographic areas are sensitive to both the price and availability of these various requirements.

The best locations today are those which not only exhibit the above features but are also suitable for single story expandable facilities. Such plants or warehouses are generally the efficiency module today, just as taller gravity-fed buildings were most efficient in the past. Thus, the land involved must be relatively level, although after a plant has been constructed it may be landscaped to look somewhat rolling to hide parking and other service areas.

Industrial use is the least compatible with residential use unless the plant's work force is drawn from walking distance. Industrial parks can, however, be designed to mitigate incompatibilities through careful planning, provided such parks involve only light industrial, warehousing and office buildings. Heavy industrial use is almost impossible to live near, although change is taking place and compliance with environmental protection requirements is increasing.

Industrial users also generally require locations with high concentrations of suitable employees within a short commuting distance. If a warehouse is involved, the lessee will require a high concentration of outlets to serve.

Management Requirements Relatively little management is required for industrial properties, because industrial lessees typically take care of indoor and outdoor maintenance and repairs. Thus, inspection of the facility may be all that is necessary beyond payment of the debt service and insurance premiums.

The exception involves industrial parks which may require an experienced leasing staff as well as intensive, experienced management to keep each facility operating within the covenants established. Maintenance of common areas and liaison with the surrounding community are necessities. Some developers turn such functions over to an industrial association after the park has been completed.

Financing The credit rating of the tenant involved will usually determine the financing available. The higher the credit rating, the more financing you can obtain and the better the terms you can negotiate. New industries are hardest to finance unless a major established and well-managed firm provides the backing. Because there are relatively few industrial tenants and there is intense competition among communities for them, there is an additional risk with smaller firms that you will not be able to replace them. Conversion of modern industrial facilities to a completely different use is difficult and often impossible, as the spaces and locations tend not to be attractive to other users.

Liquidity Liquidity generally depends on the credit rating of the tenant. The higher the credit rating, the more liquid the property will generally be. Certainly the credit rating of a General Motors, combined with the minimal management requirement, makes an investment in a net leased GM facility attractive to many buyers. However, the size of the investment which may be involved tends to limit the number of buyers in the market at any one time.

LAND

Undeveloped land is an unusual investment, most suitable for short-term capital appreciation investors or for capital turnover investors. To make a capital gain profit, unimproved land must about double in value within five years. A ten percent rate of return would require its value to double in seven years. The high holding costs will keep you from making a profit if the appreciation is less rapid.

To achieve sufficient growth in value, unimproved land must be located in the path of development. However, land in such a path is likely to be expensive. Thus, you are gambling that you can raise the price yet again without overpricing it in relation to any use that might be made of it.

Any interim incomes available, from farming, timber cutting or parking lots, at best often merely offset such expenses as property taxes and insurance premiums. Depreciation is limited to any improvements on the land such as asphalt paving or fencing.

Acquiring land for capital turnover purposes today requires the use for the land to be almost immediately achievable. Developers involved in construction of new facilities can no longer afford to stockpile land indefinitely. Thus, the demand for housing, retail, office, industrial or special purpose use must be on the horizon.

Size   The larger sizes of land, involving hundreds or thousands of acres, limit the developers to those planning a large subdivision, a planned unit development, a major shopping center or an office, industrial or recreational park. Smaller sized acreage is more likely to move onto the market sooner as there are potentially more purchasers, ranging from smaller scale developers to individual home buyers.

The larger the amount of land involved, the more involvement with government will be mandated. For one thing, the problems are likely to be greater. Traffic pollution and congestion difficulties are manifestly harder to resolve if a regional shopping center is involved than if it is a matter of two or three stores. Moreover, the burden shifts to the developer to solve such problems. Overhead will be higher as land planning must be more sophisticated, documentation more thorough and financial analysis more demanding. It will also take longer to get the necessary permits to proceed with development.

Smaller scale acreage which is suitable for development involves much less in the way of expertise and capital. Furthermore, projects planned on smaller plots of land are likely to meet with more community approval. Infill projects designed for land bypassed by previous development may meet with the highest degree of acceptability. Streets and other community services are more likely to be in place, a considerable plus in areas where government is hostile to new development because the cost of bringing municipal services to it exceeds the fees or taxes that can be collected.

Lease Provisions   Leases to interim users are generally short-term so that you do not discourage a purchaser, particularly one who plans to use the property and is thus able to pay the highest price. Buyers who may want the land for development do not want any more delays in gaining possession than can be helped. Enough delays result from obtaining government permits to build.

However, leases on ground intended to support a significant improvement tend to be relatively long, at least as long as the improvement on the land is expected to last either economically or physically. Ground leases on land supporting improvements involving top credit tenants are virtually dictated by the credit rating of the tenant. Thus, such ground leases are usually acquired by investors interested more in security of income and in appreciation than in amount of income. Ground leases involved in properties with less creditworthy tenants are more negotiable, and should give you more income for less security.

Quality and Durability of Income Interim users do not provide much in the way of durability, nor should they, as you are seeking to sell for capital gain. The quality of the income varies with the quality of the tenant. For example, some large national firms are lessees of small-scale parking lots.

Ground lease income also varies with the quality and durability of the tenant providing the income stream. Frequently, ground leases are involved in the most creditworthy projects because they cut down on the amount of capital needed for development.

Location Because of high holding costs and the lack of adequate income, most undeveloped or underdeveloped land for investment should be located where development is most likely to take place next. Anything which would help to bring that development to your particular plot of land, such as increased accessibility, water and other municipal services and appropriate topography, is highly desirable.

Particularly important is the location of your land in relation to radial transportation patterns. Almost all development has occurred along transportation spokes, as can readily be observed by examining a map showing commuter rail lines and highways. New highways which link the spokes may spark new development. A location where new development might occur after an existing improvement wears away is best if you are making a long-term investment in land subject to a ground lease.

Management Requirements Undeveloped land requires minimal maintenance, such as haying, clearing of drainage ditches and inspection to make sure no one is using it in an inappropriate way. Land subject to ground leases requires even less, perhaps only the handling of debt service payments.

Land under development, however, requires intensive management. The entire process, from planning and analysis to applications for zoning changes or for permits to actual construction if that is involved, is complex. It also requires a strong hand at the helm if all the inherent problems are not to overwhelm the project's success.

Financing Unimproved land is the least financeable type of property, for reasons we have discussed previously. At the most, institutional lenders might provide a loan against 50 percent of the value of the property. Land with an interim use is only somewhat more financeable. Obtaining an additional mortgage loan from a seller may raise your holding costs substantially.

Land under development shows a pattern of irregular cash inflow, if any, and outflow. Thus, construction loan interest payments may have to be made by the equity investors. Land subject to a ground lease to a top credit can be extremely financeable as the lender can judge the quality of the project and knows where the income for its payments is coming from.

Liquidity The closeness of the land to development determines its liquidity. The farther away the land is from development, the fewer buyers will be interested. And, if the land is ready for immediate use, the market will shrink to developers ready to develop it. Land subject to long-term ground leases tends to be liquid in relation to the credit rating of the tenant providing the income. However, income from ground leases may be relatively less marketable than income from other types of property because it has no tax shelter attached to it.

SPECIAL PURPOSE REAL ESTATE

Real estate designed for special use is easily the most difficult to start with. You face much higher risks. Not only may a small operator fail, as an individual residential, office, retail or industrial tenant may, but it is less likely that you will be able to substitute another tenant. You will also need more experience to evaluate each individual tenant.

Size Stadiums, convention centers, hospitals and transportation terminals rank among the largest special purpose properties. Smaller properties might include a fast-food operation, a small sports facility or a nursing home.

Lease Provisions Leases are highly individualized. It is harder to develop lease terms as there are not as many comparable tenants. Thus, it is more difficult to develop a norm and then adapt that norm to your and your tenant's needs. With smaller sports operators, leases with percentage rents are somewhat common. Achieving percentage rentals may, however, be difficult. Moreover, becoming involved with the many franchise operations which utilize special purpose properties may mean negotiating a lease with expert lease negotiators.

Quality and Durability of Income The income stream is only as reliable as the tenant. Individual tenants may not have high credit ratings. That may include even the franchisees of the national firms. The individual franchise holder is in some instances undercapitalized or he or she would probably establish an independent business. However, it is possible in many cases to get a guarantee from the franchisor, and, with proper lease provisions, have it maintain the real estate. But, there should be heavy penalties for failure to do business. That would provide the franchisor with a strong incentive to substitute another franchisee if one fails. An empty property, even one where an absentee tenant is paying the rent, tends to deteriorate in value.

Location Small-scale special use real estate, such as fast-food outlets, bowling alleys and tennis courts, is usually located where there is extreme visibility and extremely easy access. Many of these businesses depend on impulse buying and convenience to attract customers. Parking requirements tend to be high in areas where cars are predominant; pedestrian counts tend to be high in walk-in locations.

Other special use properties are by their nature individual. As a consequence, some, such as a stadium, need highly visible locations; others, such as hospitals, need easy access; while yet others, such as an amusement park or a tire testing track, tend to be in areas remote from habitation.

Management Requirements Management must be intensive even if the real estate is net leased. Frequent inspection and supervision of maintenance may be necessary if the business is to keep up its income sufficiently to pay the rent. Adequate advertising and signage may also have to be supervised. The more effort and the more effective the effort you can require of your tenant, the higher the odds are for maintaining your income stream.

Financing Special purpose real estate falls somewhere between unimproved land and other types of real estate in terms of financing. Lenders are understandably wary of income dependent on a limited tenant supply. Any loan you obtain from an institutional lender is likely to be low in amount and high in cost. You may, thus, have to grant a mortgage to a seller or take on additional equity partners. Raising your capital costs will require you to receive higher rents. That, in turn, may jeopardize the ability of the tenant to stay in business.

Liquidity Special purpose real estate is somewhat less liquid than other types of real estate. Within the type, liquidity depends on the size of the investment required, the quality of the tenant's credit rating and the real estate's location.

There is a general tendency for all investors in real estate to trade upward in size to command economies of scale as they continue to invest. There is also a tendency to expand the types of real estate in which they invest and thus secure diversification of risk. But, in order to accomplish growth and expansion, each investor must start somewhere. As we have indicated, we feel the best place to start a long-term involvement in real estate investment is with

WORKSHEET 8
Selection of Real Estate Type

	Residential	Retail	Office	Industrial	Land	Special Purpose
Size						
Leasing Requirements						
Income Quality and Durability						
Location						
Management Requirements						
Financing Capability						
Liquidity						
TOTAL:						
DIVIDED BY:	7	7	7	7	7	7
AVERAGE:						

POINTS:
1 - Minimal   2 - Adequate   3 - Standard   4 - High

smaller real estate from which you can learn the most, at the least cost. We have provided Worksheet 8 to help you make your choice of real estate type.

You can use Worksheet 8 to rank each type of property by its ability to meet your standards. Thus, if you will require financing in order to acquire a property, you might put one point in the financing capability boxes under both land and special purpose real estate as these kinds of real estate are the least financeable. The types of real estate which produce the highest point averages will be the ones which are most likely to satisfy your goals. Within this group, you can then decide which type most interests you.

The form of ownership you select for your real estate investment is as critical a choice as its substance. The venture itself will have a significant economic impact on the achievement of your goals within the personal perimeters you have staked out. However, the ownership structure which incorporates your investment will have not only a great effect on its economics, but also important legal consequences. Therefore, great care must be exercised in making your choice.

There are three primary questions to which you must address yourself. The first concerns the legal vehicle which will most facilitate the achievement of your objectives and your personal investment choices. The second is the question of your exposure to liability problems. The last has to do with the relationship between the amount of capital you can make available for an investment and the amount of capital required from you in order to make it. How you handle these issues will depend on the importance you attach to various aspects of your objective choice and on your investor profile.

While many different ownership vehicles exist, they are all variations on three basic themes. Each can be used to acquire any interest in real estate ranging from an equity interest to a mortgage interest. However, once you complete your evaluation of the trade-offs each ownership vehicle requires among aspects of your goals and your investor profile, you are likely to find that one form is more appropriate to the situation you face than either of the other two. The three ownership forms are:

1. Sole proprietorship

2. Partnership

3. Corporate ownership

Each of these forms of ownership is created by the law, as this is a society of laws. Strict observance of the legalities is what will allow the benefits of real estate ownership to flow to you in the manner in which you want them to flow. The laws are complex in themselves and in their formal requirements. Failure to meet a formal requirement may invalidate your choice, just as a failure to make the right choice may nullify the objectives you hoped to achieve.

Moreover, each state has its own rules for setting up each ownership vehicle and for maintaining it in existence. State and local tax laws are based on state ownership laws, as are federal tax laws which have been overlaid on the foundation of state laws governing the ownership forms. Thus, a failure to observe the rules can have a broad impact on your investment strategy. In addition, legal situations can change rapidly as a result of legislative and court decisions.

As a consequence, legal counsel is an initial and continuing necessity. Not only that, but your legal advisor must be locally oriented for you to gain the most benefit, both for the purpose of understanding the ramifications of the choices available and for the proper execution of your choice. Nothing can substitute for a lawyer's guidance in questions involving such important consequences.

We will cover the primary issues in relation to the three ownership choices, your goals and needs. You can then make a tentative choice, subject to obtaining expert guidance which reflects the localized nature of the laws governing your choices. Nothing that follows should be construed as a substitute for competent legal advice covering the details of both the local situation and your individual position.

SOLE PROPRIETORSHIP

Sole ownership ranks highest in the amount of control you can establish, which is why most real estate investors choose this form. The property in which you invest is your ship; you are the captain. All ownership and management decisions are yours to make, subject only to the requirements of the law, the market and your lender, if you have one. Thus, you have a sole owner's right to transfer property in total or in part by sale, by gift or however else you please. You also have the sole right to make management decisions.

You are accountable only to yourself and not to any partner or shareholder. It is your objective, your risk/yield and term requirements that govern. If control and the kind of security which flows from total control are what you most want, this is the best vehicle you can select.

The profits and losses which flow from the property are also yours. Thus, you have the sole right to any cash flow, tax shelter, capital turnover or appreciation which you seek from the property and which it generates. Under the tax laws, any interest deductions, depreciation write-offs, or capital gains or losses belong only to you and can be applied directly to your tax return.

Of course, if you are in sole control, you cannot share the risks or decisions with anyone, for all the counsel you may seek from your professional advisors. You alone are responsible. With smaller properties, this can expose you to management liabilities, such as a call in the middle of the night if a roof develops a leak or the plumbing breaks down. However, you can choose to handle day-to-day management problems by taking care of them yourself or by getting one of the tenants or a superintendent from a neighboring property to handle them for you. As you move up the line to larger properties, you can insert management personnel between yourself and day-to-day operations. But, under this form of ownership, you will continue to be the one who makes the more important decisions.

A more serious issue may be the question of personal liability, either operating or debt liability. The first involves operating hazards, such as injuries from falls on your property. It can be handled by a program of preventive maintenance to reduce hazards and by the purchase of sufficient personal liability insurance.

Personal debt liability must be avoided altogether. Allowing yourself to be personally responsible for paying off any mortgage loan or loans on a property exposes you to the risk of bankruptcy if something should go wrong. Several ways exist to shift this risk. The first involves the insertion of what is called an exculpatory clause in any debt agreement. Such a clause asserts that, in the event of a default under the agreement, a lender can look only to the property on which the loan was made to satisfy the debt. The clause specifically excludes a lender from having recourse to your personal assets, such as your house.

Alternatively, you could put all your personal assets into a trust or in someone else's name. You must then consider whether you can trust the other person or whether you want to have to go to someone else in order to do something with the property. In each case, however, a lender would be barred from seizing your personal assets, although the lender could still obtain a judgement and attach your salary. You can also purchase mortgage insurance or life insurance in amounts which will extinguish the loan on your death. However, as you can see, all these attempts to solve a debt liability problem have their drawbacks compared with the exculpatory clause.

While most people who invest in real estate choose to do so as sole proprietors, such a choice does reflect an ability to provide the necessary capital. Mortgaging a property and substituting your time and effort for paid labor can reduce the amount of capital you need to contribute. However, this ownership form means that you must meet any capital requirement that still exists after you have taken these two actions.

If you want to acquire a property to which more capital than you can command must be applied, you have three choices. You may consider seeking out another property which would require less equity capital. Alternatively, you may decide to take on partners or take in shareholders, although the last is rarely done in real estate investment.

PARTNERSHIP

The partnership vehicle has at least two advantages over the sole proprietorship. An investor who does not have enough capital to accomplish his or her purpose may decide to join with others who can provide the capital required. An investor who lacks expertise in certain areas may also want to set up or join a partnership where the other partner or partners can fill in any skill gaps.

Partnerships require sharing the rewards of real estate ownership, but also provide for sharing the risks. Moreover, a partnership can mean that someone will be available to mind the store if you take a vacation or are otherwise unavailable. Of course, the partnership form often involves a high degree of trust, particularly among general partners, any one of whom can obligate the others to an action or a liability.

There are two basic partnership forms: The general partnership and the limited partnership. There are also two roles partners can play. You can choose to become a general partner, which would allow you to apply your experience to an activity, or you can decide to become a limited partner, one who contributes capital. Your selection of a partnership vehicle and a partner role will depend on your capabilities, needs and objectives.

A general partnership consists only of general partners, each of whom contributes expertise, time and effort. Each or only some or none may also contribute capital. One partner may be skilled in construction management, another in obtaining financing and yet another in marketing functions. A combination allows each to participate in a venture that could not be accomplished alone or could not be accomplished as efficiently.

If you choose to set up or join a general partnership, you can maximize your chances of success by doing so with people who complement your skills. Thus, if you are a detail person, you may want to team up with someone who is good at sales. If you are an accountant, you may find the addition of a lawyer as a partner most beneficial.

A general partnership can provide for the continuity of a venture beyond the death or incapacity of a partner. A general partner in a general partnership also has ownership control in the sense that a partner can transfer her or his interest in the partnership as he or she likes.

However, general partners in a general partnership must disperse control over the investment among themselves. Of course, one of the general partners must be designated the managing partner for the partnership to function effectively. However, the other general partners retain the right to depose a managing partner and substitute another. This means that there can never be the level of central management and control which the sole ownership, corporate or limited partnership forms can provide.

Moreover, each of the general partners must be personally liable for any debt or operating deficit. However, just as in the sole proprietor form, general partners can protect themselves through such devices as an exculpatory clause in mortgage instruments and operating liability insurance.

A general partnership which resembles a corporation in only two aspects, continuity and transferability of interests, is entitled to the same tax treatment as a sole owner. Thus, the general partners can divide up the income, turnover or appreciation profits and losses, and these, along with any interest deductions, depreciation write-offs and capital gains or losses, will flow directly to them without an intervening tax liability.

The second, or limited, kind of partnership is established to combine expertise and capital in order to accomplish a goal. In most cases, the limited partnership form is chosen because it allows investors who do not have either sufficient capital, expertise or time to select the sole ownership route to participate in a venture. A general partner contributes skills, time and effort and, in some cases, capital. A limited partner generally contributes capital.

A general partner in a limited partnership is in control of management decisions, within the limits of a fiduciary relationship with the limited partners. A limited partner is forbidden by law to participate in management. In most cases, this arrangement allows a general partner the management control which a sole proprietor possesses.

However, ownership control is more limited and, thus, liquidity is less than it can be in a sole proprietorship, a general partnership or a corporation. In most cases, the partners can not freely transfer their interests as they like, as that would cause the partnership to lose the ability to pass profits, losses and tax shelter directly to the partners' tax returns. In certain cases, a limited partner may have the right under the partnership agreement to transfer his or her interest back to the group upon demand or within a set period of time. A limited partnership can also have no continuity of existence.

A general partner in a limited partnership must assume personal operating and debt liability. Again, this can be handled by the insertion of exculpatory clauses in any debt agreements and by prevention programs and the purchase of adequate operating liability insurance.

Limited partners are exempt from personal operating or debt liability above the amount of any capital contribution each may have made. Thus, if you contribute $10,000, your exposure to loss should be limited to $10,000. This ability to limit your losses may well attract you. However, unless the partnership agreement is carefully scrutinized by your legal advisor, you may be exposed to two special liabilities you may not be aware can occur.

The first may be an obligation to make additional capital contributions if the partnership needs more cash to pay for construction overruns or operating deficits. This potential exposure can be handled by rejecting any partnership proposal which contains this requirement.

The second involves a contingent tax liability. If the partnership's real estate is mortgaged and then at some point sold, you will have to count as gain the amount by which you have been relieved of a mortgage debt. Debt, as many limited partners fail to understand, raises the basis of your interest; thus its removal as a result of a sale is considered an economic benefit which must be reflected as gain. This could result in your having to pay taxes on what the taxing authorities consider "gain", even though you did not receive any cash with which to pay the taxes. You can handle this only through proper tax planning.

Another potential problem also deserves special mention. Some limited partnerships require an organization fee at the front end. This may require a high percentage of your total investment to be allocated to these fees. If the fees are high, it is obvious that your chances for making a profit are much diminished. As an example, if the front-end load is 25 percent of your contribution, the investment will first have to make up for as much as a 25 percent cut in your capital before it can produce a profit on the entire amount you initially had to invest.

The general partner of a limited partnership usually receives a fee, either a percentage of the total investment, an equity interest or both in recognition of the time, effort and expertise he or she commits to the partnership. Most developers, who set up limited partnerships to attract working capital, want both because they are taking more risk and because development requires more effort and skill. This is reasonable, but the fees should be structured in such a way that all the partners involved stand to meet their objectives. In addition, professionals who provide services to a partnership may take part of their fee in the form of an equity investment. That allows them to invest in real estate and may lower initial costs.

A limited partner generally gains an equity interest in return for contributing capital. Each interest, whether a general partner's or a limited partner's, may be designed to be disproportionate in relation to the amount of capital invested. In addition, the benefits may be divided up unequally in order to pass through to a partner the specific benefit, such as tax shelter, in which she or he may be most interested.

Profits and losses are passed through to each partner according to each partner's share under the partnership agreement. The partnership itself, although it has to file a tax return, is not a taxpayer. Thus, as in the general partnership and sole proprietorship forms, operating profits and losses can be applied directly to each partner's tax return, as can any interest deductions, depreciation write-offs or capital gain or loss to which a partner is entitled.

This treatment only obtains if a partnership avoids two of the four characteristics of a corporation. Thus, a general partnership cannot provide for central management or limited liability. A limited partnership can possess these characteristics, but cannot have free transferability of interests or continuity of existence. Expert legal assistance is necessary to make sure these rules are not inadvertently violated.

Both public and private limited partnerships are available for investment in real estate. Public partnerships take in many more partners than private ones do. Thus, the sum required for each investment unit in a public partnership is usually less, in some cases as low as $2,500. More capital is generally required to acquire a private partnership interest. However, as long as you do not violate the rules on how many partners can be in a private partnership, there is nothing to prevent you from setting up a partnership in which the price of a unit is pegged as low as $500.

Public and private partnerships are also distinguished by the knowledge each individual investor is presumed to possess. Generally, investors in a private placement are assumed to know more and, thus, to be in less need of protection. However, in many instances, both kinds must be registered with a state regulatory body and with the Securities and Exchange Commission, depending on the number of investors involved.

While both public and private partnerships are required to provide disclosure statements, these are usually not enlightening unless you are yourself an expert in legal, accounting and marketing real estate matters. A high level of expertise is necessary to understand the import of what is disclosed. For this reason, at least an expert lawyer and accountant should be asked to examine any prospectus for you.

A passive investor in either a public or a private limited partnership must rely on his or her own skilled counsel and on the experience, reputation and net worth of the general partner or partners involved. You owe yourself due diligence in investigating the general partner or partners, the properties in which the partnership plans to invest and the partnership agreement. In addition, it is important to select only those partnerships where the major objective and other characteristics, such as risk and term, match your choices. Failure to observe this simple rule has caused much unhappiness among investors.

CORPORATION

A corporation's chief advantage is the shield it can place between you and any liability, provided the corporation itself has been correctly set up and is maintained properly. There is no personal operating or debt liability if you invest in real estate through a corporate vehicle.

However, in the eyes of most real estate investors, the costs of investing in real estate in this manner outweigh the advantage of liability protection. For one thing, all profits and losses are taken at the corporate rather than the personal level. Thus, the corporation is taxed on any profit and retains any losses to offset profits. The tax advantages which real estate can produce, such as interest, depreciation and capital gains or losses, can be applied only at the corporate level.

For another, a corporation passes on its after-tax profits to you as a shareholder in the form of dividends. These can be taxed at up to a maximum rate of 70 percent, the same maximum as is applied to income from rents. However, if you are a sole proprietor or a partner, you can offset any rental income you receive with the tax shelter generated by the property involved. A shareholder does not get to do this.

Moreover, the lower tax rate applied to capital gains can only be taken at the corporate level. The profit which remains from a sale after corporate taxes on it have been paid comes to you as a shareholder, but it does so as dividend income, subject to the highest tax rate.

A corporation can also pass income to you as salary if you are an employee. This income is not taxed at the corporate level and thus will be subject only to the taxes you have to pay on it, up to a maximum rate of 50 percent. However, only a limited amount, the sum the Internal Revenue Service deems reasonable in relation to your efforts, can be paid out to you as salary.

In order to be treated as a corporation, certain rigid requirements must be met. This includes a corporate charter, actually holding required meetings and keeping minutes and records in a certain manner. If these rules are violated, a corporation can be declared null and void. Moreover, if you want a corporate entity to be the borrower in order to eliminate your liability for debt, the corporation itself must have sufficient assets to qualify for the loan in question.

In real estate, the price of incorporation tends to make the corporate form useful only to those exposed to unusual operating liabilities. This would include a management firm and a developer who is also a contractor. Both must deal intensively with labor and the public.

A corporation can provide not only for limited liability, but also for continuity, central control and free transferability of interests. The latter, of course, is subject to what may be a limited market for closed corporate shareholdings. As a single shareholder, you may exercise both ownership and management control over a real estate operation, just as a sole proprietor does.

However, if you take on additional shareholders to meet a need for capital, you will dilute your control. For example, shareholders have the right to oversee management decisions. Nonetheless, you do not lose as much control as a limited partner who must relinquish control in order to obtain limited liability protection.

The advantages and disadvantages which each form offers must be carefully evaluated in order to locate the combination of features which would most benefit your investment strategy. For example, if you desire active participation, you could choose the sole ownership form, a general partner role in either kind of partnership or the corporate officer role within a corporation. A goal of tax shelter might cause you to eliminate the corporate form unless you judge your need for the kind of limited liability a corporation affords to be a more important requirement. Similarly, the amount of capital you can make available for a specific investment opportunity may dictate a choice of either the partnership form or the corporate form with multiple share ownership.

We have provided Worksheet 9 to help you make a preliminary choice. By circling the characteristics which you find most desirable and striking out the characteristics which would negate your strategy, you are likely to find that one form stands out as best able to meet your objectives and needs. Some weighting of your selections may be necessary. However, we again emphasize that a final choice must wait until you are ready to acquire a property and have rigorously considered the legal and economic ramifications of each choice in consultation with your legal and also your accounting advisors.

WORKSHEET 9
Ownership Choices
(Circle Your Requirements Under Each Form)

	Corporation	
	Shareholder	Shareholder/ Officer
Capital Sum Required for Participation	Low to high	None to high
Continuity	High	High
Control of Real Estate		
Management	Low	High
Ownership	Shared	High to shared
Experience Requirement	None	Generally moderate to high
Liability Protection		
From Form Itself	Total	Total
From Exculpatory Clause, Prevention and Insurance		
Exposure to Loss	Limited	Limited
Ability to Satisfy Objective from Real Estate Itself		
Income	Dividend	Dividend/salary
Tax Shelter	None	None
Turnover	Dividend	Dividend/salary*
Appreciation	Dividend	Dividend/salary
Ability to Collect Management Fee	None	High
Exposure to Management Problems from		
Small-Scale Property	None	High
Larger-Scale Property	None	Low to high

* Most appropriate form for developer-contractor and management firm.

| Partnership | | | Sole Proprietorship |
| General | Limited | | |
General Partner	General	Limited	
Generally low	Generally low	Low to high	Low to high
High	Low	Low	Low
High	High	None	Total
Shared	Shared	Shared	Total
Generally moderate to high	Generally moderate to high	None	Low to high
		High	
High	High		High
High	High	Limited	High
High	High	High	High
High	High	High	High
High	High	High	High
High	High	High	High
High	High	None	High
High	High	None	High
Low to high	Low to high	None	Low to high

WORKSHEET 9 (Continued)

YOUR CHOICE OF OWNERSHIP VEHICLE:

1. CORPORATION: _____

2. GENERAL PARTNERSHIP
   a. General partner: _____

3. LIMITED PARTNERSHIP
   a. General partner: _____
   b. Limited partner: _____

4. SOLE PROPRIETORSHIP: _____

In today's complex society, you will require a team of advisors if you are to locate, evaluate, acquire, hold and dispose of a specific property that can best embody your investor profile, objective and ownership choices. How many advisors you will require and what services they will perform for you depends partly on the level of your needs and partly on society's.

In less populous and less diversified times, perhaps you would have needed someone else's services only for legal clarification of ownership rights and obligations. Owners then were apt to possess all the other necessary skills, although they might choose to hire builders or managers for their property.

However, specialization increased in step with increases in population and in the range of human activity, particularly those resulting from the Industrial Revolution. No one person now is apt to have the time to learn the skills required to become an accountant, appraiser, architect, broker, engineer, insurance expert and lawyer, to name the professional services you are most likely to need. As a result, an investor is more likely today to purchase more services.

The nature of real estate increases the need for specialists. Its role as a basic means for carrying out all human activities, from the production of raw materials such as grains and minerals through transportation to the provision of shelter for home and work, affects all aspects of life. As population grows and uses multiply, real estate becomes subject to more and more restrictions as society seeks to protect itself from potential danger.

In the past, what you could accomplish alone or with a small group, using minimal tools, was less likely to have a serious impact on others. Now new developments, such as skyscrapers, expressways and

5

which advisors will i need?

large power plants, to name but a few, are potentially far more hazardous. The size and kind of our activities over the last century or so more seriously affect the health and safety of more people.

As a result, society's need for protection has grown. This need is expressed in building codes which try to prevent building collapses, environmental protection statutes which try to prevent poisoning, and lease and ownership requirements which try to govern amicably the relations among people likely to be strangers. Such restrictions are bound to grow as society continues to grow. Good examples of such changes are new laws protecting marshlands or scenic views from encroachments, laws which express newly perceived societal needs. Moreover, society's needs today for government tend to require more taxes. Compliance with society's needs, in turn, requires more knowledge and more specialization.

Even the acquisition of a relatively passive investment, such as a stock, art, gold or bonds, usually requires at least the services of a broker or dealer and a means of safe storage or other protection against physical destruction and theft. Among astute investors, it also requires a lawyer, accountant or other financial planner to integrate the investment with a long-term financial plan, both in terms of the investment's economics and its tax implications. A passive investment may also require the periodic services of an appraiser to value it, perhaps for insurance or sale purposes, and a lender, if you need to borrow for or against the investment. While it is more unusual, it is not unheard of for passive investors interested in acquiring a limited partnership or private corporate interest to go one step further: Having the underlying physical assets investigated by an architect or engineer.

Investing passively essentially requires advisory services that relate mainly to your personal financial needs. Investing actively in real estate extends your horizons through involvement with other people in their roles as sellers, purchasers, lessees and so on. You are likely to need more services from each advisor and you may also need more advisors.

For example, in addition to the role of explaining and evaluating the implications of a contract you may enter into in order to purchase a property, you may require your lawyer to negotiate for you or to draft a lease for a specific tenant. You will definitely need at least an architect or an engineer to investigate the real estate itself. The purchase of raw land for resale might require the services of soil analysts and engineers to evaluate its potential use.

Becoming a developer raises the requirements to yet another level. Not only might you need an architect to inspect the property, but also to prepare working drawings of changes you intend to make and to supervise construction and renovation.

If it sounds as if it would take a small fortune to engage all these professionals, you may well be right. However, the cost of the services you require should be measured against the value of what you are acquiring, holding or disposing of. Professional costs should also be regarded as the price of protection. Thus, a lawyer or an accountant protects you from losing tax benefits through inadvertence, and an architect or engineer keeps you from acquiring real estate with structural defects which cannot be cured economically. Compliance with laws and codes is best thought of as a cost of doing business today.

Moreover, starting with small investments, as we advise, will shrink the bills for services rendered to manageable size. And, if the advisors are cooperative, as they should be, you may be able to reduce the costs by doing some of the work yourself, such as inspecting building department records and tax records.

Substituting your unbilled time not only saves you money. It can also increase your knowledge and understanding of real estate. That, in turn, will increase your sensitivity to opportunities. One prime investment resulted when an investor noticed that an office building was listed as fireproof. That observation opened up the property for manufacturing uses in a district that was short of manufacturing space. After acquiring the property, this investor was able to attract higher quality tenants who paid more rent, which boosted the value of his property. Understanding the implications of all aspects of real estate is the first step on the road to realizing opportunities.

There is another way you may be able to reduce the size of the bills involved, most of which must be paid before you receive money from the property with which to pay them. You can offer an equity interest in the real estate itself in lieu of part of the fee, perhaps to your lawyer, accountant, architect or engineer. That can turn out to be more expensive over the long term, but it may be worth your while for two reasons. First, you may not otherwise be in a position to afford the investment. And, second, you may engage the interest of the professional involved above and beyond his or her duty to you. The more creativity that flows from each advisor, the more opportunities you may be able to seize.

This method would not work with appraisers, real estate brokers and insurance brokers as they must be compensated in different ways. A real estate broker, however, may be willing to accept a staged payment of her or his commission. Moreover, all professional fees and commissions can now be regarded as negotiable as a result of recent decisions on restraint of trade. It can do no harm to attempt negotiating.

Do not hesitate, even with accountants and lawyers, to ask for a proposal. This proposal should include what the advisor intends to do for you and how, the nature of the assignment, the basic approach, the work program, timing, estimated costs and a place for your authorization.

The choice of which specific accountant, appraiser, architect, broker, engineer, insurer or lawyer to engage is solely up to you. There are certain choices, however, which you should evaluate before you obtain any services.

The first distinction is between professionals whose main activity is unrelated to real estate investment as opposed to those who specialize in serving investors involved in real estate. Thus, a lawyer who handles family matters in large part or a broker whose beat is residential may not be as well oriented to investing in commercial real estate as experts who have considerable experience in that field. You can, of course, do some intelligent substitution, such as having a student architect help out with minor renovation work.

As many professionals charge by the hour it can be expensive to pay them for learning what you require them to know. It can also be expensive if it causes later problems, particularly in the tax field. The less experienced you are, the more it may be necessary to seek out advisors who are experienced in the specific investment choices you have made.

Thus, if you plan to renovate a small commercial strip, your team might be composed of a lawyer who is familiar with commercial property purchase agreements and store leases as well as with construction contracts; an accountant equally well up on commercial financial arrangements; a leasing agent able to bring you potential commercial tenants; an architect who has designed stores and storefronts; an insurance broker who understands commercial risks, as well as an appraiser whose experience is founded upon the valuation of commercial real estate.

Assembling a good team will take some time, as it deserves to. The time you invest in finding the right professionals will pay many dividends later. You can start with the local professional societies, which will provide lists of specialists in your area. In case you can not find a local branch, we have included the names and addresses of national organizations you can write to as a last resort. You can also gather recommendations from business associates and friends, provided you pay close attention to the kind of work each advisor performed for them. A great divorce lawyer may not be the best real estate counselor.

Another source is your bank. The local bank or savings and loan usually knows which professionals are competent and skilled. And, while your lending officer may not directly recommend a specific professional, you may get some leads simply by listening closely to what she or he has to say.

You should feel comfortable with the people you choose. In any investment strategy, you are seeking a long-term, ongoing relationship. Any initial problem you have in being candid with a particular professional will only get worse as you go along. It is also important to keep in mind your long-term goals. These should engage the interest of any professional you select, so that you can grow together.

There is no harm in interviewing several of each kind of professional to evaluate their levels of competence and their approaches to problems. You should be comfortable with any professional's ability to explain complexities in language you understand. Initial misunderstandings are likely to multiply later on with potentially grave financial and legal consequences. You should also be sensitive to your advisors' larger obligations. They not only serve you and your purposes but are also obligated to serve society.

Your role should be clear. You are the team leader, not a follower. Your advisors are there to interpret their specialties to you, to detail the choices available, and to advise you on what they consider the best way to carry out your intentions. In most cases, they are also there to execute your decisions.

Your advisors are not there to make decisions on whether to invest, how much to invest, what property to invest in and so on. These decisions are for you to make, with due regard to the expert advice you have acquired. You must be the one in charge, the one who pulls the team together and resolves any conflicting advice. Any vacuum you leave at the top will cause disarray below, a condition not considered helpful to the success of any investment program.

The act of assembling a team of advisors transforms your potential interest in real estate investment into actual involvement. It is the first step you take to test the reality of your investment strategy.

Below we outline the chief roles these professionals are equipped to play, subject to their experience and level of specialization. We start in each case with what all real estate investors might require and then move on to what the more active investor may need. The ones we have chosen to discuss in detail will provide the most basic help you will need. As you develop your investment in real estate you may decide to add on more professionals. A list is appended to the end of the chapter.

ACCOUNTANT

Much of what an accountant does overlaps with the role of the lawyer. Both are trained to evaluate and explain the financial and tax implications of a choice of ownership. The lawyer concentrates, however, on the legal aspects of securing your rights and spelling out your obligations, aware of the economic and tax implications. The accountant concentrates on the financial and tax arrangements, aware of the legal implications. The roles are not interchangeable as only a lawyer is allowed by the state to draft legal instruments or take care of legal problems. And only an accountant is empowered to prepare an audited financial statement or analysis.

For a passive investor, the accountant is in a position to explain and evaluate the financial and tax implications of acquiring any passive interest. In addition, the accountant often does the financial and tax planning required to carry out the intentions of trusts and wills and other personal financial matters. And, of course, an accountant prepares tax returns and often defends the tax interpretation chosen before the tax authorities.

An accountant may also keep track of your net worth and analyze how much of its growth occurs as a result of inflation and how much through your own efforts. He or she can also suggest ways to improve cash flow, cut expenses and refinance profitably, both in terms of any real estate acquired and in terms of your personal situation. And he or she can produce the kind of financial documentation that lenders require and also financial reports for any equity partners you may have. An accountant may have additional responsibilities, such as auditing percentage retail leases.

The courts are in the process of interpreting the privacy of the relationship between an accountant and a client. Certainly, the legal protections are not as extensive as those protecting a lawyer-client relationship. The American Institute of Certified Public Accountants, 1221 Avenue of the Americas, New York, New York 10020, can help you find appropriate accountants in your locality.

APPRAISER

An appraiser estimates the value the market would place at a particular time on any interest you acquire. That can include, among others, a limited partnership interest, a private corporation's stock, a leasehold interest or the entire physical real estate consisting of land and any buildings. You can then use the appraiser's estimate to determine whether the price at which the interest is offered to you is a fair one in the market prevailing at the time.

An appraiser can also be called in to estimate the best price at which to sell an interest in terms of market values then current. An investment in a widely held public corporation is the only one which would not require the services of an appraiser, as the stock market itself continually establishes a stock's value.

An appraiser also estimates value for the purposes of loan submission, insurance, estate tax, liquidation, salvage value, tax-free exchanges of real estate, and any other purpose where an estimate of value is needed.

In addition to their basic role of estimating value, appraisers can also be engaged to conduct marketability studies. Such a study would be undertaken to evaluate the best way to market a new or renovated project. They may also be engaged to make recommendations such as one involving the mix of apartments in a proposed project. For example, the marketability study may indicate that the demand for two-bedroom apartments in the area is much greater than for one-bedrooms or studios. An appraiser might then suggest that the number of two-bedroom apartments be increased.

Appraisers may also develop feasibility studies for development projects. Such a study includes a marketability analysis but, in addition, involves calculations of the project's potential profitability.

Appraisers can never be advocates, but are required to be impartial. Their fees are based on hourly rates and in no instance can the remuneration be a percentage of the value reported. Professional designations include the MAI (Member of the American Institute) and the RM (Residential Member), which are awarded by the National Association of Realtors. The other professional designations are the SRA (Senior Residential Appraiser), the SREA (Senior Real Estate Analyst) and the SRPA (Senior Real Property Appraiser), awarded by the Society of Real Estate Appraisers. Both the Society and the American Institute of Real Estate Appraisers are located in Chicago: The first at 645 North Michigan Avenue, the second at 430 North Michigan. The zip code in both cases is 60611.

ARCHITECT AND ENGINEER

Either professional can assist a passive investor in inspecting the real estate underlying acquisition of a limited partnership interest or a private corporation shareholding. Either professional can also inspect real estate for an active investor who does not contemplate making structural changes.

Typically, you might engage an architect to make a preliminary estimate of structural soundness and then use the services of a structural engineer if there appear to be problems. An engineer might be the one engaged to estimate the utility of any raw land involved as to drainage and soil capacity or of the mechanical systems of a building. Either may also become involved in concert with your accountant in classifying the components of a structure if you plan to use component depreciation.

If you intend to become a developer, an architect and an engineer may become much more involved. For example, an architect may design the structures or any renovation required, prepare working drawings for contractors to use, file building plans with the proper authorities, obtain building permits, arrange for contractors and supervise construction or renovation. An engineer would undertake the same steps in connection with any engineering work required. In addition, either may be willing to take on the role of building contractor.

Both are usually paid in the form of fees billed hourly. Architects can be located through the American Institute of Architects, 1735 New York Avenue NW, Washington, D.C. 20006. And the Engineers Joint Council, 345 East 47th Street, New York, New York 10017, can help you locate the national organization of engineers which can best serve your needs. In turn, the society to which you are directed to write will furnish you with a local association's name and address.

BROKER

There are many types of brokers, ranging from the stockbroker to the broker who arranges for investment in private corporations to the real estate broker. All brokers bring together a seller and a buyer of some interest, although a stockbroker does not literally do this face to face. A stockbroker's role may include giving you information about certain stocks, executing a trade and record keeping.

The point of the broker's activity is to produce a situation where a buyer is willing to purchase and a seller is willing to sell, each knowing the same material facts and relevant information. Thus, a broker's role is primarily that of facilitating negotiations between the interested parties.

In order to do this, however, a broker may first aid in locating a parcel of real estate for purchase or buyers if you are selling. And a good broker will be helpful in supplying information on current population, housing and business trends in the locality as well as current market prices and rents.

He or she will also supply all information relevant to the property itself, such as operating expenses, mortgages placed on the property, the condition of the property and the terms of sale. All this information comes from the seller and thus should be checked independently, by yourself or your advisors. The broker may also assist you in finding suitable tenants for any rental property purchased.

A broker is usually paid by the seller on a commission basis as a percentage of the actual sale price. However, even if you will be acquiring several parcels of real estate over time rather than selling, you can build a long-term relationship with a broker. Thus, you may utilize the broker's services to investigate real estate that might not yet be on the open market. If a property becomes available as a result of such canvassing, your broker can then act for the seller as well as for you.

For smaller investments, many brokerage firms can also be used as leasing agents and as management firms. For larger ones, there are specialized leasing firms which concentrate on obtaining tenants for shopping centers or for industrial parks or apartment complexes. And there are specialized management firms which are not necessarily connected with brokerage activities. There are many specialized brokerage associations. Some of the most prominent are the National Association of Realtors, 430 North Michigan, Chicago, Illinois 60611, and the Society of Industrial Realtors, 925 15th Street NW, Washington, D.C. 20005.

INSURANCE BROKER

The passive investor in real estate does not require the services of an insurance broker as the interest acquired is not insurable, nor are there liability risks to be considered. An active investor, however, may require personal liability insurance, even for the holding of raw land. Active investors in improved properties will also require a complete line of casualty property insurance, such as fire, boiler, roof, elevator and so on.

In addition, rent interruption insurance is advisable. It provides payments which will help meet the debt service and other continuing expenses, such as property taxes, in the event of a casualty which renders the property unfit for occupancy. Fire and other casualty insurance proceeds are usually paid directly to the mortgage holder. While most lenders will cooperate in releasing the proceeds to you for reconstruction purposes, it is best to insert a clause to this effect in any debt agreement.

Your insurance broker should also become involved in an ongoing risk reduction program. Many insurance companies work with real estate owners to reduce hazards and will even suggest safer materials and designs when you are involved in construction or renovation. If hazards are reduced, the insurance premiums may also drop to reflect the increased safety of the real estate.

Insurance brokers receive commissions as part of the premium payments. A major association to which insurance brokers belong is the National Association of Insurance Brokers, 1511 K Street NW, Washington D.C. 20005.

LAWYER

For a passive investor, a lawyer's job involves meshing the acquisition or sale of any partnership interest or any corporate stock ownership with the investor's income and estate tax plan as expressed through legal documents such as wills and trusts. It is his or her job to evaluate and explain the legal, financial and tax consequences of acquiring or selling a limited partnership interest or a corporate shareholding. Particularly important in regard to these matters are the ramifications of ownership with a spouse. And while any objective requires a high level of competence, the tax shelter objective may require the most esoteric reach of expertise if the eventual costs of a decision are not to outweigh the benefits.

A lawyer's contribution to an active investor's strategy may also involve the drafting of ownership instruments, purchase and sale contracts, leases, covenants, easements, and contracts with architects who undertake construction or renovation for you, subcontractors, management firms and employees. In addition, your lawyer may undertake tenant eviction proceedings, nuisance suit settlements, and your defense in liability suits.

One of the most important roles a lawyer can play is that of negotiator. Much of what goes on between two parties to a lease or sale is resolved at the respective lawyers' level as each lawyer carries out his or her client's intentions. Another useful role involves your ability to insert a lawyer between yourself and anyone with whom you are having a dispute. This can cool tempers considerably and resolve a problem more quickly. The lawyer you choose for this role must, of course, possess the temperament to be an effective negotiator and resolver of disputes.

You may eventually need legal specialists to handle such matters as zoning hearings or property tax matters. There are also specialists who deal in various kinds of contract law and tax law.

The relationship between a lawyer and client is, by law, fully protected from disclosure. Fees are usually billed hourly, although you may arrange to have him or her on a retainer. The American Bar Association, 1155 East 60th Street, Chicago, Illinois 60637, can direct you to a specific local association of lawyers.

Other experts you may want to consult in the future include:

1. Advertising professional
2. Civil engineer
3. Environmental scientist
4. General contractor
5. Geographer
6. Land planner
7. Landscape architect
8. Leasing agent
9. Lending officer
10. Market analyst
11. Mortgage broker
12. Public relations specialist
13. Real estate economist
14. Registered surveyor
15. Site planner/engineer
16. Soils or geological engineer
17. Termite inspector
18. Traffic engineer

Most of the experts on this list, as you can see, are heavily oriented to development, either of unimproved land or of underdeveloped structures. If you plan to go into development and you work your way up to needing these experts, your primary team should be able to help you locate several of each kind of specialist in your area.

We conclude this section with Worksheet 10. The potential roles of each primary advisor are outlined and a separate column is provided for you to note what you may initially require from each advisor.

WORKSHEET 10
Advisors
(Check Your Needs)

ACCOUNTANT:

    Financial and tax explanations   _____
    Financial and tax analysis   _____
    Auditing   _____
    Tax returns   _____
    Suggestions for financing, ways to improve cash flow
    and to cut expenses   _____
    Loan documentation   _____
    Financial reports   _____

APPRAISER:

    Value estimations of:
      A limited partnership interest   _____
      A private corporation's stock   _____
      A leasehold interest   _____
      Improvements   _____
      Land   _____
      Other   _____
    For purposes of
      Acquiring   _____
      Selling   _____
      Insurance   _____
      Loan submissions   _____
      Other   _____
    Marketability study   _____
    Feasibility study   _____

ARCHITECT/ENGINEER:

    Preliminary inspection of improved property
    (architect)   _____
    Structural inspection (structural engineer)   _____
    Mechanical systems inspection (HVAC engineer*)   _____
    Land inspection (civil engineer or soils engineer)   _____
    Other inspection   _____
    Design
      Architect   _____

Engineer \
Working drawings \
  Architect \
  Engineer \
Obtain permits \
Obtain contractors \
Supervise contractors \
Act as contractor

BROKER:

Produce property to acquire \
Produce buyers if selling \
Produce information about area \
Produce information about specific real estate \
Produce tenants \
Provide management

INSURANCE BROKER:

Personal liability insurance \
Casualty insurance \
  Fire \
  Boiler \
  Roof \
  Elevator \
  Other \
Rent interruption insurance \
Risk reduction program

LAWYER:

Legal, financial and tax explanations \
Legal, financial and tax analysis \
Estate planning \
Tax shelter expertise \
Contract drafting \
Negotiating

* Heating, ventilating and air conditioning

section two: the what

6

Real estate is the physical embodiment of certain observable trends and principles. You will gain or lose according to the operations of these trends and principles. Thus, learning how they work and how one can observe them in operation is of critical importance to your success in real estate investment.

No parcel of real estate exists in isolation, just as "no man is an island, entire of itself". One can not divorce an individual parcel of real estate from its surround. Not only is the land fixed in place, but in most cases the improvement is also immovable. This universal feature of real estate has made it possible to develop a coherent body of principles which apply to individual properties as well as to neighborhoods. Your ability to apply them will enable you to determine a property's prospects for profitable realization of your investor objectives and profile.

A variety of rights is bound up in real estate. Commonly referred to as "the bundle of rights", these rights include the right to rent a property, the right to leave it to an heir, to mortgage it, to occupy it and many more. The operations of the trends and principles will affect the value and profitability of each right you may acquire. An understanding of the rights inherent in real estate in conjunction with comprehension of the trends and principles will enable you to maximize the return on the rights you acquire. We will first discuss real estate trends and then the economic principles behind the trends; finally, we will take up the bundle of rights.

TRENDS

The directions real estate trends take are so closely connected with human activity that life itself can be considered an apt metaphor to describe the processes involved. Just as a person, animal or plant is born, grows up, matures, grows old and dies, so too does real estate, both in the broad sense of area development and in the more narrow sense of the life of an individual property. Moreover, just as major surgery may extend a person's life significantly, so too can changes in real estate extend the life of a property. However, while the stages of development are similar, the time frame for the life cycle of real estate is generally much longer than that for a person.

Birth occurs when land is transformed into some use. Much of the earth's surface consists of land, but land does not become real estate, a source of wealth, until it meets with a human being who finds value in its use. For value to exist, two conditions must be satisfied. First, a particular parcel of land must to some degree be able to meet a human need better than any other parcel might. Second, the person whose needs may be met by the parcel must have both the desire to use the land and the ability to satisfy that desire. Once the requirements of utility, relative scarcity, desire and ability are met, land may be said to be born into real estate.

As far as can be discovered, this accurately describes the germination of cities. Cities got their start at sites that were capable of supporting commercial activity. The land chosen for manufacturing goods or for the exchange of goods exhibited certain characteristics. These locational features included water, often more particularly river water which met an ocean or other useful route for commerce.

Occasional manufacturing and trade may have occurred at sites without water, but water was essential if the site were to prosper and grow to city dimensions. Water obviously must be available for drinking and for irrigation, but also, and emphatically, for industry and transportation. Cities founded on navigable rivers or near the junctions of rivers with seacoasts or lake shores have tended over the course of civilization to exhibit the most growth and, during their life spans, the greatest real estate values. A glance at an atlas showing the locations of major ancient and modern cities will confirm this.

This historical account gains point when one considers the Rocky Mountain region today. Investors who think the boom which has been taking place there can continue at the same pace have fallen into the trap of overlooking a fundamental locational characteristic. In those areas of the West with limited water supplies, values are likely to be restricted to levels far below those achievable in areas with water supplies adequate for the myriad uses to which people now put water.

Manufacturers and traders, then as now, seek out land where their activities can best take place. Those who prosper can afford to acquire and defend the site, whether they own it or, under the ownership structures then or now existing, win the right to use it by paying rent to an "investor" who owns it.

The first simple structures enable the economic activity to function in some comfort and utility. Buildings to house equipment, such as ovens, furnaces and facilities for storage grow up, becoming more permanent and elaborate as time passes. More people are attracted to the site either because they seek the same locational advantage for their businesses or because they are prospecting for jobs. Suppliers of goods needed by the original settlers follow, and the community begins to grow in size and complexity.

One can see this process at work today. New economic units, or bulblets as they are known, are forming, particularly on the periphery of older cities. In some way, and the ways today can be exceedingly various, some business functions can be more profitably performed in these bulblets. More dramatic in its effects may be a decision to locate a new manufacturing plant or trading activity where transportation is good but no economic activity of any significance has yet taken place.

The economic activity attracts suppliers, workers and their families. In addition to the necessity of serving work needs, personal needs must be satisfied. Both create opportunities for real estate investors, as the needs to be met exist in or on real estate. For example, workers in a new area need housing, retailers moving in to tap the workers' wages in return for food, clothing and other articles need stores, additional industry may move in and need plants, and the new community may grow to need a firehouse, a school and other types of special use real estate.

The manufacturing or trading purpose which originates the process causes other uses to grow up around it. The most basic retail and service uses, such as a general store, follow, and then comes residential. Investors who are not sufficiently alert to this process are likely to find themselves on dangerous ground, as the experience of the "new towns" program illustrates.

New towns were designed as a total concept, including industrial, retail and residential uses. However, because residential development could be financed under government programs, residential properties were, in some cases, built first. When the hoped for industrial development did not occur, too few jobs were available to support the real estate already built. And, for the most part, the new towns were located away from areas where available jobs might have picked up the slack.

For this reason, many of the new towns proved economically unviable. In addition, the costs of putting in most of the infrastructure of a town all at once were extremely high and meant high continued carrying charges for the developers over long periods, while growth took place slowly. External factors, such as the increase in the price of oil, also spelled trouble. Some of the new towns have since collapsed into bankruptcy. The basic problem, however, lay in not allowing for natural development to grow slowly around an economic core.

The economic health of an area turns on what are known as export industries. Such industries produce more goods than their immediate area can absorb. Thus, they supply a demand from a greater distance. It is important for an investor to determine the underlying economic truth of an area: Whether the export industries in it are expanding, because of the addition of export industries moving in from other areas or as a result of internal growth, stabilized, or declining through shutting down or moving out. These industries form the base, even in our complex society, on which rests the ability of purchasers and renters of your real estate investments.

The chain of ability to pay for the use of real estate starts with the export industries. They produce goods for and sell goods to a wider area than their locality. Today, this may mean they operate in a regional, national or world market. If successful, they bring money into the local economy from outside.

As a result of their activities, the export industries gain the ability to pay their workers, their suppliers which are known as nonexport industries, and the local government for services. In turn, the workers in the export, nonexport and government sectors of the economy can afford to pay for housing, food, clothing and, if the wealth brought in from outside is sufficient, for entertainment. If whatever the export industries produce is in great enough demand, increasingly elaborate forms of goods, including forms of real estate, can be purchased or rented, up to and including support for professional baseball teams and symphony orchestras.

No matter how elaborate or complex the chain becomes, the level of activity of the export industries is what supports the real estate in which you invest. If the export industries were taken away, the ability to pay would wither away.

At this point, you may be wondering how the new retirement communities, which have no industry, survive. The answer lies in the sources of income which support both the retirees and their activities and the real estate in which these activities take place. In most instances, the incomes are derived from the government in the form of Social Security and from pensions. The taxes paid the government to fund Social Security come from business and workers and the pensions come from companies and from contributions the retirees made while they were working. If one were to trace the ultimate sources of these funds, one would discover the export industries.

You will remember our discussion in Chapter 2 of the investor whose objective is capital turnover. A turnover investor is generally most attracted to areas where land is in the process of becoming real estate, where he or she can create value out of the transformation process. In developing areas, there is usually a great need for new real estate products, such as houses and stores. The developer creates these products, which then can be sold to users, or to investors who will rent to users, for more than it cost to create them. Thus, it is capital turnover investors who take land in an area just beginning to be valued by people and turn it into a more useful and, therefore, more valuable product.

Areas undergoing transformation or birth and childhood attract not only capital turnover investors but also certain tax shelter investors. New properties often provide both large interest deductions and depreciation write-offs because their costs are so high in an inflationary environment. Opportunities for relatively high rentals from income-producing property also exist in developing areas where demand typically outstrips the creation of supply.

Risks are high in areas undergoing birth and childhood, just as they are in the early stages of human life. There is no guarantee that the economic base will take hold. And, since development can spread in many directions from the economic base, there is no guarantee that it will flow in the direction you have chosen.

As the area survives birth, childhood and adolescence, risks begin to diminish. In the process, existing development helps to channel future development. And the new development is additional, building on what has gone before, rather than purely pioneering. Land supply is no longer omnidirectional but has been absorbed or used to a point where prospective competition from new development is lessened. More people have come into the area, making more incomes available to support activities which occur in and on real estate. In fact, successive reinvestment may take place, each successful new investment on a site representing a gain in the area's ability to support the real estate involved.

Investors who have chosen the objectives of long-term substantial income or preservation of capital or both are normally most attracted to areas which have reached a stabilized maturity. In this stage of development, population has grown to a point or density where generally the largest rental incomes can be produced and the greatest values achieved from properties. Investors who are most interested in tax shelter may also be attracted. Improvements with the highest tax basis have more to depreciate. And, as a result of increased values, mortgage loans tend to be larger and thus interest deductions tend to be high. In fact, one method of increasing tax shelter, investing in new multi-family housing developments, requires the greater population density mature areas exhibit.

As a stabilized maturity is reached in a city's core, the city tends to expand on its periphery, thereby enhancing for a period the central business district's convenience and desirability. As population grows, new residential areas on the outer ring may spring up, a less valuable use seeking out less valuable land. Then, in some cases, commercial development will expand into formerly residential areas or leapfrog over residential areas to open land.

Cities also decline and decay, as happened in New England mill towns when their export industries moved away. The ability to support real estate shrinks and values decline. Cities as a whole tend to take long periods of time to grow, mature and decline. Within a city's overall life span, however, there are always smaller areas within it which are undergoing decline while others are in the process of revitalization. New economic centers within the city may grow up, causing shifts in values across the city. And now, new economic bulblets are growing up within overall metropolitan areas. These bulblets are pulling users out of the older centers. All of these shifts create opportunities for investors aware of their potential for profit.

Decayed areas may be reborn, just as individuals may regain their health. The process usually involves real estate users who kick off the renaissance by undertaking renovation work to transform older properties into ones suitable for reuse or a new use. Once work of this kind is under way and the new uses have begun to take hold, investment opportunities tend to open up.

For example, speculators may move in to buy up properties sold at price levels reflecting the former use. Their hope is to resell the properties to new users at a gain in price. Turnover investors are also likely to find opportunities to reconstruct the improvements. Not all users attracted to areas undergoing rebirth will want to do it themselves.

Redevelopment is most probable in areas which have such great locational convenience that the decline can be reversed. For businesses moving in, this may mean proximity to sources of materials, workers and customers. For new residential users, the areas must be convenient to sources of employment, a feature of many of the old commercial loft districts and of older urban residential neighborhoods. Generally, when a neighborhood within a city declines, systems of transportation and other municipal services remain in place, in a sense awaiting a new use.

Awareness of the cycles areas naturally go through is a first step toward attainment of a profit from the cycles. In addition, knowledge of how each stage works will help you find an area capable of meeting your objectives through its ability to support a certain kind of real estate activity. However, in addition to knowing the overall trend, it is important for an investor to watch for changes that cut across the general development line. These changes can both create new trend lines and enhanced opportunities for profit, as well as wreak havoc.

Two developments since World War II offer examples of changes that created great profits and wealth for investors who understood their implications. Both the creation of the interstate highway system and the advent of shopping centers altered the course of development in this country, and, in many areas, started the life cycle trend over again with a new birth.

The development of modern highways changed the patterns of goods and people movement. As the highway, because of its convenience, became the preferred mode of transportation, areas not served by highways moved into the decay stage of the cycle. Areas served by highways were reborn or moved into more valuable stages of development.

Highways caused new areas to open up for development, providing turnover investors with opportunities for profit. Industries chose to locate near highway exits; travel facilities grew up, and new residential areas boomed. Each initially offered a turnover investor a chance to transform less usable land into more usable land with improvements. In turn, enriched opportunities for other investors with different objectives emerged as the changed area grew and matured.

Highways radically changed the measurement of distance, from miles to time. Much the same pattern occurred as a result of railroad construction in the ninteenth century, but highways had an even more substantial impact. Railroads were limited to fixed tracks which meant most journeys involved more than one mode of transportation. Highways enabled one form of transportation, either trucks for goods or automobiles for people, to go off the highway "track" to accomplish more convenient door-to-door trips. In effect, they allowed the natural law of following the line of least resistance to operate.

This substitution of time for miles entered a new stage with the widespread development of air transportation, which has now become much more critical for both business and pleasure. It is now creating opportunities to invest in hotels, office buildings and industrial plants or warehouses around airports just as these uses once grew up around railroad stations.

The modern highway system also created the shopping center as we know it today. The highway allowed a retail center to draw upon a much wider geographical area for customers, as it took an equal or shorter time to reach the shopping center by highway as it had taken to travel to the older retail centers by less convenient routes. The shopping center not only altered retail patterns but also provided jobs on a larger scale than had previously been available in the areas in which it located. This in turn provided more investment opportunities as other businesses began to locate nearby.

The existence of large-scale employment centers at suburban shopping centers may have provided the impetus for office users to relocate to the suburbs where they could draw upon a new pool of employees. As a result of their moves, new economic bulblets are in the process of forming within metropolitan areas. This development is fueled by newer highways that allow goods and people to move across the transportation spokes leading in and out of the city proper.

These new economic units are independent of the city that is the center for the metropolitan area and yet interrelated. At the same time as some functions which have been associated with the city proper move to outlying economic centers, other functions may become more prominent within the city. This is renewing opportunities for investors to provide real estate to the businesses which must serve a nexus of proximate customers to survive. For example, financial and advertising services are probably best located central to both the new economic centers as well as the older center.

You may never have considered the business pages of your local newspaper a source of real estate opportunities. However, watching the ebb and flow of industry, of retail sales, and of transportation changes is identical to watching out for real estate investment opportunities.

In determining the life cycle stage in your area, you will not be able to use an equivalent of the arbitrary human benchmarks, such as legal age of maturity or retirement age. The life stages in real estate tend, unless interrupted by something like the interstate highway system, to be longer and more relative. The process is more like that of a person moving from young adult to middle age or from middle age to elderly.

It is best to start by comparing your area to others surrounding it. Then you can determine whether your area exhibits relative growth, stability, or decline in basic or export industry, business activity, population density and personal incomes. Net in-migration and net out-migration figures offer clues, as will spending patterns. In another chapter, we will develop the information you will need to identify and confirm opportunities.

You will be attempting to solve for the difference between existing real estate supply and existing and potential real estate demand for the particular type of real estate you have chosen. This difference will tell you the stage wherein this type of real estate now finds itself in your area. Existing supply consists not only of units in place, but also of those in process, such as the new office development under construction down the road or the one for which plans have been filed with the building department.

If there is greater demand for office space than there are units, an undersupply situation exists which may indicate that the area is moving into a new stage of growth. For a turnover investor, it may mean an opportunity to create more units. Conversely, if the trend over the past few years shows a decline in office population, it may mean that the office buildings in the area are in decline. It might then be time for you to consider another type of real estate whose users are increasing or to seek out office properties in an area where the trend is running in your favor.

In addition to surveying the area for its potential ability to satisfy your objective, you will have to consider particular properties as well. Each property exhibits the same trend cycle an area undergoes. When a property is new, it will experience the same growing pains as an area undergoing birth and growing up. There will inevitably be a shakedown period.

Once a rental property reaches maturity, it is likely to stabilize. Decline in the improvement may take place as a result of physical deterioration or because it has become functionally inadequate or due to changes in the area that cause values to decay.

At several points in the life cycle of the property, opportunities for rebirth may be identified by an astute investor. Renewal may occur as a result of redevelopment to a more intensive use if the density in the area has increased notably or of renovation of the present improvement to serve existing or new uses.

One or more of the appraisal methods discussed in Chapter 8 will help you analyze the property in question. The information developed through the appraisal methods will enable you to determine not only the life cycle stage of the improvement, but also that of the surrounding area. These appraisal methods apply the operations of the economic principles which follow to a property so that the life cycle stage of the property and its area can be determined and opportunities for profit identified.

PRINCIPLES

The economic principles governing real estate underlie the trendline or life cycle characteristic of real estate. Profits and losses are the result of the operations of these principles, as is value. Of critical importance to your success is your discovery of the economic principles at work behind what is happening in your area.

Six major economic principles rule the conduct of real estate.

All six are interrelated. In order to judge as accurately as possible the likelihood of the outcome you desire from any property you acquire, hold or sell, you must apply each principle to it. The six principles are:

1. Supply and demand
2. Substitution
3. Change

4. Conformity
5. Highest and best use
6. Future benefits

1. Supply and Demand   Real estate moves continuously from conditions of overdemand/undersupply to a balance between supply and demand to oversupply/underdemand to a new balance. Then, after a short or long period, the cycle starts again.

Undersupply means that there are too few units of a given kind of real estate relative to demand for those units. In other words, demand is greater than supply. This describes the birth portion of the life cycle. In the process of growing up, there are likely to be repeated episodes of more demand than supply, as supply or construction of improvements takes a certain time to accomplish.

Oversupply means that demand is too low to fill up or support the real estate involved. If it continues, it is likely to lead to declines in values. A balance implies that there is enough existing and potential demand to fill the real estate units supplied. Achievement of a lasting balance corresponds to the stage of maturity.

Of course, there will never be a balance of precisely 1,000 units demanded and 1,000 units supplied. In fact, a rigid balance is undesirable in a free market economy. If there were an exact balance in jobs and workers or real estate units and occupiers, each worker and each occupier would probably be locked forever into place. Thus, in a condition of balance, there is always a desirable level of frictional vacancy or enough empty units to allow for natural movement.

Knowing the relationship between supply and demand in your area, particularly for the type of real estate in which you are interested, is of profound importance to your financial health. The relationship will enable you to forecast, with reasonable accuracy, what is going to happen in your area in the future. Discovery of an undersupply may trigger a decision to acquire property for turnover. If you are the first investor or among the first to see demand developing, you stand to make the most money from the supply you provide. An approaching balance may stimulate a decision to buy for capital preservation or high income. And the approach of oversupply may tell you it is time to sell.

Thus, the analysis of supply and demand is not some abstract exercise designed to give you the trappings of professionalism. It is vital. Your property's ability to attract or retain tenants capable of providing you with an income stream, the appreciation you reap, your prospects for capital turnover and the yields you can draw from the property are largely a function of supply and demand.

Moreover, it is not sufficient for you to analyze the relationship of supply and demand only when you go to purchase the property. For profitable holding and for profitable sale, continual scanning of the horizon for the status of supply and demand is necessary.

Effective demand is what is sought by all real estate investors. Demand by itself is not enough, as we may all desire something we can not have. Nor is supply enough as there may be a supply of something not wanted. The existence of effective demand for the property you invest in is what will bring you the financial rewards you seek.

In general terms, effective demand arises out of three conditions: 1) A desire to use the real estate, 2) An ability to obtain what is desired, and 3) Enough scarcity to focus demand. Typically, ability takes the form of being able to pay the sales price or the rent. This is why it is so important to discover the income levels in an area. But the ability of a prospective tenant or buyer may also encompass such factors as the terms of the lease on the premises presently occupied. If the lease length remaining is long or the penalties for breaking it severe, the desire of that tenant to move to your real estate may be blocked.

Some degree of scarcity must exist in the market if desire and ability are to focus on your particular real estate. An oversupply will spread available demand over so many units that your real estate will be unlikely to obtain the share of demand it needs to be profitable. A relative undersupply will tend to move tenants or buyers in the direction of your real estate.

The free market economic cycle based on supply and demand is best exemplified in real estate. Real estate, after all, is fixed. Thus, a local oversupply can be more readily discerned and takes more time to cure. In comparison, an oversupply of television sets in one locality may be corrected rapidly by moving the sets to an area where they are in demand. More recently, the cycles in real estate have been growing shorter and shorter. This means that even more constant attention must be devoted to keeping up with the condition of supply and demand in your area.

The real estate investor who makes the greatest profit is the one who can identify what will happen as a result of supply and demand trends and who can spot opportunities created by their operations. If you anchor your investment behavior on the trends actually in process in terms of supply and demand, you will have a superior chance of success.

Certainly, you will be less likely to make the common mistake that led to a great oversupply of office space in New York a few years ago and, naturally, to a decline in values for a period. Manhattan investors, insisting that there would always be a strong demand for office space, kept producing more and more despite a decline in office population. Declining effective demand was not capable of supporting the glut produced. Saying that there will always be demand will not make it so.

It will be easier to abstain from such suicidal herd behavior if you can recognize the typical pattern of supply and demand. This can be summed up in the rule that excess demand causes excess profits which breed excessive competition. In real estate, demand for space arises from a need to replace space currently occupied or from a growth in the local population. In the first stage, supply tends to lag behind demand because it takes time to plan and construct more units. As a result, demand continues to grow and prices or rents are pushed up on available space.

Under such circumstances, the rising profits attract the attention of developers whose business is supplying the kind of space in demand. They begin to erect similar properties to take advantage of the strong effective demand. If they are first into the market with the right product, they stand to make large profits. Yet more developers are attracted and they build more space. More competition means slightly lower profits, but still plenty to go around. Demand may continue to spill over onto older properties, and their rents may begin to rise.

At this point, profits are still high and values are increasing. The process becomes visible enough to attract more developers who, confident that such strong demand can only continue, keep building more space. But these developers tend to rely on the financial results of the properties already built as if there were a rule that these profits will inevitably be duplicated on their own properties. The smell of success is likely to overlay what is actually happening to supply and demand.

An oversupply is created, vacancies soar, profits tumble and values decline. A halt in new construction takes place until demand rises to fill the supply. Supply and demand then enter a stage of balance. However, if effective demand again rises above supply and pushes profits up as a result of scarcity, the cycle will repeat itself.

One recent example of this occurred in Atlanta. Some 5,000 hotel rooms could not cope with the influx of business and convention visitors. As business travel to Atlanta increased, occupancy and profits in the existing hotels soared. Every hotel developer seemed to race to the same conclusion: Build more hotels. They did, to the tune of 7,000 more rooms, far above demand. Profits naturally plunged as demand was no longer effective; in some cases, bankruptcy ensued.

At the same time, an oversupply of office space was constructed and an undersupply of housing existed. While it might seem to have made sense for some of the hotel and office developers to switch to housing, they did not. This may have been due to the complicated nature of real estate. Developing major office and hotel buildings requires great expertise, as does the development of housing complexes on the same scale. It is seldom feasible to make a quick switch from one type to another. Too much new expertise is required, expertise that takes time to develop.

The supply and demand cycle is growing shorter as a result of two technological changes. When it took a long time to construct improvements and when information reached people more slowly, the cycle took more time, as did each of its stages. Now new buildings can be created relatively quickly.

A wider circle of developers and investors is also likely to become involved. In fact, the news that Houston was enjoying a boom economy was no sooner disseminated across the country by television than out-of-town developers arrived to start building new housing and offices. This was partly a result of the supply and demand situation in the rest of the country. The recession had depressed demand elsewhere to the point where there was a scarcity of opportunities to develop supply.

Since the cycle repeats itself, it is important to consider how to protect any real estate investment you may make. Location is a particularly critical function of demand. As we have discussed, demand develops because of locational considerations. An office building served by excellent transportation patterns is better located and thus will be in more demand than one that is inconvenient to reach.

To the extent that you select real estate in a location that has clear-cut benefits to its users compared with its competition, your property is more likely to retain its share of the market. Moreover, if the improvement itself has marked advantages, it is more likely to maintain profits and value. In addition, you can design leases to make it less likely that tenants will find it profitable to relocate.

It is just as important to consider potential as existing sources of competition. The supply of real estate, even in areas which appear saturated, is never fixed. People will always invent or create new sources of supply, such as housing in Los Angeles over the water, that create new competition for the existing supply. However, you can look for new supply to come chiefly from areas where the infrastructure already exists or is planned. It is easier to develop new sources of supply where transportation and municipal services already are or soon will be available.

The time to make large capital turnover profits is at the beginning of the supply and demand cycle. Effective demand is then strong and competition largely absent. However, the way in which developers make their profits contains the seeds of oversupply.

Developers generally make their profits by selling what they create to user-occupiers or to another investor who seeks income, tax shelter or eventual capital appreciation. Developers tend to be able to continue building and selling their products even after effective demand has begun to decline. It usually takes some time for the change in demand to become obvious to investors who do not do their homework. Thus, developers make their profits, while the next investor who owns the real estate may go through a period of high vacancies and low profits. If you decide to invest in a new property for income, tax shelter or appreciation, remember the short-term nature of the developer's interest. This should spur you into a careful analysis of the condition of supply and demand before you buy.

Investors may also want to jump into the market when property values are depressed as a result of oversupply. These investors bank on an increase in demand sufficient to shore up profits or create increased values. If investors can buy these properties at low prices relative to the value expected, they may realize a large capital gain. Or, if they hold the property during the next period when supply and demand are more in balance and during the early stages of the next cycle when demand is rising above supply, they stand to make profits from income. Investors attracted by stable incomes and interested in the preservation of capital tend to be more interested in properties in built-up areas where there is somewhat less likelihood of a great deal of new competition.

Restrictions on supply must be adjusted for. Building codes, zoning and environmental statutes all constrict supply. Moratoria on utility, sewer and water hookups or lack of energy will depress supply. Local taxes may be so stringent that they preclude profitable operation and thus restrain supply. Tenant and homeowner associations may prohibit certain uses. If effective demand exists and additions to supply are blocked, a condition of scarcity will be created. You may want to be among those property owners who will benefit from the resulting increase in values exhibited by the existing stock of improvements.

In most areas, demand and supply tend to build up over a number of years, with each particular market experiencing now more demand and now more supply. Moreover, in any community, there is likely to be a layering of markets, so that what is going on in any one market is unlikely to be exactly the same as what is going on in another market.

However, on occasion mass changes may occur in all or most markets in an area. A new plant may move in, causing additional demand for business, retail and residential real estate, or the government may buy up a forest for wilderness preservation or construct a dam. Each change may substantially alter the relationship of supply and demand in the area: It will depress or destroy the values of some properties and provide opportunities to enhance or create values in others.

Government programs are particularly prone to cause massive, rapid change. New employment centers, like those for the space program at Cape Canaveral, Florida, or at Houston, may spring up and just as quickly disappear. These sudden declines in demand are behind the decline in real estate values at the Cape as well as in areas where military bases were formerly located.

The supply of and demand for real estate is obviously important. What may not be so obvious is the importance of more general supply and demand functions. The supply of financing is critical to real estate investment. If financing is diverted from real estate to other purposes or a recession occurs, the supply of money available for real estate investment will shrink. If loans are available at all, interest rates are likely to become too high, the loan lengths too short or the downpayment requirements too stringent.

Conversely, an oversupply of money for real estate development is likely to create an oversupply of new construction. With money available and the ability to sell their products, developers rarely, if ever, restrain themselves. They are not, as you will recall, the ones who will have to operate their improvements in a market that is oversupplied.

The supply of and demand for materials and labor is also critical. Their availability and cost, for new construction, for renovation and for maintenance, will affect your profit margins. For example, in boom times, unions may push up wages; a recession may allow a new supply of less expensive labor to flourish. The new supply of nonunion labor plus the supply of union labor may produce an oversupply that causes some construction wages to decline, as happened in the mid-1970s. Then the availability and lower cost of the labor component may help spur another building boom.

Materials manufacturers also go through demand and supply cycles, ones that can strongly affect real estate. For example, a relatively long period of balance in the supply of and demand for insulation was interrupted by the decision of the Organization of the Petroleum Exporting Countries (OPEC) to raise fuel prices. Demand for insulation rose as heating prices rose. However, supply could not expand as quickly, as it takes time to plan and build more plants.

Thus, a shortage developed, prices rose and problems were created for developers of new construction who could not obtain insulation when they needed it. This caused costly delays. Owners of older real estate also needed insulation to keep their heat and air conditioning expenses competitive. If the improvement could not be economically retrofitted with insulation, it became less competitive and thus lost value.

National and international developments may affect the supply and demand function of materials and labor in your area, just as they are likely to influence the cost and availability of money. The OPEC decision is only one example. For another, a war curtails the availability of materials and labor for other purposes, as happened in the 1960s at the height of the Vietnam war. Prices rose, which affected the profitability of real estate operations. Uncertainty as to the value of the dollar, itself a function of supply and demand, will curtail demand for new plants and equipment, sending ripples through the real estate community.

You can follow the status of supply and demand of those functions underlying real estate supply and demand through newspaper coverage. National indexes track the overall supplies of money and labor; local indexes for your area may also be published. Industrial trade associations often compile information on materials; this is either published or can be obtained directly from the association listed in your library's *Encyclopedia of Associations*. Newspapers also provide coverage of such topics as the demand for loans, the value of the dollar and energy capacity. Real estate investment requires a general knowledge of all that is going on.

While what is happening in the nation's money market centers is important, local occurrences are even more critical. By its nature, real estate is immovable. Thus, what is happening on the local scene in terms of supply and demand will have the greatest impact on your fortunes as a real estate investor. As a result, you will find it necessary to specialize in information about your locality.

2. Substitution   If two similar products are on the market, and one can be obtained at less cost than the other, a purchaser will tend to buy the less costly product. You have probably seen this principle in operation at your local meat counter. Each time beef supplies decline and beef prices, as a result, rise, people substitute less costly sources of protein, perhaps poultry, fish or cheese.

The principle of substitution explains why the market for each type of property forms a continuum. In residential property, the range is from the large, single family house to single room occupancy. The extremes are not at all likely to be substituted for each other. In fact, there is less opportunity for substitution at the extreme ends of the market. The poor can not afford to move and the rich can afford to obtain what they want without having to substitute.

In the middle range, however, housing may be freely substituted. For example, someone who has not yet come up with the downpayment required for a house may rent one or an apartment or a mobile home. If the downpayment for a single family house is out of reach, the family may opt for or substitute a townhouse. An apartment tenant may substitute a two-bedroom apartment for the more costly three-bedroom or may continue searching until a less expensive three-bedroom unit is located.

Substitution is what often creates demand for older space. For example, a new lawyer may need an office, but available office space in new improvements may be too costly. She or he may then look in older improvements for similar office space which rents for less. The substitution principle also extends to creating new supplies. Thus, someone establishing a new business may not be able to afford to rent space in which to function. Turning some space at home or in a garage into an office may prove to be the substitution needed.

Substitution is a form of competition of which you may not be aware. For example, substitution options may lead businesses and property owners making excess profits to lower their prices. An area with few retail outlets and strong shopping demand may attract more retail outlets to cash in on the profits. To gain shoppers, the new competition may offer similar goods at less cost. Then the original shopkeepers may have to lower their prices as patronage flows away from them toward the newcomers.

You can sharpen your ability to protect yourself by becoming cognizant of the ways in which people can substitute one product for another that is similar. This will keep you from charging rents or setting prices at levels that strongly encourage prospective or current tenants and purchasers to seek out less costly alternatives. Moreover, by listening to prospective tenants describe their business operations, you will be able to identify certain problems before you sign them up. Thus, if a retailer intends to stock goods that are much more costly than similar products being sold in the area, you can deem it likely that he or she will not obtain enough support from customers to meet your rent.

You can also use the principle of substitution to help you define your market. If you establish the chain of choices available, some more costly than the one you are looking at, and some less expensive for a similar product, you can determine how much substitution is feasible and therefore how much competition you will have.

As you look at real estate, you might also ask yourself whether the property offers amenities which can not be substituted. This might include more light if the properties across the street are small-scale landmarks, whereas otherwise similar properties are in the shade much of the time. You could then advertise this special feature to attract tenants, who would be likely to stay as long as they could not find a substitute offering the same amenity at less cost.

Substitution options are becoming more diverse. This is chiefly a result of the increasing acceptability of different ways of life. As one example, there was a period when conformity demanded acceptance of the suburban way of life. Living in the suburbs and commuting to work in the cities meant people paid what they considered an acceptable price, both in time and money, to obtain what they wanted. In terms of money, the lower cost of housing space was combined with a higher cost of transportation.

Now, some people have decided that the price in time spent commuting is no longer acceptable. Greater diversity today has made it acceptable for them to move back into the city. There they pay more for housing space but less for transportation. As a result of this substitution, they can afford to live in the city.

Substitution can occur at any point. For example, manufactured housing is a substitute for costly stick-built housing. Factory labor is much less costly than labor employed in putting up a house piece by piece. As high housing costs have cut effective demand, some developers have responded by substituting these prefabrication techniques. Suburban low rise office buildings can also, in some cases, be seen as a substitution. Thus, office users who could function in downtown areas may choose to locate in suburban areas because the cost of land and building is less and, as a result, their operating costs are less.

Substitution is also behind the recent conversion of older urban commercial space into housing. Dollar for dollar, tenants or purchasers can often obtain larger living spaces in these commercial buildings than they can elsewhere at affordable prices. This ability to substitute a new source of housing for older sources has caused effective demand to flow in new directions and has changed the competitive situation in some areas.

Investors who undertake conversions are also applying the principle of substitution on several levels. Compared with new urban construction, conversions, with their already existing structures, call for fewer materials and less labor. In addition, it often takes less time to complete a renovation, which brings down financing and overhead costs. As a result, demand for less expensive housing can be met by producing living space at lower rentals or sales prices, but at similar profit margins.

3. Change The underlying reality in real estate is change. Real estate is always in transition from one stage to another, even if the changes are so slow as to be barely noticeable. The recurring pattern of change is one of birth, growth, maturity, decay and, in some cases, renewal. It is an evolutionary process.

However, change can also occur with relative rapidity. In order to widen a street, the state may condemn a property with an otherwise long remaining useful life. Fire may destroy an improvement. If more attractive areas open up, another area may decline more rapidly than would otherwise have been the case. What was fashionable last year may not be in style this year.

However, revolutionary change in real estate is rarely so rapid that you can not protect yourself. For example, your retail tenant's business may be falling off because youngsters no longer want beads and bangles but instead have discovered the pleasures of feathers. If the store operator does not react quickly, you are still likely to have time to suggest merchandising changes before all the youngsters follow the leaders to another store.

You will also have time to hire an expert lawyer and protest a condemnation proposal. Even if you lose, you will have a considerable period of time to reinvest the condemnation award. Zoning proposals must go through lengthy public proceedings, which will give you time to rally a protest. New developments are usually announced far in advance of actual building, which will give you the opportunity to lengthen leases or adjust rents on property you already own or to buy up property that may benefit from the change. Casualty insurance can protect you against natural disasters.

The best protection is to stay current in insurance and information. Listen to what people are saying about their preferences and their dislikes. The first person to say he can no longer stand to wear a tie may startle you if the area in which you operate has supported traditional business attire. But, if you hear several more say it and then take action, you may want to start thinking about a replacement for the tie store in the building you own.

These small occasions of surprise are the seeds from which change may grow on the social scene. If they hit fertile ground, the change is likely to take place in time. To the extent that you are aware of the change early on, you may find opportunities for profit. The only sure thing in this world of real estate is that change is ever taking place.

4. Conformity Both economic and social behavior exhibit a desire for homogeneity. If a group of things or of people are homogeneous or similar, they tend to hold the same values. Nonconforming objects surrounded by objects which are homogeneous tend to assume the value surrounding them.

You may have seen the principle of conformity at work in your own neighborhood. For example, one house may be much more expensive or larger than its neighbors. The value of this improvement is likely to fall toward the norm in the neighborhood for two reasons. First, buyers tend to buy neighborhood before they buy a particular property. Thus, people looking for homes in the neighborhood are likely to be able to afford the norm but not the over-improvement. Second, people who might be able to afford a larger or more expensive house are likely to want its surroundings to be in conformity with it.

Thus, if you buy a nonconforming overimprovement at a price much above that of its neighbors, you will have overpaid in relation to its value. Of course, if you are able to purchase the property at a price reflecting average values in the neighborhood, you will obtain more property for your dollar. Conversely, an underimprovement will tend to rise in value toward the value of the surrounding properties. If you can purchase it for less than the norm in the neighborhood, you may have an opportunity to resell it at a price closer to the average value.

Too much nonconformance can lower values in a neighborhood, a prime consideration when you are selecting a property to purchase. For example, a neighborhood combining industrial and residential uses in close proximity is likely to exhibit lower property values than neighborhoods that are exclusively industrial or residential. The price of a house next to a gas station would always tend to be lower than that of a similar house protected from such an inharmonious conjunction.

Restrictions that enhance conformity, such as zoning or private covenants, tend to enhance value. Zoning proposals that would allow too great a degree of nonconformity will tend, if allowed to go into effect, to lower property values. A property which is undermaintained in relation to its neighbors will be nonconforming and thus tend to decline in value.

However, conformity does not mean identicality. Some mixture of uses and properties is inevitable and desirable if the diversity of human needs and desires is to be met and individuality expressed. Endless rows of identical buildings have a deadening effect. The individual properties are likely to become less desirable and less valuable, as will the neighborhood. Residential neighborhoods without convenient retail facilities mixed in are also less desirable. However, the shopping area is usually confined to a definite sector within the neighborhood so that its activities do not intrude on the residential sections.

The degree of conformity deemed acceptable is undergoing change, a change which may open up new markets for you. We have already mentioned the suburbanites who move back into the city, one market you could tap. But the change is operating on a broader scale than that.

Over the past two decades, a redefinition of conformity has encompassed people of diverse religious, racial, social and economic backgrounds. No longer do property values fall if people who are not identical to the original dwellers move in. As a result, effective demand has been broadened. Moreover, this change is now widening to include acceptance of divorced or single people remaining in the suburbs or of young professional couples moving into so-called ethnic neighborhoods to renovate a house. The broader markets that result are there for investors to sell or rent properties to.

5. Highest and Best Use   In applying economic principles to real estate, you are seeking to establish the highest and best use for the land. The improvement which permits the land to earn the greatest net return will be the most valuable and will enable the land to reach its highest value.

The highest and best use for a parcel of land is defined as its legal and most probable use. However, both overimprovement and underimprovement can occur, events which can damage your investment's profitability. Both detract from the highest and best use the land could achieve. If they did not exist, the land could earn more from a more suitable improvement.

Several examples will serve to illustrate highest and best use. First, we will postulate land valued at $1.3 million, a value developed by comparing it with what similar parcels have recently sold for. The improvement on the land generates $100,000 in net income. If the return on the land must be eight percent to reflect current market conditions, some $104,000 in net income should be applied to the return on the land. As there is not even that much net income available, the improvement must be a detriment or an underimprovement. The land could earn its just reward only from an improvement which generated much more net income than this one does.

In order to establish highest and best use, an appraiser hypothesizes several potential improvements, a necessarily delicate process of assumptions. For example, a three story improvement might be assumed. It would cost $600,000 to construct and it is estimated that it would last 50 years. To recapture the investment in the improvement, a rate of two percent of its cost is required. Moreover, we will assume that the current market return on the investment in the improvement is 10 percent. Therefore, an annual rate of 12 percent of the cost of the improvement is necessary.

To provide an adequate return on and of the improvement will take $72,000 in net income, or 12 percent of $600,000. If the hypothesized improvement is estimated to produce $100,000 in net income, as similar properties are now producing, then $28,000 is left for return on the land. At the eight percent current market rate of return on similar land, the land might be capitalized or valued at $350,000 ($28,000 divided by eight percent).

In order to test this hypothesis to see whether it provides the greatest net return to the land possible, we will hypothesize an additional floor and extra parking. The additional cost might bring the total cost of developing the improvement to $950,000. Total net income might increase to $130,000. By taking 12 percent of the cost of the improvement, we discover that $114,000 of the net income must be applied to the improvement if an adequate return on and of it is to be accomplished. That leaves $16,000 for the return on the land.

Again using an eight percent return on the land, the value of the land with this improvement on it would be $200,000. This is some $150,000 less than the value without the extra story and parking. Thus, the four story improvement is an overimprovement. In this case, the three story improvement hypothesized would be the highest and best use as it returns more to the land.

Different measurements can be used to establish highest and best use, such as square feet of space or the quality of the space. Both are functions of the rents an improvement can generate. For example, we will hypothesize an improvement that, because of low ceiling heights, can only be rented at two dollars a square foot in an area where three dollars a square foot is being received. The one dollar difference per square foot indicates the amount by which this improvement undershoots the highest and best use for that parcel of land.

Another example might involve construction costs for office buildings. If one building cost $100 per square foot to construct, it undoubtedly has some unusual amenities. However, most office buildings in the area cost only $65 a square foot to develop. Rent levels which users of office space are willing to pay in the current market run to $11 a square foot. In order to obtain the same profit margin, the costlier building might have to receive $18 a square foot. However, tenants are willing to pay only $12 to $13 a square foot for the space with extra amenities.

In effect, too much capital has been applied to the more costly improvement to provide the highest and best use. The rent levels achievable can not compensate an investor for the full cost of the improvement, much less provide an adequate return to the land. Generally, only users can afford to overconstruct or overimprove, because their consideration of greatest net return is not limited to the financial aspect. For example, a corporate headquarters may be overbuilt in order to portray an image.

A great many people confuse highest and best use with the most impressive improvements. Impressive generally indicates an overimprovement. The test is the highest residual value to the land, not how tall or ornate the building is. For example, a small building surrounded by much taller ones might appear to be an underimprovement. But, looks can be deceiving. If the area is undergoing a phase of severe oversupply, it would be folly to erect a tall building on the site. Perhaps, in light of current market conditions, the present use is the highest and best one.

In another case, that small building may be encumbered with a legal restriction which prevents further development. For example, the developer of a corner site might buy up the right to develop a site in the middle of the block. The developer's ownership of that right would prevent construction of a building which might block out the light for the developer's building. The small building in place would then be the highest and best use for the land.

The principle of highest and best use subsumes the other principles we have discussed. Their application is what makes it possible to determine whether a particular improvement is the highest and best use for the land or whether it overshoots or falls short of the mark. The operations of the other principles tend to bring about realization of a given highest and best use.

Supply and demand is the test of highest and best use. What may appear to be an underdevelopment on the surface, like the small building surrounded by larger ones, may turn out to be adequate once this principle is considered. Effective demand may be low and thus putting up a larger building would simply mean constructing for vacancies. That would not provide the greatest return to the land.

Conformity also plays its part. If highest and best use is considered in the abstract, a particular parcel of land may seem appropriate for an office building. The street on which it is located may be convenient to good transportation and sources of employees, or it may be prestigious. However, the land may be zoned for small-scale retail. The neighborhoods surrounding the site may be the sort that would try to block the establishment of a large office development, thus causing expensive delay. The highest and best use in actual fact would not be for an office building but perhaps for an exclusive neighborhood shopping center.

Highest and best use is not a static concept. Real estate does not attain a highest and best use and stay there forever. The principle of change may cause what has been the highest and best use to become an under- or overimprovement. The example we cited in Chapter 2 of the resort properties located on a pre-interstate route illustrates this well.

As you will recall, an interstate highway was built parallel to the older road. Its coming set off a chain reaction which lost the resort facilities along the older road much of their business and thus resulted in their becoming overimprovements. They were no longer capable of earning enough to compensate the owner for the use of his or her land as well as for the improvement on it. At the same time, other sites located near interstate exits gained a new highest and best use. Improvements already located on such sites may have become underimprovements and therefore not able to provide the greatest net return to the land. An investor might then tear them down and erect new improvements that would boost the return to the land.

Actual or potential substitution contributes to what can be the highest and best use. A brand new luxury hotel may seem like the highest and best use that could be developed from a particular parcel of land. But, if there are many slightly less expensive luxury hotel rooms already in that market, the new hotel's occupancy rate may be so low as to render it unprofitable. The test for whether that hotel is the highest and best use is whether the residual to the land is the highest that can be achieved.

The principle of highest and best use also assumes a principle of balance. The greatest net return of all to the land is achievable when supply and demand are each sufficient, one to the other. This state corresponds to the stage of maturity. Balance can also be seen at work in the operation of conformity. When a balance among uses has been achieved, the highest values are created and sustained. Change can work to upset existing balances and thus cause values to rise or fall on their way to a new balance and a new highest and best use.

In real estate, balance refers more exactly to a proper proportion of the four active forces that work to produce a property which can make profits. Each of the four, labor, the investor/manager, improvement and land, makes a contribution to the whole value. Only when they are in balance is maximum value reached.

An overimprovement means that too large a contribution of capital has been applied to the improvement for the greatest return on the land to be earned. An underimprovement means too little capital has been applied. And if labor or supervision of the property consumes too much compensation, the capital elements of improvement and land will earn too little.

The principle of economy of scale can be applied to each of these four productive forces. Maximum value is achieved when the four are not only in balance but each is invested to the point where the greatest net return on the land is realized. Investment past that point will mean that net return declines, as was illustrated by the building to which an extra floor was added. A disproportion in one element of the property will cause the others to suffer.

In addition, one can apply this principle of balance to the whole of real estate. An increase in demand will increase supply until the two reach another balance and new highest and best uses are achieved. In a city where there is a strong reliance on industry, a decrease in industrial demand, perhaps because of relocation or overbuilding, will decrease demand for housing, retail uses and so on until a new level of highest and best use is achieved for each use.

6. Future Benefits An investor purchases the future economic benefits of a property when he or she invests. These future benefits determine a property's value. This principle is easy to forget when so much emphasis is put on examining the past performance of an investment vehicle. But, an investor can not look for her or his return from the past or present.

Any amount earned by a property or any appreciation in it, up to the point when you acquire the property, belongs to the previous owner or owners. It is no longer available to compensate you for making the investment. It is merely helpful as one guide for estimating what the property may earn in the future.

You acquire a property solely for its future benefits, those that will accrue to you. Before you purchase, you must be able to anticipate that the trends and principles affecting the property will be of benefit to you in the pursuit of your objective. Only if the property is likely to benefit in the future from their operations are you likely to profit from its acquisition.

THE BUNDLE OF RIGHTS

When most people look at real estate, they see only the physical components, such as a building, a tree and a lawn. As a result, they see only the surface of real estate and mistake it for real estate itself. There is much more to real estate which is not as visible as a building or the land. If you are to prosper, you must perceive the totality of what real estate is.

When we began this book, we defined property as a right or rights you could acquire. Real estate comprises all the rights, both tangible and intangible, which are inherent in it. When you invest in real estate, you are actually acquiring one right, several rights or many, depending on what you need to meet your objective.

The totality of real estate's rights is termed a bundle of rights or a bundle of sticks. Each stick corresponds to a legally separable right or interest you can acquire. It is because these rights can be separated from the bundle that you can acquire a particular stick or sticks which can provide you with income, tax shelter, capital turnover or capital appreciation.

The tangible sticks include the land, what is underneath the surface of the land as far as the core of the earth and what is above the land, such as the improvements, natural growth and the air. When you purchase specific real estate, you can acquire the minerals underneath the soil, the topsoil, vegetation, any improvements, air space, water, scenic views, rock formations, a bird sanctuary or any other tangible interest which may be present.

Simultaneous with the purchase of the physical rights is the acquisition of the legal rights pertaining to the physical aspect of real estate. These intangible rights include the rights to leave the physical assets to your heirs, to give them away, to mortgage them, to lease them, to develop them, to sell them, ad infinitum.

When real estate is acquired in fee, as it is known, the fee owner acquires all the rights and interests, both tangible and intangible. The fee owner has a total and absolute right to the property under this legal system, subject only to the government's right to exercise eminent domain and its police powers.

The ways in which these rights can be put to use are limited only by imagination. For example, a condominium improvement is no more than a collection of air spaces. A certain limited air space, legally defined as occupying a certain space above ground, is what the individual condominium owner acquires along with the insides of the walls bounding the space. Land in the Midwest may have several separate rights or interests in simultaneous operation: The right to dig out the coal under the land, the right to farm the land, the right to hunt, the right to occupy a house on the land, and the right to mortgage.

To further your understanding of the bundle of sticks, we have constructed a hypothetical example based on the complex Park Avenue situation discussed in Chapter 2. The following system might be developed:

1. The fee interest in the land, which includes the right to the use of the trackage below grade.

2. The right to lease certain portions of the ground and the air rights in return for rental payments.

3. The granting of a leasehold right to construct an office building on pilings between and over portions of the tracks and the land.

4. The right to mortgage the land by the fee interest.

5. The right to mortgage the improvements by the leasehold interest.

6. The right of the lenders to seize either the land or the

improvements, depending on which they loaned against, if default occurs.

7. The right of the local government to take a portion of the fee interest through eminent domain and police power for streets and water and sewer connections between the buildings and over the railroad tracks.

8. The right to grant an easement to the local electrical utility to construct electrical conduits and steam pipes under the streets and over the fee interest.

9. The right to grant a sublease provision to the land lessee.

10. The loss of certain development rights due to the government's right under eminent domain and police power to designate an improvement as a landmark.

11. The right of the fee interest to transfer the undeveloped air rights to someone else.

12. The right of the developer who acquires the air rights to develop a larger improvement on the parcel of land to which the air rights can be transferred.

This list could go on indefinitely. But it is already clear that each right must be spelled out carefully and in great legal detail. If the rights and obligations are not put into proper legal form, one party may gain a right or escape an obligation at the expense of the other parties. The legal documents, which define the rights and obligations, are where many of your best protections can be developed. The example above may be unusually complex, but even in a less complicated situation great care is warranted in developing legal documents.

For example, if you are the fee owner of the land and you lease it to another party, you may want to transfer the right to maintain the land with the right of occupancy. That would lessen your management requirement. However, you should retain the right to enforce maintenance, so that a littered appearance does not detract from the value of your interest in the real estate.

Similarly, if you, as a fee owner, transfer your right to mortgage the fee to another party, in most cases your lessee, you should retain certain rights. Then any default on the loan payments will not mean that the lender could take your fee interest from you. In such a subordination situation, it is common for the fee owner to retain the rights to make the mortgage payments and to be notified that any are past due so that her or his fee will not be foreclosed upon.

To make it more likely that you receive income to which you have a right, you may want to place restrictions on use in your leases. For example, you might require your tenant to remain open for certain hours, to stock certain merchandise, to staff the premises in such a way as to promote business efficiency and so on. The protections available are virtually endless and must be tailored to fit each situation by a lawyer who is familiar with the type of real estate involved and the problems likely to be encountered.

As a fee owner, you may be subject to certain conditions established by the owner who sold you the property. There may be deed restrictions which require you to build only one structure of a certain size on the land to conform to other improvements in the neighborhood. You may be required to keep up the improvements acquired in a certain manner. The previous fee owner may have conveyed the land to you without the right to develop the minerals, a right which may have been transferred previously to another investor. Examining the documents for such restrictions is a necessity.

Certain priorities of interests can legally be established, priorities which will affect your yield. The further down the list your interest is, or the greater the number of interests which are ahead of yours, the less secure yours will be. Thus, the market would judge it to require a higher yield.

The government's interest always takes precedence. The government has the right to collect property taxes on the physical assets and income taxes on your income from the property. If you do not pay taxes due, the governmental unit involved has the right to seize the real estate. A government also has the right to take your property under eminent domain for public purposes or if you die intestate. And it has the right to regulate the real estate to promote the general health and safety of the population through devices such as building codes and zoning ordinances. The acquisition of a fee interest in real estate in effect obligates you to pay certain dues to society before any other dues can be paid.

The fee owner's interest is next as long as the right to mortgage the real estate is not exercised. If you choose to mortgage the fee, or you subordinate your right to mortgage to the lessee and let your lessee mortgage it, the lender's rights will take precedence over your rights as the fee owner. Any second mortgage on the fee would come after the first mortgage, but before the fee owner's interest. If the leaseholder's interest were mortgaged, the leasehold mortgage would come after the fee owner's interest and before the leaseholder's interest.

As you can see, an ascending scale of risks, as perceived by the market, accompanies the descending scale of priorities of interests. The government, at the head of the line, is in the most secure position. The first lender's interest in the fee is the next most secure. The fee owner's interest is more risky than that of the lender who has loaned against the fee. As a result, the market determines that a higher yield on the fee is required than on the first mortgage loan.

In addition to the priority scale we have developed, there is one interest which may suddenly leap ahead of the others in line. As you will recall from our discussion of the principle of balance, the labor component comes before any other component of an investment. As a result, labor is due its compensation first. Thus, mechanic's liens may be accorded priority over a mortgage lender's interest and may also tie up the fee owner's right to sell the property until the bills are paid or the lien is judged by a court to be without justification. You must protect yourself by obtaining waivers from any contractor you employ, indicating that each payment of each bill for both labor and materials has been properly made.

The yield on any property right or interest is a function of the market. The interests in real estate are exceedingly diverse and the rights that are conveyed by a fee owner will be contingent on the objective sought. If the fee owner elects to mortgage the property in order to increase the yield on his or her equity or to be able to purchase real estate with a strong potential for capital appreciation, income or tax shelter, the fee owner is passing certain rights on to the lender. These have certain priorities and would command a certain yield depending on the type of property, the risk, size and liquidity involved and the management required.

All the rights can materially affect the ultimate use and the yield on a property. For example, the decision to convey the right to use a property to a leaseholder will mean giving up the right to occupy the property and the opportunity to lease it to someone else at a higher rent. The granting of a scenic easement on a property by giving away the right to develop it to the government or to a charitable organization interested in wildlife preservation will restrict the potential for a certain kind of profit, particularly that from turnover.

While the fee interest consists of absolute rights subject only to the government's rights, the fee interest can be made conditional. Thus, decisions made by the fee owner as a function of the objective sought may place a whole series of conditions on the property.

These conditions may include a mortgage, as we have discussed, or they might include offering to share the fee with partners. Each time a fee owner gives up a right, there is less control over the real estate and thus a higher yield is required. In other words, you trade a part of the control for the opportunity to participate in some immediate or long-term benefits. Leasing the property also means giving up some control.

Yields change as conditions change. Without a mortgage, the yield required to attract an investor to the real estate might be 10 percent. After the right to mortgage the fee has been exercised, the yield might have to be 12 percent as the fee owner's interest is now restricted by the lender's rights.

The yields that will attract limited partners may be lower than the yield required on a general partner's interest because no management is required of the limited partners and because more risk is assumed by a general partner. Again, you might be a fee owner who decides to pass along your right to manage the real estate to your lessee through a net lease. The yield then required on your fee would decline to reflect the lower management requirement.

Real estate's inherent bundle of rights is what provides you with the opportunity to select the stick or sticks you want to acquire. Thus, a pension fund, itself a tax shelter, does not need to acquire the tax shelter stick. To meet its income objective at least cost, it might choose to acquire the land underneath an improvement, an interest which generates no depreciation write-off. That would make the tax shelter stick of the improvement available for other investors.

Each stick in the bundle is affected by the trends and principles discussed earlier in this chapter. To name just a few examples: The government, having too low a supply of tax dollars, may raise taxes on your fee interest or on the income from your property in order to meet public demands for services. A lender may have too great a supply of dollars in relation to the demand for loans and thus make money available at more favorable terms to a fee owner or lessee.

The right to receive payments from a lessee may be jeopardized if the tenant, through misapprehension of the market, switches from stocking the kind of merchandise the neighborhood wants to nonconforming merchandise. Operating expenses may rise to a point where the imbalance threatens the fee owner's return.

You must understand exactly what rights you will have to acquire in order to pursue your objective. For example, you may have to acquire the fee interest subject to a mortgage or a limited partner's portion of the fee interest. You may have to acquire the right to lease the space on the current market in order to meet an income objective. If so, you will need a property unencumbered by an existing leasehold interest. You may also be able to maximize achievement of your objective by acquiring only certain sticks and not others.

Evaluate the rights and their attendant obligations in terms of your objectives: What rights must you have in your bundle? What will it cost you to acquire them? What rights will you give up and at what price? What position will you take? What rights should you retain to meet your objective and protect your position? How does your compensation for taking a certain position meet your objectives? What obligations, such as the fee owner's obligation to pay taxes, will result from taking a particular position? What obligations attend on the acquisition of rights from you by other parties? How can you enforce these obligations?

Finally, weigh how the trends and principles of real estate affect the interest you plan to acquire and how they are likely to affect it in the future. The operations of the trends and principles will in large measure cause the value of your interest to grow or decline over the period during which you own the interest or interests you acquire.

Real estate is the base for everything we do. Literally. Our material nature ensures that no human activity can take place without in some way involving real estate. As a result, it is our activities which afford real estate investors opportunities for profit. And it is the multiplicity of our activities which will assure you of many properties capable of meeting your individual mix of objectives and investor profile.

The integral linkage between real estate and all levels of human activity (past, present and future) is what differentiates a real estate investment from all other kinds of investment. In all types of investment, an investor does well to know what impacts upon a particular investment he or she makes. But, if real estate is not the investment involved, the investor's focus is essentially a narrow one. Each day an investor is likely to undertake many activities and will learn of many other people's activities that have nothing whatever to do with her or his investment. But this is not the case with real estate.

Real estate is so all encompassing that investing in it requires a dramatically different mode of thinking. If you are to recognize opportunities successfully, you must learn to perceive the real estate behind each surface activity. Instead of thinking of business as business, you must begin to see a business as occupying a certain type of real estate which facilitates its activities. Rather than thinking of buying an appliance solely as a personal shopping expedition, think of it in terms of the real estate necessary for your purchase to take place.

Your thinking must transcend any individual activity if you are to understand that real estate is in back of it, under it or around it. Thought of in this manner, even poetry is not poetry but the real estate where inspiration, writing and poetry readings take place.

7

what makes real estate investment different?

Everything you do and everything that everybody else does is done in or on real estate. In order to recognize when these activities create opportunities for you, an obviously key aspect of real estate investment, you will need to apply your interest in real estate investing. Your interest will first enable you to notice and acquire information about what may previously have seemed unrelated, even uninteresting, spheres of activity. Second, your interest will allow you to think through the real estate consequences of each activity about which you acquire information.

Both the earliest and the latest forms of human activity will illustrate the omnipresence of real estate. Analyzing them offers you an opportunity to begin to transform your normal mode of thinking about different aspects of life into real estate investment thinking. The first, probably the search for sustenance, certainly involved land capable of supporting edible growth and a place where people ate the produce gathered.

Today, the much longer and more complex chain of food supply involves real estate at each point in the process: 1) The farms or ranches where grains or animals are grown; 2) The rail, truck or barge way for transporting them to a processor; 3) The processing plant; 4) The railroad or highway necessary to transport the processed foods to a wholesaler; 5) The wholesaler's warehouse; 6) The highway and local streets for trucks carrying foodstuffs to a retailer; 7) The grocery store; 8) The streets and sidewalks that permit a purchaser to get to the store and bring the food home; and 9) The cooking and dining areas within a home.

Many more examples of real estate's role in the food chain could be adduced. We have not, for example, even mentioned the mines where fertilizer is produced, the factory where cans are made, the commodity exchanges where those involved in the food chain try to protect themselves against adverse price moves, nor the real estate required to deliver the electricity for food refrigeration.

However, it is clear enough that what we tend to think of as a food chain, if we think of it at all, can just as readily be thought of as a real estate chain and, more pertinently, as a real estate investment chain. Some person or entity owned, now owns or will own all the real estate involved.

Humanity's latest venture, the exploration of space, also requires real estate at each stage in the process of launching a spacecraft. Just a few instances would include: 1) Buildings for offices and research laboratories; 2) Mines where metals are produced; 3) The rights-of-way needed to get raw materials to factories; 4) The different fabricating plants for everything from aluminum to transistors; 5) The assembly point; 6) The launching pad; 7) The control tower; and 8) The tracking stations around the world and their supply systems. Even the process of sending a rocket out past the point where current real estate ownership ends is both immediately and ultimately real estate. Undoubtedly, many investors have made and are making real estate profits at different stages of the process.

Everything you do at work also involves real estate. The office building, plant, store, farm or dock where you work is certainly real estate. So is the telephone system you use to gather or give business information during your working hours. Someone granted easements for underground or overhead lines, while others owned the land for or built the switching stations, the plants which manufacture cable and telephone instruments and the laboratories where new methods of transmitting sound are invented. The paper on which you write memoranda would not be available for your use without land for timber to grow, pulp mills, warehouses, and stockrooms near your office. Filing cabinets too must be manufactured, shipped and stored somewhere, and each somewhere is owned by someone.

All the places in which you seek entertainment are real estate. A short list might include ski trails, fishing streams, summer theatres, scuba-diving areas, circuses, movie theatres, opera houses and the den in which you watch television. Someone made or is making a real estate profit somewhere along the way to your enjoyment of your favorite recreation.

Airborne travel obviously requires mundane real estate for runways, hangars to store the airplanes when they are not aloft, passenger and freight terminals, control towers and access roads. But air travel also needs real estate far from the airport, such as ticket offices, bus terminals, limousine garages and tanker terminals for jet fuel, as well as the offices of credit card companies to which payments are sent.

In short there is no aspect of human life that does not involve real estate in some way. You, in order to operate your own car, depend on streets, gas stations, and parking spaces. In fact, you can not get away from real estate. When you pick up your child at school, you are involved in real estate. So, too, are you making use of real estate when you go to a shopping center or to visit someone in a hospital.

To start transforming your thinking, ask yourself what kinds of opportunity existed in the past for properties around you, what presently exist and what kinds may exist in the future. Put another way, the question for you to answer is how the real estate behind all these activities, the real estate you may suddenly be perceiving for the first time, meets real estate investment objectives.

For example, some of the real estate you encounter is owned or leased by the government, such as highways, bridges, streets, fire stations, offices, launching pads, some grazing land in the West, and airports. The ultimate human activity involved is governmental policymaking in pursuit of some public purpose. This kind of activity can affect real estate opportunities significantly.

Any governmental decision may mean an opportunity for a turn-over investor to convert a building to public use or to construct a public building. An income, appreciation or tax shelter investor may find it promising to lease real estate to a governmental agency charged with carrying out a decision.

Other decisions may mean a cutback in some public activity which has supported certain real estate. A pending decline in activity may indicate that the time has come to shift from an investment which benefited from previous decisions to one that will benefit from some other decision or trend. It is your clear understanding of how these activities impact upon real estate which will give you time to dispose of real estate that may be adversely affected.

Not only governmental decisions, and their resulting activity, impact on real estate investments. Private decisions also result in activities that create opportunities. For example, some privately owned real estate may be readied for development as a result of a nearby plant opening, and that may mean turnover opportunities. The users of other properties may generate activities around them which will give real estate investors the opportunity to make a profit to meet income, appreciation or tax shelter objectives.

To train yourself to recognize opportunities, you may want to consider your own activities for a day or a week. If you write down everything you do and next to each activity note the real estate involved, you will greatly sharpen your perception of real estate. For example, your list might start with the activity of eating breakfast. If you eat it at home, you may be doing so in a place where a turnover investor made a profit. If you are renting your home, you may be eating your breakfast where a turnover investor made and an income investor is making a profit.

If you take breakfast in a coffee shop, a turnover investor may have made a profit from building it for either a user or an investor. If the coffee shop is in a highrise office building, the odds are that an investor interested in income, tax shelter or appreciation leases it to the coffee shop operator. If your favorite coffee shop is in a series of one story shops in a built-up area, the investor involved may be receiving income while holding the property for appreciation from future development.

By making your list of activities as comprehensive as possible, you will learn to see not only the real estate behind each activity, but also the possible profit opportunities generated by the activity. Moreover, if you also note down any activities in which you would like to engage but can not, you may spot an opportunity to fill an activity gap. For example, you may often wish there were a nearby coffee shop, but none is conveniently situated. After conducting a market analysis as described in Chapter 11, you may decide to reap a profit from the existence of demand you have uncovered and confirmed. You can then purchase or lease a suitable property in order to lease it to a coffee shop operator to meet your investment objective.

Successful real estate investors live real estate. They continually listen and look for opportunities even in the most casual of conversation or reading. In talking to people about their activities, they are alert to the real estate needed to carry out the activities mentioned. Then they think about the objectives which might be met through the real estate concerned.

For example, you may hear a group of doctors talking about their need for additional office space and their inability to find suitable space. Upon analysis, you may find an opportunity to create space for them and make a turnover profit. Or, after a building has been constructed to suit the doctors' requirements, you may want to purchase it for income, tax shelter or appreciation purposes.

The clue may be less obvious. The doctors may be talking about the advantages of group practice which, although they do not mention it, would require real estate that could accommodate several doctors practicing together. It is important always to be alert to the real estate implications behind information you acquire.

Real estate is unique because it shelters all human activities. Those we have listed and others all offer shelter of one kind or another. Farms shelter growing food; industrial land and plants shelter one kind of work activity, and other kinds of real estate shelter recreational pursuits. Even scenic easements offer psychological shelter.

Perceiving the real estate behind the activity which is sheltered by it also involves understanding how real estate expresses ways of life and indeed to a great degree dictates them. Once a person has chosen a location, that location will dictate a particular way of life. If you select one location in which to live, your life will necessarily be different than it would have been had you chosen another. Living in a suburban house requires mowing the lawn; living in a brownstone may mean sweeping the sidewalks.

Different activities are implied by the way in which real estate is used in different geographic areas. Thus, a suburban location implies a demand for lawn mowers and a potential opportunity to rent to retailers who sell them. Suburban life also implies the necessity of owning a car, which in turn implies opportunities for specific tenancies, including those that can supply automotive needs. A relative lack of car ownership in a city may mean that more money is available for recreation, as may the reasons city life is chosen. That may imply more opportunities to rent to tenants which supply away-from-home recreation. Thinking through the implications of real estate activities is another way of alerting yourself to opportunities.

Hey - We Missed You!

YES - Please renew my subscription.

SAVE 25% OFF NEWSTAND PRICE

It's not too late to renew your subscription to America's most exciting and inspiring magazine, **COUNTRY FOLK ART MAGAZINE™** !

☐ 8 Issues – $28.95

☐ 6 Issues – $22.95   ☐ 4 Issues – $14.95

Payment must accompany subscription order

8393 E. Holly Road, Holly, MI 48442

Name

Address

City   State   Zip

☐ Check/Money Order Enclosed   ☐ MasterCard   ☐ VISA

Card #:   Exp. Date:

Signature:

Country Folk Art
MAGAZINE

Country Folk Art
MAGAZINE

8393 E. Holly Road
Holly, MI 48442

1ST CLASS
Pre-Sort
U.S. POSTAGE
PAID
Holly, MI
Permit No. PO8

Please make any

50236

Remainin

HARD229   465060203 1891 02/04/92
NOTIFY SENDER OF NEW ADDRESS
HARDY
1687 DOUGLAS RD
BREMEN IN 46506-9603

The reciprocal relationship between human activity and real estate, pointed out in Chapter 6, explains why the life of real estate resembles human life. Shifts in human activity bring real estate to birth and cause it to grow, mature, decay and to be reborn. Understanding how changes in an activity impact upon real estate can maximize your opportunities. Real estate is as dynamic as life itself and continually undergoes change.

If you are beginning to realize that real estate is involved in everything we do and that each activity may offer you the opportunity you are seeking, you are starting to think as a successful real estate investor does. You will see certain human activities winding down in one place and therefore recognize that investment opportunities are in the process of shrinking. You will also begin to spot activities shifting to other areas and realize the growth in investment opportunities which that implies.

Seeing the world dynamically in terms of real estate also means not thinking of the physical world of real estate as a given. Anything physical can always be changed (assuming it meets economic criteria) to meet the needs of an activity. For that matter, any intangible right can also be changed if the same economic criteria are met. Realizing this will widen your opportunities for profit.

For instance, you may spot certain pointers in an area, such as an absence of "for rent" signs and an increased incidence of people seeking apartments. If the signs point to an increase in demand, your market analysis may be able to confirm that an unmet demand exists. However, if you fail to think dynamically, you may assume that a lack of land justifies stopping dead in your tracks.

You would be justified in ignoring this opportunity only if your mental definition of land is an open space of a certain dimension, a rather static concept. Not taking that definition for granted may allow you to see an opportunity like one an investor pursued in one of the West Coast gateway cities. This investor decked over an industrial area to create the "land" he needed to meet a demand for housing.

What is being done with a property today does not necessarily mean that the same thing must always be done with it. For example, you may be looking at a 300- acre farm, of which 240 are planted with crops. Fences, pastures, a house and ponds may occupy the remaining acreage. However, if the fences were removed, the planted portion of the farm could be increased to 280 acres. Perhaps that change would mean the difference between an adequate return on your investment and an unusually profitable return.

Social attitudes are also dynamic in nature. Today's mores make remaining single, divorcing and living together acceptable. Similarly, the norm of young people staying home until marriage and widows and widowers moving in with their children has changed. In addition, more people are changing lifestyles upon reaching retirement. Changes of this kind make a considerable impact on real estate. Certainly, housing markets have been significantly altered. If you recognize how a change in attitude can alter the use of real estate, you may spot opportunities to serve the new markets with certain apartments, mobile homes or retirement homes or, indeed, with certain kinds of shops.

If real estate is everything, then information about changes in any human activity may spotlight opportunities for you close to home. Particularly rewarding sources of information include reports from your local planning commission showing where and why development is expected to occur, announcements from local, state or federal agencies of transportation developments, and information from the local zoning department on changes. Other sources, such as *Shopping Center World, Shopping Center Digest* and the *Dollars and Cents of Shopping Centers,* will give you clues to changes in retail opportunities. In addition, *Multi-Housing News* and *Dodge Construction News,* as well as others, may alert you to new ideas or opportunities.

Professional publications carry articles about current happenings. For example, accounting journals would alert you to something like the replacement cost accounting change, which might mean you could increase the value of a property and then sell it. Or a law journal article alerting you to changes in the way courts are deciding zoning cases may be applicable to land near you. The real estate section of your local newspaper will also focus on activity changes that may spell opportunities for you.

To help you see what we mean by equating information about

activities with opportunity, we have selected three case studies. Each shows how a change in activity can impact on the real estate around you. We have deliberately chosen information which was conspicuously in the public domain where you or any other real estate investor could have put it to use. Similar information, which you can collect from public and private sources in the course of your daily life, will indicate opportunities worth your investigation or areas of real estate worth staying away from for a period.

CASE STUDY I
Employment Center Moves In

Illustration 1

Giant Johns-Manville Firm Moving to Denver

By Jack Phinney
Denver Post Business Writer

Johns-Manville Corp., a company with annual sales in excess of $500 million, said Wednesday it is moving its corporate headquarters from New York to Denver.

The move, to be completed by September 1972, is expected to involve up to 1,500 persons now employed in New York City and Finderne, N.J.

John Fuller, president of the Denver Chamber of Commerce, hailed the move at a Wednesday press conference. He said it's the first time in Denver's history that a major corporation has decided to relocate completely here.

Fuller and Mayor Bill McNichols praised the work of the chamber's Forward Metro Denver team in presenting Denver's attractions to the Johns-Manville management.

W. R. Goodwin, president of Johns-Manville, said in New York that the transfer of employes will begin this summer. "We intend to develop at Denver one of the most outstanding corporate headquarters facilities in the country," Goodwin said.

The site is to be the Greenwood Plaza office park being developed in Arapahoe County by the John Madden Co.

Asked why Denver was chosen, J. B. Jobe, executive vice president of operations, said that when Johns-Manville management decided the company's operating efficiency could be improved by moving out of the New York area, a number of locations across the nation were surveyed.

"The final study—involving the scope and method of Johns-Manville operations, and considering the long-term growth of the company—showed Denver to be the best headquarters location," Jobe said.

The company now has its headquarters at 22 E. 40th St. in New York and its research, engineering, data processing and accounting operations at Finderne.

A key factor in the decision to move, said Francis H. May Jr., executive vice president of finance and administration, was the need for "consolidating the company's administrative and service functions to bring about improved operating efficiency." He said the company will keep some offices in the New York area "to maintain long-established relationships."

Johns-Manville manufactures products for the construction market—including roofing, insulation and siding. The company is the world's largest producer of asbestos, and manufactures asbestos-cement pipe and glass fiber and asphalt products.

The firm has plants in Florence and Antonito, Colo., and a regional sales office in Denver.

Sales and earnings of the company this year are expected to top the 1970 levels, management said recently. Johns-Manville had net income last year of $33.4 million on sales of $578 million. The firm has more than 21,000 employes worldwide and more than 25,000 shareholders.

A month ago Johns-Manville announced a joint venture to extend the Sun Valley resort in Idaho. The Company will work with William C. Janss on the project, involving 1,900 acres.

Courtesy of *The Denver Post* from the May 19, 1971 issue.

Illustration 2

Work Begins On
$43 Million J-M 'Quarters

Johns-Manville Corp. (J-M), Denver, held a groundbreaking Tuesday for the company's world headquarters to be built on its 10,000 acre Ken Caryl Ranch southwest of Denver.

Colorado Atty. Gen. John P. Moore and J-M's president, W.R. Goodwin, headed the ceremony. Moore said he was "dumbstruck" on seeing the headquarters site for the first time Tuesday. He said "until you've seen this spot, you haven't seen anything Colorado has to offer."

Goodwin said "what you see here is pretty much the way it's going to remain." He said J-M plans to preserve all of the ranch's inner valley with the world headquarters as the only development. He said "it will give us a beautiful front yard."

Goodwin put the overall construction cost at $43 million, including roads. Excavation will begin in 30 days.

"You only build a world headquarters once," Goodwin said in explaining the cost. He said the shape of the building will resemble that of a grand piano.

Construction manager for the project will be Turner Construction Co. of Los Angeles. Denver architect Carl F. Groos, Jr., will work with the Architects' Collaborate of Cambridge, Mass., which was selected in a design competition in spring 1973.

Johns-Manville plans to occupy the world headquarters by fall 1976. Some 1,600 employees will work there.

Courtesy of *The Denver Post*, October 9, 1973.

Illustration 3

Fleeing Cities, a Company Finds
Suburbs Encroaching

By Paul Goldberger

Surely no building in the United States has as dramatic an approach as the new headquarters of the Johns-Manville Corporation on a 10,000-acre ranch 22 miles southwest of Denver. The last few miles are traveled along a country road that winds through a valley; the road makes a sudden turnoff through a mountain pass, then winds upward past great formations of red rock that sit beside the road like sculptures. Suddenly the road makes another turn, and there, set across the valley like a squared-off aluminum spaceship come to rest in the foothills of the Rockies, sits the building.

It is as sleek and gleaming an object as any architect ever dreamed of creating, and it sits in the rough mountain landscape with the self-assuredness of a Greek temple. The architect was the Architects Collaborative of Cambridge, Mass., whose design was chosen in 1973 as the result of an architectural competition sponsored by Johns-Manville.

Serious Questions Raised

The building has absolutely nothing to do with its site—it is a machine-made object, and every detail of its precise, shiny facade shouts that fact. One's first instinct is to wonder why there was not more of an effort made to relate to the site, but then it becomes clear that the right route was taken—that this site is so extraordinarily beautiful that to "relate" in the usual way through the use of natural materials or a more modest physical form would have been futile. The only answer was to celebrate the site by also celebrating technology, and letting the machine-made object sit gently in the natural landscape.

That said, however, both the building itself and the philosophy behind the Johns-Manville headquarters raise serious questions, with relevance far beyond this splendid, stunning piece of land. The building is perhaps the ultimate new corporate environment in the nation—it is the farthest extreme to which any major corporation has gone to create its own environment. This shiny structure in the foothills is sealed off, both literally and figuratively, from the world around it.

Johns-Manville had formerly been based in New York and New Jersey. Its executives, like those of so many corporations, grew tired of problems of the Northeast and chose to flee, not just out of the city, but also out of the region. And the company, once it had chosen to move to Colorado, made it clear that it did not want to try city life again, either—Johns-Manville not only didn't want to be in New York, it didn't think much more of Denver.

So the company bought the former Ken-Caryl cattle ranch, a safe hour's drive from downtown Denver, and its officials talked excitedly about the problem-free land to which they were moving.

Really That Different?

All well and good in theory. But the reality is a bit harder to accept. Much of the land between Johns-Manville's sprawling site and the city of Denver has been farmland until recently, but the coming of the corporation, with almost 2,000 workers—which means 2,000 households—has changed all that. Real-estate developers bought up the farmland in anticipation of Johns-Manville's arrival and now much of the land has been built up with suburban subdivisions, just like those one would see anywhere else.

So Johns-Manville, which wanted to trade the crowded Northeast for the land where the buffaloes roam, has ended up causing a lot of that land to be turned into something not so very different from the place it left. The company itself is apart from this suburban sprawl, of course—its enormous site affords it protection from the changed landscape. The views from the executives' windows are of a pure, perfect virgin landscape. But over the ridge, it is something else.

Company executives come and go by helicopter; others are forced to travel the long distance by car, so that here again, the company that sought to find a trouble-free environment has helped to seriously alter that environment. The question inevitably arises: Is this the most socially responsible kind of architecture we can expect from a corporation with the vast resources of Johns-Manville?

If stealing away to a palace in the mountains is not the most responsible course of action Johns-Manville can take in terms of its overall effect on society, one wonders if it can be justified in terms of the company's own operations. Only Johns-Manville's employees know, of course, and the company naturally maintains official pleasure at the results of the move.

A Matter of Isolation

But it is hard not to wonder if the extreme isolation does not have some sort of effect on the people who work at Johns-Manville. They do not have any place to shop, and they do not have any place to eat except in company facilities. They have no one to talk to except fellow employees, and never in their work lives is there ever the chance for that sort of accidental encounter with a friend or a colleague or even a competitor that can yield a new idea. Johns-Manville is so isolated that it makes Greenwich, Conn., look like Times Square.

Curiously, it is these issues that come to mind after a visit to this headquarters complex, not questions of architecture. As pure architecture, the building is good—perhaps as good a structure as the Architects Collaborative has done—although it blazes no really new trails.

Like so many buildings of the 1960's and 1970's, the form traces its descent from LaTourette, Le Corbusier's famous monastery in France of 1955. As at LaTourette, there are horizontal floors set atop pillars, and the entire structure is set gracefully into the side of a hill.

Johns-Manville takes the LaTourette form, alters it, and stretches it to the point of near-absurdity—the building is more than 1,000 feet along, a fifth of a mile. Some corridors inside run for the full length, and they are astonishingly dramatic and powerful spaces—we almost never see that kind of space stretched out like a tunnel, and the effect is genuinely exciting.

The building breaks away from its LaTourette beginnings in other ways besides its size. It is sheathed entirely in aluminum, making it responsive to what is really an altogether different esthetic from Le Corbusier's harsh, raw concrete. Most of the other aspects of the design relate well to that sleek, aluminum esthetic—the major form of the building is shaped like a wedge so that there is one sharp corner that deftly jabs the sky, and there is an immense, drumlike wing of aluminum just behind the main wing that provides an important formal counterpoint to the larger form.

The inside is so enormous that there are floor plans every few hundred feet to help keep one's direction straight. The offices, designed by the Space Design Group, are comfortable and attractive and are laid out so that most employees get to share in at least a bit of the view. There are a number of fine modern prints on the walls—among them several etchings of New York buildings by Richard Haas, which seem like touching bits of nostalgia.

There are lavish facilities—gyms, dining rooms, a swimming pool—for the use of the employees. Indeed, the pleasures this building provides are such that it is difficult to imagine a worker not being relatively content. And after all, there is only one price he or she must pay for all of this—the lack of contact with the real world.

© 1978 by The New York Times Company. Reprinted by permission.

When the Johns-Manville Corporation first announced that it would move its headquarters operations from New York City and New Jersey to Denver, developers in Denver undoubtedly took note. According to an article in the *Denver Post* on May 19, 1971, reprinted as Illustration 1, up to 1,500 employees were to be transferred. That meant some 1,500 households would need places to live, to shop, to enjoy themselves and to satisfy all the other requirements of today's way of living.

The company first moved into a new office park. Then it bought ranch land some 20 miles from Denver. An alert developer who was checking land transfers in the course of his or her investigation of turnover possibilities may well have spotted the sale and the opportunity it created for real estate development. In addition, the company was apparently making no secret of its desire to leave city life completely behind. Another developer or an equity partner of a developer may well have heard about that. In any case, the announcement of an architectural design competition for a world headquarters building as mentioned in Illustration 2 must certainly have alerted developers.

As a result of these signs of activity, developers bought up farmland around the Johns-Manville site in order to meet the anticipated demand for housing reasonably close to the new place of employment. Housing tracts were constructed, as described in Illustration 3. The developers who were alert made turnover profits. Other developers undoubtedly read the same signals and piggybacked new retail stores on the housing developments.

CASE STUDY II
Retail Chain Goes Bankrupt

Illustration 4

Grant Will Close
Nine WNY Stores

By Jim McAvey

Nine of the 17 W.T. Grant stores in Western New York will be among 133 more stores the bankrupt company will close, Robert H. Anderson, chairman of the retail chain, announced on Monday. A total of at least 270 jobs will be lost.

The new round of closings will include 37 stores in New York State and will leave Grant's with 359 stores in 14 Mid-Atlantic and Northeastern states. The company operated 1,074 stores in 40 states before it filed under Chapter 11 of the Federal Bankruptcy Act in October.

Western New York stores to be closed after the close of business on Wednesday are in the Northtown Shopping Center, Amherst; Garden Village Plaza, Cheektowaga; Mid-City Plaza, North Tonawanda; Transit Rd. Plaza, Lockport; Albion in Orleans County, and Warsaw in Wyoming County.

Others which will close are: Grant City, Bolivar Rd., Wellsville; 58 E. Main St.,

Westfield; and 44 Main St., Perry. A store at 117 W. 3rd St., Jamestown, was closed previously.

Staying Open

Buffalo area stores which will remain open are at Main and Huron, Buffalo University Plaza, Amherst; Thruway Plaza, Cheektowaga; Grant City, North Tonawanda; Main and Transit, Williamsville; Depew; Hamburg, and East Aurora.

Other stores remaining open include W. State Rd., Allegany; 135 N. Union St., Olean; and, Dunkirk-Fredonia Thruway Plaza, Dunkirk.

In filing under the voluntary Chapter 11 bankruptcy proceedings on Oct. 2, Grant's listed debts in excess of $1 billion. Under Chapter 11 provisions, the company is permitted to stay in business and prepare a plan for payment of its debts.

Store closings will result in the loss of 32 jobs at Northtown, 93 at the Garden Village Plaza, 97 in Lockport, 16 in North Tonawanda, 17 in Albion, and 12 in Warsaw.

A loss of 5,036 jobs will result from the latest closing of 133 stores, 1,554 of the jobs in the 37 additional stores to be closed in New York State.

Some of the 133 stores will be reopened briefly in January for clearance sales. The Lockport and the Garden Village Plaza store are the only two in this area in which January clearance sales will be held.

Anderson said the latest closings will enable Grant's to concentrate efforts in those areas where its merchandising has been most successful.

"This planned reduction will establish for Grant an operating base of 359 stores located in 14 Mid-Atlantic and Northeastern states," he said. "These are markets in which Grant has long been well known and well received by its primary customer—the family shopper."

Following is a list of the states where Grant now operates, the number of stores to close and the number that will remain open:

Connecticut, 5, 32; Delaware, two, six; Maine, 4, 22; Maryland, six, nine; Massachusetts, 15, 36; New Hampshire, three, nine; New Jersey, 13, 44; New York, 37, 85; Ohio, 11, 6; Pennsylvania, 27, 87.

And Rhode Island, one, nine; Vermont, four, five; Virginia, four, five; West Virginia, one, four.

Courtesy of The Buffalo Courier-Express, December 23, 1975.

Illustration 5

Gautieri Buys Former Grant Store

Courier-Express Batavia Bureau

BATAVIA—Vito J. Gautieri, Batavia contractor, has purchased the former W. T. Grant Co. store at the corner of Main and Center in downtown Batavia for a reported $225,000.

According to the new owner, the purchase of the building from Cornell University was through a holding company, Batavia Liquor Store Inc. The East River Bank of New York City reportedly holds the mortgage for the purchase.

Gautieri has leased the building since the Grant store closed and has remodeled and has all but about 2,000 sq. ft. of space leased out.

The major tenant is Western Regional Off-Track Betting which has its executive offices on the second floor of the building and a betting parlor on the first floor.

Other tenants include a restaurant and an Endicott Johnson shoe store scheduled to open within a week. Gautieri said the remaining 2,000 sq. ft. should be rented within two months.

Courtesy of The Buffalo Courier-Express, May 1, 1976.

If the arrival of a new employment center on the outskirts of Denver meant profits for housing developers, the 1975 departure of W. T. Grant from the ranks of major retail chains meant a different kind of opportunity in New York's Buffalo area. All that year, Grant had announced store closings in what turned out to be a futile attempt to avoid bankruptcy. After it filed a voluntary bankruptcy petition in October 1975, it sought to consolidate operations east of Cleveland.

As Illustration 4 shows, Grant failed in its effort to keep all the remaining stores open. A *Buffalo-Courier Express* article of December 1975 listed nine store closings in its area alone. Just as previous store closings had in other locations, those in western New York created opportunities for investors. Some were probably prepared to seize the moment because they had followed the declining fortunes of the Grant chain and understood the implications of the previous announcements.

Certainly, a Batavia contractor was quick off the mark. By May 1, 1976, as Illustration 5 shows, he had already remodeled a Grant store for smaller tenants and leased almost all of it to them.

The May 1976 article also displays a real estate acquisition technique you may wish to incorporate in your own investment strategy. According to the article, the contractor involved leased the premises until he could remodel and produce an income stream from tenants to whom he sublet. Only at that point did he purchase the property. While it can only be a supposition, it is reasonable to assume that the property had to produce an acceptable income stream before a purchaser could obtain financing or obtain it on favorable terms. Moreover, leasing can reduce the capital required at the front end of an investment. Thus, it can enable an investor with insufficient acquisition capital to invest or it can release more capital for renovation purposes.

CASE STUDY III
Highway Realignment Opens Real Estate Opportunities

Illustration 6

Fight Down the Road to Improve Ill. 53

By John McCarron

OPPONENTS DUB it the "cornfield Crosstown"—calling it an unnecessary expressway that would scar one of the last expanses of open space within 30 miles of Chicago.

Proponents say the road is needed "for the orderly development of central Lake County."

THE FIGHT OVER whether to extend the improved Ill. Hwy. 53 from its current terminus near Arlington Heights to Grayslake in northern Lake County has all the elements of a classic:

• Environment—Opponents complain the road would destroy marsh and bog lands that are not only nice to look at but necessary to recharge dwindling ground water supplies in the area.

• Traffic jams—Continuing the expressway into Lake County would eliminate the rush-hour snarl where three lanes of northbound cars crowd onto the exit ramp at Dundee Road. Some opponents charge that state highway planners "designed in" the bottleneck to generate a public outcry for completion of the road to Grayslake.

• Politics—The extension of Ill. 53 north of the Northwest Tollway has been a political hot potato since the early 1960s, when the expressway was built and critics charged it was constructed to benefit the owners of Arlington Park Race Track. Opponents now claim that several Lake County landowners who stand to gain from further extension are big donors to both political parties.

• Chicken or egg—The project typifies one of the growing controversies in urban planning: Should roads and sewer lines be built to service areas of expected growth, or do these public projects actually cause urbanization of outlying areas?

Like Chicago's Crosstown, the Ill. 53 project has been on the drawing boards for more than two decades, and like the Crosstown, it goes under several different names.

THE LAKE COUNTY extension would be the northern 14 miles of what area planners call the Lake-Will Corridor.

Federal, state, and regional transportation plans for the area all call for a north-south expressway to serve the far western suburbs.

The corridor would roughly follow the path of Ill. Hwy. 53 from Grayslake to Joliet, although the only major portion completed to date goes from Dundee Road in northern Cook County to Army Trail Road in Du Page County.

The "old" Ill. 53 in Lake County is a two lane highway that winds north from Dundee Road for about 3 miles into the county, where it merges with Ill. Hwy. 83, which continues to the Wisconsin border.

THE LAKE COUNTY extension of the corridor has been designated by the Federal Highway Administration as Federal Aid Project (FAP) 432, meaning the U.S. government will pay 70 percent of construction costs if the state can put up 30 per cent.

State highway planners say inflation has pushed the total cost of FAP 432 to well over $100 million.

That is a problem, since nearly all the money in the state's Supplemental Freeway System fund has been earmarked for other, critical, projects.

The money pinch recently caused the Illinois Transportation Study Commission—the agency that recommends future state highway construction—to trim the state's agenda for new freeways from 2,150 miles to 397 miles.

BUT FAP 432 was included in that high-priority list, and the commission recommended that if no money is available to build it as a federal-state freeway, it should be built as a state tollway.

"The need for the extension is already there," said Fred Schoenfeld, executive director of the commission. "The land-use pattern is set, the development is coming."

Either method of building the road would require action by the governor and state legislature, Schoenfeld said.

If the road is to be built as a freeway under the 70-30 federal matching program, the state would have to gather additional highway money—probably by raising the motor fuel tax.

IF THE ROAD is to be built by the Illinois Toll Highway Authority, the legislature would have to amend the state Tollway Act to include the project before bonds could be sold.

Schoenfeld said the legislature probably won't act on either plan until after the 1978 elections.

He said tollway status would be the quickest way to begin construction—perhaps within two to four years—because only state funds would be involved.

Another cog that would have to fall into place before construction could begin is completion of an environmental impact statement required by the Federal Highway Administration.

The FHA approved a draft impact statement in 1975 but asked the Illinois Department of Transportation to redo part of it after local officials complained it did not fully assess the impact on the wetlands in the road's path.

A REVISED impact statement will be finished early in 1978, according to an IDOT spokesman.

Officials from the Village of Long Grove, with a population of 1,600, have led opposition to the project since 1964.

"What we're talking about here is the massive destruction of land," said D.M. "Cal" Doughty, Long Grove village administrator.

The proposed highway would cut through the undeveloped western edge of the town, including an area called the Long Grove marsh.

Doughty said the town prides itself on being an "open space" community and homes generally cost more than $100,000 and are built on lots of at least two acres.

The downtown, which is also a historical district, is dominated by a covered bridge and storefronts of 19th Century design.

"THE PLANS FOR this highway are 10 years old, and a lot has happened since then," Doughty said.

"How about the environment? How about changes in what people are looking for in the quality of their lives? How about the energy crisis?"

Robert Coffin, mayor of Long Grove, insists the traffic needs of central Lake County could be served by connecting Ill. 53 with U.S. 12 (Rand Road), which the state has already upgraded to four lanes nearly all the way from Arlington Heights to the Wisconsin border. He recommends the connection be made near the Lake-Cook border south of Long Grove.

"Don't, in the name of a highway we don't need and shouldn't afford, destroy one of the last great tracts of natural open space, water retention, water recharge, and natural wildlife habitat." Coffin told highway planners at a public hearing on the project last year.

OTHER TOWNS in southern Lake County don't see it that way.

"Something has to be done about those traffic jams where (Ill. Hwy.) 53 empties onto Dundee Road," said Verna Clayton, village clerk of Buffalo Grove, which is on record as favoring the project as long as environmental precautions are taken.

She said commuters in her village are angry at the delays in getting on and off Ill. 53, which is their main access to downtown Chicago.

The same reasons were cited by a Buffalo Grove newspaper's editorial earlier this month that concluded: "It's time to get on with the project."

TO THE WEST OF Long Grove, Lake Zurich officials favor completion of the project lest planners take Coffin's advice and route the Ill. 53 traffic north on Rand Road through Lake Zurich.

"That would only shift the traffic jam over to us," said Lake Zurich village administrator John Petrie of the Long Grove proposal.

Most of the rolling farmland within the expressway corridor was bought years ago by developers and is being leased back to farmers until the time is ripe for subdividing, according to Lake County officials.

One of the largest landholders, Kemper Insurance Company, owns about 900 acres where the corridor intersects Ill. Hwy. 22 north of Long Grove.

PART OF THE land is being used for Kemper headquarters, but the company is also building a championship golf course there and has obtained zoning changes for other, as yet unspecified, development.

"Yes, we're for it," said a Kemper spokesman of the Ill. 53 extension. "If it isn't built, there will be a hodge-podge up here."

"Development is coming," another Kemper official said. "Long Grove can stamp its feet, but the world has got to go on.

"A few rich people have staked out a claim and want to keep the rest of the world out," he said of the Long Grove opponents.

THE KEMPER spokesman would not say how much the Ill. 53 extension would raise the value of the company's land, but other real estate experts say the increase would be dramatic, especially since the project calls for an interchange at Ill. 22.

Long Grove's Mayor Coffin has little doubt why landowners in central Lake County are pushing for the road.

"Once you build such a road, a corridor of development follows it. The highway is not the result of the need, the need comes as a result of the construction of the highway," he said.

Coffin charged that the development pattern is to "buy farm land at low prices, stimulate a highway at taxpayer's expense, and then sell to make a killing."

DESPITE COFFIN'S objections, most area planners believe the Ill. 53 extension will eventually be built to Grayslake.

Two reasons are most often mentioned: First, the project is "on the planning boards," and second, the development of central Lake County appears inevitable.

Opponents continue to insist that nothing is inevitable, that roads bring developments, and the chicken brings the eggs.

Reprinted courtesy of *The Chicago Tribune*, September 22, 1977.

Illustration 7

Shopping Center Planned

A 13-store shopping center is planned at Baldwin and Dundee roads in Palatine Township.

The developer is Ted Schwartz, part owner of Musicraft, a company that owns six audio sales shops in the suburban Chicago area.

The 5.25-acre tract is zoned for commercial use but building permits still have not been issued by the county. Schwartz said he hopes the complex will be complete by November.

PARKING LOTS will be built on the front, side and rear of the center and there will be entrances on both Baldwin and Dundee roads, Schwartz said.

Stores will include a Musicraft shop and a real estate office and Schwartz said he will favor tenants whose customers are "youth oriented," such as record, jeans and t-shirt shops, as well as interior decorators. As many as 13 stores could be included, Schwartz said.

There are 1,700 townhouses, condominiums and apartments that house 4,000 persons along Baldwin Road. Plans to build at least 500 more units are pending.

Residents have complained about 20-car backups along Baldwin onto Dundee at rush hour and the state highway department said the number of accidents at the corner is "significantly higher than the state average for that type of intersection."

Township officials have asked the state to install a traffic signal at Baldwin Road but it will not be operating until late summer.

Schwartz said he is aware that the area already is crowded. "We're not saying we don't care what happens in Cook County. Dundee Road is a busy street but that's why we want to be there."

WITHIN ONE BLOCK of the proposed shopping center a Dunkin' Donuts restaurant and National Pride self-service car wash will open soon, adding to the area's traffic.

Palatine Township Supervisor Howard Olsen said, "The area already is zoned commercial but if they were asking for a variance we would object. This will tend to add to traffic and bring still more cars into the area."

Courtesy of *The Daily Herald Palatine*, March 25, 1978.

Proposals to build a new road or upgrade an existing one attract the attention of real estate investors for more reasons than one, as the accompanying articles show. The first announcement many years ago that plans were afoot for a major highway extension north of Chicago galvanized investors, who bought up undeveloped land to hold for future development.

Illustration 6 shows the two objectives involved. Some of the investors appear to have bought land in hopes of realizing capital appreciation by reselling the land to a developer when actual development was on the horizon. Others bought for capital turnover. They planned to add more value to the land by creating housing, changing zoning, selling small parcels and other like activities. In the interim, both kinds of investors seem to have protected themselves by leasing the land to farmers in return for income that would cover their holding costs.

These investors observed a potential market activity developing in the area. We will take you through market analysis requirements in Chapter 11. However, any market analysis starts with observation of what is going on in an area. Then, the trade area involved is delineated and a demand and supply analysis applied to it. Here, it is obvious that these investors were spurred on by the potential activity level they saw implied by the road announcement.

The investment opportunities that prevailed before everyone realized what a new road would mean have passed in the Route 53 case. However, this has not meant an end to all opportunities. Development in parts of Lake County is now in full swing, as can be seen from Illustration 7. Four thousand people have been added in only one location, about one half mile west of the proposed Route 53 extension, and more are coming. Whether the county likes it or not, development has arrived. This makes the construction of Route 53 more likely because a greater demand will develop as more people gain a stake in faster and easier transportation.

This article illustrates the kinds of opportunities that exist provided you are an astute investor who is alert to the implications of what you read, hear or see. The developer mentioned in Illustration 7 obviously observed the existing housing developments, the new construction under way and the announcements for housing development. He determined that the teenage and young adult market was growing. He plans to make a profit by creating a retail property which will serve the surrounding residential developments.

This single development by no means eliminates all the opportunities which may exist near this site or others in the county. For example, if your market analysis had confirmed this developer's demographics, you would probably have found an effective demand for other retail uses, such as fast-food outlets. There are many fast-food franchises which would complement the Dunkin' Donuts facility. In fact, between the date the first article illustrated appeared and spring of the next year, more than ten fast-food outlets moved in.

Moreover, the demographics for the trade area might have revealed that most of the young people still live with their parents. If that were so, there might be opportunities to create stores which would serve a somewhat older clientele. For example, there could be effective demand for an auto parts store near the car wash. In fact, this is just what occurred. Once you start observing what goes on around you, opportunities like these will leap out at you.

The article also shows precisely why the developer chose his site. Not only is there a large housing complex right next door, but the nonlocal resident retail intercept potential is high because of the heavy traffic carried on Dundee Road.

The investors who will make money in this area form several layers. The first includes the long-term holders of undeveloped farmland who spotted the announcements of a proposed road years ago and investigated the possibility that development would eventually take place. The second is made up of those who initiated housing developments. The third consists of investors who are hitching a ride on the primary developments to create retail properties to serve the new residential market. When the time is right, another layer may come into existence to develop nearby offices in which the residential population can be employed. Even if Route 53 is never built, there are now multiple sources of support for changes in land use within the county.

A prime challenge to real estate investors is buying right. Acquiring a property at too high a price relative to its value will unduly increase your capital requirements and cause yield to decline, perhaps below adequacy. Moreover, the only way to know whether you have gained the advantages of acquiring a property at a low price relative to value is to know what its value is.

MARKET VALUE

Value may seem a highly subjective quality. Pebbles, a tattered ribbon and a bird's nest may be valuable objects to a child, but worthless to an adult. Another child may, however, find these objects so valuable that he is willing to pay a price for them. For value to exist, there must be a need which a particular object can satisfy, a desire for the object, and also an ability to obtain it.

The definitions of value become more meaningful when different kinds are examined. For example, there is the value of something in use, perhaps a business. If the company is a going concern, its value will be higher than it will be the moment it ceases to function. The value of the company's real property, its plant and machinery for example, is likely to be at its peak during the firm's operating life. If the business were to cease operation, the plant and the machinery could become less valuable unless, as rarely happens, another user were to find the real property exactly what its needs called for.

Other kinds of value include scrap value, value for insurance purposes, taxable value and exchange value. Each kind has a precise purpose, which determines the valuation reached.

In real estate, the investor is usually concerned

with market value. This is generally considered to be the congru-
ence between what the average well-informed buyer will pay for a
property and the average well-informed seller will accept for a
property, both knowing all the uses to which the property can be put
and all material facts, with neither party acting under duress.

This is a definition of great consequence. Not only does it affect
purchase and disposition decisions but it is the essence of what the
Internal Revenue Service and the courts use to consider condemnation awards and to aid in establishing tax liability, among other
decisions which are likely to affect the investor materially.

Without this general definition of market value, an individual's
objective would become the measurement of value. The clear im-
possibility of ascertaining in advance the particular objectives of
unknown individuals necessitates a workable definition based on
what motivates the bulk of buyers and sellers.

The market value definition breaks down into several components, each of which must be understood if the concept of market
value is to be applied effectively to your transactions. First is the
average buyer. A somewhat mythical figure, the average buyer
should not be confused with yourself. The average buyer is not an
individual who buys for a special need or purpose. He or she is
assumed to have no dominant motive for the acquisition. In most
transactions, value equals price, and value is what most buyers pay
for a property.

Actual buyers, such as yourself, are characterized by special
circumstances, as each actual buyer is an individual in a highly
distinctive position at any given moment. There are several kinds
of actual buyers in conformity with the layering of motivations we
will discuss in Chapter 10.

There are actual buyers who are primarily interested in income,
in tax shelter for its own sake, in turnover or in preservation of
capital. Each has a different perception of an investment, as we
developed in Chapter 2. In each case, a buyer's personal tax situation may affect his or her perception of price. There are also
the buyers who acquire the million- or multi-million-dollar interests.
They constitute a different market from those who purchase smaller
properties.

A particular acquisition's price will relate to the law of supply and demand and to the particular investor's objectives and profile. The actual market, as opposed to the hypothetical average market, for a property will tend to be composed of buyers who share certain characteristics which will reflect what that property will be able to do for their particular objectives.

Average sellers are also presumed not to be motivated by a specific need. In reality, sellers sell for a variety of specific reasons. One might sell because he or she has lost a tax advantage. Another may have decided that it is time to switch from a property that has satisfied income needs to one that will satisfy a new need for capital preservation. Yet others might have more personal reasons: She plans to move; he is tired of management responsibility.

The definition of market value stresses the participation of informed parties. Unless one presumes equal awareness among the parties that make up the market, an estimation of value would consist of only so much guesswork. No one estimating value could ascertain which particular blind spot or combination of blind spots might sway a potential but unknown purchaser, just as market value can not recognize the effects of a particular purchaser's tax status. There would be too many undiscoverable variables.

To be sure, many actual investors know too little of the complexities of real estate investment. They are unlikely to be as aware as you now are of the overlapping nature of the economic principles underlying the behavior of investment real estate. Nor do they tend to take into account in an informed manner the major influences of financing and governmental action, as well as other seemingly external considerations.

Instead, most investors concentrate exclusively on their own personal situations, not realizing how that is likely to skew their perception of value. Nonetheless, and despite the prevalence of ignorance, market value must assume that due diligence will be exercised by sellers and buyers. This can create opportunities for those who employ their abilities to acquire information and an understanding of how economic principles work.

Market value also includes the concept of lack of coercion. Duress may exist in a quick sale needed to settle an estate either because one of the heirs needs money immediately or because taxes are due. It may also be present due to a seller's personal financial emergency. The buyer may be under pressure to complete an acquisition rapidly to take advantage of a tax break before a law changes. Any element of duress, which usually implies an abnormally short exposure of the property to the market, is likely to result in a price that departs, sometimes radically, from the property's market value. When duress exists, one party is likely to gain unduly at the expense of the other.

Market value is the price which could have been achieved if the period during which the property was for sale had been reasonably long enough to attract a sufficient number of buyers, the seller could afford to wait for the right buyer, and the parties involved were well informed as to the nature and probability of the property's risks and rewards. Forced sales, by adding in the element of duress or distress, can create price opportunities for astute investors who understand market value.

PRICE

Market value is the benchmark against which you, as an investor in real estate, must measure price. Price, however, is what you will pay if you acquire a property. The sum agreed upon is not what you might pay for a property if you were an average buyer, but what you have to pay as a specific purchaser.

You will pay the price that allows you to meet your objective. For example, ten people might each be willing to pay one dollar for an object. One dollar might then be the object's market value. However, one person who needs to use the object for a specific purpose may come along. That person may be willing to pay $1.10 to make sure he or she obtains the object. Price is what you must pay to meet special, particular, individual objectives and needs.

To establish the price you can afford to pay, it is most important that you understand the distinction between the user and the investor. What you will pay as an investor will depend not only on the property's use, but also on the yield it can produce for you based on your own specific investment objectives. In contrast, a user or occupier is generally willing to pay more than an investor to meet certain use objectives. We will elaborate on the difference between use and investment objectives in Chapter 10.

A willingness to pay more is what makes selling to a user so attractive. It tends to bring you the best price. A user must pay the price that will enable the user to get on with the primary business in which he or she is involved, whether it is living on the premises or operating a business from the property. A user may also pay more to obtain extra amenities, which can range from a view to an unusually efficient truck loading dock.

In some cases, a user will pay a great deal more than market value if the property is the only one which can meet certain personal or business objectives. For example, a user who must locate near a certain limited source of raw material in order to continue in business would have a compelling need, indeed be operating under a certain duress, to pay a premium for a property which allows access to the resource.

In certain instances, an investor may be willing to pay a little more than market value to meet an investor objective and profile. For example, an investor might want to select properties all in one area for ease of management. If the area were relatively small, few properties within it might come on the market. As a result, this investor may be willing to pay more to snap up the few which do.

Another investor may decide to diversify and thus pay more than market value to obtain a property that meets certain diversification specifications. Yet another investor may be willing to pay more or less than market value depending on how the investment impacts on his or her tax situation.

An assemblage is another investment enterprise in which the price paid may exceed market value. If 20 parcels of land are involved, the first 12 may be purchased for relatively low prices. But, once the situation is assessed by the remaining owners, the last eight parcels may be offered at a premium. There may even be a holdout for an extremely high price, one who causes the whole assemblage to collapse.

The astute assembler understands this process and tries to option all the parcels as quickly as possible. If simultaneous options are not feasible, it is then important for the assembler to determine the prices she or he can afford to pay for the last pieces in relation to the cost of the entire project and the income stream which can be created. To the extent that the project will still bring an economic benefit, the assembler may be required and be able to pay a higher price than market value for the last necessary plot.

The investor, unlike the user, has only the real estate to look to for advantage. The user may be able and willing to pay more because he or she will gain a non-real estate advantage in the user's business or personal life. However, to the investor, these amenities are worth paying more for only if they will produce more in rent or a higher sales price from users. Thus, the price an investor pays must be closely related to the market value of the property.

In a turnover situation involving undeveloped land, the price the investor can afford to pay for the land must not be more than the retail price of the lots sold off, less provisions for expenses, absorption rate and a reasonable profit. To establish the affordable price, a turnover investor must first take the price at which the lots could be sold after they have been developed and project that price into the future to take account of the time over which development and sales will occur. He or she then estimates the absorption rate or the number of sales which are likely to occur in a given time period.

Once the future sales price and the absorption rate are estimated, the investor establishes the annual income flow and subtracts the cost of development as well as provisions for overhead and profit. This net figure, which will be achieved in the future, must then be discounted back to the present to arrive at the price an investor can afford to pay today for the land. This method allows an investor to test the offering price of undeveloped land.

For an income-producing property, the price should not be more than what an informed buyer will pay for the right to receive the future income stream from the property plus the right to the residual value at the end of a period of time. Unless some special circumstance is involved, the price the investor pays should be as close to market value as possible or, preferably, less than market value.

The effects of different acquisition prices on matters of great importance to an investor can be seen in Table 4. We assume that the market value of the property in the example is $100,000, what an average buyer would pay. We further assume three different prices at which you might acquire the property: 1) $110,000 because you need it for a specific purpose; 2) $100,000 or right on the market value; and 3) $90,000 because you obtain the property from a seller responsible for settling an estate. In each case, you are able to obtain a mortgage loan for 75 percent of the property's market value, at 9¼ percent interest for 25 years.

Paying more than market value for the property would diminish your chances of success. Buying at the particular wrong price of $110,000 in Case 1, Table 4 increases the equity requirement by $10,000 and reduces the yield to eight percent, less than the mortgage loan interest rate.

Purchasing at market value in Case 2 produces a yield higher than the mortgage loan rate and thus more commensurate with the risk of taking the equity position. By purchasing below the

TABLE 4
Effects of Different Purchase Prices

	Case 1	Case 2	Case 3
Price	$110,000	$100,000	$90,000
Mortgage Loan	− 75,000	− 75,000	−75,000
Original Cash Equity	$ 35,000	$ 25,000	$15,000
Net Income	10,500	10,500	10,500
Debt Service	− 7,710	− 7,710	− 7,710
Cash Flow	$ 2,790	$ 2,790	$ 2,790
First Year Return on Equity	8%	11.2%	18.6%

market value in Case 3, the equity requirement declines by $10,000 and the yield rises to 18.6 percent, a considerable difference in profit.

The potential for capital appreciation has also been affected: In Case 1, you would have paid for $10,000 worth of appreciation which has not yet occurred and which may never occur. In Case 2, any appreciation above current market value would be pure gain for you, while in Case 3 you would start off with $10,000 in enhanced equity for which you did not pay.

THE APPRAISER'S APPROACHES TO VALUE

In order to apply the distinction between value and price to your advantage, you will find it useful to understand how value is estimated by an appraiser, a professional valuer. There are three distinct approaches: 1) The Cost Approach; 2) The Income Approach; and 3) The Market Data Approach. Each is most appropriately used in certain situations, but all three may be, and often are, used to estimate the value of a particular property. In that case, the value estimated by each method serves as a check on the values estimated by the other two methods.

1. The Cost Approach Generally, the cost approach sets an upper limit on what a purchaser will pay for a property. Few, if any, investors are willing to pay more for a property than the amount it would cost to reproduce the property new, less any depreciation. In some instances, a user may pay more than cost, less depreciation. However, if the firm offering price on a property is higher than the value arrived at through the use of the cost approach, investors would generally choose to substitute another similar but less expensive property.

In the cost method of analysis, the land is valued separately as if it were unimproved. Using the market data approach, the appraiser attempts to gather information on recent sales of land in close proximity to the land being appraised. The sales should be similar in size, topography, zoning and availability of municipal services; they must also have similar utility, amenities and configuration in order to be comparable.

In the process of gathering specific data about comparable sales, information about conditions concerning the sale, such as price, zoning and financing, is obtained from various sources. These sources include public records, the buyer, seller and broker, the banks and the savings and loan institutions. The prices actually paid are then analyzed to ascertain the differences between the sale properties and the subject property. This is accomplished through a composite analysis so that adjustments for the differences can be noted and made. A common method of developing the composite analysis is through such units of measurement as price per acre, per square foot or per front foot.

If there have been no recent comparable sales, the process of estimating value is much more complex. It may involve the allocation of known sales prices between land and improvements for application to the site in question. If the land has not yet been subdivided, the analytical technique involved could consist of a subdivision analysis where the value is estimated by projecting retail prices for the lots and then making appropriate deductions for development costs, absorption rates and overhead and profit items.

One additional method that can be incorporated is the land residual technique. It involves developing a series of hypothetical improvements and translating the income and expenses of the hypothetical buildings into a residual value to the land. However, this is a very sensitive technique and can only be used where reliable data are available for the return on and of the improvements hypothesized. In most cases, however, the market data approach will suffice to estimate land value.

Once land value has been estimated, the appraiser moves on to estimating how much it would cost today to reproduce the improvements as they are, even if this means an outmoded gazebo must be included. Various cost manuals and also local contractors' estimates based on their current experience can be utilized. The costs developed are then applied to the improvement in question.

In those instances where consideration of depreciation or obsolescence on either new or older improvements is warranted, additional steps of analysis must be taken to reflect the impact on the improvement. Depreciation normally occurs as a result of physical deterioration. If the improvement has experienced the effects of wear and tear, some downward revision of the current cost estimate of reproduction must be made. This is an entirely different concept than depreciation for tax purposes. Tax depreciation is an accounting technique which, for the most part, does not reflect actual physical deterioration.

In addition to physical deterioration, two other forms of potential value loss may affect overall value. These are functional and economic obsolescence.

Functional obsolescence refers to inadequacies within the improvement itself. For example, ten-foot ceilings in a warehouse are not as functional today as much higher ceilings under which a forklift truck or stack crane can be employed. Given current and future market expectations regarding the provision of elevators, a three story apartment building without an elevator may now be considered functionally obsolete. In view of today's host of belongings, limited closet space is no longer functional.

However, sometimes a feature that was considered nonfunctional for a period comes back into demand. An example is an apartment building with ceiling heights above the modern standard of eight feet. Functional obsolescence can sometimes be cured by renovation. The question is whether it can be cured economically with sufficient return on and of the investment made to cure it.

Economic obsolescence may prove more intractable. It stems from factors external to the improvement itself. For example, incompatible uses may penetrate a neighborhood, as when a plant moves too close to a residential area. A gas station located next to a single family home may render the home economically obsolete to a degree because it has become less desirable than other readily substitutable homes. This could provide you with an opportunity to change the home's zoning to commercial use and then to modify the property to suit that use. Another example would be a small commercial building which, formerly located beside a highway that has been rerouted, may now be partially obsolete.

Economic obsolescence in terms of one use for the property may provide opportunities to convert the property to a new use. Thus, the single family home may be turned into an office or retail property, if zoning permission can be obtained. The small commercial building might prove attractive for residential or office use if the highway rerouting has produced quieter surroundings.

In arriving at a value through the use of the cost approach, the appraiser takes into account the land value, the cost of reproducing the improvements new and the effects of any depreciation or obsolescence. The cost approach is not only useful because it tends to set an upper limit on the price an investor is willing to pay, but the analysis required may highlight renovation possibilities capable of increasing income, reducing operating expenses and enhancing value.

2. The Income Approach An economic analysis of all the factors that go into the production of actual and prospective net income is the basis for this approach. The net income which has been stabilized after analysis is then utilized as one function in the estimation of value. As we pointed out earlier in this chapter, an investor who purchases an income-producing property is actually acquiring the right to the future income stream and the residual value of the property. How much both are worth then becomes the critical question.

Gross income, vacancy and collection losses, effective gross income and operating expenses, all must be examined in terms of quantity, quality and durability. All four must be compared with the experience of similar properties. Then they must be stabilized before the resulting net income can be capitalized to arrive at value.

For example, gross income, also known as the rent roll, must be compared with the current economic rents similar income-producing properties can now command on the market. Leases on the property in question may provide for a contract rent that is greater or less than the current rent levels in the market. Some adjustments must be made for these differences between the subject property and other comparable sales or offerings.

A leasehold interest might be developed in a property encumbered with leases at less than current economic rent. The likelihood that gross income will continue or change must be analyzed. Opportunities to increase rents may be identified. Comparisons are generally stated in terms of apartment room counts, number of square feet of retail or office space, land-to-building ratios, floor area ratios or other units of measurement which offer the opportunity to compare like property with like property.

A reasonable provision for vacancy and collection losses must be established on the basis of what the appraiser thinks can be expected as a result of current and future market conditions. Supply may be on the increase, demand may be declining or other competitive factors may be in operation. Analyzing this factor is important, as gross rent is not always what you actually receive in rent or what you may receive in the future. For example, a property may currently be enjoying 100 percent occupancy. However, if a new complex is developed nearby, some of the tenants in the existing development might find the amenities in the new project so useful or attractive that they might decide to move.

Effective gross rent, as we established in Section I, is the rent you actually collect. Once it has been evaluated through an analysis of gross income and vacancy and collection losses, operating expenses must be stabilized. The analysis will include both the degree to which tenants are obligated to pay future expense increases and the trend of expenses. For example, property taxes and heating costs may show an upward trend in the area, while water and sewer charges may be stable. A new labor contract with the janitors may be due for negotiation next year. Prospective changes such as these must be taken into account.

Expenses must also be compared with those experienced by other, similar properties in order to identify items which are out of line and which may unnecessarily reduce income. Methods of reducing expenses in order to increase or protect net income and, thus, value might be developed and analyzed. For example, labor costs might be reduced by instituting management that matches the more efficient properties in the area or by substituting capital equipment for labor. Heating costs might decline as a result of the addition of insulation. Renovation may be required to cure any physical deterioration and functional obsolescence that is causing operating expenses to rise above the norm. The cost of these opportunities to increase or protect net income must be evaluated in the same manner as any other investment: By the return of and on the capital required to make the improvement.

Stabilized net income is the result of these evaluations of gross income, vacancy and collection losses and expenses in light of the experience of comparable properties in the current market. It is also the result of how these three items may be affected by the trends underway in the market. Net income is thus stabilized before any provision for debt service or depreciation for tax purposes.

Both debt service and depreciation for tax purposes allow for some recapture of the investment to provide for return of the investment, one of an investor's financial goals. However, the effects of both on a particular property are so individualistic that they can not be utilized as a function of value. For example, debt service is a function of the loan-to-value ratio. This ratio may have started out at 75 percent of the value of a particular property but, after ten years, the loan may have been reduced to 65 percent of value. Even if the mortgage loans on other comparable properties had started at exactly the same time, a highly unlikely coincidence, some of these loans may have had a shorter term. Thus, after ten years the ratio on the other properties could be 60 percent or some other figure.

In addition, the actual economic life that can reasonably be expected for the property as a result of market conditions seldom, if ever, coincides with the Internal Revenue Service's standards for economic life that must be applied for tax purposes to properties across the nation. Each individual improvement will, in fact, be subject to different actual rates of physical deterioration and functional and economic obsolescence. Moreover, both the debt service requirement and the depreciation schedules generally change with new ownership.

For these reasons, net income before debt service and depreciation for tax purposes is utilized to estimate value. Recapture of the investment will be handled, along with return on the investment, by the overall capitalization rate used to process net income into value. Net income is what is available to an investor to provide both a return on the investment as well as return of the investment. Net income is thus what is attributable to a return on and of the property. It reflects both the yield on investment as well as the recapture of it.

The calculation required to estimate value is both highly subjective and complex. For example, only a return on the investment attributable to the land is necessary. There is no need for net income to provide for a return of the investment because land is not considered a wasting asset. The land is what will always be returned to you.

Both return on and return of the investment in the improvements is necessary, as the improvements are a wasting asset. Thus, net income and current yield or return on the investment must be processed into a capitalization rate which will provide you with a rate of return on *and* of your investment in the improvements.

The subjectivity involved in selecting an appropriate capitalization rate can be reduced by looking to the actual behavior of the market for derivation of the various functions utilized. The availability of long-term financing has made the task much easier, as we shall see.

First, we will examine how an investor recaptured an investment before long-term financing was available. The technique is called the straight-line building residual method. To begin with, it requires estimating the economic life of the property. If we observe that improvements similar to the subject property have an economic life of 50 years, we may use that figure as a reasonable one. It would then take a rate of two percent of the investment each year for recapture to take place by the end of the useful life of the building. If an economic life of 20 years is assumed as a result of market experience, then five percent each year would have to be recaptured.

If return on investment or yield is estimated at ten percent in a situation where no mortgage exists, a capitalization rate of 12 percent to provide for both return on and return of the investment over 50 years would be required. A capitalization rate of 15 percent would be necessary over a 20-year period with the same ten percent yield requirement.

To look at it in another way, we will assume that the investment totals $100,000. You would have to receive a net income of $10,000 a year for a ten percent return on the investment and $2,000 each year as return of the investment over 50 years. Over a 20-year economic life, you would have to receive $10,000 as return on the investment and $5,000 as return of the investment each year.

Establishing a capitalization rate that is realistic and available in the market place is made easier today by the ability to use the terms of currently available financing as functions. This is possible because building up equity as you amortize the loan will provide you with a large measure of recapture of the investment.

The market rate of return on and of a mortgage loan is easily discoverable by consulting with several lenders to find out their current loan-to-value ratio requirements and their current constants. The constant, as we will elaborate on in Chapter 9, comprises the loan's interest (return on) and amortization (return of). The process of estimating value by incorporating the currently available financing constant and the loan-to-value ratio requirement as functions in the valuation process is known as the mortgage-equity band of investment technique. It is the most common method in use today.

We will assume that we discovered a prevailing loan-to-value ratio requirement on properties like the one in question of 75 percent and an annual constant of .1028, which represents 9¼ percent interest over a 25-year period. Thus, the mortgage part of the equation to reach the overall capitalization rate would be:

.75 (ratio of loan-to-value) × .1028 (constant of 9¼ percent interest over 25 years) = .077, or
.75 × .1028 = .077

We now know what 75 percent of the investment must produce in order to provide a return on and of the investment. The next problem to solve for is what the yield must be on the remaining 25 percent of the investment, which is the equity-to-value ratio.

We are aided by knowing, as we learned from the discussion in Chapter 6 of the priorities of different rights, that the return on your investment in most instances must be higher than the mortgage loan interest rate to make it worth your while to invest. After all, the return on the loan portion of the investment is guaranteed to the lender by contract. If you do not provide the lender with a return on its capital, the lender can seize the property. You have no such guarantee protecting your equity. Thus, your risk is higher. As a result, your yield must be higher than the yield on the loan.

If lenders will currently accept a 9¼ percent return on their capital, you require more than 9¼ percent. To determine how much your yield must be, yields on comparable properties must be obtained from the market place. We will assume for the purposes of this discussion that the current yield required to attract investors to comparable properties is 11 percent. We have now obtained two parts of the equation involving equity from the market: The ratio of equity-to-value, derived from current lending requirements, and the yield.

What remains to be discovered is the return of your investment. Because most of the investment will be returned to you in the form of equity build up or amortization, the remaining amount needed to provide you with a return of your equity over the economic life of the property may be relatively small.

The economic life of the property must be determined by going to the market again. Lenders almost always lend on the basis of a shorter time period than the estimated economic life of a property in order to increase the security of their repayment. In this example, lenders are willing to make loans on similar properties for 25 years. The economic life as estimated from the experience of similar properties may be around 30 years. Recapture must then be at about the rate of 3⅓ percent a year. A 25 percent equity would mean taking 25 percent of 3⅓ percent to obtain a rate of .008. This rate would accomplish recapture of the equity portion of the investment. With all parts of the equity equation assembled, the equation itself would look like this:

.25 (ratio of equity-to-value) × (.11 current yield + .008
recapture over 30 years) = .029, or
.25 × .118 = .029

The equation to establish an overall capitalization rate, one that reflects both the financed portion and the equity position, would look like this*:

Mortgage: .75 × .1028 = .077

Equity: .25 × .118 = +.029

Overall capitalization rate: .106 or 10.6 percent

Each function and each component used to arrive at the overall capitalization rate was derived from the market. This includes the loan-to-value ratio requirement, the constant on available mortgage loans, the equity-to-value ratio, and the return on and of the equity.

Experience is required to select an appropriate yield and recapture rate. Nonetheless, subjectivity can be reduced by obtaining each figure from the market activities of several lenders, sellers and purchasers who are putting money behind their beliefs as to appropriate yields and other functions. The function of net income, used in the next stage of estimating value, is also derived from the experience of comparable properties in terms of quantity, quality and durability. Of course, these aspects also served to determine the yield requirement the market would apply to this property.

Once the overall capitalization rate has been developed, it is applied to net income. The process involves dividing net income by the overall capitalization rate. Thus, in an example where the net income is $10,500 and the overall capitalization rate is 10.6 percent, the value of the property would be estimated at $99,056 or $99,000.

You may have noted that the example we have used here is the same as that developed in Case 2 of Table 4 in the earlier part of this chapter. There the value of the property was set at $100,000. Here we have arrived at a value of $99,000, a difference of one percent. A difference of up to ten percent is not atypical and is not critical when one considers all the factors of judgement which go into the

---

*To make this process clearer, we have not here detailed an allocation between land and improvement.

function selection process. Here, the difference might be explained by a judgement on the part of the appraiser that the yield on the property is likely to decline to the 11 percent typical of the area's comparable properties, rather than remain at 11.1 percent.

3. The Market Data Approach As we discovered in our discussion of how land is valued under the cost approach, the market data approach involves a careful comparison of the property being valued with the current sales prices of other, comparable properties.

The comparison shopping involved should be familiar to you. You may have utilized it to purchase coffee when prices went through the roof. You probably comparison shop for major appliances, for your car and certainly for any home you purchase. If you are purchasing a car, you may compare the steering, ride or luggage space of several automobiles in order to make a decision to purchase.

Just so does an appraiser shop the market. The major criteria for comparison are physical condition, time and location. The appraiser looks first for several properties that have sold recently in order to keep the effects of change over time manageable. The appraiser also checks to make sure that the sales were not made under any duress or special circumstance which would invalidate the comparison.

The properties selected as comparables must be as similar to the one under valuation as possible. Thus, the appraiser looks closely at location, size, amenities, functional and economic obsolescence, quality of construction, maintenance, lease terms and other factors which might affect value. The appraiser also investigates the effects of the various economic principles, particularly supply and demand, to determine whether values for the kind of real estate under valuation are rising, stable or declining. Such an approach may be particularly helpful in determining actual and potential sources of competition. And, from the comparisons made, ideas for attracting tenants may be developed or difficulties uncovered that can not be overcome.

The final step taken to arrive at an estimate of market value is the correlation of the three approaches. This does not mean that the three values which have been estimated are averaged. One approach may be given more weight than the others. For example, the income approach would not be used for owner-occupier property such as a single family home unless the home will actually be rented. Instead, the market data approach may be the most useful.

A company-owned headquarters building with unusual amenities is also unlikely to be valued through the income approach. There may be no one who is willing to pay the price of the extra amenities in rent. Perhaps the cost approach would be most suitable in this situation.

However, the cost approach may not apply to a very old building. The depreciation and obsolescence estimations required may become too judgemental over a long period of time rather than be sufficiently factual. The market data approach may not be suitable for a very unusual property. For example, some special use properties are so seldom sold that there are no comparable sales to analyze.

Generally, the approach that best describes the actual situation is selected as the final estimate of value. However, undertaking the processes required for the remaining approaches, unless obviously not called for, is seldom a waste of time. All three approaches should produce values within 10 to 15 percent of each other. If one value figure is considerably out of line, it indicates that the assumptions and facts used should be checked carefully.

Knowing the market value of a property for sale will help you determine the price you can and want to pay to obtain its economic benefits. Of course, you may choose to pay more than market value in order to obtain a special benefit. In that case, however, you should determine how you will be compensated for having paid extra. Will you be able to raise rents because of the additional amenity or is the benefit a matter of convenience to you?

Knowing the market value when you are ready to sell is just as important. If you set a price much lower than market value, you may lose out on a portion of the total yield. You will remember from our discussion in Chapter 2 that the total yield on your investment can not be determined until after a property is disposed of. Only then will all the different equities be assembled and the actual rate of recapture of investment known. Too low a selling price relative to value may cause your total yield to be smaller than the one you might achieve with a price closer to value. You may, of course, have a special reason to sell at a lower price. If so, knowing market value will help you assess the cost to you of that special circumstance.

Understanding the processes of estimating value will also help you spot opportunities for profit. We have mentioned the expense analysis and how you can use it to discover where the expenses of a property are out of line compared to the experience of other properties. You may be able to reduce those expenses to increase your net income and yield. Or you may spot an opportunity to make a capital improvement that would cause operating expenses to decline.

Other opportunities for profit may be revealed by the valuation processes. For example, the cost approach may disclose that the present improvement on the land is not the one that would bring you the most profit. This disclosure may trigger consideration of razing the building and erecting a new, more profitable one. The market data approach may indicate that the price at which a property is being offered for sale is a bargain. Or an unusual feature may be uncovered that would increase the property's appeal to tenants or to owner-occupiers who might buy the property from you on resale. At each stage of the analysis involved in the three approaches to estimating value, you may discover an opportunity you can turn to advantage.

One reason why investment in real estate can be accomplished by people who are not already very wealthy is the availability of long-term financing. Both the ability to acquire property for relatively small sums and the ability to pay back the amount borrowed for acquisition over a long period are the result of a relatively recent revolution in financing practices.

Acquisition of real estate was once confined to those who could afford to pay cash or a combination of cash and short-term financing. A purchase could not be consummated without the ready cash necessary to pay the whole amount required either immediately or within a very short period. This condition still obtains over much of the world.

But, in the United States, starting in the thirties, development of the long-term amortized mortgage loan was stimulated by the Federal government to facilitate homeownership. This device permitted individuals to purchase a home by making a downpayment in cash of only a percentage of the total price. The remainder could be borrowed and paid off or amortized over the term of the loan.

THE DELIGHTS OF LEVERAGE

Not only has the amortized mortgage loan allowed an individual to acquire a home worth $80,000 for as little as $16,000 down, but it has been responsible for greatly widening opportunities to acquire real estate for investment purposes. This is known as the ability to leverage, one of the most important aspects of real estate investment. Leveraging your capital, if done properly, allows you to acquire properties you could not otherwise afford, to acquire more properties than you could otherwise command, and to increase your yield.

The major reason investors borrow is to increase the means at their disposal to accomplish their goals. For example, by financing 75 percent of a property's value, you can leverage $25,000 in equity to acquire a property worth not $25,000 but $100,000. Or, by borrowing for development, you can increase the funds available to you for renovation or construction of real estate, thereby obtaining the ability to create value above the cost of its creation.

By borrowing, you also obtain any appreciation in value at less cost. Appreciation of real estate accrues to its owner whether it is financed or not. For example, a property now worth $100,000 may appreciate to $125,000 within two or three years. Your judgement of the rapidity of appreciation may, if your objective is appreciation, cause you to acquire this property. Your yield will be materially affected by the amount of appreciation that occurs.

If you acquired the property without financing, you would have paid $100,000 to obtain the $25,000 appreciation, a 25 percent increase in your capital. But, if you had financed the property as outlined above, you would have paid $25,000 and obtained a $25,000 gain, for a 100 percent increase in your capital.

Additionally, if you finance properly, you can increase your current yield. To demonstrate what financing can achieve for you, we will develop several examples based on a property worth $100,000. For purposes of the illustrations in Table 5, we will assume that only simple interest must be paid to the lender.

In the case in Table 5 with no mortgage loan, the yield on your equity is ten percent. However, you would have had to produce $100,000 in capital to obtain it. With a mortgage loan with ten percent interest, your first year yield is still ten percent, but it cost you only $25,000 in capital because the property was financed. If you lacked $100,000 in cash, you might have been able to make the purchase by financing it. If you had $100,000 at hand and used financing, you could purchase four properties, worth four times as much, instead of only one, and you could look to inflation to make some money on the four. With a mortgage loan at eight percent interest, you would have been able not only to acquire the property for less equity capital than if there had been no mortgage,

TABLE 5
Effects of Leverage

	No Mortgage	With a Mortgage At 10% Interest	With a Mortgage At 8% Interest
Value	$100,000	$100,000	$100,000
Loan Amount		− 75,000	− 75,000
Equity	$100,000	$ 25,000	$25,000
Net Income	10,000	10,000	10,000
Debt Service (interest only)		− 7,500	− 6,000
Cash Flow	$ 10,000	$ 2,500	$ 4,000
First Year Return (cash flow divided by equity)	10%	10%	16%

but also to increase the first year yield on your equity from 10 to 16 percent.

Financing can result in two additional benefits for investors. First, the interest paid to compensate the lender for making the loan is deductible. If the interest paid in the first year, as in the example where the mortgage interest was eight percent, is $6,000 and you are in the 40 percent bracket, the government is, in effect, paying for 40 percent, or $2,400, of the interest. Thus, you must give up only $3,600, not $6,000, to meet the interest cost. Costly as financing can be, it is made less so by the ability to take interest deductions.

Moreover, the interest deductions provide you with more ready cash to spend or to keep. In today's inflationary environment, as we discussed in Chapter 2, the dollars you retain today are worth more than dollars you will receive in the future.

The second benefit also has to do with inflation. The dollars you obtain from financing today have greater purchasing power than those you pay back in the future will have; this is the basis of the concept of present worth. Furthermore, the amount due the lender remains fixed by contract while your income from the property may be rising. Thus, with inflation, the loan payments may come to form a smaller and smaller percentage of net income in the future.

THE LENDER'S POSITION

Of course, lenders have caught on to inflation's effects on their creditor position. What to you are benefits are deterrents to lenders. They have thus devised several methods to increase their compensation in order to make up for the eroded value of the dollars that are returned to them.

One method is to charge higher rates of interest because the value of their money is more at risk. However, lenders in some states may be prevented by usury laws from charging interest rates that would fully compensate them for inflation's effects.

In those states, the lenders may charge you the highest rate of interest that is legally permissible, plus points. Usually this fee runs to one or two percentage points of the loan amount. Points are payable at the time you take out the loan.

In effect, the lender has less actual money on loan to you (although you must still pay back the total loan amount agreed upon). For example, you may borrow $50,000, subject to a two percent fee. By giving the lender $1,000 at the same time the lender provides you with $50,000, a net amount of only $49,000 is on loan. The lender obtains the $1,000 in current dollars, which are worth more than if it had to wait to get them later. Moreover, the lender can then relend at interest the $1,000 it has received in points, thus raising its effective yield. The lender is receiving interest not only on the $50,000, but also on the $1,000.

Another method, which has gained favor among sophisticated lenders, is to require participation in the investment real estate venture. In order to approve a loan, the lender may demand that a percentage of the equity with rights to income, appreciation and/or tax shelter be granted to it. Such requirements may have to be met to obtain financing or to obtain it on the terms you prefer, but each requirement must be carefully analyzed from your point of view to make sure it does not destroy the economics of the investment. Participation should be regarded as an increase in debt service. It can also increase or dilute equity. In some cases, participation requirements may be so great that your yield will significantly decline or disappear.

Because financing is a major key to investing in real estate, it is complex and its requirements are stringent. A lender looks first, second, third, fourth and fifth at the ability of the investor to repay the loan and at the property itself. Lenders have no interest in becoming charitable institutions by making gifts of money that will not be repaid. Ability to repay is considered a function of the quantity, quality and durability of the income stream of the property, its location and the reputation of its sponsors.

For example, if the property is an apartment building composed of studios in an area devoted to single family homes, the quality and durability of its income may be considered low, its location misjudged and its marketability likely to be nil. No lenders worth their underwriting standards are likely to lend on the property. On the other hand, if the project is well conceived and well located, with effective demand for what it offers, and if its sponsors have demonstrated responsible financial behavior, a lender is more likely to underwrite a loan on it.

Money available for real estate investments comes in two forms: short- and long-term. Short-term financing is generally used for turnover projects. A construction loan may cover much of the cost of renovating or of building an improvement. Only interest is usually charged over the period of the loan. Points are normally paid at the front end. As development is a very risky undertaking, the interest and points are likely to be very high.

The principal repayment may come when the property is sold. Much of the money from the buyer's mortgage loan and downpayment would be used to pay off the construction loan. Or the construction lender may be repaid when a property is rented up and money from a long-term mortgage loan is made available.

Sometimes rent-up or sale takes longer than anticipated. There may be a gap between the end of the construction loan and the date when the long-term mortgage loan is due to begin. Certain performance standards must usually be met, such as 80 percent occupancy of apartment units or 51 percent of condominium units sold, before a permanent mortgage loan commences. Gap financing may cover the period in between and any gap in amount as well. Generally, a construction loan will not be granted unless there is a lender who has made a commitment to write a long-term loan on the property. There may be a requirement for a gap financing commitment as well.

A long-term mortgage loan is referred to as a permanent one, although it, of course, does not run to perpetuity. Permanent mortgage loans usually run 20 to 35 years. The longer the term, generally the more favorable the results of the investment will be, because you can lower debt service and obtain more cash flow. However, a long-term or permanent mortgage loan usually runs for less than the expected economic life of the property or for less than the term the property is leased to a major tenant. This requirement serves the lender's need for reasonable expectation of repayment.

A real estate lender looks to the real estate itself to return the capital loaned and to provide a return on the loan. This can be accomplished in different ways. For example, in a turnover situation where homes are under construction, a construction lender would look to the equity owners' working capital position for payment of the return on the loan in the form of interest and points. The equity owners would, in turn, look to the sales proceeds from the property to pay them back. And, as we have pointed out, repayment of the construction loan would normally come from money made available by a permanent mortgage lender to the homeowners.

The permanent mortgage lender would look in the first instance to the income stream of the property to provide both a return on and a return of its capital. If the property is to be sold to someone who will occupy it, the lender would examine the user's income to see whether it is likely to be sufficient. In the case of an income-producing investment property, a lender would examine the net income produced from the rents after operating expenses are met.

In addition, both kinds of lenders or mortgagees would consider the real estate itself the security available to repay the loan in the event default occurs. For example, a construction lender attempts to provide money only up to the value of the construction in place each time it makes a payment to a builder. In the event of default, both lenders hope to get back the money loaned from the sale of the property. Thus, the property must be considered to have enough value to accomplish the return of the capital lent if it must be sold.

To secure the loan, two instruments are created, as shown in Illustrations 8 and 9. One is a note evidencing the creation of a debt and containing the terms of the loan. The second, the mortgage itself, pledges the property as security for the loan.

The mortgagor (borrower) grants a mortgage on the property to the mortgagee (lender) in order to obtain the loan. Your ability to pledge the property can relieve you of a personal obligation to repay a loan.

One of the most important elements of real estate investment is the opportunity it offers for non-recourse financing. This can best be understood by contrasting non-recourse financing with what happens when you take out a personal loan. Signing a personal note obligates you to meet the loan payments. In the event of default, the lender can, after receiving court approval, seize part of your salary, your bank accounts or other assets of yours in order to make good on the loan amount in default.

In real estate, a lender can be limited to seizing the property pledged if payments are not made on a loan, taxes, insurance and any other obligations specified. This feature prohibiting personal recourse can protect you from personal liability for repayment of a loan. In order to prevent personal recourse if you become the fee owner or a general partner, you must make sure that an exculpatory clause is added to the mortgage and note. Such a clause states that the owner of the property is not liable for the loan payments, but that the lender will rather look to the property itself for satisfaction of the debt.

Signing personally, as you would be doing without the insertion of an exculpatory provision, is an invitation to failure in real estate

Illustration 8

Note form. Courtesy of Talman Federal Savings and Loan Association, Chicago.

Note

Dated this   day of   A.D. 19   Loan No.

FOR VALUE RECEIVED, (money borrowed), we hereby promise to pay to

Talman Federal Savings and Loan Association of Chicago

a corporation organized and existing under the laws of the United States or to its successors and assigns, hereinafter referred to as the Mortgagee, at its Office in the city of Chicago, Illinois, or at such other place as the holder may designate, the principal sum of

Dollars ($)

together with interest thereon at the rate of   per centum per annum, said principal and interest to be payable in monthly installments as follows:

Dollars ($

or more on the first day of   A.D. 19   , and a like sum or more on the first day of each month thereafter until this note is fully paid, subject to the following provisions:

MORTGAGE LOAN PAYMENTS

TAX AND INSURANCE PAYMENTS

1. We further promise to pay to the Mortgagee on each monthly payment date an additional amount equal to 1/12th of the annual taxes and assessments levied against the mortgaged premises, and 1/12th of the annual premiums for all insurance covering said premises, all as esti-

purpose of accumulating funds for the payment of said items, or any other indebtedness owing the Mortgagee.

APPLICATION OF PAYMENTS

2. All payments received by the Mortgagee in accordance with the terms of this Note shall be applied first to the Tax and Insurance Account for required taxes and insurance, then to interest, and the remainder to principal. Whenever we fail to make a payment, or pay less than the required amount during any month, or elect to skip payments in accordance with the privileges in paragraph 6 and 7, we hereby authorize the Mortgagee to add to the unpaid balance of our loan account at the end of that month, the amount necessary to provide for taxes, insurance and interest and the equivalent of the tax and insurance charge will be deposited by the Mortgagee into the Mortgagor's Tax and Insurance Account.

CALCULATION OF INTEREST

3. Each month interest shall be charged for the use of funds due and owing the Association during the month of the interest charge, it being understood and agreed that said interest charge shall be calculated at the rate of 1/12th of the annual rate on the unpaid balance due as of the last day of the month preceding the month of the charge.

GRACE PERIOD

4. Payments may be made any time during the first 15 days of each month.

PREPAYMENT PRIVILEGE

5. The whole or any part of the indebtedness may be prepaid at any time without prepayment charge.

FLEXIBLE PREPAYMENT AND GRACE PROVISION

6. In the event of any prepayment, this Note shall not be treated as in default at any time so long as the unpaid balance of principal, additional advances under this Note or the instrument securing the same, and interest (and in such case accruing interest from month to month shall be treated as unpaid principal) is less than the amount that said indebtedness would have been had the monthly payments been made as first specified above; provided that monthly payments shall be continued in the event of any credit of proceeds of insurance or condemnation.

GRACE PERIOD FOR BORROWER IN NEED

7. In the event of the Mortgagor's unemployment, illness or an accident to him or other emergency affecting his ability to pay at any time after three years from date, upon written notice from the Mortgagor to the Mortgagee hereof of intention to do so, and upon verification of the fact of such emergency by the Mortgagee, the Mortgagor shall have the right from time to time to lapse one or more payments but not exceeding a total of four regular monthly payments first hereinabove provided for, and such lapse of payments shall not be treated as a default upon this obligation, but nevertheless the full amount of principal and interest shall be payable within the period required to pay this obligation, principal and interest, by regular monthly installments as first hereinabove provided.

43   10/76   **1-4 FAMILY**

Illustration 8 (Cont.)

ADVANCES

8. Additional sums may be advanced to us by the Mortgagee and in the event of such additional advances the amount of the monthly installments and the rate of interest on the entire mortgage indebtedness are to be agreed upon at the time of such advance.

TAXES AND INSURANCE AGREEMENT

9. The Mortgagee is hereby authorized and directed to use monies collected under the provisions of Paragraph 1 for the payment of taxes, assessments, insurance premiums or other charges, and may be paid in such amounts as are shown by its own records or by bills issued by the proper authority or on the basis of any other information received by the Mortgagee. In the event such monies are insufficient for the purpose and we fail to pay to the Mortgagee without demand the amount of such deficiency, then the Mortgagee at its sole option may at any time pay the whole or any part of such items from its own funds; any such payment from its own funds shall constitute an advance on our account and shall be added to the principal sum. Such advance shall bear interest from the date thereof. It shall not be obligatory upon the Mortgagee to inquire into the validity or accuracy of any of said items before making payment of the same and nothing herein contained shall be construed as requiring the Mortgagee to advance other monies for said purposes. The Mortgagee has the right to pay the entire real estate tax bill as soon as it is available notwithstanding the fact it is shown payable in installments. The Mortgagee may commingle with its general funds any monies received by it pursuant to the provisions of this agreement, and shall not be liable for any payment of any interest thereon, nor shall the Mortgagee incur any liability to the Mortgagor, or any other party on account of such monies, except to account for funds received and funds disbursed under the terms hereof. Any monies received pursuant to the provisions of this agreement are hereby pledged to the Mortgagee to further secure the mortgage indebtedness.

RETIREMENT OF MORTGAGE THROUGH LIFE INSURANCE

10. We further agree that if any of us shall secure and assign to said Mortgagee disability insurance and life insurance in a company and in a form acceptable to said Mortgagee, the Mortgagee has the right to advance the first annual premium for such insurance and add such payment to the unpaid balance of the loan as of the then current month, and it shall become additional indebtedness secured by this Note. It is further understood that if the Mortgagee advances said insurance premium, we agreed to pay each month, in addition to the installments required herein, a sum equivalent to 1/12th of the annual insurance premiums, such sums to be accumulated by the Mortgagee in the Tax and Insurance Account and used only for the payment of subsequent annual premiums as they become due.

LATE CHARGE

11. A Late Charge shall be assessed against any monthly mortgage loan payment which is received after the fifteenth of the month for which it is due, provided however, that if the fifteenth of the month shall occur on a weekend or holiday, then any payment received on the next succeeding business day shall not be assessed a Late Charge. A payment shall be deemed late if the entire payment is not received by the fifteenth of the month, as aforesaid, even though a partial payment has been made. The amount of the Late Charge shall be equal to five (5%) per cent of the monthly mortgage loan payment of principal and interest. The Mortgagee shall have the right to waive a Late Charge with respect to any individual monthly mortgage loan payment which is late and such waiver shall not be construed as a waiver of the Mortgagee's right to assess a Late Charge with respect to any subsequent late payment.

WAIVER OF NOTICE

12. The makers, sureties, guarantors and endorsers of this Note, jointly and severally, hereby waive notice of and consent to any and all extensions of this Note or any part thereof, without notice, and each hereby waive demand, presentment for payment, notice of nonpayment and protest, and any and all notice of whatever kind or nature and the exhaustion of legal remedies hereon.

13. This Note is secured by a Mortgage bearing even date herewith to said Mortgagee on real estate therein described. All of the terms and conditions of said Mortgage are hereby incorporated and made a part of this Note, and any waiver of any payment or breach of any covenants hereunder or under the instrument securing this Note at any time, shall not, at any other time, be taken to be a waiver of the terms hereunder.

14. This Note shall be the joint and several obligation of all makers, sureties, guarantors and endorsers, and shall be binding upon them, their heirs, personal representatives and assigns.

IN WITNESS WHEREOF, we have hereunto set our hands and seals, the day and year first above written.

....(SEAL)

....(SEAL)

....(SEAL)

....(SEAL)

43   7/76   **1–4 FAMILY**

Illustration 9

Mortgage form. Courtesy of Talman Federal Savings and Loan Association, Chicago.

Mortgage

Dated this   **day of**   **A.D. 19**   **Loan No.**

THIS INDENTURE WITNESSETH: THAT THE UNDERSIGNED,

of the   of   County of   , State of Illinois, hereinafter referred to as the Mortgagor, does hereby mortgage and warrant to

Talman Federal Savings and Loan Association of Chicago a corporation organized and existing under the laws of the United States or to its successors and assigns, hereinafter referred to as the Mortgagee, the following real estate situated in the County of   in the State of Illinois, to wit:

TOGETHER with all buildings, improvements, fixtures or appurtenances now or hereafter erected theron, including all apparatus, equipment, fixtures or articles, whether in single units or centrally controlled, used to supply heat, gas, air conditioning, water, light, power, refrigeration, ventilation or other services and any other thing now or hereafter therein or thereon the furnishing of which by lessors to lessees is customary or appropriate, including screens, venetian blinds, window shades, storm doors and windows, floor coverings, screen doors, in-a-door beds, awnings, stoves and water heaters (all of which are declared to be a part of said real estate whether physically attached thereto or not), together with all easements and the rents, issues and profits of every name, nature and kind, it being the intention hereby to establish an absolute transfer and assignment to the Mortgagee of all leases and avails of said premises and the furnishings and equipment therein. Such rents, issues and profits shall be applied first to the payment of all costs and expenses of acting under such assignment, including taxes and assessments, and second to the payment of any indebtedness then due and or incurred hereunder.

TO HAVE AND TO HOLD all of said property with said appurtenances, apparatus, fixtures and other equipment unto said Mortgagee forever, for the uses herein set forth, free from all rights and benefits under the Homestead Exemption Laws of the State of Illinois, which said rights and benefits said Mortgagor does hereby release and waive.

TO SECURE (1) The payment of a note and the performance of the obligations therein contained, executed and delivered concurrently herewith by the Mortgagor to the Mortgagee in the principal sum of

Dollars ($),

which is payable as provided in said note, and (2) any additional advances made by the Mortgagee to the Mortgagor, or his successors in title for any purpose, at any time before the release and cancellation of this mortgage, but at no time shall this mortgage secure advances on account of said original note and such additional advances in a sum in excess of

Dollars ($

such additional advances shall be evidenced by a Note or other agreement executed by the Mortgagor or his successors in title as being secured by this mortgage, provided that, nothing herein contained shall be considered as limiting the amounts that shall be secured hereby when advanced to protect the security

THIS MORTGAGE CONSISTS OF TWO PAGES. THE COVENANTS, CONDITIONS AND PROVISIONS APPEARING ON PAGE 2 (the reverse side of this mortgage) ARE INCORPORATED HEREIN BY REFERENCE AND ARE A PART HEREOF AND SHALL BE BINDING ON THE MORTGAGORS, THEIR HEIRS, SUCCESSORS AND ASSIGNS.

IN WITNESS WHEREOF, we have hereunto set our hands and seals, the day and year first above written.

_____(SEAL)   _____(SEAL)

_____(SEAL)   _____(SEAL)

State of Illinois
County of Cook } ss.

I, THE UNDERSIGNED, a Notary Public in and for said County, in the State aforesaid, DO HEREBY CERTIFY that the above named persons personally known to me to be the same persons whose names are subscribed to the foregoing Instrument, appeared before me this day in person, and acknowledged that they signed, sealed and delivered the said Instrument as their free and voluntary act, for the uses and purposes therein set forth, including the release and waiver of the right of homestead. GIVEN under my hand and Notarial Seal, this   day of   ,
A.D. 19

_____
NOTARY PUBLIC

THIS INSTRUMENT WAS PREPARED BY

5501 S. Kedzie Ave., Chgo., Ill. 60629

48 7/76   1-4 FAMILY

Page 1

Illustration 9 (Cont.)

Page 2

THE COVENANTS, CONDITIONS AND PROVISIONS REFERRED TO ON Page 1 (the reverse side of this mortgage):

A. THE MORTGAGOR COVENANTS:

(1) To pay all taxes, and assessments levied or assessed upon said property or any part thereof under any existing or future law in accordance with the terms of the Note of even date herewith; (2) To keep the improvements now or hereafter upon said premises insured against such hazards or liability, as the Mortgagee may require in such companies, and in such form as shall be approved by the Mortgagee. All such insurance policies shall contain proper mortgage clauses and the policies shall be retained by the Mortgagee until the loan is fully repaid; (3) In the event such insurance policies are cancelled for any reason whatsoever and no new insurance policies are presented to the Mortgagee on or before the date of termination of the notice of cancellation, then the Mortgagee shall have the right to declare the total indebtedness due and payable immediately and the Mortgagee shall have the right to commence foreclosure proceedings as provided hereinafter; (4) To promptly repair, restore or rebuild any buildings or improvement now or hereafter on the premises which may become damaged or destroyed; (5) To operate said premises and keep them in good condition and repair in accordance with the building, fire, zoning, health and sanitation laws and ordinances of the Municipality and any other governmental board, authority or agency having jurisdiction over the mortgaged premises; (6) Not to suffer or permit any unlawful use of or any nuisance to exist on said property nor to diminish nor impair its value by any act or omission to act; (7) Not to suffer or permit, without the written permission or consent of the Mortgagee being first had and obtained, (a) any use of said property for a purpose other than for which the same is now used, (b) any alterations, additions to, demolition or removal of any of the improvements, apparatus, fixtures or equipment now or hereafter upon said property, (c) the Mortgagor will not suffer or permit any change in the nature or character of the operation of said premises which will increase the intensity of the use thereof, save and except upon the written approval and consent of the Mortgagee, and further, will not suffer or permit to be changed or altered the exterior and interior structural arrangement including (but not to the exclusion of others) walls, rooms and halls without first obtaining the written consent of the Mortgagee; (8) The Mortgagee shall have the right to inspect the premises at all reasonable times and access thereto shall be permitted for that purpose.

B. THE MORTGAGOR FURTHER COVENANTS:

(1) That in case of his failure to perform any of his covenants herein, the Mortgagee may do on his behalf everything so covenanted; that said Mortgagee may also do any act it may deem necessary to protect the lien of this mortgage; and that he will immediately repay any monies paid or disbursed by the Mortgagee for any of the above purposes, and such monies shall be added to the unpaid balance of the aforesaid Note as of the first day of the then current month and become so much additional indebtedness secured by this mortgage and may be included in any decree foreclosing this mortgage and be paid out of the rents or proceeds of the sale of said premises, if not otherwise paid by him; that it shall not, be obligatory upon the Mortgagee to inquire into the validity of any lien, encumbrance or claim in advancing monies in that behalf as above authorized, but nothing herein contained shall be construed as requiring the Mortgagee to advance any monies for any purpose nor to do any act hereunder; that the Mortgagee shall not incur personal liability because of anything it may do or omit to do hereunder;

(2) That it is the intent hereof to secure payment of said Note whether the entire amount shall have been advanced to the Mortgagor at the date hereof or at a later date, and to secure any other amount or amounts that may be added to the mortgage indebtedness under the terms of this mortgage;

(3) That if the Mortgagor shall secure, and assign to said Mortgagee, disability insurance and life insurance in a company acceptable to said Mortgagee, and in a form acceptable to it, the Mortgagee has the right to advance the first annual premium for such insurance and add each such payment to the unpaid balance of the loan as of the first day of the then current month, and it shall become additional indebtedness secured by the Mortgagee;

(4) That in the event the ownership of said property or any part thereof becomes vested in a person other than the Mortgagor, the Mortgagee may, without notice to the Mortgagor, deal with such successor or successors in interest with reference to this mortgage and the debt hereby secured in the same manner as with the Mortgagor, and may forbear to sue or may extend time for payment of the debt secured hereby without discharging or in any way affecting the liability of the Mortgagor hereunder or upon the debt hereby secured;

(5) That if the Mortgagor conveys, sells, transfers or assigns or causes to be conveyed, sold, transferred or assigned or enters into any contract or agreement to convey, sell, transfer or assign or to cause to be conveyed, sold, transferred or assigned the title to the property, his equity of redemption in and to the property or the beneficial interest in any trust holding title to the property, without Mortgagee's prior written consent, excluding (a) the creation of a lien or encumbrance subordinate to this Mortgage, (b) the creation of a purchase money security interest for household appliances, (c) a transfer by devise, descent or operation of law upon the death of a joint tenant or (d) the grant of any leasehold interest of three years or less not containing an option to purchase. Mortgagee may at Mortgagee's option declare all the sums secured to be immediately due and payable. Mortgagee shall have waived such option to accelerate if, prior to the sale or transfer, Mortgagee and the person to whom the property is to be sold or transferred reach agreement in writing that the credit of such person is satisfactory to Mortgagee and that the interest payable on the sums secured by this Mortgage shall be at such rate as Mortgagee shall request. If Mortgagee has waived the option to accelerate provided in this paragraph and if Mortgagor's successor in interest has executed a written assumption agreement accepted in writing by Mortgagee, Mortgagee shall release Mortgagor from all obligations under this mortgage and the Note;

(6) That time is of the essence hereof and if default be made in performance of any covenant herein contained or in case of default in making any payment under said Note or any extension or renewal thereof, or if proceedings be instituted to enforce any other lien or charge upon any of said property, or upon the filing of a proceeding in bankruptcy by or against the Mortgagor, or if the Mortgagor shall make an assignment for the benefit of his creditors or if his property be placed under control or in custody of any court or officer of the government, or if the Mortgagor abandons any of said property, then and in any of said events, the Mortgagee is hereby authorized and empowered, at its option, and without affecting the lien hereby created or the priority of said lien or any right of the Mortgagee hereunder, to declare, without notice, all sums secured hereby immediately due and payable, whether or not such default be remedied by the Mortgagor, and apply toward the payment of said mortgage indebtedness any indebtedness of the Mortgagee to the Mortgagor, and said Mortgagee may also immediately proceed to foreclose this mortgage;

(7) That upon the commencement of any foreclosure proceeding hereunder, the Court in which such bill is filed may, at any time, either before or after sale, and without notice to the Mortgagor, or any party claiming under him; and without regard to the solvency of the Mortgagor or the then value of said premises, or whether the same shall then be occupied by the owner of the equity of redemption as a homestead, appoint a receiver (who may be the Mortgagee or its agent) with power to manage and rent and to collect the rents, issues and profits of said premises during the pendency of such foreclosure suit and the statutory period of redemption, and such rents, issues and profits, when collected, may be applied before as well as after the sale, towards the payment of the indebtedness, costs, taxes, insurance or other items necessary for the protection and preservation of the property, including the expenses of such receivership, or on any deficiency decree whether there be a decree therefor in personam or not, and if a receiver shall be appointed he shall remain in possession until the expiration of the full period allowed by statute for redemption, whether there be redemption or not, and until the issuance of deed in case of sale, but if no deed be issued, until expiration of the statutory period during which it may be issued, and no lease of said premises shall be nullified by the appointment or entry in possession of a receiver but he may elect to terminate any lease junior to the lien hereof;

(8) That the Mortgagee may employ counsel for advice or other legal service at the Mortgagee's discretion in connection with any dispute as to the debt hereby secured or the lien of this Instrument, or any litigation to which the Mortgagee may be made a party on account of this lien or which may affect the title to the property securing the indebtedness hereby secured or which may affect said debt or lien and any reasonable attorney's fees so incurred shall be added to and be a part of the debt hereby secured. Any costs and expenses reasonably incurred in the foreclosure of this mortgage and sale of the property securing the same and in connection with any other dispute or litigation affecting said debt or lien, including, but not limited to, receivership fees, publication costs and costs (which may be estimated as to and include items to be expended after the entry of the decree) of procuring abstracts of title, title searches, examinations and reports, guaranty policies, Torrens certificates and similar data and assurances with respect to title, shall be added to and be a part of the debt hereby secured. All such amounts shall be payable by the Mortgagor to the Mortgagee on demand, and if not paid shall be included in any decree or judgment as a part of said mortgage debt and shall include interest at the highest contract rate, or if no such contract rate then at the legal rate. In the event of a foreclosure sale of said premises there shall first be paid out of the proceeds thereof all of the aforesaid amounts, then the entire indebtedness whether due and payable by the terms hereof or not and the interest due thereon up to the time of such sale, and the over-plus, if any, shall be paid to the Mortgagor, and purchaser shall not be obliged to see to the application of the purchase money;

(9) In case the mortgaged property or any part thereof is damaged, or destroyed by fire or any other cause, or taken by condemnation, then the Mortgagee is hereby empowered to receive any compensation which may be paid. Any monies so received shall be applied by the Mortgagee as it may elect, to the immediate reduction or payment in full of the indebtedness secured hereby, or to the repair and restoration of the property. In the event the Mortgagee makes inspections and disbursements during the repair and restoration of the property, the Mortgagee may make a charge not to exceed 2% of the amount of such disbursement;

(10) This mortgage shall be released upon payment to Mortgagee of the indebtedness secured hereby and payment of Mortgagee's reasonable fee for preparing the release;

(11) That each right, power and remedy herein conferred upon the Mortgagee is cumulative of every other right or remedy of the Mortgagee, whether herein or by law conferred, and may be enforced concurrently therewith; that no waiver by the Mortgagee of performance of any covenant herein or in said note contained shall thereafter in any manner affect the right of Mortgagee to require or enforce performance of the same or any other of said covenants; that wherever the context hereof requires, the masculine gender, as used herein, shall include the feminine, and the singular number, as used herein, shall include the plural, and that all rights and obligations under this mortgage shall extend to and be binding on the respective heirs, executors, administrators, successors and assigns of the Mortgagor and Mortgagee.

48 7/76 **1-4 FAMILY**

Box 930

MORTGAGE

To

TALMAN FEDERAL SAVINGS AND LOAN ASSOCIATION

5501 S. KEDZIE AVENUE
CHICAGO, ILLINOIS 60629
PHONE: 434-3322

Recorder's Stamp:

investing. Loan amounts are often large relative to an investor's personal assets. Thus, if you have committed the cardinal real estate error of permitting a lender personal recourse, you may find yourself in personal bankruptcy if proceedings against you are undertaken.

The credibility of the property and its location will weigh heavily in the lender's decision-making process. So too will the source of repayment, whether from sales or from rent. In the case of sales, the lender will consider the project's marketability. In the case of rents, the lender will primarily evaluate the income's quantity, quality and durability.

LOAN TERMS

The factors previously discussed will determine not only whether a loan will be granted, but also the terms on which it will be granted. The terms generally consist of four elements: 1) The size of the downpayment; 2) The interest cost; 3) The term or length of the loan; and 4) The points, other fees or participation. These variables fluctuate with money market conditions, the goals of the lender, the condition of its loan portfolio and legal limitations on the lender and its lending practices.

Thus, when the supply of money is plentiful relative to loan demand, the downpayment required may be less than when the reverse conditions apply. If the lender's cost of obtaining money from depositors and the government is high, the loan amount available may shrink and the interest rate offered to you may rise.

If lenders anticipate that future costs of money will rise or calculate that they have too many long-term loans on their books at a fixed low rate of interest, they may raise interest rates on new loans to make up for these conditions. In periods of great uncertainty, lenders may not want to extend 30-year loans, preferring instead loans of shorter maturity.

Each lender's particular mix of money costs and loan portfolio differs from any other lender's. Moreover, each kind of lender is subject to different government regulations. This makes it desirable to shop around to obtain the best terms among those that are offered. It is also the reason why any investor is well advised to have access to several lenders. At any particular moment, one lender or another may be fully loaned out, or may offer terms which are disadvantageous to your prospects for a profit.

Downpayment A cash equity requirement is determined by a lender's loan-to-value ratio, which in turn is set by both government regulation and the lender's needs. The higher the loan-to-value ratio, the lower your downpayment will be. Thus, if a lender makes a loan for 80 percent of the value of a property, you would be required to come up with less cash equity than if the prevailing loan-to-value ratio were 75 percent.

Generally speaking, lenders like to set a lower loan-to-value ratio for investor-owned property than on owner-occupied property. In their experience, owner-occupiers exhibit a higher degree of commitment to meeting payments. To put it another way, a higher cash equity requirement for investors is seen by lenders as a good device to enforce the interest of an investor in making a property work financially, so that the lender is repaid without having to foreclose on it.

Moreover, a higher equity requirement puts the debt service at less risk from income and expense fluctuations. As we discussed in Section I, an increase in expenses or a decrease in gross income can cut severely into net income, which is the source of debt service. If the net income is just barely enough to cover the debt service in the first place, any decline in it is likely to jeopardize the debt service too much for a lender to contemplate with equanimity.

As a result, lenders develop what they call debt service coverage requirements. This might mean that a lender would want to see net income that was a certain number times the debt service. Thus, if a property's net income were $10,000 and the debt service $8,000, its debt service coverage would be 1.3. To arrive at the coverage, the net income is divided by the debt service.

In this case, there is at least $2,000 that could disappear from gross income or be used to pay increased expenses before the debt service would be placed in jeopardy. The higher the coverage, the safer the debt payments are. The particular coverage applied to a property will vary by lender, type of real estate, and the financial credibility of the borrower.

A relatively high debt service coverage offers you a measure of protection as well. It could be considered your margin of safety. In inflationary periods, incomes are likely to rise. This can provide you with an additional measure of safety if you have negotiated leases that allow for income increases. Moreover, if expenses are rising more rapidly than income, an adequate margin between debt service and net income will give you room to maneuver and may stave off default and loss of the property until you can remedy the situation. In deflationary periods, when less well protected incomes may be subject to decline, adequate cash flow again gives you more room before default looms.

During periods of deflation, the advantage is considered to pass to the creditor position. The lender will be paid back with dollars worth more than those that were lent. To a degree, receiving the net income left over after debt service, or the cash flow, will allow you to participate in this advantage. Thus, the rent dollars you are paid for the loan of your property to a lessee will have greater purchasing power. The greater the margin between net income and debt service, the more you will receive in more valuable dollars.

Constant Beside the downpayment requirement, two other financing variables are most likely to affect your yield and cash flow. These are interest costs and the term of the loan. Any increase or decrease in either can make or break your profitability. They combine to determine the constant you will have to pay on the most common type of mortgage loan, the self-amortized variety. The constant is the percentage of the original loan needed in any period to provide the lender with a return on and of its capital over the period of the loan.

To illustrate the workings of a constant, we will first assume that you borrowed $10,000 for ten years at ten percent interest. Without a constant, you would have to repay $1,000 of the principal each year and ten percent interest annually on the amount outstanding.

In the first year, you would repay $1,000 of the principal and

$1,000 in interest, or a total of $2,000. In the second year, the loan outstanding has been reduced to $9,000: You must repay another $1,000 and $900 in interest, or a total of $1,900. In the third year, the loan amount has been amortized or paid down to $8,000: You are obligated to pay $1,000 of the principal and $800 in interest, for a total payment of $1,800. This pattern of payment might be useful to you if a property's income were expected to decline in a steady progression, perhaps as a result of lease terms.

However, the need of the lender to keep interest payments flowing so that it can relend its proceeds at a profit and your probable need to reduce debt service to more manageable proportions are more likely to make the application of a constant mortgage payment desirable. The constant percentage on a $10,000 loan for ten years at ten percent interest is 16.28 percent. Each annual payment would total $1,628. The payment of $1,628 each year would be enough to provide a ten percent return on the amount loaned and to repay the loan in ten years. The example in Table 6 illustrates how this is accomplished if payments are made at the end of each year.

You can clearly see the equity build up pattern in Table 6. In the beginning of the loan, the level or constant payment will consist of more interest than amortization or principal repayment. At some point in every loan's life, the initial payment pattern will cross over and more principal than interest will be paid. Here it occurs in the fourth year. As that point approaches, investors interested in the tax shelter provided by interest deductions generally refinance or sell the property to investors who will finance it anew. In both cases, the loan payments would start over again and consist initially of higher interest than amortization for a number of years.

To show the effects of changing each of these key variables—downpayment, interest and term of the loan—we have created several examples in Tables 7, 8 and 9. Each assumes a property worth $100,000.

In Table 7, where downpayment is the variable, the higher equity requirement in Cases 2 and 3 produces several effects: 1) Debt service is lower because the loan amount is less; 2) Cash flow is greater because debt service is less; and 3) Yield on equity declines.

TABLE 6
Application of a Constant

First year		
Principal amount outstanding		$10,000
Interest	$1,000	
Amortization	628	
	$1,628	
Second year		
Principal amount outstanding		$10,000 − 628 = $ 9,372
Interest	$ 937	
Amortization	691	
	$1,628	
Third year		
Principal amount outstanding		$ 9,372 − 691 = $ 8,681
Interest	$ 868	
Amortization	760	
	$1,628	
Fourth year*		
Principal amount outstanding		$ 8,681 − 760 = $ 7,921
Interest	$ 792	
Amortization	836	
	$1,628	
Fifth year		
Principal amount outstanding		$ 7,921 − 836 = $ 7,085
Interest	$ 708	
Amortization	920	
	$1,628	
Sixth year		
Principal amount outstanding		$ 7,085 − 920 = $ 6,165
Interest	$ 616	
Amortization	1,012	
	$1,628	
Seventh year		
Principal amount outstanding		$ 6,165 − 1,012 = $ 5,153
Interest	$ 515	
Amortization	1,113	
	$1,628	

Eighth year
Principal amount outstanding
Interest $ 404
Amortization   1,224
                $1,628

$$\$ 5,153 - 1,113 = \$ 4,040$$

Ninth year
Principal amount outstanding
Interest $ 281
Amortization   1,347
                $1,628

$$\$ 4,040 - 1,224 = \$ 2,816$$

Tenth year
Principal amount outstanding
Interest $ 146
Amortization   1,482†
                $1,628

$$\$ 2,816 - 1,347 = \$ 1,469†$$

---

*Crossover point where interest is less than equity build up.

†Difference due to rounding; the last actual payment would be the precise amount due rather than any overpayment.

However, you may decide to accept a higher equity requirement as part of your strategy. For example, if that is what is available on the market, accepting it means you could acquire a property in order to pursue your objective. If your objective is current income, you may like the fact that a smaller loan uses up less net income. However, if you do not have sufficient equity, you may be able to find another lender with a less stringent downpayment requirement. This might allow you to acquire a property without having to put up quite so much cash. Alternatively, you may be able to find an equity partner to help you purchase a property.

In Table 8, where interest rate is the variable, Cases 2 and 3 illustrate how an increase in the interest rate results in a decline in cash flow and yield on equity. There is very little you can do with rates in the way of tactics to enhance your strategy's outcome, except to shop around for the best rate you can find. A high interest rate does not even help a tax strategy much. Here, you would gain

TABLE 7
Variable: Downpayment

	Case 1	Case 2	Case 3
Value of Property	$100,000	$100,000	$100,000
Loan-to-Value Ratio	80%	75%	70%
Loan Amount	$ 80,000	$ 75,000	$ 70,000
Equity Required	20,000	25,000	30,000
Net Income	12,000	12,000	12,000
Debt Service (9.75% interest for 25 years; constant .1070)	− 8,560	− 8,025	− 7,490
Cash Flow	$ 3,440	$ 3,975	$ 4,510
First Year Return on Equity	17.2%	15.9%	15.0%

only $150 extra in tax deductions in Case 2 and about the same amount more in Case 3.

In Table 9, where term is the variable, the shorter term in Cases 1 and 2 results in an increase in debt service and a reduction in cash flow and yield on equity. In this table and in the one involving interest rates, you can observe how the change in constant changes the financial results.

As part of your objective strategy, you may want to negotiate with a lender for the longest possible term. That would increase your cash flow or the current income you receive as in Case 3 of Table 9. However, it would mean putting off receiving all of the net income for a longer period of time.

Alternatively, you may want to pursue a retirement strategy. If you are able to arrange for the term of the loan to coincide with the number of years remaining before you plan to retire, you would then be able to receive a larger stream of income just when you may need it. For example, you may plan to retire in 20 years. If you arranged the financing to resemble that in Case 1 of Table 9, you would receive less current income for the next 20 years. But you would have all of the net income at your disposal starting with the twenty-first year after acquiring the property.

Another strategy consideration can involve taxes. During the course of your working career, you have your own income on which to rely. Adding more income from a real estate investment may cause you to pay more in taxes than you want to pay. Instead, you may develop a strategy for receipt of income in order to take advantage of a tax bracket which is likely to be lower after your retirement.

When considering loan terms, do not take the numbers for granted. For example, the most advantageous financing you can

TABLE 8
Variable: Interest Rate

	Case 1	Case 2	Case 3
Value of Property	$100,000	$100,000	$100,000
Loan-to-Value Ratio	75%	75%	75%
Loan Amount	$ 75,000	$ 75,000	$ 75,000
Equity	25,000	25,000	25,000
Net Income	12,000	12,000	12,000
Interest Rate	9%	9.25%	9.50%
Term	25 years	25 years	25 years
Constant	.1008	.1028	.1049
Debt Service	− 7,560	− 7,710	− 7,867
Cash Flow	$ 4,440	$ 4,290	$ 4,133
First Year Return on Equity	17.8%	17.2%	16.5%

TABLE 9
Variable: Term of Loan

	Case 1	Case 2	Case 3
Value of Property	$100,000	$100,000	$100,000
Loan-to-Value Ratio	75%	75%	75%
Loan Amount	$ 75,000	$ 75,000	$ 75,000
Equity	25,000	25,000	25,000
Net Income	12,000	12,000	12,000
Interest Rate	9.50%	9.50%	9.50%
Term	20 years	25 years	30 years
Constant	.1119	.1049	.1010
Debt Service	− 8,392	− 7,867	− 7,575
Cash Flow	$ 3,608	$ 4,133	$ 4,425
First Year Return on Equity	14.4%	16.5%	17.7%

obtain may consist of a low downpayment requirement and a low constant, within reason. Certainly, in each of the accompanying sets of examples, the highest current yield resulted from the lowest downpayment requirement or from the lowest constant. A low constant is achieved either by lengthening the term over which the loan must be paid back or by lowering the interest rate.

However, that is the most advantageous financing only if you are pursuing current income or a high current yield. If you have another strategy, another form of financing may be more advantageous. In the retirement example above, you may find that your yield is raised above what it would otherwise be when you take into consideration the present worth of receiving a net income of $12,000 starting with the twenty-first rather than the thirty-first year after acquisition.

The sole important consideration is how the financing will advance your objective. In order to calculate how financing will affect the profitability you desire, you must learn to think in terms of relative loan-to-value ratios, constants (and the terms comprised by a constant), and the present worth of sums to be received in the future.

It is also important to realize that financing, as one of the key variables in a real estate investment, can significantly affect value. A change in the term or the interest rate may make the investment feasible. A change in downpayment may make it possible to acquire a property. A change in any of these terms may change the yield to meet your requirements. In addition, you may also be able to pay more for a property if the cash flow from it is increased by negotiating a longer term or a lower interest rate.

In addition, other costs must be considered. As we have mentioned, points or a percentage of the loan may be charged as a method of increasing the lender's yield. In that case, they are considered interest. However, in some cases points may be service fees, designed to cover loan processing costs. There may also be other fees for such items as mortgage recording. And, of course, participation, as discussed previously, may cut into your equity and yield.

THE DANGER OF LEVERAGE

The advantages of reasonable leverage are manifold. However, leverage, as with anything carried to excess, can turn against you. There is an adage that it is better to be alive at a high interest rate than dead at a low one, but this can be carried only so far with financing's key variables before you face the risk that the property's economics will die on you.

If the loan-to-value ratio is too high and, thus, the debt service coverage is too low, or if the constant and the participation requirement are too high, your yield may crumble away to nothing. The temptation to accept unrealistic terms can be very strong, as many investors discovered the hard way in the early part of the

1970s. But it rests on nothing more certain than the hope that some fortuitous circumstance will occur to bail out a property and an investor. An example of what can happen, known as reverse or negative leverage, is developed in Table 10.

In a reverse leverage situation such as that in Table 10, the lender is receiving a 12 percent return on its capital, almost double the 6.2 percent return on the equity-investor's capital. This is the reverse of the result which should occur. As you will remember from our discussion of priorities of interests in Chapter 6, the mortgage lender's investment comes before the equity-investor's interest and is, in every way, more secure. As a result, the yield on the financed portion of the investment should be less than the

TABLE 10
Reverse Leverage

	Without Financing	With Financing
Value of Property	$100,000	$100,000
Loan-to-Value Ratio		90%
Loan Amount		$ 90,000
Equity	100,000	10,000
Net Income	12,000	12,000
Interest		12%
Term		25 years
Constant		.1264
Debt Service		11,376
Cash Flow	$ 12,000	$ 624
		($12,000 − $11,376)
First Year Return on Equity	12%	6.2%

yield on the equity portion. Moreover, leverage should work to increase your yield above what it would be if you did not finance. Financing which involves reverse leverage causes your yield to decline significantly and may mean you have to pay the debt service out of your own pocket.

The debt service coverage here is highly insecure. The property produces only $624 a year to stand between the debt service and any increase in expenses or decrease in gross income. If expenses on this property rise by $624 or its gross income decreases by that amount, a not unlikely event, the equity investor will have to start dipping into his or her own pocket to cover the debt service in order to save the investment. Otherwise, the property may be foreclosed upon for failure to meet debt service.

You may think it highly unlikely that a lender would underwrite a loan that is so inadequately covered. Lenders, however, have been known to push out money almost regardless of the merits of the loans when pressures to lend money are great. When these pressures build up to the point of unreason, it will be up to you to examine the financing offered to see whether it conforms to economic sense or if it would put your goals in jeopardy.

KINDS OF FINANCING

A variety of mortgage loans have been developed to serve different purposes. In this chapter, we will discuss some of the most prevalent ones. The most common financing vehicle is the self-amortized mortgage which we have already discussed. It consists, as we have seen, of constant or level annual payments to the lender that incorporate both the return on (interest) and the return of (amortization) the capital loaned in order to accomplish complete repayment by the time the final payment is made.

Balloon Another type of mortgage loan is one with level payments that do not include enough amortization to complete repayment over its term. In this type of loan, there will be an outstanding balance, called a balloon payment, due at the end of the term. For example, a balloon mortgage loan might require repayment of only some 20 percent of principal during its term. At the end, some 80 percent of the principal would come due in a lump sum. As a result, most of the level payments consist of interest.

Generally, a lender offers a balloon loan when it does not want to make a loan for a long enough period for complete amortization to occur at an affordable annual cost. For his or her part, a borrower might want to negotiate a balloon mortgage not only to lower annual debt service requirements, but also in the expectation that more advantageous terms would be available at the end of the mortgage term.

Balloon payments are usually met through refinancing. The danger, of course, is that the balloon may come due as money conditions worsen. Thus, refinancing may not be available when it is needed or the terms may be worse than expected.

Interest-Only For a limited period, a lender may agree to let you pay only interest without having to repay principal. This is typical of a short-term construction loan. It may also occur if a property is in trouble and the lender is willing to negotiate a period of interest-only payments. The lender may allow you to pay only interest if it expects the property to regain its financial strength within a reasonable time and, thus, full payments to resume. Interest-only loans may also be obtained from sellers to facilitate a sale. Such loans can be highly desirable as they free up more cash for your personal use or to renovate a property to bring its income stream up to a higher standard that would allow principal payments to be made.

Purchase Money A mortgage you grant to a seller is called a purchase money mortgage. It is usually used in cases where a buyer has inadequate funds and a seller is willing to take a mortgage rather than cash for most or all of the purchase price. Although you have not paid the full purchase price either with your cash or with a combination of your cash and an institutional loan, title to the property passes to you. A purchase money loan may be an interest-only one, but in most cases it includes some provision for amortization.

A purchase money mortgage loan is a major method of financing land purchases because institutional lenders are not generally willing either to make loans on unimproved land and some improved land or to make them at a desirable loan-to-value ratio. However, a purchase money mortgage may also be granted on any type of property provided a seller is willing.

A seller may be motivated to agree to a purchase money mortgage for several reasons. It may provide him or her with a secure source of income, without the management responsibility that goes with owning the property. It may also enable a seller to reduce any capital gains taxes due as a result of a sale by providing for installment payments of the purchase price. As the capital gains tax is a progressive one, spreading the payments over several years through a purchase money mortgage arrangement may cut the overall tax due.

In some cases, the terms of a purchase money mortgage loan may be more generous than those an institutional mortgagee would consider. A seller may lower the interest rate or the downpayment requirement in order to complete a sale. The term, however, is likely to be shorter than that on available institutional mortgage loans because the seller in most cases is an individual and is less likely to want to tie up her or his money for long periods.

A purchase money mortgage loan, when used in conjunction with an institutional mortgage loan, is a prime method of reducing capital needs. It must, however, take the second mortgage position if an institutional lender is involved. In many states, institutional lenders are prohibited from writing a second mortgage loan. In other areas, institutions are not willing to consider a more risky lending position than that of a first mortgage loan priority because of their fiduciary responsibility to their depositors and investors.

If you grant a purchase money mortgage to a seller before you are able to obtain an institutional mortgage loan, you must make sure you obtain the right to subordinate it to any new first mortgage you grant. As a result of subordination, the purchase money mortgage would slip to the second or subordinate lien position behind the new institutional loan. Without your having the ability to subordinate the purchase money mortgage, it is unlikely that an institution would make you a loan on the property.

Juniors Mortgages with a lien priority less than that of the first mortgage are called junior mortgages, and, depending on their priority position, are also known as second mortgages, third mortgages and even fourth or fifth mortgages. A subordinated purchase money mortgage granted to a seller is a junior mortgage. But such mortgages can also be obtained from investors whose business they are.

However, when a junior mortgage loan is obtained from mortgage investors, the interest rate is likely to be extremely high. Certainly the rate will be higher than that on any first mortgage loan because a mortgage junior to the first takes a riskier position. Moreover, these investors do not have the incentives a seller does to lower the interest rate to conclude a sale. Nor do they obtain the tax advantages from an installment sale that might offset a lower interest rate.

All financing arrangements must be analyzed carefully to compare the risks and rewards attendant on them. For example, you might find an investment where the mortgage loan outstanding on the property can be assumed by its purchaser. However, the loan may have been amortized to the point where a downpayment larger than your available cash is required. In that case, you might consider a second mortgage or refinancing. The example in Table 11, using a property worth $100,000, shows a method of comparison.

In Table 11, several considerations emerge: 1) The total equity requirement was reduced by obtaining the second mortgage loan. 2) The debt service coverage remained relatively secure despite the higher debt service required as a result of combining the remaining original mortgage loan with a second. 3) Interest deductions under the refinancing method were higher, as more of the total payment was composed of interest. By the time the original loan in this table had been paid down to $60,000, most of the high initial interest

TABLE 11
A Second Mortgage Loan Versus Refinancing*

	Remaining Original Mortgage Loan	Second Mortgage Loan	Total	Refinancing
Loan-to-Value Ratio	60% +	20% =	80%	75%
Loan Amount	$60,000† +	20,000 =	$80,000	$75,000
Equity	$40,000 −	20,000 =	$20,000	25,000
Net Income			12,000	12,000
Interest	5 ½%‡	12%		9 ½%
Term	25 years‡	10 years		25 years
Constant	.0737‡	.1722		.1049
Debt Service	5,896 +	3,444 =	9,340	7,867
Cash Flow (Net Income − Debt Service)			$ 2,660	$ 4,133
First Year Return on Equity			13.4%	16.5%
Debt Service Coverage			1.3	1.5
Interest Deductible First Year (Approximate)			$ 5,200	$ 7,000

*This is just one example of how these financing methods might work out. Each situation must be analyzed individually.

†Original loan amount was $80,000.

‡Original loan terms.

deductions would have disappeared and more of the current payment would be nondeductible amortization. 4) The refinancing method increased both cash flow and yield.

When the choice is available, your needs and goals will dictate whether you select refinancing or a loan combination of original mortgage plus a second mortgage. Here, your cash position might be such that you must take the original mortgage plus second mortgage loan combination. If property values are rising, you may in the future be able to increase your equity to the point where you can refinance advantageously.

Two additional elements should be analyzed before you make any decision. The first involves a prepayment penalty. In some cases, no prepayment is allowed. A check of the existing note will disclose whether a penalty will be levied if the loan is paid off prematurely. Such a penalty may require payments of up to three percent of the outstanding balance to compensate the lender for letting you extinguish the loan before its term ends. Generally, if a loan prepayment penalty exists, it is written so that the payment required declines as the loan ages or matures. The penalty requirement may disappear altogether as the loan comes closer to maturity. Practically speaking, you are likely to find that a lender will be most willing to waive a penalty payment on a loan with an interest rate well below current interest rates, as the money received from early repayment can then be lent again at a higher yield.

The second element to be analyzed involves discovering whether any points or fees must be paid before a new mortgage can be written. If points or other service fees will be charged, these must be added to the other front-end costs, such as legal fees and title search charges. Upon analysis, you may find that these additional penalties, fees and charges make obtaining a new first mortgage too costly a proposition.

Wraparound Another choice which may be available to you is called a wraparound mortgage loan. For it to work, there must be an existing first mortgage loan with a relatively long remaining term and a low interest rate. In practical terms, a second mortgage loan is wrapped around the first loan by a second institutional lender.

However, the second loan does not truly take a second mortgage position in terms of risk. In the normal course of events, a junior or second mortgagee is not likely to get repaid in the event default occurs on the first loan. Typically, if a default on the first loan's payments occurs, the first lender forecloses and sells the property for the balance of the first loan. In a wraparound situation, the second lender assumes the obligation of paying the first lender the amount due. Thus, the second lender, by effectively guaranteeing the payments to the first lender and making default less likely, achieves a more secure position.

The wraparound lender gives a larger loan than the balance remaining on the original loan. As a result, you obtain additional financing. However, because there is already a loan on the property for part of the new total, the second lender has to pay out only the difference between the original loan balance and the new total. This device is particularly useful when the supply of money is short, because the amount lent is less than a new first loan might have to be.

Moreover, a wraparound arrangement should cause the second lender's yield to increase on the amount actually lent to you, above the stated interest rate for the total amount. The higher yield potential is a lender's motive for granting a wraparound loan. The example in Table 12 will serve to clarify how a wraparound mortgage loan works.

In the example presented, the mortgage financing method least costly to you is the wraparound, by a small margin over refinancing. The wraparound lender was able to apply an eight percent interest rate on the $100,000 face amount of the loan, substantially lower than the prevailing 9¼ percent rate reflected in the refinancing example. The wraparound lender could offer this because it actually lent only $50,000. As it is applying an eight percent interest rate to $100,000 but has on loan to you only $50,000, its first year yield on its $50,000 is approximately ten percent, more than it could have obtained on a new first mortgage loan at the 9¼ percent rate.

TABLE 12
A Wraparound Comparison

	Remaining Original Mortgage Loan	Second + Mortgage Loan	Refinancing	Wraparound
				$ 50,000 Original
				50,000 Additional
Loan Amount	$50,000	$50,000	$100,000	$100,000
Interest	6%	12%	9¼%	8%
Term	15 years	10 years	15 years	15 years
Constant	.1013	.1722	.1236	.1147
Debt Service	5,065	8,610		
		Total		
		$13,675	$ 12,360	$ 11,470

In some cases, a wraparound may be written with a balloon. That would cause your annual debt service requirement to decrease even further, but expose you to the hazard of handling the balloon payment at some time in the future.

Leasehold   Yet another kind of financing involves a leasehold interest. A lessee may be able to obtain a loan on the difference between the contract rent called for according to the terms of its lease and the economic rent achievable from the current market. As we have indicated, the two are likely to diverge unless there are provisions in the lease for frequent re-evaluation of the contract rent to reflect current economic rent levels. If they do diverge, a leasehold interest which can be financed may develop.

For example, the lease may call for two dollars a square foot in rent. Current rents may be five dollars a square foot. If the lessee has the right to sublet, it could re-lease the space for five dollars a square foot to a sublessee. If we assume that the original tenant has 50,000 square feet of space, the difference between what the original lessee has to pay, $100,000, and what its subtenant has to pay, $250,000, is financeable.

Leasehold financing is more typically used in instances where a developer is building on leased ground. Leasehold financing is then used for construction purposes and also for the permanent loan on the improvement.

A leasehold interest is financed in much the way a receivable is factored. Generally, a lender would make a loan on a leasehold interest at a relatively low loan-to-value ratio, because a leasehold interest is more risky than a fee interest. Sometimes a whole series of leasehold interests develops, each of which may be financeable.

Another situation is also possible. You may decide to lease a property rather than purchase it in order to reduce the amount of capital required. Then you might re-lease the property to somebody else, at a higher rent than you have to pay. In this instance, you adopt what is called a sandwich position, one between the fee owner and the sublessee or user of the property.

Along with your lease, you may also be able to obtain the right to mortgage the fee from the fee owner. If your negotiations are successful, the fee owner would subordinate his or her rights to mortgage the real estate to you, the lessee. You can then mortgage the fee and obtain a loan that is likely to be at more favorable terms, as the interest being mortgaged is a less risky one than the leasehold interest which belongs to you.

However, the fee owner should retain the right to make the payments on the loan in the event that you default and the right to be informed that the payments are behind schedule. If these rights are not retained, the lender could foreclose on the fee and thus wipe out the fee owner's position before the fee owner even knows that a problem exists. This is something to remember if you ever take the fee owner's position and decide to subordinate your right to mortgage the fee to a lessee.

New forms of financing are likely to emerge in the future, just as many of the forms we have discussed here did not exist too long ago. One that may develop is the variable interest rate mortgage. In times of tight money, lenders may decide that they can make money available for mortgage loans only if they can be sure of getting top dollar for their money over the term of the loan. Thus, they may tie the interest rate to a money market index which reflects changes in interest rates across a broad range of investments. This has already occurred in the market for home mortgage loans in some areas of the country. The interest rate would rise during certain periods and presumably decline in others.

This concept is similar to tying the interest rate on construction loans to the prime rate. A construction loan rate tied to the prime rate fluctuates with the interest rate at which the most creditworthy corporations can borrow. During the last recession, when the prime rate rose to unprecedented heights, construction loan rates soared even higher. Developers, whose loan rates were pegged at several percentage points above the prime, watched their interest costs rise well into the double-digit range. At that point, rates were too high for any construction to be profitable, to put it mildly. Short-term rates, such as the prime and construction loan rates, are more likely to fluctuate rapidly than are long-term rates.

If a variable interest rate is what will make money available in certain periods, an investor would be well advised to try to negotiate a ceiling on the rate level. The range of fluctuation must be kept to a level that will permit the property to survive the interest charges. Otherwise, variable rate loans are likely to be too risky.

You can use common threads to unravel the economics of different financing techniques. The key points are the benefits, the costs and the safety.

The first question you might ask is what particular investment purpose the loan serves. Will it enable you to purchase a property you could not otherwise afford? Will it improve your yield or your cash flow? Will it provide you with a certain level of interest deductions? Even more important, how will the financing provisions positively affect your strategy?

Once you have located the benefits, you can then assess their costs. How much net income will you have to give up? What will that do to your cash flow? Is there another method of financing that would improve your cash flow and your yield? Can you negotiate for a longer term or a lower interest rate or both to reduce the constant? How will the costs affect your strategy?

Third, how safe will your position be after you obtain the loan? What is the debt service coverage? By how much can net income decline before a danger point is reached? How likely is it that net income will decline? Can your cash flow needs be satisfied with what remains of net income after debt service has been met? Will there be a balloon mortgage payment? How likely is it that the arrangement you envision for handling it will occur?

To keep the rewards of leverage in perspective, you must analyze the risks. The loan-to-value ratio, debt service coverage, constant and yield on your equity are the key figures. We have included a table of constants at the end of this chapter for your use. In order to find the constant figure that is used as a multiplier of the loan amount, simply go down one column in Table 13 and across a line to where a given interest rate and a given term of years meet.

For example, if the terms of the mortgage loan on your house were nine percent interest for 20 years, the constant annual percentage calculated on a monthly in arrears basis would be 10.80 percent. If the loan were for $40,000, your annual constant payment would be $4,320. In order to obtain the monthly payments, the annual figure must be divided by 12. In this case, each monthly payment would be $360. By using a table of constants, you can see for yourself how your mortgage loan payment was figured by your lender.

There are many such tables available, each using different assumptions as to when payments will be made. The most common one, included here, assumes that you will make payments at the end of each month. Other tables assume you will pay each month in advance, or that you will pay quarterly, semi-annually or annually either at the end of the period in question or in advance of it. For example, the constant in Table 6 comes from an annual constant table with payments made at the end of each year. You will note that the constant required, 16.28 percent, is higher than the 15.86 percent constant (ten years at ten percent interest) in the monthly constant table at the end of this chapter because the lender has to wait longer to get its money.

To increase your familiarity with financing analysis, you might ask your local lending institutions for current quotations on refinancing your home. You can then develop a series of examples to which you can apply your strategic analysis. Inquiring about current lending practices on investment properties will also provide you with information that is realistic in terms of the downpayment you may be required to deliver and the other terms you may have to meet.

TABLE 13
Level Constant Payment Plans (Monthly Payments)*

RATE YEARS	7	7 1/4	7 1/2	7 3/4	8	8 1/4	8 1/2	8 3/4	9	9 1/4	9 1/2	9 3/4	10	10 1/4	10 1/2	10 3/4	11	11 1/4	11 1/2	11 3/4	12	RATE YEARS
5	23.77	23.91	24.05	24.19	24.34	24.48	24.62	24.77	24.92	25.06	25.21	25.35	25.50	25.65	25.80	25.95	26.10	26.25	26.40	26.55	26.70	5
6	20.46	20.61	20.75	20.90	21.04	21.19	21.34	21.49	21.64	21.78	21.93	22.09	22.24	22.39	22.54	22.69	22.85	23.00	23.15	23.31	23.47	6
7	18.12	18.26	18.41	18.56	18.71	18.86	19.01	19.16	19.31	19.46	19.62	19.77	19.93	20.08	20.24	20.39	20.55	20.71	20.87	21.03	21.19	7
8	16.37	16.52	16.67	16.82	16.97	17.12	17.28	17.43	17.59	17.74	17.90	18.06	18.21	18.37	18.53	18.69	18.86	19.02	19.18	19.34	19.51	8
9	15.01	15.16	15.32	15.47	15.63	15.78	15.94	16.10	16.25	16.42	16.58	16.74	16.90	17.06	17.23	17.39	17.56	17.72	17.89	18.06	18.23	9
10	13.94	14.09	14.25	14.41	14.56	14.72	14.88	15.04	15.21	15.37	15.53	15.70	15.86	16.03	16.20	16.37	16.54	16.71	16.88	17.05	17.22	10
11	13.07	13.22	13.38	13.54	13.70	13.87	14.03	14.19	14.36	14.52	14.69	14.86	15.03	15.20	15.37	15.54	15.72	15.89	16.07	16.24	16.42	11
12	12.35	12.51	12.67	12.83	12.99	13.16	13.33	13.49	13.66	13.83	14.00	14.17	14.35	14.52	14.69	14.87	15.05	15.23	15.40	15.58	15.77	12
13	11.74	11.91	12.07	12.24	12.40	12.57	12.74	12.91	13.08	13.25	13.43	13.60	13.78	13.96	14.14	14.31	14.50	14.68	14.86	15.04	15.23	13
14	11.23	11.40	11.56	11.73	11.90	12.07	12.24	12.42	12.59	12.77	12.95	13.12	13.30	13.48	13.67	13.85	14.03	14.22	14.41	14.59	14.78	14
15	10.79	10.96	11.13	11.30	11.47	11.65	11.82	12.00	12.18	12.36	12.54	12.72	12.90	13.08	13.27	13.46	13.64	13.83	14.02	14.21	14.41	15
16	10.41	10.58	10.75	10.93	11.10	11.28	11.46	11.64	11.82	12.00	12.18	12.37	12.56	12.74	12.93	13.12	13.31	13.51	13.70	13.89	14.09	16
17	10.08	10.25	10.43	10.61	10.78	10.96	11.14	11.32	11.51	11.69	11.88	12.07	12.26	12.45	12.64	12.84	13.03	13.23	13.42	13.62	13.82	17
18	9.81	9.97	10.14	10.32	10.50	10.69	10.87	11.06	11.24	11.43	11.62	11.81	12.00	12.20	12.39	12.59	12.78	12.98	13.18	13.38	13.59	18
19	9.54	9.71	9.89	10.08	10.26	10.44	10.63	10.81	11.01	11.19	11.39	11.58	11.78	11.98	12.17	12.39	12.57	12.78	12.98	13.18	13.39	19
20	9.31	9.49	9.67	9.86	10.04	10.23	10.42	10.61	10.80	11.00	11.19	11.39	11.59	11.78	11.99	12.19	12.39	12.60	12.80	13.01	13.22	20
21	9.11	9.29	9.47	9.66	9.85	10.04	10.23	10.43	10.62	10.82	11.01	11.21	11.41	11.62	11.82	12.03	12.23	12.44	12.65	12.86	13.07	21
22	8.93	9.11	9.30	9.49	9.68	9.87	10.07	10.26	10.46	10.66	10.86	11.06	11.26	11.47	11.67	11.88	12.09	12.30	12.51	12.73	12.94	22
23	8.76	8.95	9.14	9.33	9.53	9.72	9.92	10.12	10.32	10.52	10.72	10.93	11.13	11.34	11.54	11.76	11.97	12.18	12.40	12.61	12.83	23
24	8.62	8.81	9.00	9.19	9.39	9.59	9.79	9.99	10.19	10.40	10.60	10.81	11.02	11.23	11.43	11.65	11.86	12.08	12.29	12.51	12.73	24
25	8.49	8.68	8.87	9.07	9.27	9.47	9.67	9.87	10.08	10.28	10.49	10.70	10.91	11.12	11.34	11.55	11.77	11.98	12.20	12.42	12.64	25
26	8.37	8.56	8.76	8.96	9.16	9.36	9.56	9.77	9.97	10.18	10.38	10.60	10.82	11.03	11.25	11.46	11.68	11.90	12.12	12.35	12.57	26
27	8.26	8.46	8.65	8.85	9.06	9.26	9.47	9.67	9.88	10.09	10.31	10.52	10.73	10.95	11.17	11.39	11.61	11.83	12.05	12.28	12.50	27
28	8.16	8.36	8.56	8.76	8.97	9.17	9.38	9.59	9.80	10.01	10.23	10.44	10.66	10.88	11.10	11.32	11.54	11.77	11.99	12.22	12.44	28
29	8.07	8.27	8.47	8.68	8.88	9.09	9.30	9.51	9.73	9.94	10.16	10.38	10.59	10.82	11.04	11.26	11.48	11.71	11.94	12.16	12.39	29
30	7.99	8.19	8.40	8.60	8.81	9.02	9.23	9.45	9.66	9.88	10.09	10.31	10.54	10.76	10.98	11.21	11.43	11.66	11.89	12.12	12.35	30
31	7.91	8.12	8.32	8.53	8.74	8.95	9.17	9.38	9.60	9.82	10.04	10.26	10.48	10.71	10.93	11.16	11.39	11.62	11.85	12.08	12.31	31
32	7.85	8.05	8.26	8.47	8.68	8.90	9.11	9.34	9.55	9.77	9.99	10.21	10.44	10.66	10.89	11.12	11.35	11.58	11.81	12.04	12.27	32
33	7.78	7.99	8.20	8.41	8.63	8.84	9.06	9.28	9.50	9.72	9.94	10.17	10.39	10.62	10.85	11.08	11.31	11.54	11.77	12.01	12.24	33
34	7.72	7.93	8.15	8.36	8.57	8.79	9.01	9.23	9.45	9.68	9.90	10.13	10.36	10.58	10.81	11.05	11.28	11.51	11.74	11.98	12.22	34
35	7.67	7.88	8.10	8.31	8.53	8.75	8.97	9.19	9.41	9.64	9.86	10.09	10.32	10.55	10.78	11.02	11.25	11.48	11.72	11.95	12.19	35
36	7.62	7.84	8.05	8.27	8.49	8.71	8.93	9.15	9.38	9.60	9.83	10.06	10.29	10.52	10.75	10.99	11.22	11.46	11.69	11.93	12.17	36
37	7.58	7.79	8.01	8.23	8.45	8.67	8.89	9.12	9.34	9.57	9.80	10.03	10.26	10.50	10.73	10.96	11.20	11.44	11.67	11.91	12.15	37
38	7.54	7.75	7.97	8.19	8.41	8.63	8.86	9.09	9.31	9.54	9.77	10.00	10.24	10.47	10.71	10.94	11.18	11.42	11.66	11.89	12.13	38
39	7.50	7.72	7.93	8.16	8.38	8.60	8.83	9.06	9.29	9.52	9.75	9.98	10.22	10.45	10.69	10.91	11.16	11.40	11.64	11.88	12.12	39
40	7.46	7.68	7.90	8.12	8.35	8.57	8.80	9.03	9.26	9.49	9.73	9.96	10.19	10.43	10.67	10.91	11.14	11.38	11.62	11.87	12.11	40
41	7.43	7.65	7.87	8.10	8.32	8.55	8.78	9.01	9.24	9.47	9.71	9.94	10.18	10.41	10.65	10.89	11.13	11.37	11.61	11.85	12.10	41
42	7.40	7.62	7.84	8.07	8.30	8.52	8.75	8.99	9.22	9.45	9.69	9.92	10.16	10.40	10.64	10.88	11.12	11.36	11.60	11.84	12.09	42
43	7.37	7.59	7.82	8.05	8.27	8.50	8.73	8.97	9.20	9.43	9.67	9.91	10.15	10.38	10.62	10.86	11.11	11.35	11.59	11.83	12.08	43
44	7.35	7.57	7.80	8.02	8.25	8.48	8.71	8.95	9.18	9.42	9.66	9.89	10.13	10.37	10.61	10.85	11.09	11.34	11.58	11.82	12.07	44
45	7.32	7.55	7.77	8.00	8.23	8.46	8.70	8.93	9.17	9.40	9.64	9.88	10.12	10.36	10.60	10.84	11.09	11.33	11.57	11.82	12.06	45

* A table of percent needed to amortize a principal amount, calculated on a monthly basis. (Divide by 12 to determine amount of monthly payments.) Source: Financial Publishing Company, Boston, Ma.

section three: the how

There they are, all the countless people who rent or buy real estate in order to occupy it. But none of these individuals or companies will be of the slightest use to you unless you or your general partners know how to transform them into your tenants or buyers. Only when you have captured tenants or buyers for either a new or an existing project can you profit from your investment in real estate.

Learning what will move tenants or buyers toward your real estate investment first requires understanding how their objectives differ from yours. However, keep in mind while reading the following pages that at some point in the future you may reverse roles. For example, if you become a buyer, your understanding of what a seller looks for will prove extremely useful.

Knowing the difference in motivation will aid you in the fine art of negotiation. Moreover, it will help you identify your market, determine whether the market is a viable one, pull in the tenants or buyers you have identified or retain tenants. In addition, if you intend to become a limited partner, your comprehension of what motivates tenants or buyers will enable you to test the realism of your potential general partner's marketing plans.

LAYERING OF OBJECTIVES: INVESTMENT VERSUS USE

The difference between investment and use real estate is a function of the remarkable layering of objectives or motivations available in real estate. Real estate can satisfy a variety of objectives, with the layering ranging along a continuum from the occupier to the investor. For the investor, real estate is the primary issue. More particularly, what most interests you as an investor is the ability of the real estate to meet your particular investor profile and financial objectives. As a result, you look exclusively to the real estate for satisfaction.

We have discussed your ranking of the four financial objectives real estate investment can satisfy. How you ranked them will differentiate you from another investor who chose a different order. So too will your choices among the investment parameters, as will your selection of a type of real estate in which to invest.

For example, your objective may be current income and your choice of means to reach that goal multi-family residential, or apartments. But your investment philosophy, particularly your willingness to take risks, may determine that you are in the market for a complex serving young adults. This choice generally means higher rents, but also a higher risk of losses from vacancies and from collection problems. It may also mean expenditures for glitter. Alternatively, if your desire for security were higher, you might select an apartment building serving more stable, middle-aged tenants. Your prospects for steady income might increase at the cost of providing a higher quality environment for your tenants.

Your decision effectively means that you have selected a layer to occupy. As we have pointed out, your ability to define the layer that fits you will enable you to steer a straight course for it. Moreover, your knowledge of the right layer for you, in all its ramifications, will help you keep to your course in difficult negotiations. In the process of determining your goals, you will define what you must specifically negotiate for if a property is to satisfy them. Of course, as an investor, you will be looking for a return on and a return of your investment no matter which investor layer you select.

For the occupiers or users of real estate, the real estate involved is a secondary issue. What concerns users is how the real estate can promote or enhance their non-real estate objectives. Thus, real estate users look beyond the real estate itself for satisfaction of their objectives. For example, a home buyer may be motivated to purchase a particular house in which to live because it is near a good school.

At their end of the spectrum, users occupy layers within each type of real estate, just as investors do at their end. Generally, the choice of the most suitable layer rests on acceptability and affordability. An individual or company may find owning and occupying real estate the most acceptable and affordable means of obtaining an objective. Another user may prefer to become a single tenant, one who wants the measure of control achievable through being the only user, but who does not want ownership. Finally, there is the tenant who seeks out multi-occupancy operations. The latter may not want maintenance duties or may not be able to afford the rent on a single tenant property or the costs of owner-occupancy, or this tenant may need only a small amount of space.

While these three categories form the major use layers, each divides into smaller segments or slices. For example, any of the three may want a layer that gives them prestige or convenience, or that is the least costly slice within the major classification they have chosen. An owner-user, single tenant or multi-tenant user may want a certain amount of space, a desire that will further define the layer into which such users fit. One home buyer may want low maintenance and thus might fit into a layer labeled owner-occupier, aluminum siding or owner-occupier, small lawn. Another home buyer may want wood because it appeals to him aesthetically, enough to overcome any objection to the higher maintenance requirement of wood.

One of your first jobs will be to determine two characteristics of the market you want to aim for: 1) Its major layer classification and 2) The factors that primarily motivate it. Once you have selected, for example, single tenant users, you know you are looking for single tenant properties within the type of real estate you have chosen. Then you can further define the layer you are after by considering the slices within that layer and what differentiates one slice from another. After conducting a market analysis to test for market viability, you can then look for properties that can satisfy your specific market layer's objectives.

OWNER-OCCUPIERS

At one extreme of the continuum are the owner-occupiers. They tend to want real estate that would be uneconomic for you, as an investor, to own and operate. As an example, consider a nineteenth-century bank building. It was meant to signal a high degree of rectitude and a high level of wealth to current and potential depositors. A bank improvement's solidity and ornate decoration cost much more to produce than did standard office structures. However, banks could afford to construct and own these improvements because their returns came from a non-real estate source. Their returns came from an image of security which drew in depositors and business and enhanced the profits they could make from their primary concern, banking.

Old style railroad stations present the same problem to investors. Many were built as monuments to the image the railroad builders sought to project. Real estate considerations were obviously secondary to a certain dignified and munificent image and to the train operations. As a result, rail magnates could afford to develop unusable and thus unrentable space in soaring main halls. In fact, the more unusable and unrentable it was, the better it was for their purposes.

In contrast, an investor can not afford to invest in too high a proportion of unrentable or unsalable space. His or her return must come from the real estate, not from image, train operations, tool manufacture or a view. Investors who have purchased major railroad terminals in the last few years have bought with the intention of decking over or of otherwise converting the halls into rent-producing space. An investor may even be able to realize increased rentals from the prestige factor involved in ornate or unusually spacious architecture, rentals which might make paying for the excess worthwhile. However, careful analysis of the market is needed to make sure tenants are willing to pay enough to justify acquiring these more costly features.

Today, major company headquarters clearly exhibit the same search for non-real estate benefits. Buildings of unusual architecture, such as the pyramid edifice in San Francisco, the mirrorlike building in Dallas, the Sears Tower in Chicago, and the latest AT&T improvement in New York can not generally compensate an investor adequately because rents can not, in most cases, be set at levels that would recapture the extra expense involved. Campuslike suburban office headquarters buildings with extensive cafeteria and recreation space for employees offer another example of amenities for which profitable rents can not generally be obtained.

These corporate owner-occupiers receive their returns in various forms: From enhanced prestige, from increased consumer identification, from their ability to capture a larger share of the labor market or to reduce labor turnover or from whatever purpose they designed the facility to serve. An investor can not tap these extra-real estate returns and thus can not be compensated adequately for investing in them for current income. In fact, these use structures are not intended to provide income, and the amenities they do provide are the basic objectives of their users.

The same layer of motivations can be found at work in other types of real estate. For example, a government may create special use real estate such as stadiums or convention centers at vast public expense. The expenditure may be so great compared with the direct return obtainable from renting the facility that no investor could become involved in owning and operating it. However, the government figures its return on the basis of attracting visitors to the Olympics or to a winning football team or to business meetings. These visitors, it is hoped, will leave behind sufficient money to encourage growth in the local economy and the production of more tax revenues to compensate the government for its investment.

Certainly all fast-food franchisors seek high visibility and instant identification to promote their business objective. As a result, certain franchisors have erected improvements with special, expensive roofs to draw in their market. In this case, too, the real estate is overbuilt if considered as a pure real estate investment.

Owner-occupier real estate generally offers limited investment potential. Only at the point of sale are there likely to be real estate profits. If you are interested in realizing capital appreciation, you may reap your profit by selling real estate to owner-occupiers. Or, if you intend to become a turnover investor, you can profit from developing owner-occupier real estate and selling it to this type of user. In fact, if your objective is turnover or appreciation, your best markets may be found among the owner-occupier layers.

Owner-occupiers tend to pay the highest prices for real estate.

This is largely a function of their extra-real estate objective. Unlike the investor, they do not have to make their real estate balance sheets work for them. They have to make their lives or their businesses work for them.

Thus, a franchisor may need to penetrate a certain market. In order to boost its sales, it may buy up sites at a higher price than a real estate investor could afford to pay if the real estate investment numbers are to come out right. Or a homeowner may pay extra for a view which he or she will be there to enjoy but which an investor can not benefit from. In addition, ownership in itself is an amenity, as it allows more control of an individual's or company's operations. Watching out for the amenities that enable individuals or companies to function better or which may appeal to their emotions can reward the investor who wants to reach the owner-occupier market.

Generally, you can not touch this layer of the market for income from rents, except in two special circumstances. First, owner-occupiers may be obliged to rent for a short period while they find the real estate they want to purchase or while waiting for it to be constructed. This may provide you with an opportunity for short-term income, perhaps from an employee who is transferred to your area and who rents a house from you.

Second, owner-occupiers, particularly businesses, may prefer to rent the land underneath the improvements they own in order to reduce their investment. This may provide you with an opportunity to receive a long-term income stream from a ground lease and possible appreciation later on.

MIXED MOTIVES

In some instances there is only a fine line between use real estate and investment real estate. For example, when fast-food businesses began, they generally had to franchise most of their outlets because they lacked the capital to own and operate them. Their decision to concentrate their capital on enhancing their fast-food operations through advertising and support services created opportunities for two kinds of investors. First, it allowed people to invest directly in a fast-food business by purchasing a franchise. Second, it allowed other investors to rent real estate to the franchisees.

Now, some franchisors' capabilities and objectives appear to have changed. Increasingly, they are purchasing real estate for new outlets and running their own fast-food operations directly. In some cases, they are attempting to buy back the franchises they sold at the start. This strategy enables the franchisors to pursue profits from their real estate operations in the form of tax shelter and appreciation as well as profits from their fast-food operations.

In the process, some real estate investors, mainly those interested in current income, are being cut out. However, the changed strategy is creating more opportunities for turnover investors to create units for the companies who are expanding their ownership of real estate.

Mixed motives can arise much closer to home. In fact, you are likely to change from one layer to another in the process of owning your own home. When you purchased your home, your overriding motive in all likelihood involved one of the amenities. You may have wanted to live in a particular section of the community, in parklike surroundings, near your parents-in-law who were ill, or at a certain distance from your work. You may have needed a four-bedroom house to accommodate your family. You may have had a very positive reaction to the wooded terrain that could be viewed from the house. If you examine your reasons for acquiring your present house, you are likely to find that your primary objective falls into the use end of the spectrum.

You may protest that you are not so much a user of your home as an investor in it. After all, you have considerable capital in it. Certainly one of the past decade's most frequently heard statements has been "my home is my best investment."

It is not surprising that most people perceive their homes as investments. The operations of recent trends and principles have, in the case of most single family homes, been favorable. As a result, home values and equities have risen sharply.

Prices shot up over the decade because of an undersupply of new single family housing. In addition, war production drew materials and labor away from home construction just as demand was growing rapidly. Construction costs rose to capture the supply that was left. Moreover, house values increased because houses are tangible property and, during inflationary periods, people seek out the tangible. As a result, your home is certainly likely to be your most valuable possession. However, it can not be your best investment until you no longer need to use it.

Unlike an investment property, the home you occupy can not fulfill your need for income, its tax shelter is limited to deductions for interest and property taxes, and you can not turn it over or reap much capital appreciation as long as you need to use it or a house like it. Of course, you can realize some of the wealth in your home by refinancing or taking out a second mortgage. This, in fact, may be a good source of capital for your investment purposes. However, again unlike investment real estate, the home you occupy will not generate income to meet the additional loan payments. Instead, you will have to dip into your own pocket to come up with the debt service.

You can shift your home from use real estate to investment real estate only when you are ready to sell or rent for income. When you sell your home at the right price, you can realize all the equities involved, including your original cash equity, the mortgage equity build up, any inflation equity, and any equity in a capital improvement you may have made. Only here will you have a financial advantage over investment real estate, as any gain from selling your home will not be taxed immediately provided you reinvest the proceeds in another home within the required time period.

However, when you sell investment real estate, your profit is available for any purpose. You can spend it, save it or reinvest it. Not so with the profit from selling your own home or other use real estate. If you need another home to occupy, the use to which you can put your profit is limited to purchasing another home. In fact, most or all of your profit will be used up in making another home purchase. The same trends and principles which have boosted the value of your present home are likely to have been in operation on the home you must purchase, increasing its value similarly.

You could theoretically increase any amount you have left over for purposes other than purchasing a replacement home by substituting much more modest space. However, there is clearly a practical limit to how far you can go in this direction. If you still need four bedrooms, you will not find a studio apartment an adequate substitute. Only when your children leave home or you retire will you have a major opportunity when you sell to free up capital for any use to which you want to put it.

Use real estate, such as your home or your company's plant or offices, is only an investment up to a certain point. Primarily it is for your use, and the return you receive for the money you have put into it comes largely from its amenities. A return in the form of the appropriate number of bedrooms, prestige or higher business profits can more than adequately compensate you for tying up your capital in use real estate.

Unfortunately, however, a failure to understand the different forms of return that result from different objectives can lead to great disappointment. You or your friends may have experienced this problem with vacation homes. To the extent that the use motive dominates the acquisition of a vacation home, the investment results are likely to be poor. And vice versa.

For example, you may have decided to purchase a second home for your own use on vacations and weekends and hold it for rent to tenants for the remainder of the season or year. If you choose to occupy the vacation home in August or during the peak of the season, you will not be able to collect rents for that peak period. Your use limitation may reduce the financial results to the point where you barely break even, if you break even at all. Alternatively, you may forego your favorite vacation period and rent the property for that time span. Your financial results will improve but your use of the property will be restricted, perhaps to the point where you can no longer fulfill your use objective.

You may also have another problem with this mixed motive property. If you are primarily its user, you may have purchased the vacation home for certain amenities you wanted to enjoy, not as a strict dollars and cents proposition. In order to obtain the amenities you desired, you may have paid more for the real estate than the numbers would justify for an investment.

Paying more for user amenities may mean you can not recover

your investment and earn an adequate return on it in the short time the property is available for rent each year. Tenants, also, are usually unwilling to pay the high rents that would be needed in this situation to produce acceptable investment results. Instead, you may be adequately recompensed only when you sell, provided you have chosen real estate that continues to be in demand and which may appreciate enough to provide an adequate profit when you come to sell.

The same limitation on investment results would apply if you were to purchase a home surrounded by 40 acres of land. You might intend to occupy the house and retain five acres for your own use. Then you could turn investor by subdividing the remainder and selling off the lots. The lots created could be sold as amenities either to other users who would build or to a homebuilder who would build for users. You could earn a user's return on the real estate you retain and an investor's return on the land you sell. But, your investment return would be limited by your decision to keep your house and five acres off the market.

Yet another way to combine user and investor motivations is for your business to acquire the real estate in which it operates. You may have noticed the many professional groups which have done this in the suburbs. Their primary motivation is to acquire the amenities of space and location that are most conducive to earning a profit from their professional activities. But, these professionals add to their business profits certain rewards as a result of owning the real estate, such as the rights to tax shelter and potential appreciation.

If you clearly understand the returns that can be expected from each objective layer, you can make a mixture of layers work to synergize your returns. Moreover, an analysis of objectives from this perspective should help you uncover which end of the spectrum predominates. If it is the use purpose, most of your return will come from the amenities, to which you can add some return from the real estate involved. If the investment objective is dominant, most of your return will be financial.

This is not to say that real estate acquired mainly for its investment prospects does not involve consideration of certain amenities.

For an extreme example, most investors are not attracted to the role of slumlord, despite the reputed high profits, because they do not want to project that image of themselves. Taking pride in real estate you own or even being able to admit you own it can be an amenity worth pursuing.

Amenities can be valuable to an investor. However, they must be examined carefully to discover how your desire for them affects the economics of your investment. Awareness of these various layers of objectives within yourself will sharpen your ability to evaluate the trade-offs. For example, you may find that pursuit of a convenience amenity means you must select real estate with lower yields than other real estate located a little further away. At that point, you must decide how much you are willing to give up in yield to obtain the amenity.

TENANTS

Careful observation of the layers at the use end of the spectrum will help you determine what attracts or repels certain buyers or tenants. For example, tenant users are just as motivated by amenities, both utilitarian and emotional, as owner-occupier users are. However, tenants may be differentiated from owner-occupiers along the spectrum by their choice not to tie up capital in ownership or by their inability to afford ownership. The tenants who choose the single user layer are likely to be better capitalized and more willing to assume maintenance responsibilities than tenants who select the multi-tenant layer.

These are valuable clues for you to examine when looking at people in a locality. For example, who appears to be motivated by ownership amenities, single tenant user amenities or multi-tenant kinds of amenities? Are they talking about low maintenance responsibilities, as tenants and condominium or cooperative owners do? Are they discussing projecting certain kinds of images for their businesses or through their homes? Where would these images place them among the use slices? What kind of real estate use would the market you are examining find most acceptable and affordable? And what properties can meet these use objectives?

Defining the use layer you want to attract will also arm you with information for advertising campaigns. Your understanding of what motivates those occupying different slices will keep you from using language suitable to one slice when you are aiming at another. For example, "your spacious lawn" may motivate single family owner-occupiers but completely turn off apartment tenants and condominium or cooperative owner-users because it implies a high degree of maintenance commitment. The latter layers might be much more attracted by "the handsomely landscaped grounds surrounding your individual apartment or condominium or cooperative" because the language used implies that they will have to take care of only a single unit. Stressing the amenities which move the market segment you have chosen will make it much more likely that you obtain tenants or buyers for your investment.

The choices users make are not set in concrete for all time, as the franchising example shows. Nor will each user necessarily be restricted to only one choice at a time. For example, a corporation may occupy several use layers of real estate at different points in its operations. It may be an owner-user of its headquarters improvement or of its major plants or stores. It may be a single tenant user for certain offices, stores or plants. At the same time, it may lease space in a multi-tenant improvement for a service or sales office. Each use layer provides real estate investors who occupy different investment layers with their own special kinds of opportunities.

DEVELOPING A USER PROFILE

In order to profile the tenants or buyers you hope to attract, you must first determine the strengths and weaknesses of the economic unit in which you find yourself. Because it is beyond the scope of this book to present an in-depth treatment of market analysis, which would itself require several books, we have chosen to present it as if you would be undertaking the analysis. There are indeed functions which you or a partner will definitely be analyzing, such as activity signals. However, much of the rest must be left to a market analyst if you are to get the professional results desired.

We recognize that this creates a dilemma for those starting, as we have suggested, with small-scale properties, as a professional analyst's services may not at that point be affordable. In those cases, we recommend that you check the information you or your partner can gather thoroughly and that you consult as many sources of information about the area in which you plan to invest as possible. The trade-off for an inability to afford a professional market analysis lies with the small-scale nature of the property. It will have a much smaller impact on the total market and thus possible negative impacts can be overcome by the investor through the exercise of more diligent controls, such as adjustments of rent levels, decorating or other methods of meeting the market.

As we discussed in Chapter 6, it is the export industries in an economy which will ultimately support the real estate in which you decide to invest. Thus, one of your first tasks is to define the economic unit and discover the trends apparent in the export industries within it.

Next, the demand factors implicit in employment trends, income trends, population trends, household trends, family size trends, age trends and buying preferences must be delineated. By breaking down the statistics, demand for a particular layer of housing, retail, office, industrial, land or special purpose real estate can be measured. Overlaying that on the supply side of the equation, which includes the net inventory of existing real estate of that type and construction activity, will produce a measure of the effective demand for a specific use of real estate.

In addition, locating the strengths of the economic unit may provide you with strong indicators of special markets which may be benefiting more than others from these strengths. For example, the addition of research and development firms to an economic unit is likely to mean a strong housing demand from upper-income employees. Buying up housing for resale in neighborhoods with amenities sought by such users or creating housing for them if there is an insufficient supply could be very profitable. The specific locality must also be analyzed to uncover its demand and supply trends.

You will find that this work more than justifies itself. First, the information you develop and analyze will enable you to make a rational judgement on whether to invest in a particular area and in a particular kind of real estate within that area.

For example, if you uncover trends which are favorably affecting both the economic unit and a locality within it, you will have strong factual evidence to justify proceeding to the selection of an individual property within that area. If only the locality shows a positive trend, you will have to find unusually strong reasons why you think the locality is capable of bucking the overall trend. If a locality's trends come up negative but overall trends are favorable, you will be able to relocate your investment impulse to a more promising locality. If you purchased a property before conducting a market analysis, you might be locked into disappointing financial results or have to take a loss to enable you to invest in a more favorable area.

Second, the material you or your partners develop can be used to interest lenders, prospective equity partners and lessees. Nothing so supports a loan application or a prospectus as solid, factual material that clearly shows trends which support the real estate involved. Moreover, potential buyers or lessees, or lessees facing lease renewal decisions, can be motivated to buy, rent or re-lease by material showing how the area's trends can benefit them.

As an example, you may uncover evidence that property tax stabilization is likely to occur. Perhaps the population breakdown shows that school age children are declining in number and new schools will not have to be built. Lenders and equity investors will see this information as an indication that operating expenses will be less likely to get out of hand and endanger their investment returns. Buyers or tenants may see it as evidence that their costs are less likely to rise in this area as compared to other areas where they might decide to locate.

Gathering such information may also alert you to investment possibilities. A decrease in school enrollment may mean you can acquire a school building that will no longer be needed. If there is a strong demand for apartments or offices in their neighborhood, residents are far less likely to object to a conversion in an existing improvement than to protest new construction.

With an analysis of the market, you are entering the final stage of the real estate investing process. Having discovered what you can seek and receive from real estate investment, how best you might choose to achieve your goals, and the basic workings of real estate investing, you are now ready to position yourself for the acquisition of a specific property.

Market analysis tests demand against supply so that you can make an intelligent, rational decision as to whether effective demand exists. Only if a viable use layer is discovered for your kind of real estate will it be worthwhile to proceed to property selection and a financial feasibility analysis in order to determine a specific property's ability to meet your financial objectives. A market analysis, if properly conducted, rests on solid facts to which careful judgement has been applied.

Market analysis comprises five elements, the first of which must, in effect, be validated by the other four if you are to have a firm basis upon which to make a decision to pursue a potential opportunity. The five steps are:

1. Activity identification

2. Market area delineation

3. Demographic description

4. Demand analysis

5. Supply analysis

Market analysis for each type of real estate follows the same basic steps. Land is a special case only in that an end use of it for one of the other types must be analyzed. While the process is the same for each type, the techniques differ, just as surgery and psychoanalysis are different. Both are motivated by healing and based on the practice of medicine. However, a surgeon utilizes certain skills to effect a cure or ameliorate a condition, while a psychoanalyst uses different procedures for the same ends.

The market analysis required for each type of real estate has in common the goal of establishing whether a viable market exists. Each kind of market analysis uses the same base, demographics. In order to identify the market, people's activities must be seen as the cause of demand, and people themselves must be considered as a supply source for all real estate. However, the methodologies involved in applying demographic data differ according to the type of real estate analyzed.

The same steps and procedures apply to both small-scale and large-scale real estate within a layer of a type of real estate. As we noted, you or a more experienced working partner may be able to conduct the preliminary market analysis required for a small-scale property. However, a larger scale investment will call for the services of a professional market analyst, as the data to be analyzed grow in complexity as the scale increases. The risk of failing to meet the market with a product also tends to rise. Fortunately, the ability of an investment to support professional services is apt to increase with size.

We shall first discuss each of the steps in order to elucidate the market analysis process. Within this discussion, we will cover certain preliminary applications to the different types of real estate. It is not the intent of this chapter to make you a market analyst but rather to give you a familiarity with the concepts and techniques. Then, we will apply the more general discussion of the process to residential and retail uses.

1. Activity Identification Before undertaking a formal market study, you must locate an area for which one would be worthwhile. Thus, your first requirement is a neighborhood or other unit in which positive activity appears to be taking place.

Looking around at neighborhoods near your home and areas close to your place of work or places that you otherwise frequent can offer you unusual opportunities to spot activities related to the kind of real estate in which you are interested. Alternatively, if you have already acquired property, perhaps through inheritance, you can observe activities in its vicinity which will help you define the market it might best serve. In both cases, you are in a better position to spot positive trends and changes which may be occurring simply because you have so much information already within your purview.

You are seeking activity signals which tell you that the area will either continue to prosper or that it is changing in ways that can meet your objectives through the alterations' impact on the real estate type you have chosen or already acquired. The signals may be relatively visible, such as new construction, or relatively invisible, such as a decline in freight rates. The signs can be either a cause or a result of some activity which has or will have a favorable impact.

For example, you may see "for rent" or "for sale" signs which quickly disappear. Apartment for rent advertisements may now be eclipsed by apartment wanted advertisements, where a year ago the opposite was true. Renovations may be underway, new kinds of uses may be appearing, a street widening may be in progress, or new construction may be on its way. These can all be signals of actual or potential demand.

Overtime may be increasing or union wage rates decreasing; a new sewage plant may be announced; rents may be rising. Each of these signs may mean the creation of conditions for certain other activities to take place. For example, extensive office overtime may mean that new hiring is on its way. In turn, that may cause firms requiring additional office space to expand into larger quarters.

Increasing rents may mean that operating expenses are going up. It could also mean that demand exceeds supply and, as a result, is pushing up rents on the available supply. A truck rate change, more favorable labor conditions, or an increase in the ability of a municipality to handle industrial waste may cause industry to expand. A street widening may mean more traffic to intercept for shopping and, thus, a need for larger retail premises.

New construction of a plant may mean an increase in employment. In turn, more employment is likely to mean demand for additional residential, office and retail real estate. A new housing project may mean more demand for retail users to capture.

However, an investor should be wary of making a connection between investing and an activity which is booming. If a particular use is already at its peak, prices for the kind of real estate serving that use will be at their highest because everyone can see what is happening and too many will want to be in on it. In addition, waiting to invest until boom conditions are obvious could mean that you will make your investment just as the boom is about to run out.

You may serve your objectives better by stepping back from a boom in one use to observe how it is likely to affect another use or uses. Your analysis may show that a soaring demand for housing and the supply that is coming in to meet it will cause more demand for convenience stores. If this effect is not yet evident in any major way, properties with existing convenience store tenants, properties which can be changed to suit them, or available appropriate land may still exhibit relatively low prices. Buying in at low prices or building to meet new demand will enable you to ride up a boom in this use at the most profit.

The focus must be on the conditions which cause activity to occur. This focus will allow you to invest before everyone catches on because everyone can so clearly see what has resulted. Activity never takes place in a vacuum. There are always positive reasons why industrial plants, other businesses or residences are doing well or expanding in an area. The question is whether the signals you see, read or hear about mean business or residential users are finding or will find it beneficial to be in an area. If there are benefits to be derived from an area, then activity is likely to occur or to continue.

Activities of the kind which impact positively on real estate impart an air of vibrancy to an area. Positive reasons for being there and an air of prosperity, change or excitement, or any of these, distinguish an area in which it may be worth investing from one in which it is not. Neighborhoods which exhibit neglect and few or negative activity signals are not worth wasting time and effort on. Areas where tattered "for rent" or "for sale" signs are ubiquitous and maintenance has clearly been deferred for too long are signaling you to stay away.

A single investor just starting out can not afford to create positive reasons for activity to take place in a neighborhood where they do not already exist or the ambience which will attract tenants or buyers. If an area in decline holds unusual promise because of good transportation or some other fundamental characteristic, users may eventually discover it and start turning it around. Until then, you can only keep an eye on the area so that you will be ready to invest well before prices reach their maximum.

At the start, you are most likely to spot positive changes in an area with which you are familiar. You are also most likely to know the positive reasons why people or businesses seek the neighborhood or remain in it, if you but examine why you or people you know are there. By comparing the area today with its past, you will also be able to protect yourself better because you will know whether a use or prosperity itself is declining within it.

If you are new to an area, you can make up for your lack of personal knowledge by talking with long-term residents, merchants, business owners, letter carriers and others about changes they perceive in the area and the reasons they consider it a positive or negative place in which to be. You should in any case be talking to people about their businesses, employment conditions, homes, prices, rents, occupancy levels and anything else which will give you clues to activity levels within a neighborhood. You can also consult old and new maps from oil companies, planning commissions and zoning departments in order to see where development has taken place since the older maps were drawn up. This will highlight for you positive flows of people and businesses and, thus, effective demand flows.

2. Market Area Delineation   Once you find an area with many actual or potential activity signals for the kind of real estate in which you are interested, your next step is to define its size. The area you delimit on a map will be the unit for which you gather facts in order to test your observations and intuition.

There must be an area from which a property you might select can draw home buyers, apartment tenants, mobile home occupiers, office tenants, customers to support retailers, industrial users, or customers for the users of special purpose properties, whichever kind attracts you. The market area delineated must encompass the area from which users come or will come and the amenities users of the properties will need to facilitate their business or residential use.

You can start estimating the size of the market area by reference to your own feelings. Simply by living, working or visiting in a neighborhood, you have certain actual or intuitive boundaries to go by. A boundary may be natural, such as a river, or artificial, such as a major traffic artery. The area may be politically or occupationally defined or bounded by the transportation lines it uses. It may be defined in terms of retail competition or of psychology, or zoning may control. You may simply know that where one style of architecture is replaced by another a different neighborhood results. Whatever marks out one area from another tends to define size.

The important consideration is the taking in of the area which provides primary support for the real estate activities you have located. For industrial uses, this would encompass an area from which most of the industry comes and where industry can find appropriate levels of employees. It also includes the other major requirements of industry, such as freight, fire and police protection districts. These may form boundaries, particularly if one district is superior in its ability to supply the needs of industrial users or does so at less cost than another district. The same holds true for the availability and cost of gas, electricity, water and special sewage treatment, which may define barriers across which industry will not move.

In addition, one industrial area may be distinguished from another by special zoning, industrial performance standards and building code restrictions. These can act to enhance an area's attractiveness to industry, as they protect each industrial user's operations from interference which might be caused by other users. Compatibility of uses may also define an area. If the other requirements can be met equally well in several areas, the availability, convenience and cost of transportation will best serve to define an industrial area's limits, as transportation is the key to industrial activity and location.

The size of the market in which office buildings compete with one another may be determined by zoning restrictions and the availability of an appropriate workforce. It may also be defined by prestige, rent levels or by similarity of use, as when lawyers group themselves in a particular area. Again, the positive reasons for seeking out an office area, such as proximity to a courthouse, are likely to govern the area's boundaries.

The area you delineate may be as small as two blocks or as large as 150 miles, depending on the patterns in your area. In fact, some market areas encompass not only the nation, but also the world. For example, some prestige specialty stores sell to a worldwide clientele. Certain financial districts are as likely to have users and customers that come from the Far East as from the next block. Certain stores in a locality draw across a city or a metropolitan region. These are the most complex to analyze and should initially be avoided.

A market area can best be understood if its boundaries are penciled in on a current map. The market will break down into primary and secondary areas. More of the users or customers will tend to come from nearer locations than will a scattered few who come from outlying places relative to the core of the market area. Thus, your map will show a primary area delineation and, surrounding it, a secondary area. Those who come from this secondary area may be just as able or find it equally attractive to go to a neighboring market area.

3. Demographic Description Once you have mapped out the boundaries of the area affected by the activity signals you have spotted, you will need to find out at your library which census tracts encompass or are included within the area. Census tracts form the smallest statistical units for which you can develop factual information. You will also require information from these census tracts and others to compare standards from comparable areas in order to test the proposed market area you have selected as a potential investment opportunity. In addition, you will be using statistics for the city and/or county, the metropolitan region, the state and nation for further tests.

You are attempting to construct a thorough profile of the area's past, present and future. To accomplish that, you will need to know everything which has happened, is happening and is likely to happen. Past censuses, current enumerations and available forecasts will be your tools.

At this stage, the focus is on the whole picture, particularly on population, employment and incomes. You will need to know how many people have resided or worked in the area, are now in the area, and how many are expected to be in the area in the future. In addition, you will need to study the composition of the area's population. By concentrating on occupational and income levels, age distribution, the ratio of males to females, household size, and family formation, you will become acquainted with the layers and form the ability to layer out the market in your area.

Setting up a grid or graph system for each part of the statistical description of the area's population will enable you to plot out a profile of the population which exists in the area, how it got to be that way, and how the area's population may be changing. Such a system will also show how rapidly change is taking place. Moreover, this method will allow you to compare your area more easily with other local areas and with the larger statistical units. That will enable you to spot trends in your area which are more positive than those in the other units. These trends are the ones to pursue.

At the same time as you are developing a profile of the demand side of the equation, you should also collect all the information you can about the past, present and future state of supply. For example, a past census and present enumeration may show how much office space has existed and now exists. Other information, such as a sewer moratorium announcement, may indicate that new construction will stop.

In addition, all the general economic characteristics of the wider economic unit, such as a metropolis, can be gleaned from economic base studies prepared by planning commissions, industrial development councils, port authorities, chambers of commerce, universities, real estate boards, utilities and some banks. Any circumstance within a larger economic unit can affect supply and demand as well as other conditions within an area which forms a part of the whole. The reports will discuss changes which are underway and which are expected to continue and give the reasoning behind the forecasts. Then you can apply your judgement to these forecasts to test them for reasonableness and applicability to the area you have delineated.

In addition to an economic description of the larger unit, an employment analysis may also be required in order to understand the trends in process. This type of study covers employment and changes in it over time for an entire economic unit, usually a Standard Metropolitan Statistical Area (SMSA), as employment incomes from an entire metropolis play a part in supporting each locality's real estate. The analysis reveals both the strength of the support and identifies where it is coming from.

In order to conduct the study, employment statistics, broken out for each major employment group, are analyzed. Figures on past employment for each group are compared with present and forecasted figures. In the locational quotient portion of the study, a group's percentage share of total SMSA employment is established and then compared with the group's percentage share of national employment. In this way, those industries which are exporting, importing or adequately serving the metropolitan population can be identified.

For example, if the percentage share of instrument manufacturing employment is larger in the SMSA than it is in the nation, that group is defined as one that exports from the SMSA. It is producing more than is needed to serve the local demand for instruments. Instrument sales to areas outside the metropolitan region will bring incomes back into the SMSA where they will support local activities, including real estate. If the total number of employees who form this group has grown from one period to another and is forecasted to grow still more, the group is one that is well worth seeking out. Then other data, such as figures on income and age, will serve to indicate which real estate products this group would find acceptable and affordable.

A more sophisticated approach is the shift-share analysis. Through the use of several formulas, it identifies both those industries which are growing and contributing more to a unit's economic health than others and those which are negative factors. It also reveals which employment groups are shifting into or out of the area by comparing SMSA employment activities with those on a national scale. The employment groups it identifies as growing are those likeliest to need additional real estate in which to work, live or shop. This can highlight turnover opportunities when correlated with data for the areas which attract these employment groups. Conversely, a finding that an employment sector is declining may mean an opportunity to change the use of real estate it has been occupying for various purposes.

The employment groups identified as stable or growing in numbers are those most likely to continue to support the real estate they use and are, thus, the groups most worth pursuing. The information developed about occupational levels will also serve to help you layer out the market in the next stage of analysis. For example, the finance, insurance and real estate category of employment may be growing and be expected to continue growing. Growth may mean that not only additional offices, but perhaps also more housing, will be needed. This finding of growth may confirm your intuition that demand for housing is coming from this group. It also tells you something about the kind of housing which might be in demand. Because the employees concerned are office workers, they are likely to find only certain definite layers of housing acceptable and affordable within certain preferred areas.

4. Demand Analysis Having collected all the relevant data and familiarized yourself with overall employment and population trends, you must now focus in on a specific kind of market, such as office or retail. The first step is to establish aggregate demand. This involves developing an aggregate figure for the type, such as office, and then distributing it across its layers to establish their aggregate figures.

Past population figures for an area, present population and projected population are used to establish aggregate demand for the type. Perhaps some 20,000 people worked in an office area ten years ago, some 30,000 work there today and an additional 10,000 may be projected over the next ten years.

However, these gross figures tell you nothing about the actual offices workers now occupy and will occupy in the future. Thus, the figures must be divided up according to the population profile you have already drawn for the market area. One slice might involve incomes; another might be the type of office employment, such as that for medical or other service offices.

Once you have an aggregate demand figure for each slice, you can convert the figure for the slice or slices you judge the most promising into some measurement unit for space. For offices, the number of square feet per employee is the conversion factor. Today, this averages 200 square feet per office employee and is higher than it was some years ago when there was less office machinery.

Once you multiply the number of people in a layer by the conversion figure, you will have a figure for aggregate office space that indicates the number of square feet in demand from a particular layer. You can then estimate a conversion factor, according to office rental agents' best judgements of trends in space needs, for application to the projected population number. You will then arrive at the amount of space which will be needed by this layer in the future.

5. Supply Analysis The same process applies to the supply side of the equation. In order to reveal trends, the total amount of supply for a type of real estate must be calculated for a point in the past and for the present. The amount of past supply can be found in the last census. Current supply includes what exists today, planned construction or conversions and land now zoned for the use in question.

If a current survey does not exist, a field inspection to calculate existing square feet or some other appropriate unit of measurement, such as the number of apartments, may be required. A check of building department permits and zoning maps will reveal supply in process or land available for new construction. Building department records will also show the amount of supply lost since the last census due to demolitions, fires or other causes.

You may find that some four million square feet of office space existed in the past and that there has been a net addition of some two million square feet since then. However, once again these gross figures must be divided up into the aggregate figures which apply to each layer.

The layering process generally starts with a discussion of rent or sale price levels with rental agents in the area. A distribution between owner-occupier and rental real estate must be applied, so that you will be able to discard the figures which relate to a layer in which you are not interested. In some cases, a further distinction can be made between single occupancy and multiple occupancy rental properties. Rent or sale price levels and space sizes consistently serve to distribute the market for all types of real estate. So, too, do amenities, although the kinds of amenities which are important for each type differ.

Once you have established aggregate supply figures for different layers, you can match them up with the aggregate demand figure for each layer. This will allow you to identify whether a state of oversupply, undersupply or balance between supply and demand exists now or will exist in the future.

A comparison of existing demand and existing supply layers may show that an undersupply situation, which you could meet with new supply, exists. Alternatively, the analysis may show that although demand from a layer is being met on a current basis, population projections for the slice indicate that new supply may be needed in the future. Conversely, supply may now exceed demand, but the demand forecasted may outstrip supply in the future. If you want to buy at a low price pursuant to your objective, a condition of current oversupply and future undersupply is the finding you may most want to follow up. The current oversupply condition will tend to depress prices, while a future undersupply will tend to raise the value of the property over time.

If you have established that there is an existing or potential effective demand, you can then begin a more thorough analysis to refine the layers. This process encompasses not only the numerical descriptions you can produce from the statistics, but also social, political and emotional factors. Even more careful judgement is required at this stage.

You will also have to draw conclusions from all the material you have gathered and analyzed. No piece of information exists in isolation. As a result of the interrelated nature of the data, judgement of all the pieces in toto is necessary. Your judgement of the situation is what counts, as that is what you will back with a decision both to investigate a specific property and to invest in one.

The final step is to calculate how much demand from a layer a particular property might be able to capture as its site share. This involves selecting a property for characteristics which would most attract the layer and then further defining the layer to estimate the site share which the property is likely to be able to attract. We shall now apply this overall process to both residential and retail uses.

RESIDENTIAL

Activity signals for the residential type of real estate can include increases in rent, construction, an absence of "for rent" signs and a relative lack of advertisements of houses or apartments for sale or rent. You may also find signs that demand is increasing by talking with realtors or bankers. You may read about a change in zoning that will restrict the amount of land available in an area for housing or observe a catastrophe, such as a storm, which knocks down some of the existing supply.

A housing area tends to be delineated by amenities. The positive reasons for locating in an area are the controlling factors. Particularly important may be proximity to a school, a religious institution, appropriate shopping, employment and other facilities which motivate people to live in the area.

Social factors are also important, such as the relative prestige of an area and the kind of space it offers. Both these differences and the employment and income levels they reflect can be used to delineate a housing area.

The third stage, demographic description, we have already discussed. The requirements are the same for housing as for any other type of real estate. We will assume that certain employment sectors are growing and that the process of familiarizing yourself with the demographics and other material about the economic unit revealed no disproportionately negative features, such as massive plant abandonment, which would cause you to discard the idea of investing anywhere in the total unit.

On the demand side of the analysis, aggregate population figures for the area may show that total population in the past was 4,000 and is now 6,000. Projections may indicate that 2,000 more people are likely to move into the area over the next five years, a greater population increase than indicated for the test areas.

Income levels will help you distribute the population across layers, which will reveal the price range each layer can afford. The conversion factor here is the amount of income a person can devote to housing, a factor which averages about 30 percent for the nation. Thus, if the predominant income level in the area is $300 a week, the kind of housing which is affordable would cost about $90 a week. This will be an average, and therefore you must again slice it more thinly to discover the percentage which can afford housing that costs perhaps $50 or $150 a week.

These income levels can be matched against the employment groups that are growing in order to determine which income layer you should be pursuing. Age and educational levels will also start setting parameters on the kind of housing which will be acceptable. For example, some 20 percent of the area's population who can afford $120 a week may be of an age which tends to prefer rental real estate. Particularly important will be the trend in household size, as it is the factor used to correlate demand with supply.

Once you have defined the demand side for the past, present and future, you can turn your attention to the supply side. The number and dollar value of units listed on the construction or conversion permits filed at the building department will provide you with a cross check on the income levels that the supply is being built to meet.

A comparison of the current number of households and the housing inventory you have established will reveal the present relationship between supply and demand. For example, if you find that the average number of people in a household in the area is 3.3, you can calculate that the existing population of 6,000 people needs about 1,800 housing units. There may now be some 1,800 units in existence, which would confirm the lack of vacancies you detected. You can then distribute the number of people per household in such a way that you discover the number of those people within a household category who can afford and would find a certain supply layer acceptable. In talking with rental agents, you may also have spotted a trend toward smaller numbers of people per household. Thus, the projected demand figures might have to be converted into household units by using another figure for number of people per household.

Both supply and demand must be distributed across the owner-occupier and tenant housing continuum to see how many units of each will be needed. There may have been an overbuilding of single family houses over the last few years in the area. The relative undersupply of apartment units may mean that some people are now having to rent houses or double up with other households in order to have a place to live. This could mean that most of the new housing units to be constructed should be rental units. Thus, this undersupply could be met, and the balance people in the area find most desirable could be achieved.

A finding that some 70 percent of the new units should be apartments must be further refined to discover the kinds of apartments which will be in demand. To do this, the use layers are sliced more thinly in order to discover a demand for a certain number of studios, one-bedrooms or two-bedrooms. The distributions of age, income and household size, rather than the averages for these factors, will have much to do with any decision as to the right apartment sizes for the market.

Once you have sliced the layers as thinly as possible, you can locate a particular property or properties and apply all the characterisitics you have developed for the layer you want to pursue.

You must carefully weigh the factors which will motivate users to buy or rent space from you or which would allow you to retain tenants.

The decision you come to must reflect both obvious and subtle factors so that you may judge how well a property will meet what moves the market. Property tax levels will obviously move the market toward certain districts and away from others. However, the factor may be considerably less obvious, perhaps one involving dining rooms. The population slice you have defined may insist on a separate dining room rather than a dining area within another room. A failure to recognize that this amenity will motivate the market you have defined could doom the project. The important nonstatistical features, which can be developed by talking with tenants or home buyers, superintendents, rental agents, banks and other investors, breathe life into the statistics.

RETAIL

Activity signs for new or changing retail uses include an active housing or office market, new construction, increases in density, the widening of a street, a low number of vacancies and other such visible signs. Announcements of new utility extensions or an upgrading of the existing utility infrastructure can be particularly good signs of anticipated growth because utility companies prepare careful forecasts of demand and their activities usually precede new supply.

For existing retail uses, the signals incorporate high density, absence of vacancies, well-kept properties, a high count of automobile traffic pulling in and out, installation of traffic lights which will facilitate shoppers' ingress or egress, and street widening. The quality of stores, summer hiring and even something as simple as clean windows are also positive signs.

A retail trade area is generally defined in terms of time distance. Thus, convenience stores may draw in shoppers who are only a few minutes away by foot or car. A somewhat larger shopping center might draw in people from an area within 15 minutes' driving distance, while a major shopping center will rely on a trade area bounded by about 30 to 45 minutes' driving time.

The density of the area will determine the method of transportation people use. In midtown New York or Chicago, people walk to stores or take public transport depending on the type of store involved. In the suburbs of cities, and in small towns across the nation, cars tend to be preferred. Utilizing the appropriate transportation method, you can walk or drive in all directions from an approximate store location for the amount of time applicable to its size. This will help to establish boundaries. They are likely to be irregular in shape, as it takes different times to traverse different kinds of roads.

In some parts of the country, the trade area still reflects only the older measure of distance. For example, it may serve customers within a radius of as much as 150 miles, as it would take the population which exists in an area that large to support major stores. Where the major shift to time distance has not been made, population must be mapped out in such a way that the incomes available in an area for a given type of retail store or line of merchandise should support the stores in question.

You can determine whether your judgement of the size of a trade area is realistic by developing population concentration tests. One way to do this is to conduct a consumer survey in stores in the area in order to pinpoint the locations from which the consumers originate. You can also undertake a license plate count in order to plot out on a map where people come from to shop at a particular location. If you are thinking of developing a new store or stores, you can do a license plate survey for similar properties and then apply the size of the trade area you discover to the subject site.

The boundary delineation can consist of natural or artificial obstacles to travel, or it can be competitive in nature. Thus, in the course of making a survey you are likely to discover that a point is reached from which the population involved could shop equally conveniently in the area in which you are interested or in an area adjacent to it. As you pass that mapped point, the population will be decreasingly likely to shop in the trade area in which you are interested. Therefore, this point is likely to form part of a trade area's boundaries. Locations from which a majority of the shoppers originate will form a primary trading area, while a lesser number of originations will define a secondary market area.

One of the most direct relationships in market analysis is that of retail spending to population and incomes. A high income, low density area may produce the same amount of sales as a low income, high density area, although the merchandise on which the income is spent will differ.

Aggregate demand figures for retail are based on spendable incomes. The sum left for purchases after basic expenditures are made, such as those for housing and taxes, provides the dollars available to support retail trade. Total sales for a metropolitan area reflect spendable incomes and can be found in the Census of Retail Trade. When total sales are divided by total metropolitan population, a per capita expenditure figure is established.

The per capita figure is then multiplied by the population figure for the trade area you have delineated to arrive at the area's aggregate sales. If a trade area's profile differs in income and basic obligations from that of the metropolitan region, adjustments will have to be made. Local savings and loan institutions are one source among many that can usually provide information relevant to spendable incomes.

The total sales figure can then be cut into layers of aggregate sales figures for specific merchandise lines or store types, according to information available from the *Census of Retail Trade*. The same procedure for developing a total aggregate sales figure for an area is used to determine an aggregate sales figure for type of merchandise or type of store within the area. Local newspaper surveys will provide updated figures, while many planning departments produce sales forecasts. A comparison of the population, spendable incomes, and per capita expenditures for the area and the larger units over time will show the relative growth, decline or stability of a merchandise line or store type.

In order to measure aggregate demand for retail space, some yardstick must be established. This generally takes the form of sales volume per square foot. The aggregate sales figure for a type of merchandise or a store type is divided by the volume figure per square foot to establish the number of square feet in demand. Various trade publications produce estimates of sales volume per square foot by product type.

For example, you may have noticed congestion at local menswear stores in a definite area. Then, you may have established that the aggregate trade area expenditure for menswear is two million dollars. If the sales volume figure for menswear stores is $100 a square foot, a division of this number into the aggregate expenditure figure will give you the number of square feet in demand. In this case, there is demand for about 20,000 gross square feet of menswear space.

Future demand for retail space of any kind can be calculated by using the population and income projections in available forecasts in order to estimate potential spendable income at some point in the future. In addition, a careful check of the second function in retail trade publications will reveal whether the sales volume figure per square foot is changing or can be expected to change by the future date you have chosen. In some instances, adjustments for the effects of inflation must be made.

Actual supply can be established by pacing off competitive stores in the trade area, by checking construction permits and by examining zoning maps for vacant land which can be used for retail purposes. You may find that a total aggregate supply of 15,000 square feet is now indicated for existing men's clothing stores. This is some 5,000 square feet less than the aggregate demand figure necessary for menswear space. If you turn up no evidence that anyone else plans to supply the unmet demand, you may be able to meet it by renovating a store property, buying a vacant property, or constructing a facility that could fill the unmet demand.

However, as we have established, it is not enough to reach a point where you can demonstrate that there is an unmet demand for 5,000 square feet of menswear clothing space. You must also apply all you know about the people in the area, and the competition, to determine the best site for a new menswear store. Perhaps one is needed at Fourth and Main or at Seventh and South Streets. Major clues for a decision will surface as you observe the composition of existing traffic at both locations and of the population concentrations in the vicinity.

Market share is a function of projected incomes, competition, and development around a location of a complementary or negative nature. In addition, physical and locational characteristics help to determine the sales volume which is capturable at a specific location. Key retail issues involve accessibility, easy ingress and egress, parking (in areas dependent on automobile transportation), visibility, and attractiveness. For example, the placement of median strips or stoplights can either facilitate or hinder a site's accessibility.

Before applying these site selection functions to a decision on property selection, further work on layering the market will be needed. The demographic statistics which you collected earlier will now help you divide the market up into age, household size, education and income slices. The area's ratio of men to women will also help you calculate the size of the market.

You can then apply the slices you develop to the existing stores and the merchandise they offer. Certain kinds of merchandise are age sensitive; certain stores carry prestige items, while others do not. As a result, you must apply judgement and experience to an analysis of the statistics to decide how much actual and potential demand is or will be available to support a certain kind of store or merchandise layer.

For example, you may discover that the number of males who could afford the merchandise carried by a quality menswear shop and would find it acceptable is growing. If the opposite is true, it would be a signal to switch to a retail layer that is affordable by and acceptable to the demand layer which offers you the best market.

Having sliced the layers as thinly as possible and having made a preliminary selection of a property, you can then calculate the share of sales volume which a menswear store in that location could hope to capture. For example, part of the spendable income now being spent on menswear may be going to the menswear section of a junior department store down the road. The rest may be going to two more local shops.

The site you have selected may be more conveniently located

than one of the other stores to a major population concentration point. Thus, a store in that location may be able to shift a percentage of an existing store's sales volume to itself. The merchandise in one of the other stores may not yet have caught up with the changes in taste you have detected. All these considerations will go into establishing the size of the market which can be captured to support a particular retail property.

The material you have developed for the market analysis can also serve two other functions. One, which we have previously mentioned, is the capture of a tenant and the design of a consumer advertising and merchandise stock profile which will help that tenant to prosper. The second has to do with the rent you decide to charge for the use of the space. The indicators you develop for sales volumes, production volumes and income levels can be applied to the appropriate type of real estate and can, thereby, set the level of minimum rents and any potential participation in a tenant's business.

You will remember that an investor acquires a property because he or she anticipates future benefits. Thus, a market analysis should be built on past and present factual information, but be directed toward estimating future demand and supply relationships. If you allow yourself to get stuck in the caboose, you will be able to see only where a market has been. A good market analysis conducted by one who is versed in the particular property type you have selected will put you in the engineer's seat, so that you can see where you and the market are going.

It is not a goal in itself to meet existing or projected effective market demand from a specific use layer for a particular segment of real estate, that is, not unless you consider yourself a philanthropist. Meeting demand must make *economic sense*. If it does not, your investment objectives will be defeated. Thus, a property which meets the test of market demand but fails your economic tests merits rejection.

We have built our entire explication of real estate investment upon the four financial objectives such investments can help you achieve. Now, we reach the crux. Everything you have learned up to this point and will continue to learn about real estate must be channeled into a financial feasibility analysis of a specific property.

The property must be tested to discover whether it can satisfy the objective you have chosen. That may be income, tax shelter, capital turnover or appreciation, as you have modified these objectives in light of your investor profile.

Financial feasibility analysis tests:

1. Incomes

2. Vacancy and collection losses

3. Expenses

4. Net income

The analysis starts with the stabilization of these four financial categories. Particularly important to the process of stabilization is a close examination of any leases. Their conditions often govern financial results. We will discuss lease provisions in some detail in Chapter 13. Once the four categories have been stabilized, a pro forma statement can be constructed. This analysis, in turn, will dictate the financing. In addition, it will focus on the cake, cash flow, and its frosting, tax savings.

A potential turnover investment involves the same analysis, although other descriptive terms are often used. Thus, incomes are from sales rather than rents. A provision for vacancy and collection losses corresponds to holding costs. Net income is a turnover investor's net profit. The kind of financial feasibility analysis we will develop also applies to an investment for long-term appreciation, as it allows you to test whether a property will pay for itself during a holding period.

A financial feasibility analysis will tell you how a property's income stream comes about. The overall categories can be considered the same for each type of property. However, each will contain different items, as each type's income sources, vacancy and collection patterns and expense management can be as different as apples and oranges.

For example, a shopping center and an apartment building will both produce base rents. But, the center may also generate overage income, while the apartment building may provide income from laundry machines or pool usage. The center may handle increases in expenses by having some tenants on net leases, while others pay escalators. The apartment complex may use periodic increases in base rents to accomplish the same end.

We will take you through an analysis of an existing shopping center and a new apartment building. We will concentrate on the financial results which can be expected in the first year of owning each property exemplified. These results must make economic sense. If they do, the odds are that the property will make economic sense over the long haul. However, this must not be taken for granted, as you invest in reasonable anticipation of the receipt of future benefits.

You and your accountant will need to expand the pro forma statement illustrated in this chapter as far out as the figures can justifiably be expected to go or until you plan to dispose of the property in question, if you already know when that will be. If you understand the rudiments of what is involved in the first year analysis, you can then calculate the remainder of what is required. In this effort, remember that both the expectation of future rental income (or sales, if you have chosen a turnover objective) and the prospect of capital appreciation must be tested by reference to the current and future state of supply and demand.

As we discussed in Chapter 11, what makes up a market or the force of positive reasons for buyers or tenants to seek out or remain in an area and a property must be assessed. In addition, a close look at how the market which has been identified is changing and is likely to change in the future is necessary for making a rational judgement of the prospects of achieving the income for which you are investing.

The data needed to conduct a financial feasibility analysis come from many sources. In the case of an existing property, a real estate broker's setup, which lists information on a property for sale, is usually the starting point. The information in a setup comes primarily from the seller and is organized by the broker involved. Similarly, a prospectus for a limited partnership contains information developed by a general partner or partners for the purpose of selling partnership interests in a property.

To verify a seller's material, figures can be obtained from taxing authorities, heating fuel vendors, utility companies, tenants and others privy to facts that will affect a property's operations. A comparison of the property in question with other properties like it will serve as a major check on the soundness of the operating figures. In our examples, we will consider the following:

1. Property description

2. Market analysis summary

3. Leases

4. Income analysis

5. Vacancy and collection losses

6. Expense analysis

7. Net income

8. Capitalization rate development

9. Value of property

10. Debt service

11. Cash flow

12. Real estate taxable income or loss

APARTMENT BUILDING ANALYSIS

1. Property Description   The property consists of a new three story 12-unit apartment building constructed of steel and masonry. It occupies 100' × 40' on a site measuring 100' × 130'. There are eight four-room apartments (living room, kitchen, two bedrooms) and four three-room apartments (living room, kitchen, one bedroom). Utilities are metered separately. The laundry area in the basement is attractive and secure. Parking for 24 cars is located on the side of the building nearest the entrance and is lighted, paved and striped. The site has low maintenance landscaping. The property is on the market at an asking price of $250,000.

2. Market Analysis Summary   The property is located in a medium-size town of 50,000 people. It is well located to serve its market, as it is near shopping and only two blocks from a road which provides good access to the town's thriving employment center. There is a good demand for apartments currently. It is expected that a high occupancy level will continue because of a lack of available land for apartment development. The apartment units of the subject property were rented immediately upon completion of the structure. In fact, they were pre-leased, which indicates a strong market. The market consists of singles and young marrieds who can afford the units at current prices and whose incomes are rising faster than the norm.

3. Leases   One or two year leases are currently being offered in the neighborhood. They are the standard real estate board variety, and provide for both security and cleaning deposits.

WORKSHEET 11
Apartment Building Income Analysis

Units	Monthly Rental	Monthly Rent Contract	Monthly Rent Other*	Lease Expiration	Stabilized
8 - 4 (LK2BR)	@ 285	$2,280		6/80	$ 2,280
4 - 3 (LK1BR)	@ 250	1,000		6/80	+ 1,000
			Total Monthly Rent:		$ 3,280
			Total Yearly Rent:		$39,360
			*Laundry Income (Net):		+ 1,500
			Total Income:		$40,860

4. Income Analysis No operating history is available and therefore all financial data must be stabilized. Current economic rents on apartments with equivalent amenities are $250 a month for one-bedrooms and $285 a month for two-bedrooms, as can be seen on Worksheet 11. Thus, the eight two-bedroom units can be projected to produce $2,280 a month, while the four one-bedroom units would bring in $1,000 a month. The total monthly rent is expected to amount to $3,280. On an annual basis, full occupancy gross income is $39,360. In addition, laundry machines in surrounding properties are yielding $1,500 annually on a net basis.

The strength of the existing and projected market demand for units of this type now dictates offering one year leases. Shorter leases will provide an earlier opportunity to raise rents.

5. Vacancy and Collection Losses While no unusual risk is evident, a slightly high provision for collection problems must be made, as the tenants involved will generally be young adults who may not yet have formed responsible financial habits. Moreover, the short-term nature of the leases dictates a provision for vacancy. In this case, a short hiatus between tenants to allow for cleaning and painting a unit is most likely. Properties in the vicinity with similar tenants can handle these normal collection and vacancy projections with a 5 percent provision. This would amount to $2,000 annually.

6. Expense Analysis With the exception of the property tax item, the projected expenses listed on Worksheet 12 have been developed from the experience of comparable properties and are, as a result, stabilized. On the basis of discussions with the tax assessor and the members of the local taxing body, sentiment appears to be strongly in favor of rescinding a scheduled increase in the property tax rate, which would have caused the tax item for the property to be $5,800. The California vote on Proposition 13 against high property taxes is still much on the minds of elected officials and voters in the community. Thus, it seems likely that property taxes will be $4,850, rather than the $5,800 slated.

No unusual problems appear to be developing. Moreover, the quality of the construction is high enough to mean that the property will probably show slightly lower expenses in the future than some

WORKSHEET 12
Apartment Building Expense Analysis

Item	As Given	Stabilized
Insurance	$ 770	$
Real Estate Taxes	5,800	4,850*
Management	1,200	
Repairs	1,100	
Water	450	
Heat	300	
Electricity	600	
Supplies	200	
Scavenger	300	
Janitor	1,800	
Painting/Decorating	1,000	
Plowing	150	
Reserve for Replacements	480	
Exterminating	100	
Other	200	
+		+
	$14,450	$13,500

* Changed because of moves to rescind scheduled tax increase.

others nearby which were built at a time of construction shortages and material substitution. The owner is responsible for paying all operating expenses. The tenants pay separately only for gas and electricity used within their apartment units.

7. Net Income   The net income projected can be accepted because it has been carefully developed from the experience of comparable properties in the vicinity. Thus, a net income of $25,360 is indicated.

WORKSHEET 13
Apartment Building Pro Forma Analysis

	As Given	Stabilized
Income (From Worksheet 11)		
Contract Rent	$39,360	$39,360
Other (Laundry)	+ 1,500	+ 1,500
Gross Income	$40,860	$40,860
Vacancy and Collection Loss	− 2,000	− 2,000
Effective Gross Income	$38,860	$38,860
Expenses (From Worksheet 12)	− 14,450	− 13,500
Net Income	$24,410	$25,360

Development of Capitalization Rate:

Mortgage Ratio × Constant	.75 × .1038 (9¾% for 29 years)	.0779
Equity Ratio × Return On/ Return Of	.25 × .10	+ .0250
	Overall Rate:	.1029

Value Estimate:

Net Income: $ 25,360 ÷ .1029 = $246,452

Or: $245,000

Land	$ 60,000
Improvements	+185,000
Total:	$245,000
Offering Price:	$250,000

Estimated Economic Life: 30 Years

Debt Service Requirement:

Constant × Mortgage Amount

.1038 × $180,000 = $18,684

Debt Service Coverage: 1.35

Cash Flow:

Net Income	$25,360
Debt Service	− 18,684
Cash Flow	$ 6,676
Yield on Equity	10.27%

$$\left(\frac{\$6,676 \text{ Cash Flow}}{\$65,000 \text{ Equity*}} \right)$$

Real Estate Taxable Income or Loss:

Net Income		$ 25,360
Mortgage Interest (9¾% of $180,000)	$17,550	
Depreciation (Double Declining 30 Year life on $185,000 Improvements)	+12,320	
Total:	$29,870	− 29,870
Real Estate Taxable Income (Loss)		($ 4,510)†

*Assumes purchase price or cost of $245,000 and improvement cost allocation of $185,000.
†Requires an investor to incorporate his or her effective tax rate to calculate after-tax yield.

8. Capitalization Rate Development Investors are currently requiring a ten percent return on and of their equity. Local savings and loans are offering loans at 9¾ percent interest for 29 years, which would result in a constant of 10.38 percent according to Table 13, which is located at the end of Chapter 9. The current loan-to-value ratio is 75 percent.

The mortgage loan portion of the equation to develop a capitalization rate is .75 (loan-to-value ratio) × .1038 (constant) = .0779. The equity portion requires a ten percent return on and of the investment. Thus, the equity portion of the equation is .25 (equity-to-value ratio) × .10 (return on and of) = .0250. The total equation as shown on Worksheet 13 is:

$$.75 \times .1038 = .0779$$
$$.25 \times .10 = + .0250$$
$$\text{Capitalization Rate} = .1029 \text{ or } 10.29\%$$

9. Value of Property The net income developed at the top of Worksheet 13 is $25,360. When this is divided by the capitalization rate developed above, a value estimate of $246,452, say $245,000, results. This value estimate is some $5,000 less than the asking price, a small enough difference to make price negotiation likely to be successful.

10. Debt Service A mortgage loan of 75 percent of the value estimate would come to approximately $180,000. The equity requirement would then be $65,000 ($245,000 purchase price − $180,000 mortgage loan = $65,000 equity). Terms of 9¾ percent interest for 29 years produce a constant of 10.38 percent, or .1038. When the loan amount is multiplied by the constant, the debt service requirement will result. In this case, it is $18,684. Perhaps this amount could be reduced by locating a lender who will offer a lower interest rate or extend the term of the loan. The resulting increase in cash flow might make it possible to pay a slightly higher price than $245,000.

The debt service coverage comes to 1.35 ($25,360 net income ÷ $18,684 debt service). This meets the current requirement of lenders in the area on properties with no major tenants. It also provides you with a sufficient margin of safety.

11. Cash Flow The amount of income you can pocket is a result of subtracting debt service from net income. Thus, subtracting $18,684 from $25,360 indicates a cash flow of $6,676.

The cash flow figure is used, along with the amount of equity, to calculate current yield. In this case, the $6,676 in cash flow is divided by the amount of equity, $65,000. That results in a yield of 10.27 percent.

12. Real Estate Taxable Income or Loss As you will remember, debt service comprises both interest and amortization payments. The latter increase your equity and, thus, are of economic benefit to you. To calculate amortization, you must first figure the interest payment. Here, the loan amount of $180,000 is multiplied by the 9¾ percent interest rate. Interest for the first year comes to approximately $17,550. This means that $1,134 of the $18,684 mortgage payment is amortization.

The last step requires you to establish whether a property will throw off taxable income or a tax loss which can be used to shelter other income. The tax shelter generated by a property, such as interest deductions and depreciation write-offs, is subtracted from net income.

In this case, we have already developed an interest deduction figure of approximately $17,550 for the first year of ownership. The depreciation technique we have chosen to illustrate is the double declining balance method, which can be used on a new multi-family residential property like the subject property. It increases the amount of depreciation which can be written off in the earlier years of the investment.

To develop the depreciation figure, we will assume as reasonable a 30-year life for the property and an improvement cost of $185,000. The straight-line method would allow you to write off 3⅓ percent a year (100 ÷ 30 years) of the cost of the property. This would amount to $6,160 each year. The double declining balance method allows you to double this for the first year of ownership. Thus, the first year depreciation figure is $12,320.

Adding interest and depreciation together, we have $29,870, which can be subtracted from the net income as shown on Worksheet 13. The net income in this example is $25,360; as a result a first year tax loss of $4,510 is indicated. This sum can be used to reduce the amount of taxes due on your other income. How much it will reduce them will depend on your personal tax situation. Thus, we will not figure out an after-tax yield, as it is meaningless unless it reflects your own tax picture. In addition, carrying the pro forma forward to subsequent years will change the results, as the amount of interest and of depreciation will decline from the first year on.

The market and financial analyses might prompt a decision to buy for income, tax shelter or appreciation. There is a good yield on equity and an attractive income stream. However, an income investor who could not use the tax shelter would be well advised to select another property on which there was no unnecessary benefit to be paid for.

The strong demand for apartments in the area, coupled with the limits placed on supply by a lack of land on which to develop more apartment buildings, may mean an opportunity to redevelop the site for a larger apartment building in the future. For a capital appreciation investor, there also appear to be good opportunities to protect value by raising the rents periodically. Again, however, an investor interested in capital appreciation and adequate interim income would do well to examine whether the tax shelter is a necessary part of her or his strategy, particularly if the plan is to sell at some point. If the property is sold, some of the accelerated depreciation which had been taken may be recaptured from the sale proceeds as ordinary income.

SHOPPING CENTER ANALYSIS

1. Property Description The property consists of a site containing 40,000 square feet and measuring 200' × 200'. The center is a two year old one story masonry building 98' × 90', with 8,000 square feet of net rentable area. A remaining economic life of 25 years for the center is estimated.

There is a full basement for storage and heating equipment. Heat and cooling are supplied by individual heating and air conditioning units. Utilities are metered separately. A parking area provides space for 60 cars across the front and sides of the center and the parking area is lighted, paved and striped. A receiving area for deliveries is located at the rear of the building. The site is attractively landscaped and concrete walks parallel the streets. The property fronts on a highway.

The center is for sale at $475,000. The owners are selling because of illness in the family, which has forced a decision to move.

2. Market Analysis Summary The center is well located with good future potential. The neighborhood consists of middle class single family homes, with a cluster of low rise apartment buildings extending for three blocks on either side of the center and across the street from it.

The majority of households are headed by managers, professionals and technical personnel employed by a wide array of research and development firms clustered around a nearby university. A high proportion of the research and development work performed by these companies results from industrial contracts, not from volatile government-funded research programs.

In addition, a significant number of those employed work downtown for financial, insurance and real estate companies. Both sectors of the economy are growing and are projected to continue growing as the local economy takes on more of the functions of a regional economic center for several surrounding counties and as the research and development firms carry out plans to expand.

Most of the population in the area consists of families with school age children. Young singles and married couples without children occupy most of the apartment units. Incomes for the area range from $13,000 to $22,000, averaging $17,000 per household, an amount adequate to support the volumes necessary to achieve gross sales projected at the center.

There is a neighborhood shopping center with a grocery store and a cleaner one mile down the highway from the center in question. The major market layer served by the latter is oriented toward convenience and service and comes from within the area. Some of the sales volume is generated from buyers who are traveling along the main road. Population projections show that future demand could support two additional centers of the same size.

The trade area is bounded on two sides by major access roads, one leading downtown and one to the university. The center is located on a major artery which cuts diagonally through the neighborhood to connect the two. The third side is occupied by a well-maintained state park. As a result of the types of employment which are growing within the city and projected population increases, it is likely that development will take place in the fourth direction within five years. Vacant land exists at that end of the neighborhood, with zoning, topography and ambience identical to that of the existing community.

3. Leases Two of the tenants are credit rated and lease a total of 5,500 square feet. There are 23 years remaining on their leases. Three strong local tenants lease a total of 2,500 square feet, with

8 years remaining on their leases. Neither assignment nor subletting is permitted, and the provision forbidding abandonment of the premises is a strong one in each lease. Insurance is up-to-date as required by the leases and names both tenant and landlord as beneficiaries. The usual provisions relating to rebuilding in the event of destruction or a taking by the government are contained in the leases so that no unusual contingent liability exists.

Strong provisions concerning the use of the property and interior maintenance conform to what the professional middle class population finds appropriate and acceptable. In addition, the hours stipulated, the kinds of merchandise required and the staffing level are well thought out to meet the needs of the kinds of shoppers frequenting the center. The tenants have joined together to create a joint promotion effort.

Contract and economic rents are still identical. One credit rated tenant is paying six dollars a square foot; the other pays $6.25. The local tenants each pay seven dollars a square foot. Overages have averaged $6,000 a year for the two years the center has been operating. The one credit rated tenant which pays an overage of 4 percent of any gross sales over $420,000 has been achieving sales of $520,000 annually. This works out to a sales volume of $148 a square foot. This type of store averages about $120 a square foot annually. As a consequence, this tenant is doing extremely well. The local tenants pay overages of 3 percent of gross sales in excess of $290,000. They have jointly achieved a little more than $65,000 each year above the base amount to produce their $2,000 overage contribution. They are achieving $142 a square foot in sales volume, while the average for stores of their type is $116 a square foot.

Of course, if you were conducting an actual financial feasibility analysis, you would want to break out the local tenants' sales figures to make sure that the average was not concealing a tenant whose business was going bad. This is part of what management is about: Identifying problems before they occur.

Gross sales have consistently exceeded the guaranteed rent requirement and, based upon the market analysis, it is projected that the current overage payments will continue for the foreseeable future at approximately the same levels. The overage rent clause requires the tenants to keep sales records for two years. The owner has the records audited at the tenants' expense.

The leases specify that the owner pay a maximum of 75 cents a square foot, regardless of vacancies, for all expenses, including real estate taxes, insurance, maintenance, legal and accounting fees and every other expense item. The tenants pay for all expenses above 75 cents a square foot on a square foot pro rata basis. Management requirements are low, as the company which manages the gas station next door takes care of any necessary work. This includes snow removal, cleanup, maintenance and repairs.

4. Income Analysis   As can be seen from Worksheet 14, tenant B's sales volume has not achieved the level originally projected; thus tenant B does not pay overage rent. It is not projected that a sales volume which would produce overages will occur. An astute lessor would have designed leases that provided for increases in rents if projected sales volumes and overages were not achieved.

The term of the local tenants' leases will require re-leasing or renting to other tenants in eight years. Because of the uncertainty of the market at that date, some provision for the market conditions at that time must be made. However, if the market analysis is right in estimating relatively strong demand for the life of the center, re-leasing or renting to new tenants should be no problem. In fact, there may be an opportunity to let the space at higher rents.

5. Vacancy and Collection Losses   The caliber of the tenants involved requires no provision for rent collection problems. The credit rated tenants' leases cover all but a minor portion of the expected life of the center and, as it is probable that renovation or redevelopment will occur at the end of their leases, no vacancy provision for their units is necessary.

However, three stores may be vacant eight years down the road. A vacancy provision of five percent of the local tenants' annual gross rent (five percent of $19,500) would give you $975 annually, or $7,800 over eight years, as a reserve against the possibility of vacancies when their leases run out. When the earnings on this

WORKSHEET 14
Shopping Center Income Analysis

Tenant	Unit (Square Feet)	Base Rent	Rent Contract	Rent Overage*	Rent Other	Lease Expiration	Stabilized
Credit Tenant A	3,500	@ $6.00/sq. ft.	$21,000	$4,000		8/02	$25,000
Credit Tenant B	2,000	@ $6.25/sq. ft.	12,500			8/02	12,500
Local Tenants	2,500	@ $7.00/sq. ft.	17,500	2,000		8/87	+ 19,500
						Total Rent:	$57,000

*Tenant A: 4 percent over $420,000 gross sales.

Local Tenants: 3 percent over $290,000 gross sales.

reserve are taken into account, it would cover a period of about five months.

A business decision must be made as to whether five months' coverage of lost income is reasonable. In this case, the market analysis estimates strong demand and a favorable climate for re-leasing or renting the three stores to new tenants. Moreover, the August expiration dates provide enough time to get new tenants in and settled before the Christmas sales season. That may mean the vacancy provision is too high. If a decision is made that re-leasing or renting to new tenants is likely to occur in less than five months, some of the amount intended for a reserve can be pocketed as current income.

6. Expense Analysis As Worksheet 15 shows, the owner's expense exposure amounts to 75 cents per square foot for all expenses except debt service. The landlord is obligated to make replacements when necessary. This would amount to about a nickel a square foot of net rentable area, which the 75 cents figure covers. The only ex-posure on the expense side would come from abnormal replace-ment requirements, which are covered by warranties for machinery failure or by lease provisions requiring lessees to take proper care of the equipment. The base amount the owner has to pay also includes a provision for legal and accounting services.

A careful examination of operating expense trends in the area reveals no cause to believe that any increases of unusual magnitude are on the horizon. Thus, expense increases are unlikely to jeop-ardize a tenant's ability to pay rent.

7. Net Income Stabilized net income for the subject property is the same as given net income because: 1) The minimum rental is guaranteed by strong tenants subject to strong lease provisions. In addition, the market analysis projects a continuation of overages due to strong current and future market demand. 2) Few collection problems can be anticipated because of the quality of the tenants involved. The vacancy provision appears sufficient for the purpose required of it. 3) Expenses are in line with those of other properties and are not expected to increase in an unusual manner. The

WORKSHEET 15
Shopping Center Expense Analysis

Item	As Given	Stabilized
Insurance	$	$
Real Estate Taxes		
Management		
Repairs		
Water		
Heat		
Electricity		
Supplies		
Scavenger		
Janitor		
Painting/Decorating		
Plowing		
Reserve for Replacements		
Exterminating		
Other		
Owner Pays 75 Cents/Sq. Ft.	+ 6,000	+
	$ 6,000	$ 6,000

owner's responsibility for expenses is limited to a maximum of 75 cents a square foot. Thus, the net income of $50,025 shown on Worksheet 16 can be accepted.

8. Capitalization Rate Development   Investors in the area are currently requiring an average of 12 percent on equity to accomplish both return of and on their investment. Lenders in the area are offering loans on similar properties in the amount of 75 percent

WORKSHEET 16
Shopping Center Pro Forma Analysis

	As Given	Stabilized
Income (From Worksheet 14)		
Contract Rent	$51,000	$
Overage Rent	6,000	
Other Income	+`	+
Gross Income	$57,000	$
Vacancy and Collection Loss	975	−
Effective Gross Income	$56,025	$
Expenses (From Worksheet 15)	−6,000	−
Net Income	$50,025	$ Same

Development of Capitalization Rate:

Mortgage Portion: .75   × .1049 (9½% for 25 yrs) = .0787
                  Mortgage Ratio × Constant

Equity Portion:

    Contract Rents

        Credit Tenants   .11   ×   11/16 = .076

        Local Tenants   .135   ×   5/16 +.042
                  Return On/   Space ————
                  Return Of   Proportion .118

                .25   ×   .12   = + .0300
                  Equity Ratio   Return On/   ————
                                  Return Of
                                  Overall Rate   .1087

    Overage Rent   .12 Yield

Value Estimate:

Contract Net Income:	$44,025 ÷ .1087 = $405,014
Overage Rent:	$ 6,000 ÷ .12 =+ 50,000

Total Value Estimate: $455,014

Or: $455,000

Land	$100,000
Improvements	+ 360,000
Total:	$460,000*
Offering Price:	$475,000

Estimated Economic Life: 25 Years

Debt Service Requirement:

$$\text{Constant} \times \text{Mortgage Amount}$$
$$.1049 \times \$340,000 \qquad = \$35,666$$

Debt Service Coverage: 1.2
(Based on Contract Rent)

Cash Flow:

Net Income	$50,025
Debt Service	− 35,666
Cash Flow	$14,359
Yield on Equity	12%

$$\left(\frac{\$14,359 \text{ Cash Flow}}{\$120,000 \text{ Equity*}} \right)$$

Real Estate Taxable Income or Loss:

Net Income		$50,025
Mortgage Interest (9½% of $340,000)	$32,300	
Depreciation (25 Year Life, Straight-Line 4% of $360,000*)	+ 14,400	
Total:	$46,700	− 46,700
Real Estate Taxable Income:		$3,325†

*Assumes purchase price or cost of $460,000 and improvement cost allocation of $360,000.
† Requires an investor to incorporate own effective tax rate to calculate after-tax yield.

of value at an interest rate of 9½ percent for 25 years on a monthly in arrears payment schedule. Current terms would produce a constant of 10.49 percent, according to Table 13. The current term of loans is slightly longer than the estimated economic life of the property and the remaining term on the major leases, but lenders in the area are figuring on redevelopment and future expansion in the neighborhood.

The mortgage loan portion of the equation to develop a capitalization rate is .75 (mortgage-to-value ratio) × .1049 (constant) = .0787. The remaining equation for the equity portion is complicated by the existence of different credit ratings and different kinds of rents.

The credit rated tenants require an 11 percent return on and of for application to their contract rents. They occupy 5,500 square feet in the center and thus account for 11/16 of the space. The local tenants require a 13.5 percent return on and of for application to their contract rents. They occupy 2,500 square feet or 5/16 of the total space. The difference in the return on and of requirements reflects credit ratings and the terms of the leases involved.

The first part of the equity portion of the equation is:

Credit Tenants: .110 (return on and of) × 11/16 = .076

Local Tenants: .135 (return on and of) × 5/16 = +.042

$$\overline{.118}$$

With rounding, the equity portion of the equation, the part applicable to contract rents, is .25 (equity-to-value ratio) × .12 (return on and of) = .0300.

The total equation to establish the capitalization rate which can be applied to contract rent is:

.75 × .1049 = .0787

.25 × .12 = +.0300

Overall Rate =   .1087 or 10.87%

The return on the overage rent is 12 percent to reflect some additional risk. No provision for return of the investment applies to the overage rents because the capitalization rate developed for the contract rents already provides for it.

9. Value of the Property As can be anticipated if you have been following Worksheet 16, several mathematical calculations will be needed to estimate the value of the property. The 10.87 percent capitalization rate must be applied to the net income which results from contract rent. Thus, vacancy and collection losses and expenses must be subtracted from that portion of the gross income attributable to contract rent. The result is $44,025. At the same time, overage rent must be segregated. It amounts to $6,000. The next step is to divide the different kinds of rent by the two different functions we developed above.

A value estimate of $405,014 results from dividing $44,025 by .1087. Added to that is a value estimate of $50,000 from dividing overage rent of $6,000 by a .12 yield. The total value estimate comes to $455,014, say $455,000. The equations required are shown on Worksheet 16.

The value estimate of some $455,000 is $20,000 less than the offering price of $475,000. A bargaining point you might use to reduce the price would be the failure of the owner to negotiate an increase in rent from tenant B in the event that this tenant failed to reach projected sales volume. We will assume that an agreement is reached on a sale price of $460,000, which is only some one percent above the value estimate. A differential in value of up to ten percent is considered acceptable. Therefore, a price of $460,000 would be quite close to value. In a half-million dollar venture, five to ten thousand dollars is relatively immaterial. The impact on yield is minor.

10. Debt Service The mortgage loan, which is assumable by a purchaser, now amounts to $340,000, close to 75 percent of the estimated value of the property. The equity requirement is $120,000 ($460,000 purchase price - $340,000 loan = $120,000 equity). We have assumed in our analysis that the purchase price could be reduced to $460,000. The constant on the mortgage loan comprises 9½ percent interest for 25 years, the same as the terms available on new loans. These terms produce a constant of 10.49 percent or .1049, as a check of Table 13 will show.

Multiplying the loan amount of $340,000 by .1049 gives a debt service requirement of $35,666 a year. The net income attributable to contract rents is $44,025. Thus, the debt service coverage is 1.2 ($44,025 ÷ $35,666), which is considered secure for a property of this type. It is even more secure when you consider that the credit rated tenants' contract rents, after expenses have been subtracted, cover much of the debt service requirement.

11. Cash Flow With a total net income of $50,025 and debt service of $35,666, the difference amounts to $14,359 in cash flow. If we assume a purchase price close to the estimated value of the property, the equity requirement would be $120,000. Cash flow divided by equity gives a current yield on equity of 12 percent. This yield is quite a bit higher than investors are currently seeking, as their 12 percent requirement incorporates both yield and return of their investment. Thus, this investment looks exceptionally good. Of course, a purchase price which is higher than $460,000 would bring the 12 percent yield down.

12. Real Estate Taxable Income or Loss As shown on Worksheet 16, the interest portion of debt service amounts to $32,300 (9½ percent interest on a loan balance of $340,000). That leaves $3,366 of the total debt service payment for amortization in the first year.

The amount of interest will decline each year as interest forms a smaller and smaller proportion of debt service payments. To calculate depreciation for a shopping center, the straight-line method can be applied and a 25 year estimated life for the improvement is assumed. Depreciation will come to 4 percent of the improvements' cost or $14,400 each year.

Interest and depreciation together total $46,700. When that amount is subtracted from the net income, a positive real estate taxable income of $3,325 results. It is this amount which must be reported as taxable income from the property's operations. However, you may be able to use component depreciation to boost the depreciation write-offs in the early years of your investment in order to reduce the amount of taxable income. The taxes you may pay will depend on your personal tax situation. Thus, it is for you to decide what after-tax income is worth after you have estimated each year's total tax bill.

At a purchase price of $460,000, the shopping center rates as an unusually good acquisition to achieve current income. It would still be an excellent purchase at a somewhat higher price. Moreover, the area's dynamics are such that it should also prove to be a good capital appreciation buy, particularly as redevelopment seems likely. In both the shopping center and apartment building examples, we have chosen to show you what a good investment property's financial pro forma statement looks like, so that you can recognize how each test result affects the other portions of the analysis.

If you have followed Worksheet 13 and Worksheet 16 closely or looked at the blank worksheets we have provided for you at the end of this chapter, you have probably noticed that the net income figure is the base for all other comparisons. Thus, it is one function in the estimation of value, which tests the offering price on a property. It is also the figure from which debt service is subtracted to arrive at cash flow, the dollar amount you can pocket. In turn, cash flow is used to develop yield on equity, another test of the property's financial feasibility. In addition, the net income figure is a prerequisite of the calculation to establish real estate taxable income or loss. Because net income has such a major impact on so many economic determinants, its stabilization is critical.

A major difference between the professional and the amateur investor in real estate is a failure on the latter's part to provide for all the expenses which will have to be covered and for contingencies. In the short run, this failure will boost the net income figure. In any but the shortest run, it is likely to create major problems which will affect both income and capital appreciation results. Certainly, an inadequate allowance for maintenance will cause a property to lose value. An improvident allowance for vacancy and collection losses may result in a severe income loss when you can least afford it. You can examine the operating information developed by various property owners' associations in your effort to cover as many bases as possible. It is then possible to stabilize the figures by direct comparison with other properties in the vicinity and by applying careful judgement to the property in question.

A thoughtful analysis of a property's financial feasibility may result in a decision to forego acquiring the property. In fact, it is quite likely that this will occur several times. You can reduce its likelihood by making your goal and investor profile clear to a broker. Nonetheless, you will probably have to test the financial feasibility of several properties before you locate the one which is right for you. Don't become discouraged. A professional will often analyze the financial feasibility of 20 or more properties before finding the one which meets his or her objectives and desires.

WORKSHEET 17
Income Analysis

Tenants/Unit Size/ @ Base Rental	Rent			Lease	
	Contract	Overage	Other	Expiration	Stabilized

WORKSHEET 18
Expense Analysis

Item	As Given	Stabilized
Insurance	$	$
Real Estate Taxes		
Management		
Repairs		
Water		
Heat		
Electricity		
Supplies		
Scavenger		
Janitor		
Painting/Decorating		
Plowing		
Reserve for Replacements		
Exterminating		
Other		
	+	+
Total:	$	$

WORKSHEET 19
Pro Forma Analysis

	As Given	Stabilized
Income (From Worksheet 17)		
Contract Rent	$	$
Overage Rent		
Other Income	+ _____	+ _____
Gross Income	$	$
Vacancy and Collection Loss	− _____	− _____
Effective Gross Income	$	$
Expenses (From Worksheet 18)	− _____	− _____
Net Income	$	$

Development of Capitalization Rate:

Mortgage Portion   _____ × _____ =
                Loan-to-Value   Constant
                Ratio

Equity Portion   _____ × _____ = + _____
                Equity-to-Value   Return On/
                Ratio   Return Of

                Capitalization Rate: _____

Value Estimate:

   $ _____ ÷ _____ = $ _____
      Net Income   Capitalization   Value
                Rate   Estimate

           Or: $ _____

Land: $

Improvements: + _____

   Total: $

Offering Price: $

Estimated Economic Life: _____ Years

Debt Service Requirement:

Constant × Mortgage Amount

_____ × _____ = $

Debt Service Coverage:

$\left(\dfrac{\text{Net Income}}{\text{Debt Service}}\right)$

Cash Flow:

Net Income $

Debt Service − _____

Cash Flow $

Yield on Equity:

$\left(\dfrac{\text{Cash Flow}}{\text{Equity}}\right)$

Real Estate Taxable Income or Loss:

Net Income $

Mortgage Interest $

Depreciation   + _____   −

Total: $

Real Estate Taxable Income or Loss: $

Leases can be your highway to achieving success or they can be a fatal roadblock. Which it will be depends on the care you and your attorney expend on their design and on your ability to negotiate. Because the impact of lease provisions on the profitability of income-producing property is frequently neglected at great cost, leases deserve your special attention.

A lease represents an agreement which transfers certain rights from a property owner to another party. The lease itself is a legal document which effects the conveyance from one party to another of the rights specified, usually the rights to occupy and use the premises. For giving up certain rights or interests, a property owner is entitled to compensation and also to protection of the rights she or he retains.

The compensation and protection level required to induce a lessor to give up rights will depend upon the lessor's objectives. A lessee also has objectives, such as the use of premises for a particular purpose, whether residential or business in nature. Moreover, a lessee may need certain kinds of protection to ensure that its objectives can be satisfied.

At the start of negotiations, the objectives and protections sought by each party are opposed. For example, a landlord tends to want high rent for the loan of his or her property and may want a lessee to assume maintenance responsibility. A tenant naturally wants to pay the least possible compensation and may or may not want to undertake maintenance.

The opposing positions generally require negotiation. The negotiating process can be quite intense or it can be casual. In some cases, a statement from a lessee that the premises are satisfactory and acceptable on the terms offered is all that is necessary. Apartment rentals usually fall into the take-it-or-leave-it category and employ standardized leases developed by a real estate board to which few, if any, provisions are added. However, business leases are generally more complex. In many cases, they are negotiated clause by clause so that the legal document which results is uniquely suited to the needs and desires of both parties.

The relative strength of the parties will, to some degree, dictate the terms of a lease. A major tenant often has the ability to draft the terms much as it wants because the lessor generally receives non-rental benefits. Thus, a major tenant's name on a lease increases the value of a property, the amount of financing which can be obtained and often the attractiveness of the financing terms which are offered. If a low credit tenant is involved, the advantage tends to lie with the landlord.

A natural limit to the pursuit of an advantage exists. The stronger party can not set terms which destroy the ability of the other party to meet its objectives and still expect the lease to be accepted. Even if such terms are accepted, through ignorance or for some other reason, it will be to little avail. If rent is set too high or the kinds of merchandise which can be sold are defined too narrowly, a tenant's business may fail. Conversely, if the rents or various protections are not sufficient, an owner may lose a property to a lender. A lessor and a lessee must both be able to prosper.

As a consequence, a lease is a compromise which results from negotiations intended to arrive at conditions which can satisfy the objectives of both parties. Because these objectives always encompass both the present and the future, a lease should reflect the parties' best estimates of current and future conditions. As an example, for the past 30 years, the key issue has involved the question of the future direction of the entire real estate market. Thus, the negotiated document protects both the present and the long-term features of the objectives of the parties to the lease.

Before negotiating any lease, or indeed any contract, you should consider exactly what you must have, what you would like to obtain, and what you must reject in order to achieve your current and future objectives. For example, your objective strategy may make it important to sign a franchisor rather than a franchisee because you would then have a better credit on the lease and a more valuable property. This requirement would mean negotiating with the franchisor and, perhaps, having to trade off some other condition for its signature.

At the same time, you should think through what a tenant's objectives are likely to be and what you may have to give up if a tenant is to survive and prosper. This analysis will aid you at a bargaining table where you are in the lessor position. It will also serve you well in the future if you change sides to become a lessee.

Planning ahead allows you to determine the best method of accomplishing what you want to achieve now and in the future. The various methods by which you can seek to achieve a goal are a function of objectives, the economics of a situation, relative strength and the type of property involved. For example, expense exposure solutions range from the net lease appropriate to a single user property through the escalators applied to certain multi-tenant operations to the short leases typical of other kinds of property.

Great attention must be given to thinking out changes which might occur over time. While the future can not be predicted exactly, it is certain that change will take place. Discussions with leasing agents, attorneys and accountants may alert you to changes now in progress. In addition, each clause in a lease should be tested for its ability to cover contingencies that now seem remote, but which may impact significantly on future returns.

A lease is a legal contract which is binding as of a certain date and for a stated period of time in the future. This quality renders a lease static unless you and your professional advisors consciously attempt to design its provisions to reflect the dynamic nature of real estate and people's activities. The changes which may occur can be social or economic, political or technological. Each clause must be evaluated not only to discover how the present condition of these four variables impacts on a lease and, thus, on a property, but also how well the lease provisions will be able to handle any changes in these conditions.

For example, it was common 20 years ago for leases to provide for decreasing rentals at renewal time. The theory then held that premises deteriorated over the period of a lease and thus would be worth less to a user in the future. In an inflationary environment, the exact opposite is true. Thus, many of today's leases provide for increased rentals at renewal.

Also common many years ago was the requirement that a landlord pay all expenses. Today, a major way for a landlord to protect her or his income is to place responsibility for expenses on a tenant. A major shift in economic analysis was required to effect this change. This shift encompassed the recognition that a business tenant has access to income which increases for the same reasons that expense charges do. In any economic environment in which inflation plays a part, inflation will increase both a property's operating expenses and a tenant's ability to raise prices on its source of income. Thus, price increases on industrial production, services and retail merchandise serve to reimburse tenants for increased costs due to inflation.

Unless a lease makes some provision for inflation, a property owner's income and yield will decline as inflation pushes expenses up. For example, if a property's cash flow were $10,000 and cash equity amounted to $100,000, its owner's yield would be ten percent. As you will recall, an increase in an owner's expenses will cause the owner's income and yield to decline proportionately. Thus, in this case, a $5,000 jump in expenses would cut cash flow by $5,000 and yield to five percent; that is, it would halve cash flow and yield.

The current expense theory revolves around keeping a landlord at least whole as a minimum requirement for him or her to commit capital to a property. In multi-housing investments, this means the landlord must have the opportunity to raise rents periodically to capture enough of the tenants' increasing personal incomes to keep yield constant. With business tenants whose incomes are the direct result of the use of a property, it means tapping into these sources of income and/or shifting expenses wholly to tenants.

Thus, a landlord attempts to shift expenses to a tenant because the tenant is the party who is benefiting from the use of the property and who has the ability to absorb expense increases. Moreover, a landlord also tries to offset inflation's impact on the purchasing power of net income by participating in a tenant's business through retail overage rentals or a percentage share in industrial production. Analyzing the economic assumptions behind lease provisions in terms of inflationary and deflationary effects will help you draft lease provisions which protect your position in either situation.

Your posture is also critical. If you are overeager to sign a tenant, you will weaken your position at the bargaining table. To prevent this from happening, a reserve of sufficient working capital is often necessary. It will enable you to reject a tenant who is likely to defeat your purposes in favor of one who will further them. For example, a feature of your objective strategy may require the pursuit of higher quality tenants. Waiting to obtain them or renovating to attract them will be facilitated by an adequate working capital position.

In a book of this size, we can not hope to cover all the lease clauses you may someday need to negotiate. Some leases have 350 provisions, each of which is important now or may in the future be critical to the success of the parties concerned. Those which we have chosen to discuss apply to a wide variety of properties and cover many of the major points. You can apply the analysis developed here to most of the lease conditions you may need or encounter in the future. The 25 basic provisions include the following:

1. Date of lease and parties
2. Description of property
3. Construction
4. Alterations, additions and improvements
5. Term
6. Rent
7. Recordkeeping
8. Options
9. Assignments and subletting
10. Type of business
11. Use of premises
12. Utilities

13. Insurance

14. Maintenance and repairs

15. Signs

16. Association

17. Eminent domain

18. Destruction of property

19. Notice

20. Access

21. Subordination

22. Remedies for default

23. Surrender

24. Security deposits

25. Miscellaneous

1. Date of Lease and Parties A lease becomes a contract only when there is an offer by one party, it is accepted by the other party, and both sign. There may be a difference between the date the contract is signed and the date the lease terms become effective. If that is the case, it is important to spell out in the lease the responsibilities, if any, of either party in the event something changes between the two dates, such as destruction of the premises by fire. Otherwise, one party may owe the other something not intended, such as a reconstructed building.

The parties to a lease are the ones who must sign it. Thus, one party may be a franchisor or franchisee, depending on your objective and your ability to have one or the other sign. In the case of an individual apartment tenant about whose ability to pay you are doubtful, you may want to have a parent or other financially responsible party co-sign. That would provide you with a backup for payments if the tenant defaults.

2. Description of Property The premises to which the rights of use and occupancy apply must be accurately defined. Each feature of the property should be described in the lease or shown on an accurate map or floor plan attached to the lease. Relevant features include location, size of lot, size of improvements, kinds of improvements, and whatever else is part of the property to be rented. The description must also clearly define the terms employed which will affect rent or use. For example, the provisions for calculating gross area, net leasable area or any other term on which rent will be based must be specified.

All rights must be defined. This includes ingress and egress rights and easements the lessor may already have granted to a third party or retain the right to grant in the future. In addition, the right to enter the property to service a third party's advertising sign or for any other purpose must be specified.

3. Construction   If new construction or renovation is involved, the lease should define in detail the specific responsibilities of the parties. Construction or renovation specifications should be attached to the lease to define the amount, quality and kind of work which will be done. The lease should also cover the date of possession, the condition in which the premises will be delivered to the lessee, and the circumstances which might cause the start of the lease to be delayed without rendering it void. For example, the lease should specify exactly what is to happen if the improvements are destroyed before the lease term commences, so that no unintentional liability is created for either rental payments or capital commitments.

4. Alterations, Additions and Improvements   If a change in the property is to be made by a tenant, the lease should cover how damages to the property will be handled, either at the time the changes are made or at the end of the lease. Each change should require approval in advance from the lessor, including approval of the workforce which will perform the alterations, additions or improvements. These generally become the property of the lessor at the end of a lease, but this too should be spelled out. You may want to add a clause giving the landlord the option at the termination of the lease of requiring the tenant to remove any changes made.

Alterations, additions and improvements, depending on their nature, can have considerable impact on a property's value and income stream. You may get back a property which has additional space that you can then lease at a higher rental. Alternatively, you may get back a property which has been so changed as to render it unusable by any other tenant without extensive work. You can rely on either a clause which allows you to refuse permission to make any changes or one which requires heavy penalties for failure to return the premises in the condition in which they were leased. The former gives you the leeway to approve changes that will impact favorably on the property's financial results.

This provision can also be utilized to effect a renovation you want undertaken at your tenant's expense. Tying down the amount, quality and kind of work in the lease will serve to protect your property and to achieve the kind of renovation you want accomplished. A provision which requires an architect of your choice to approve each stage of work will serve to enforce your wishes. How you handle this provision will depend on your objectives. A shoddy renovation will lower the value of a property, but might allow you to obtain the level of interim income you are seeking.

5. Term Rent levels are generally tied to the term of a lease. Thus, the term negotiated is a critical component of any lease. To some extent, the term depends on the type of tenant to which you rent. Apartment tenants and small business tenants generally have short-term leases, while single tenant users on net leases have longer term leases.

However, within these perimeters you have room to apply your strategic objectives. For example, you may decide to offer a very low first year rental to a new business in which you have confidence in order to give the business time to establish itself. Each subsequent year of the lease, you can require a higher rent. By structuring the terms and the rents in this manner, you can give yourself an opportunity to participate in any success at a much higher overall rent than if you had given the tenant a lease with a single term at a flat, fixed rental.

A short-term lease allows you to change the contract rent to reflect economic rent at frequent intervals. But, your risks are twofold: You are more exposed to vacancy losses and economic rent may decline in the future. A long-term lease with a strong tenant will transfer the vacancy risk to the end of a longer period, but can expose you to a significant differential between economic rent and contract rent.

Lease terms can be for one specific period of time, such as an apartment lease which terminates in two years, with no obligation in most jurisdictions on the part of the landlord to offer a new lease. The term can also include options providing for the same rental, higher rent or declining rent, depending on your objective and your assessment of future conditions.

A strategy requiring an increase in income at stated intervals can be handled by having the term of the lease end at the first interval. If economic conditions have improved, you may then be able to re-lease the premises at a higher rental. This strategy could also be achieved by negotiating stepped increases in rent or the right to re-evaluate the rent at stated intervals within the overall term of the lease to bring contract rent into line with economic rent on the dates specified.

The terms of existing leases on a property you may acquire should be evaluated in a like manner. For example, the leases may all expire at the same time, which would expose you to a higher vacancy risk. Existing leases with options to renew or extend the term should be tested as to whether you think the tenants are likely to renew or extend and what their decision would do to your chances of achieving your objective.

Acquiring a property with existing leases obligates you to honor them. If you are investing for turnover purposes, you may require a property on which all the leases will terminate within a short period so that you can enter the premises to start construction or renovation. Alternatively, you may want to see staggered terminations because your capital position requires you to stage the work. A special problem can arise with residential tenants who do not always vacate the premises when their leases end or when their non-lease status is revoked. As residential leases do not usually contain heavy penalties for failure to vacate, you must protect yourself by acquiring the property subject to gaining possession as of a certain date. If the tenants fail to leave as of that date, the sale is nullified and you have protected yourself from exposure to heavy carrying charges while you attempted to remove them.

6. Rent There are many kinds of rent. The basic distinction is between rent you are guaranteed because the exact amount is stipulated in the lease and all other sources of income from a property. The latter includes service income, such as charges for the use of a pool or laundry machines in an apartment or mobile home property and fees for providing office cleaning services.

Additional income from business tenants can include a charge for heating, ventilating and air conditioning (HVAC) and payments for common area maintenance. Selling utility services to tenants can also boost income. In the latter case, you may want to have the tenants individually metered. Then, you can purchase gas or electricity from a utility at a bulk rate on your mass meter and resell it at a higher retail rate according to usage recorded on the tenants' individual meters.

If you have chosen retail real estate, you may want to combine a minimum guaranteed rent with overage rent from gross sales if you think you can better achieve your objective by participating in a tenant's business. Depending upon your analysis of the sales volume projections for a tenant's business, you may want to make the minimum rent relatively low or high, with contrary overage provisions.

In order to meet your objectives, you may decide to accept a lower yield because of a current low rental and to pay more for a property. You could lease to a tenant who will renovate and, thereby, increase your property's value. This will require considering whether to let the tenant pay no rent for the renovation period or a lower rent than it would otherwise have been charged. Alternatively, you may rent to a higher quality tenant and receive less current income in return for the desired boost in value.

Stops or escalators on business leases, which are used to handle expenses on multi-tenant properties, can also be considered additional rent. Escalators require a landlord to pay a base amount for expenses, perhaps 50 cents a square foot at a time when expenses are running one dollar a square foot. The tenants pay the difference between the capped amount the landlord pays and actual expenses. This could be just the 50 cents difference as above or it could involve much more if expenses go up. Property taxes may be handled by a tax escalator provision above a tax stop, which is the base amount the landlord is obligated to pay. Sometimes the terms are used interchangeably. One issue to check carefully is whether the tenants are obligated to pick up all expenses over the base amount regardless of vacancies or whether the landlord will be exposed to all expenses allocable to a vacant unit.

On a single user property, you may be able to negotiate a net lease that makes all expenses the tenant's responsibility, without even a base amount obligation on the landlord. The degree to which the net lease is loophole-proof will have a major impact on the rent you receive from the property.

A cost-of-living clause to protect income from inflation is likely to result in additional income. Another way to achieve the same end may be to provide for raising the rent at stated intervals in proportion to any increase in the property's value. This provision would require a reappraisal of the property, the expense of which you may be able to pass off to a tenant.

If your goal is high current income, you may be most concerned with its quantity. Conversely, if your goal involves selling or refinancing a property in order to obtain a lump sum, you may want to concentrate on the income's quality. Your strategy may require negotiating a delayed commencement of rent payments or a certain income stream, in the form of either monthly, quarterly, semi-annual or annual payments. The longer you have to wait for your income in an inflationary environment, the less it is likely to be worth in purchasing power. Thus, the amount may have to increase to correct for inflation's effects.

Each of the different forms of rent and expense pass-throughs will greatly affect the amount of net income you receive. You will remember that the amount of rent brought down to net income is one function in estimating value and the amount of financing a lender may be willing to advance you. You must also take into account the annual amount of rent which can be brought down to after-tax income in order to calculate your profit.

7. Recordkeeping Requiring a tenant to keep certain records is advisable when any kind of participation income above a guaranteed rent is possible. This includes rent tied to retail sales, occupancy levels at hotels, industrial production levels, and crop yields for farmlands.

The provision should require a tenant to keep records which will enable a landlord to calculate the additional rental to which he or she is entitled and to check that the figure on which the additional rent is based is an accurate one. Thus, this clause usually provides for certification of monthly, quarterly, semi-annual or annual reports by someone the landlord agrees to accept and allows the landlord to have an accountant conduct an audit at the lessee's expense. It can also include the right to have an auditor actually check cash registers or other units in operation to estimate daily sales volume or other production measurement.

Related to this is the need for a careful definition of the unit of measurement upon which additional rent will be based. In retail situations, this means that the term gross sales must specifically exclude such items as returns.

8. Options The real issue involved in offering options to a tenant or acquiring a property encumbered with leases which have options is your estimate of future economic conditions. If you think inflation will continue, you want to be able to receive higher income in the future. You would certainly not want to offer a tenant a fixed rental for a future period or continue the same rental, as it is impossible to predict exactly how much inflation will ensue. If you think rents will go down in the future, you may want to lock a tenant into today's current economic rent for as long a period as possible. As in so much related to real estate, you will have to back your best judgement.

There are three ways to handle a longer term than the initial period specified. One is simply to have no option in the lease. You and the lessee will then have the opportunity to come to an agreement on a new lease when the original one expires. The second provides for an option to renew. The conditions can be either the same as or different from those controlling the first period. The third method involves an option to extend, which gives a tenant the right to extend a lease under the same conditions for a stated period.

The tenant is usually the one to exercise an option. A provision should be included that requires a tenant with an option to inform the landlord of its intentions sufficiently in advance of the exercise date to allow the landlord a reasonable period in which to seek out a new tenant if the option is not going to be exercised.

9. Assignments and Subletting Anything which decreases the control a landlord has over a property may be detrimental to the achievement of her or his objectives. Either an assignment by a tenant of its entire interest in a lease to another party or a subletting, where a portion of the tenant's rights are passed to a sublessee but the original tenant remains liable for meeting the provisions of its lease, can mean that an undesirable tenant will occupy and use the premises. This in turn can lower the value of the property or jeopardize the receipt of income.

As a result, you may want to forbid both or you may require any right to assign or sublet to be subject to your written approval. The latter could mean that the original tenant will be obligated to undertake the task of finding a new tenant if for some reason the sublessee must vacate the premises. This could save you considerable time and effort. If you do permit a change in tenant under a subleasing provision, you may also want to make it an occasion to raise the original tenant's rent so that you can participate in the going economic rent.

A tenant to whom a lease is assigned assumes the exact terms of the original lease. However, a sublease's terms may be completely different from the conditions of the original lease as long as the sublease does not violate the original lease in any way. A lessee which negotiates a sublease with a sublessee can receive higher rent or otherwise change the sublease's terms to benefit the lessee. This can provide a worthwhile opportunity to create a sandwich position in which you lease a fee from its owner under certain conditions and then sublease the premises to a user at more advantageous terms.

The assignments and subletting clause can be drafted to provide a lessee with major protections. It can prevent the unregulated substitution of tenants, which might disturb the compatibility of a retail center's tenant mix, the quiet enjoyment of premises in an office or apartment building, or the ability of some industrial tenants to function.

10. Type of Business The nature of the business which can be conducted on the premises should be stipulated and any change in it should require the written consent of the landlord. In addition, the lease should forbid illegal or immoral business uses, to protect the landlord from any damages that might arise from the nature of illegal or immoral businesses. For example, you may rent premises to an ink manufacturer and subsequently discover that this use is illegal because of zoning. This could cause your insurance policies to be invalidated if they exclude illegal or immoral uses.

This provision can protect both landlord and tenant. For example, a landlord may want to exclude a blueprint operation on the grounds that the odor it produces would lessen the attractiveness of the property to other tenants. A manufacturing business above an office which you wanted to rent to a doctor would effectively render the premises unsuitable for a medical office. A landlord should also exclude any business which might damage a property. Thus, a tenant utilizing large amounts of water should be prohibited from floors located above ground level.

In addition, compatibility of uses has a direct effect on rents and, therefore, value. Preplanning for a multi-tenant business property should include an analysis of the kinds of businesses which will enhance overall tenant operations and, thus, tend to increase the amount of business they do and the rent they can pay. In retail properties, neither too broad nor too narrow a definition of the merchandise which can be sold or the store types which can occupy the premises is most conducive to achieving objectives. Thus, a provision which allows a supermarket to merchandise all the food sold within a shopping center would require you to give up a later opportunity to rent space to a restaurant, a use which would be likely to increase the center's overall sales volumes.

11. Use of Premises This provision can be developed into a major source of protection for both lessor and lessee. It should detail both the use or uses to which a tenant is obligated to put the premises and those that are forbidden.

In a retail lease, this provision can be used to specify hours of operation, adequate maintenance of stock and an appropriate number of employees to ensure that a business will be conducted in a manner which will enable gross sales to reach projected volumes. In addition, it can require merchandise to be offered at retail prices and forbid warehousing which would lower sales, and also fire sales.

In a residential lease, a tenant may be forbidden to conduct a business in an apartment unit which would make it likely that the other tenants would not renew their leases. This provision can also require acceptable behavior in any common areas. An industrial lease may include a provision to protect an industrial tenant which uses sensitive instruments in its operations from adjacent uses that would disrupt the first tenant's ability to function.

Of major importance is a clause forbidding abandonment of the premises while the tenant is still paying rent. Vacant space quickly causes a decline in a property's appearance and therefore can lower its value. Vacancy may also attract vandalism.

The tenant should also be required to use the premises in such a manner that its operation will not impact unfavorably on any insurance carried on the property. This includes improper storage of paints and other dangerous materials. In appropriate circumstances, a lessor may also want to use this provision to forbid noise that can be heard outside the premises, alcoholic beverages or anything else which would tend to lower the value of the property.

12. Utilities The lease should make clear which party is obligated to pay for electricity, gas, water and sewer charges, fuel and air conditioning. If the tenant will be responsible, the lease should also specify the basis, such as lineal front foot, cubic foot, metered or other, upon which the charges will be made as well as the rate that will be applied.

This provision can be used to require a lessee to supply air conditioning or other utility units or to conserve energy and water. If tenants will share some common area, such as a parking lot or an entrance to a shopping mall, the lease can specify how they will divide up responsibility for lighting, heating or air conditioning the space. You may even need to write in a provision which penalizes shopping center tenants for using common area heating or air conditioning to heat or cool their own premises.

13. Insurance You may want to insist on an apartment tenant's purchase of contents insurance. That could prevent a claim for damage in the event of a fire which incidentally destroys a tenant's belongings.

In a business lease, the responsibility for carrying insurance should be defined. For example, a lessee may be obligated to carry certain amounts of public liability, plate glass, property damage and boiler insurance and also appropriate insurance on its own fixtures. A lessor may be required to carry property insurance and public liability insurance for common areas.

Except for the insurance policy covering a tenant's fixtures, policies should normally name both the lessor and the lessee as payees to increase the protection of each party's rights. Moreover, the provision should specify the insurance amounts which must be carried, the party responsible for paying premiums and the way in which renewals will be handled. In a net lease situation, you may prefer that insurance premiums be sent to you for you to transmit to the insurance company. You can then be certain that the insurance is being kept current. An inadequate insurance clause may mean that your property could be destroyed without adequate compensation.

14. Maintenance and Repairs Again, responsibility is the key issue. In apartment leases, a tenant can be required only to keep the interior of an apartment in as good condition as it was received from the landlord, subject to normal wear and tear like scuffed paint. The lessor is obligated to make any repairs necessary to keep an apartment habitable. In a multi-tenant property, the lessor is also generally required to maintain any common areas, such as hallways, stairs and elevators.

With business tenants, the responsibility can be negotiated to place it entirely on the lessor or the lessee, or to share it. Each obligation, such as the replacement of broken glass, painting frequency and air conditioning equipment servicing must be listed, and the party responsible specified. A particularly strong clause may be needed to prevent littering from building up around certain retail operations and causing a decline in value.

If you are negotiating a single user net lease, do not overlook the question of responsibility for structural repairs. If structural repairs to the interior, exterior or to sidewalks and other improvements are not made the responsibility of the tenant, an expense exposure is created for the landlord. As structural repairs are likely to be needed over the term of a net lease, income could be severely affected.

The point at which repairs and maintenance end and replacement begins should be defined, particularly if repairs and maintenance are the tenant's responsibility and replacement is the landlord's. You may also want to require the use of union labor on any work to be done.

The consequences of any failure to maintain and repair the property as the lease requires should be set out. For example, a lessee may have the right to make repairs which are the landlord's responsibility and then deduct an appropriate amount from the rent. The lessor may want the right to make repairs if necessary and then bill the tenant for their cost. Strong remedies are desirable as the soundness and appearance of a property will affect both a firm's ability to conduct a business and a landlord's return on her or his investment.

If you are seeking light management responsibilities to satisfy your investor profile, you may require a net lease which shifts all maintenance and repair responsibilities to a tenant. As you will be providing fewer services, a somewhat lower rent payment is likely to result. In contrast, you may want to increase your income by offering maintenance services to a tenant for an additional fee.

15. Signs How this provision is handled will affect the value of your property. The clause should make clear the kinds of signs which can be erected, their size, lettering style and placement. For example, you may want to forbid the hanging of signs out windows and on doors of an apartment building.

Signs are important to business users because they serve to attract and retain business. Thus, their placement and attractiveness can have a major impact on the operations of a business. Generally, uniformity of style bespeaks a higher quality of operation.

The clause should specify the party responsible for erecting and maintaining the signs and for securing any necessary permits. Awnings should also be covered as they can have a similar effect on business and on the value of a property. You know yourself what attracts you to certain stores and not to others.

16. Association This provision applies to multi-tenant operations. It provides tenants who live or operate businesses in one property a means to achieve an objective or lessen the potential for disputes.

In shopping centers, merchants may find it useful to group together to handle common area maintenance and promotion of the center. An association provision can obligate each tenant to join the merchants' association and pay dues or other assessments based on some fair share measurement. To a great degree, an association can create a center's public image. It can also be the body responsible for determining operating hours and setting the amount each tenant must spend on advertising an individual store. It can require the advertisements to mention both the shopping center and its address in order to build public identification.

An industrial assocation can be formed to enforce covenants that protect industrial tenants in an industrial park. Office tenants may want an association to maintain some control over security. A residential association may serve to promote group activities and to handle complaints or problems.

A successful association tends to produce effective standards. If you decide to set one up, you should spell out its activities in such a way that its effects on a property will be most beneficial. In addition, both you and the association should have the right under each lease to sue a lessee which does not cooperate or pay a fair contribution. The lease should also make failure to contribute or to cooperate a cause for lease termination.

17. Eminent Domain   The lease should provide for the possibility that the government will take all or part of a property. For example, you may want to terminate a lease when the government takes all of the property, but provide for payment of rent to the date on which the government takes title. If a partial taking occurs, you may want to terminate the lease as to the part taken and continue the lease on the portion remaining, subject to a proportionate rent abatement. This provision should also cover any reconstruction that might be necessary, such as a new entrance or new parking spaces, the party responsible for undertaking the work, and the period in which the reconstruction is to be completed.

18. Destruction of Property   A lease usually provides for cancellation by either party if a property is totally destroyed. Whether or not you elect to rebuild or have a tenant rebuild in the event of a partial destruction may depend on the extent of the damage. The lease should specify the party responsible for any work, the party which will pay for it, its quality and any conditions of the lease which you may want to change as a result of a partial destruction and rebuilding. This provision should also require the removal of fixtures which might impede construction work and specify the amount of rent to be paid during the rebuilding process.

19. Notice   This provision is used to prevent a claim that a party was improperly notified of something which affects its interest. This can include an obligation to repair, or an intent to renew. It can also be used to cover the possibility that a tenant which is supposed to be making payments directly to a mortgagee has let them lapse. The addresses of both parties, the method of informing the other party that an address has changed, the form of the notice such as registered mail, and the proper person to whom notices should be sent must be specified. In addition, if a time limit applies to any required response, as it frequently does, its commencement should be mutually defined, perhaps by using a postmark date or a meter's time stamping as a protection.

20. Access A tenant has the right to exclusive possession of the premises unless otherwise specified. A landlord can legitimately claim the right of access to the premises for the purposes, among others, of showing a prospective tenant around, making repairs or inspections, or servicing a roof sign. However, these reserved rights must be written into a lease with the purposes for which access is sought clearly stated.

21. Subordination Because a lease may be recorded prior to obtaining a mortgage loan, it could take priority over a mortgage recording and thus prevent the granting of a loan. A lease should contain a provision requiring a lessee to subordinate the lease to any mortgage at the request of a mortgagee. In fairness, this provision should also state that a tenant has a right to nondisturbance of occupancy and use as long as the tenant is not in default under the terms of the lease. This provision will generally prevent a tenant from losing its interest in the event of foreclosure.

22. Remedies for Default This provision contains reasons for terminating a lease and a lessee's right to occupy or use the premises. It usually covers a failure to pay rent for over ten days, failure to perform other obligations for over 30 days, a bankruptcy judgement, a lessee's assignment of its lease to creditors or a writ of execution or attachment against the leasehold or a lessee's property which is not released within a stated period, and also a vacancy or abandonment of the premises caused by a lessee.

The provision should also define the way in which extensions of time for the purpose of curing defaults will be handled. Another essential clause is one allowing a lessor the right under the provisions of the lease to re-enter the premises to take possession as well as a right to accelerate any rent payments due and to relet the premises. In addition, the provision may permit a landlord to place a lien on a lessee's property to ensure a lessee's compliance with all terms of the lease.

23. Surrender A lessee is generally required to surrender premises to a lessor in a certain condition at the end of a lease term. A lease may provide for continuation on a month-to-month or year-to-year basis at the lessor's option. If the lessor decides to allow continuation, then he or she may charge double rent to prompt the tenant to leave by the end of the continuation.

If you think you can re-lease the premises to another tenant at an increased rental at the end of a lease, you will require the specification of severe penalties with regard to holdover. In addition, care should be taken to specify the removal of any fixtures, additions, alterations and improvements you may want removed and to provide for repair of any damage caused by removal. The condition of the premises as they are returned to you will affect the value of the property and its future rentability.

24. Security Deposits Deposits are primarily a means of protection against damage to a property. If you consider it likely that repairs will be necessary when you get the property back, perhaps because small children have had the use of it, you may want to insist on a relatively large deposit. In some areas, residential security deposits must be held apart from a landlord's funds and interest must be paid on them. You may also want to obtain a cleaning deposit to cover the cost of any abnormal cleaning required to get premises ready for re-leasing.

The size of the deposits you can obtain from business tenants generally depends on your strength, the credit of the tenant and the purpose you foresee for them. If you require security deposits, you will want to make certain a clause is inserted in any lease you write which will prevent you from becoming embroiled in any dispute over the handling of security deposits in the event a new owner takes title to the property. This clause will prevent you from being followed by disputes which occur after you have sold a property.

25. Miscellaneous This clause or series of clauses can include any item deemed necessary to achieve your objectives or necessary to protect your property. One provision might be payment by a lessee of all fees and expenses due to default. Another might cover a broker's commission. A third might be a disclaimer that a lessor was the partner of a retail lessee, despite participation in gross sales, to prevent any liability on the lessor's part arising from the lessee's operations. An important provision would be one denying a tenant the right to create a leasehold interest in your property. The purpose of each clause is to provide protection of one kind or another.

This section of a lease can also be used to develop what is called an escape clause. Such a clause places a requirement on a tenant which can not be met. In most cases, the condition is never enforced. However, if circumstances arise in which it is necessary to break a lease, this clause may allow you to do so legally and without penalty.

A further legal point involves antidiscrimination laws. You can not under any circumstances discriminate against any person on the basis of race, religion, color, ethnic origin or any other quality covered by federal, state or local laws. In fact, there is no correlation between any of these qualities and a tenant's willingness and ability to meet lease terms.

Antidiscrimination laws are changing to cover more groups, as present attempts to prevent a landlord from refusing to rent to families with children illustrate. In addition, recent court decisions have made it harder to regulate the mix of tenants in retail centers. Nonetheless, you have the right to set use criteria as long as you make them explicit before you show a property so no one can claim that you are practicing illegal discrimination.

From the landlord's point of view, the purpose of a lease is to obtain compensation for giving up the rights to occupy and use the premises and to get the property back at the end of the lease in good condition. From a lessee's point of view, the purpose of a lease is to obtain premises which will facilitate a personal or business objective.

One example of how these goals can be compromised to benefit both parties is the sale-leaseback. An owner-occupier of a property may decide to sell it to an investor and then lease the premises back. The former owner-occupier retains the use of the property, but gains capital and the ability to deduct all the costs of using the property in the form of its rental payments. The rental payment includes a provision to the new owner to cover return on and of his or her investment, but the tenant is able to deduct the total amount of rent being paid as a business expense. The investor gains an income stream, the right to use any tax shelter the property generates, and any increase in value which may occur.

For both parties to a lease, it is beneficial to have all rights and obligations spelled out as precisely as possible to prevent disappointments and unnecessary disputes. To that end, every conceivable contingency should be covered in a manner that will further both parties' objectives. Covering all eventualities is also important because a lease endures for a certain period into the future when conditions may differ from those of today.

The value of an income-producing property is the present worth of receiving the future benefits of an income stream plus the residual value of a property when it is returned by a lessee. Most lease provisions bear directly on either the income stream or the value of a property at the end of the lease or on both. The other provisions, such as the notice clause, make it easier to carry out the intent of the lease.

In addition, the acceptance of one lessee will prevent you from renting the premises to another for the term of the lease. This dictates careful examination of an existing or potential tenant's credit and reputation with a view to their effect on the quantity, quality and durability of income, your yield, and the value of your property.

Particular attention should be paid to the composition of the income and to the means provided for maintaining or increasing the value of a property in order to meet your objectives and your investor profile. You may have a high level of security uppermost in your mind or a definite amount of cash flow with receipts at certain preferred intervals, perhaps to pay college expenses for your children. You may have your eye more on capital appreciation than on current income or tax shelter. Your choices should dictate what you attempt to achieve through negotiation.

We have exerted every effort in this book to map out the inner workings of the real estate investment process so that you can make informed decisions on the direction you intend to take. We hope we have made it clear that *your* objective is the principal key to designing a successful real estate investment strategy. If you elect to invest in real estate or to expand your real estate investment program, your individual objective choices will allow you to control a route which will lead to an increase in your net worth or disposable income.

The process of identifying your objectives will require you to draw heavily upon your investor profile. This, in turn, requires you to analyze your own present and future needs and motivations. Since the development of your profile will enable you both to identify objectives and to flesh out your choices, any effort this activity requires is well worthwhile. Your design of a complete picture, incorporating your profile and your objective, can then be used to help you determine all subsequent moves.

Thus, your profile may involve: High risks, a very short investment term, some technical ability to renovate a house, and a desire for a lump sum of capital almost immediately. If that is the case, you have effectively defined for yourself an objective of a certain kind of capital turnover. This profile may cause you to focus upon somewhat rundown properties which you can acquire and, after making only cosmetic changes, quickly sell to produce the kind of profit you want.

Your personal choices will also dictate whether or not you will need outside assistance. You can select a real estate broker who can help you locate suitable properties and an architect who can check out their physical soundness and perhaps make design or material suggestions which will save you time and effort. Your choice also means that you will need a lawyer to go over and draw up sales contracts and alert you to any legal restrictions on a property which might interfere with your purpose in acquiring it. You may also need an accountant to help you establish the financial feasibility of a specific property. If property values are changing rapidly, you may want to have an appraiser give you an estimate of value when you are ready to sell.

You can begin to observe what is happening to real estate in the area which interests you and may discover that users are fixing up older properties. You may hear a great deal of talk from users and brokers about the special Victorian detailwork in and on the older properties. You may also notice that income levels are changing. In addition, a more convenient bus schedule may have been announced for the bus line which serves the neighborhood. You can then use this information to start identifying opportunities. The higher incomes may mean that renovation of retail stores on the bus route would be an effective way to meet your objectives. Or perhaps there seems to be enough demand for houses with Victorian decoration to warrant analyzing the potential investment opportunity.

Starting small with a slightly dilapidated house may mean you can afford to select the sole proprietor vehicle of ownership in order to have complete control over your investment. However, if a check with lenders reveals that you will need more capital than you have at present in order to acquire even the smallest property, you might start to think about optioning or leasing a property for a period that will be long enough to complete renovation. You could also turn over in your mind whether you want to become the general partner in a limited partnership composed of friends.

Just as your investor profile and objective served to help you select a type of property, your informed interest in it will concentrate your attention so that you can observe the entire activity level relating to it. If the signals you observe are positive, you can follow up with a market analysis keyed to discovering whether there is effective demand for purchasing newly renovated properties. In turn, if the market analysis produces positive results, you can then use the detailed understanding it has helped you develop of the market layer's wants, needs and income levels to direct your selection of a property. The market analysis can also help you define more precisely the kind of renovation work, such as retention of old-fashioned claw leg tubs, which would appeal to the viable layer you have discovered.

At this point in the process, your broker can be instructed to start turning up properties which you can test for financial feasibility. If market demand is strong enough to support the sale of a property almost immediately after you have fixed it up for a sum which will yield you the profit you seek, you can enter into negotiations to purchase it.

Your capital position, your understanding of value and price and the results of a financial analysis will provide you with a figure which will set a cap on what you can pay and still reach your goal. In addition, your capital position and your choice of ownership vehicle will dictate certain of your negotiating points. For example, you may need to have the seller agree to a purchase money mortgage, or an option or lease to enable you to acquire the rights which will further your objective. If you decide the latter two are what you need, you can focus on the protections which should be contained in the lease relating to the renovation process. Thus, an option to acquire the property as of a set date must provide for renovation delays and for an appropriate marketing period.

If you have built this entire process solidly on the foundation of your investor profile and objective, the odds for your success will be much higher than they otherwise would have been. The same process as described above applies if you are seeking income, tax shelter or capital appreciation from any type of property. Your analytical portrait of yourself will direct you along the series of choices necessary to put an investment together.

In addition, your investigation of yourself will guide you through the process of analyzing all the components of real estate. Each choice concerning a component must relate back to your investor profile and your objective. For example, you will need to think through the maintenance and repair component. How a property is or has been constructed will impact on future maintenance and repair expenses. A well-built property tends to cost somewhat more to acquire, but has the capacity to reduce maintenance and repair costs over the long term to protect an income stream. Good construction also increases the value of a property over the long haul and, thus, impacts upon your future net worth. You will have to choose between a current capital commitment and a higher long-term operating expense level before you can put this piece of real estate into the jigsaw puzzle you are constructing.

If, on the basis of your self-portrait, you decide to pay more now in order to have more in the future, the question of your current capital position may have to be re-examined. As we have mentioned in different contexts within this book, real estate investment need not take a large sum of capital. In fact, there are five major methods investors use to reduce capital needs. Moreover, the application of your imagination to much of what we have discussed will undoubtedly turn up some other ways to trim capital requirements.

The first method involves the use of financing. An institutional mortgage loan may be all that is required for you to acquire a property. However, if an institutional loan will not be sufficient, you may be able to meet any remaining need for more capital than you possess through a combination of an institutional loan and another loan. This could be a purchase money mortgage or another junior mortgage loan from a mortgage investment firm.

You can also boost the capital sum you can apply to a property by choosing the partnership vehicle. In fact, you may not need to produce any capital at all if you can obtain an equity position in a partnership for the work you contribute. You may also be able to reduce capital needs by creating what is called sweat equity. A substitution of your own work and time for hired labor may provide you with the margin you need to acquire and fix up a property. Moreover, you may reduce the cost of professional advisors by doing some of the legwork yourself. Thus, you could check building plans and undertake a title search. In addition, your advisors may be willing to accept an equity interest in lieu of some of their cash fee requirements.

Another method of capital reduction involves taking a sandwich position between a fee owner and a sublessee. If a fee owner desires steady income but no longer wants management responsibility, you may be able to persuade him or her to lease a property to you. If you can then re-lease the premises to a user at a higher rent than you have to pay, you will have created an income stream for yourself for only the cost of your professional advisors' services.

Yet another way to reduce capital requirements is to option a property for long enough to sell it to another party for more than the original purchase price. You will have to put up earnest money to obtain the option, but earnest money is usually far less than a downpayment would be. Closings with the person selling to you and with the party buying from you are usually simultaneous activities, accomplished through the use of an escrow. Through this technique, you can wind up with a significant net profit without committing a large sum of capital. This will give you current cash. The choice you make of a method to meet capital requirements will relate directly to your needs and objectives.

Your investment in real estate must lean heavily on your own common sense. If your intuition tells you that supply and demand are out of balance in a way that would defeat your goals or you have spotted a change which you do not feel is reflected in any market analysis you commission or which is provided you as part of a limited partnership prospectus, you should bend every effort to pick apart its assumptions. In the end, you should trust your own judgement on all aspects of an investment.

Your advisors will, of course, help you with their facts and judgements. If you make it clear to them at the start that you desire a long-term relationship, their facts and judgements should be as good as they can make them. However, after weighing what they tell you and conducting all the tests you can, you will have to make up your own mind. You are the one who has to back any judgement with your money, effort or time, not theirs. Thus, attending to your own common sense and judgement is a necessity.

Your position will require you to put the real estate jigsaw puzzle together after you and your advisors have taken it apart to analyze each piece. Even if you choose to become a passive investor in a limited partnership because of your participation or liability protection requirements, you will still have to decide whether a particular venture makes sense when it is assembled in a package for you.

In this primer, we have provided the basic knowledge required to undertake putting together an investment in real estate. We have also attempted to organize the book in such a way that you will be able to spot where you may need further information. If there is an area where you feel you could use more knowledge, the act of defining the area will lead you to appropriate sources for what you need. For example, a desire for more financing information will direct you to discussions with local lenders and real estate brokers. A need for more information about leasing patterns in your area will lead you to local leasing agents and property owners.

Only if you possess an understanding based on knowledge can you feel comfortable with the process of investing in real estate. Moreover, only through such a base can you gain control of the process. We hope that the act of reading this book has elevated your understanding of real estate investment in its complex entirety. If the book has succeeded in its objective, you will be able to exert more control over the process of meeting your objectives. Each additional piece of information that you gather will further increase your control.

In turn, your control of the process is what allows you to affect the value of a property you acquire in ways that will further your goal. Thus, your understanding of your objectives and the effects of different maintenance levels will allow you to determine whether you ought to defer some maintenance on your property in order to obtain a higher current income for a short period of time or whether you ought to increase maintenance to increase the property's value over the long run.

The value of the property you acquire is critical to your success. Its value rests almost entirely on the decisions you, or your working partners, make. Because of the nature of real estate, you can have more control over a property's financial results than you will have if you choose to invest in most other types of investment. In real estate, it is within your power to provide the occasions for value increases. This includes decisions to hold out for properties which best meet the market, to upgrade management, to renovate to attract certain tenants, to refinance at more attractive terms, to handcraft leases, and a host of other decisions you can make.

Your interest is the key to achieving value increases or any other goal. Your basic interest and drive can produce the effort necessary to increase your wealth. There is an old farmer's tale which illustrates how this comes about. It goes this way:

One farmer's cows consistently produced both more and richer milk than the other farmers' cows. The others naturally tried to figure out how this could be. They investigated the kind of cows, the equipment and the pasturage. All were the same as their own. Finally, they were reduced to watching the successful farmer call in his cows. He spoke to Dečani and scratched behind her ears and he murmured something to July the Third and patted her head. So it went down the line of cows marching into the milking barn.

The other farmers asked him how he could possibly remember the name of each cow and where each cow liked to be scratched or patted. Their cows were simply numbered. He replied that he guessed he just took an interest in what he was doing. Applying this story to real estate investment is not difficult. You must establish a relationship between yourself and all that encompasses a property which can help you reach your goal. If you are as interested in it as the farmer was in his cows, you and it will jointly produce a richer outcome.

It is your interest, and your interest alone, which will enable you to take in and apply the details of real estate investing. Because real estate investment is based on real property and people's activities, it is composed of many small details ranging from the size of laundry machines in relation to typical family usages, to the design of lobbies and the placement of lighting fixtures. Subtleties like these are a key to producing superior results.

Your interest can also provide you with the strength required to resist anything which might defeat your purposes. When you invest, one of the hardest things to resist is the temptation to follow the crowd. As we have discussed, real estate investment goes in cycles which are caused by monetary or other economic and social changes. Today, changes are occurring more frequently and thus the cycles are growing shorter.

At a certain time, with a certain property type, in a certain area, everyone will seem to jump on a bandwagon and rush into real estate. These boom conditions are always exciting and extremely seductive. However, once such a bandwagon effect occurs, properties reach their maximum price. This peak is generally not sustainable for any long period of time. The kinds of activities likely to result in boom conditions tend to involve fads. People eventually tend to switch their attention to some other activity than the one supporting a boom. Thus, properties bought at peak value produce less than satisfactory financial results over the long term.

Your sustained interest in and knowledge of real estate investment will give you the courage necessary to back your judgement of the supply and demand cycle in effect. You can then turn your attention to a type of real estate you desire when it reaches a point near the bottom of the cycle. If your timing is correct and you have perceived market conditions clearly enough, the value of the property you acquire should increase. Buying low is a major, perhaps the major, component of success, no matter what your goal. This is obvious in the case of a long-term capital appreciation goal, as buying low provides you with the opportunity to achieve a greater amount of appreciation.

It may not be as obvious why it is desirable for you to buy low if your objective is capital turnover, income or tax shelter. However, if you are a capital turnover investor, buying low will increase your chances of obtaining a price from the market above the amount which it cost you to acquire the property and change it. It also means you will have a better chance of achieving the profit margin you desire. If you were to buy high and then add on more value, you might discover that the price which would then be required to compensate you would cause the potential market to shrink dramatically.

An income investor who pays a price higher than market value is generally willing to take a lower yield in order to accomplish his or her objectives. The same holds true for a tax shelter investor. Paying the highest price will probably give you larger depreciation write-offs and interest deductions. But, the real question is your yield, not the absolute numbers.

Early in this book, we pointed out that you can not know your total return until you dispose of a property. Part of your return comes from any income or tax shelter generated while you are holding a property. But a certain portion, perhaps a large share, of your total return will come from any profit you make as a result of disposition. Thus, buying low and selling close to the peak of the next or a future cycle will tend to produce higher overall profits.

If you do not intend to sell but want to realize an increase in wealth from refinancing, you may obtain a larger sum by purchasing a property which can produce a greater value increase. Recognition of the cycles which occur, having the courage to buy in at a point when a cycle is starting on its way up and the courage to stick it out until value increases will bring you greater rewards.

In this book, we have attempted to outline a strategy which will most help you achieve your objectives. Thus, we have advised you to start any investing program you undertake on a small scale so that the process of learning more about the complex interrelationships of the real estate investment components can be accomplished at less risk to your financial position. We have emphasized that all the complexities can be successfully unraveled only from the standpoint of your objectives, needs and desires. You must be the pivot, or none of what you learn will help you achieve your objectives.

Of primary importance is watching what is going on around you, all of which impacts on real estate, in order to identify activity signals which, in turn, can be used to alert you to opportunities. Continual scanning of the activity level around you and on the horizon is a necessary part of the everyday life of the real estate investor who is striving to make a success of her or his ventures. We have provided you with many examples of signals to watch for, of signs that something worth investigating is taking place around you.

We hope that when you put down this book to pick up a newspaper or turn on your radio, you will read or listen with a new awareness of all the items which impact on real estate. More importantly, we hope you will make the connection between what you read, see or hear about and your objectives. The required new mode of thinking takes practice, but it will become automatic if you open your mind to it.

Once you have established your objectives, identified opportunities, conducted a market analysis, and selected an available property, you will face the most important test: Financial feasibility. Unless an investment makes economic sense, you will not be able to meet what are, after all, financial objectives. Nor will you be likely to locate a lender willing to make you a loan on a property with doubtful financial capacities. Financial feasibility is the final test of an opportunity's reality.

We repeat our advice about not becoming discouraged if the first property you select fails to meet your financial tests. There will always be another opportunity which will be even better than the first or the fifth.

Our aim in this book was to explain the workings of real estate and real estate investment in as basic a way as is possible. We know that once you understand the basis of each of the puzzle pieces and gain the capacity to put them together in the right order, you will find it much easier to tackle more complicated and sophisticated analytical techniques. We also know that computer printouts are useless unless you have assimilated enough knowledge to understand the skeletal frame on which they are draped.

Our objective was to develop a book which covers what you most need to know before you start to invest or expand your investment in real estate. Once we had identified an opportunity to serve you in this way, we tested the book's market and its feasibility. The book met our tests. We hope and trust that it meets yours. Whatever decisions you may have reached in the course of reading this book, we wish you well on your journey toward achieving your objectives.

Accelerated Depreciation   An accounting procedure which speeds up or increases the amount of depreciation which can be written off in the earlier years of an investment; accomplished by using either the declining balance method or the sum-of-the-years digits method; now allowed on new or renovated multi-family improvements. See Appendix for examples. See also Depreciation Recapture.

Aggregate Demand   The total demand for a real estate type within a given area delineation at a specific point in time. Aggregate demand can be divided into specific layering components by such functions as income, age distribution and employment.

Aggregate Supply   The total supply of a real estate type within a given area delineation at a specific point in time. Aggregate supply can be divided into specific layering components. The availability of undeveloped or underdeveloped properties will impact on total supply.

Amortization   Periodic repayment of principal over time; usually designed to extinguish the sum owed by the end of the term of the loan; one component of debt service; sometimes denotes payment of both principal and interest.

Amortized Mortgage Loan   A loan against real property which requires repayment of principal periodically over the term of the loan. The loan's terms may require that: 1) Each payment be composed of a constant amount of principal repayment and a decreasing amount of interest over the loan term, or 2) Each payment be a constant amount composed of decreasing amounts of interest and increasing amounts of principal repayment over the term of the loan.

Appreciation Equity   An increase in the difference between the value of a property and any debt on the property due to circumstances external to the property.

Assemblage   The act of combining separately owned but adjoining properties into a larger property so that they may be used together, perhaps as a single building lot; a process which creates greater utility and, thus, a higher value; in most cases, the items assembled are parcels of land.

Balloon Mortgage Loan A loan against real property which is not fully amortized at the end of its term; one requiring part of the principal repayment at its end, through what is known as a balloon payment. For example, a lender may write a loan for $10,000 but require only 25 percent of it to be repaid by the end of the loan's term. When that date is reached, the borrower would have to come up with the balance, 75 percent of $10,000, or $7,500.

Bond Net Lease A net lease under which a tenant is obligated to pay absolutely all expenses; the term "bond" emphasizes the similarities of this type of lease to a bond investment, such as a lack of management effort and protection from expense items and their possible increases. However, this term does not imply the fixed capital reversion that occurs when a bond investment is held to maturity; appreciation in a property is still possible and would accrue to the property owner if it does occur.

Building Residual Technique A method of estimating an improvement's value when land value can accurately be established through comparable sales; the entire property's net income can then be allocated between the improvement and the land, and the residual net income to the improvement can be capitalized to estimate the improvement's value.

Bulblets Either new or old secondary employment and economic centers within a metropolitan area.

Bundle of Rights The tangible and intangible elements which pertain to real estate and its ownership; both the physical and legal attributes inherent in real estate.

Capital Appreciation 1. An increase in value due to circumstances external to a particular property, such as an increase in demand, inflation, changes in transportation patterns, new construction and actions of government and real estate owners in the vicinity of the property. 2. A strategy to preserve and increase wealth over the long term by acquiring real estate which is most likely to increase in value in the future.

Capital Gains The profit from the sale of real property; the difference between a property's adjusted cost and the net sales proceeds. Capital gains are presently taxed at a much lower rate than profit from rents, interest or dividends and at a lower rate than that on earned income.

Capital Turnover An increase in capital as a result of changes made in a property to increase its utility and, thus, its value to either user-purchasers or to investor-purchasers.

Capitalization Rate A composite of a return on the land investment and a return on and of an investment in an improvement or improvements on the land at a given point in time; when used to process net income, it provides an estimate of value.

Cash Equity The amount of cash that may have to be invested to acquire a property above any borrowing used to finance the property; also the amount of cash invested in any capital improvement of the property.

Cash Flow The amount of net income which will remain after debt service has been met.

Comparable Sales Properties similar to a subject property in such value factors as physical condition, location, utility and amenities whose recent sales prices, incomes and other conditions can be used for comparison in order to estimate the subject property's value.

Component Depreciation An accounting method which allows an investor to increase the amount of depreciation which can be written off in the early years of ownership by using shorter lives on specific segments of an improvement; it can produce the same results as accelerated depreciation, i.e., an increase in write-offs early in the investment, if an improvement is composed of a high proportion of components with shorter lives, but avoids the problem of depreciation recapture because the straight-line method is used for each component.

Constant A percentage comprising a loan's interest rate and term, which, when the original loan amount is multiplied by it, gives the amount of debt service required in each period to provide a lender with complete repayment of principal by the end of the loan and with the stated return on the loan. A loan with an interest rate of 8½ percent and a term of 25 years with payments made on a monthly in arrears basis requires a constant of 9.67 percent or .0967, as can be ascertained from a check of Table 13 at the end of Chapter 9.

Construction Loan Financing extended to a borrower for the purpose of improving land or of renovating an already existing improvement, usually secured by the work in progress. Repayment is generally accomplished through use of a permanent mortgage loan. The points and interest costs incurred are paid currently out of working capital.

Contract Rent The payments specified in a lease for the use of a property; sometimes distinguishable from economic rent.

Contract Sale A sale by contract under the terms of which title does not pass to the buyer until all contract terms have been met.

Corporation An entity which is owned by a shareholder or shareholders and which meets the tests of continuity, free transferability of interests, central management and limited liability; currently subject to tax liabilities at both the corporate and shareholder levels.

Cost Approach to Value A method of estimating value which generally utilizes the market data approach for estimating the land's value and the reproduction cost of the improvements after allowance for any depreciation (physical deterioration or obsolescence). The value estimated by this method is generally considered to set the maximum an investor would be willing to pay to purchase property.

Cost-of-Living Clause A provision in a lease requiring an increase in rental payments in the amount of a percentage increase in the government's cost-of-living index; a protection against erosion of income due to inflation.

Crossover The point at which an advantage in tax shelter is lost; more specifically, the point at which accelerated or component depreciation write-offs cease to exceed straight-line depreciation write-offs and the point at which interest payments cease to exceed amortization payments; usually the point at which an investor interested in tax shelter refinances or sells a property in order to start over again on another property with high interest deductions or depreciation write-offs or both. (See Table 6 and the Appendix for examples.)

Debt Service A combination of payment of interest on the capital borrowed and repayment of the principal owed. From the lender's point of view, debt service provides for both return on and return of the sum lent.

Debt Service Coverage A measure of the margin between a property's net income and the debt service required on a loan against the property; calculated by dividing net income by debt service. The higher the debt service coverage, the safer both debt service and continued ownership of the property are. For example, if a property's net income were $10,000 and the debt service on a loan came to $8,000, a division of $10,000 by $8,000 would result in a debt service coverage of 1.25. This may meet a lender's safety requirements for granting a loan on a property. Your margin of safety would be $2,000. Thus, you could lose that amount from rents or because expenses increased before you would have to dig into your pocket to cover debt service if you wanted to save the property.

Declining Balance An accelerated depreciation method which allows an investor to write off a higher percentage of the cost of an improvement in the earlier years of ownership, e.g., with 200 percent or double declining balance, the first write-off allowed on a $100,000 property with a life of 25 years would be $8,000; the next year the write-off would be $7,360; in each subsequent year, the write-off would decline and at some point it would fall below the write-off allowed under the straight-line method. Percentages allowed are 200 percent of straight-line and 150 percent. See Appendix for an example.

Depreciation 1. Actual physical deterioration. In appraisal practice, depreciation includes physical deterioration and functional and economic obsolescence; not to be confused with depreciation for tax purposes (sense 2) which allows an investor to write off deterioration according to a set schedule which generally does not reflect actual deterioration. 2. A periodic allowance for deterioration; restricted to write-offs of the cost of an improvement, not land, over a set period of time. See Accelerated Depreciation, Component Depreciation, Declining Balance, Depreciation Recapture, Straight-Line Depreciation, and Sum-of-the-Years Digits. Also see Appendix for examples.

Depreciation Recapture A problem to investors who select an accelerated depreciation method, one which may cause some of any gain on sale to be taxed at ordinary income rates to allow the government to take back or recapture benefits from the use of accelerated methods. Without use of an accelerated method, all of the gain on sale would be taxed at the lower capital gains tax rates.

Developer An investor who is the catalyst and acts to bring everything together to effect a change in the utility of real estate for a capital turnover profit.

Developer's Equity Any creation of value which can be attributed to a change brought about by a developer.

Downpayment The amount of cash equity which must be paid at closing to a seller; the difference between the original loan amount and the purchase price of a property.

Easement The granting of a right to limited use of a property by an owner, such as a grant of a right to a utility company to use a property for its transmission lines or a grant to the public of a right-of-way; one of the sticks in the bundle of rights which a property owner has.

Economic Base Study An analysis of an economic unit's economic strengths and weaknesses which stresses basic and nonbasic employment components in order to forecast population and other functions which affect real estate utilization.

Economic Obsolescence A form of value loss due to factors external to a property.

Economic Principles The operating laws which describe economic behavior. They include, but are not limited to, the principles of balance, change, conformity, future benefits, highest and best use, substitution, and supply and demand.

Economic Rent The amount which is most likely to be obtained from a tenant signing a lease under current economic conditions; can be the same as, or higher or lower than, the contract rent specified under an already existing lease on a property.

Effective Gross Income The amount of rent after a reasonable allowance for losses due to vacancies and/or collection problems has been made. Such an allowance may or may not be needed to cover vacancies or collection problems over the ownership period, but some provision for what can or is likely to happen should be made.

Equity The value of a property less any debt on the property; total equity can consist of several kinds of equity. See Appreciation Equity, Cash Equity, Developer's Equity, Equity Build Up, Inflation Equity and Sweat Equity.

Equity Build Up An increase in the difference between the value of a property and the debt on it as a result of repayment of principal borrowed or amortization; more generally, it can also include increases due to changes in a property's value.

Equity-to-Value Ratio A ratio of downpayment to the value of a property; the percentage figure by which the amount of equity required as a downpayment at purchase can be calculated; derived from the loan-to-value ratio. For example, if a property's value is $100,000 and a lender's current loan-to-value ratio is 75 percent, the equity-to-value ratio would be 25 percent and the down payment required would be 25 percent of value, or $25,000.

Escalator Clause   A provision in a lease which requires a lessee to pay all operating expenses over a certain base amount paid by the lessor; a protection of a landlord's income against expense increases.

Exculpatory Clause   A provision which can be inserted in a mortgage and note to direct a lender to look to the property, rather than to an investor's personal assets, for repayment of a loan in the event of default on any payments required.

Export Industries   Production concerns which supply demand from extralocal sources and thus bring money in from outside to support the local economy and real estate; also known as basic industries, which now can include tourism, service industries and other export economic generators.

Fee Ownership   Possession of the physical real estate with all inherent legal rights; absolute ownership of real estate subject only to the government's rights and to rights contracted away.

Functional Obsolescence   A form of value loss due to inadequacies within the property itself.

Gap Financing   A loan which provides a financing bridge between one loan and the permanent mortgage loan; most commonly used in a construction situation.

General Partner   A partner in either a general or a limited partnership who pools his or her abilities, effort, time and, in some cases, capital; the managing partner in a limited partnership.

General Partnership   A partnership which has general partners who contribute skills, effort, time and, sometimes, capital to accomplish a joint purpose; one which has the corporate characteristics of continuity and free transferability of interests, but lacks central management and limited liability.

Gross Income   The amount of money which could be collected if a property were operating at maximum efficiency; the rent schedule for 100 percent occupancy plus any other sources of income from the property.

Gross Sales   The amount, after agreed-upon deductions for such items as returns, of a retail tenant's sales on which percentage rentals are calculated.

Improved Property   Land to which something constructed has been added, such as drainage, housing, an office building, tennis courts, etc.

Improvement Any permanent or semipermanent structure such as a building; real estate, not including the land to which an improvement is attached.

Income Money or other form of gain received periodically. See Cash Flow, Effective Gross Income, Gross Income, Net Income and Income Stream.

Income Approach to Value A method of estimating the value of an income-producing property by processing stabilized net income, yield and re-capture of the investment into an estimate of value. The latter two functions are incorporated into a capitalization rate which is then used to process net income. Once all functions have been derived from the market, net income is divided by the capitalization rate to arrive at an estimate of a property's present value.

Income Stream The timing and form of periodic income, i.e. net income under a net lease once a year at the beginning, end or other time of the year, apartment rents once a month whether under a lease or not, etc.

Inflation Equity A kind of appreciation equity where an increase in value due to inflation brings about an increase in the difference between value and any debt.

Installment Sale A sale under the terms of which portions of the purchase price are paid at stated intervals. If the strict requirements of the Internal Revenue Service are met, such as payment of less than 30 percent of the purchase price in the first year, the seller can spread the proceeds over several years and thus reduce the amount of any capital gains tax due. Title may or may not pass to the purchaser depending on local custom until all payments have been made.

Interest 1. A right or property an investor can acquire in any manner, as through purchase, inheritance, leasing, etc. 2. A sum charged for the use of money borrowed; one component of debt service.

Interest-Only Mortgage Loan A loan requiring payment of a lender's return on capital loaned without any amortization, also known as a straight or a standing mortgage loan. Usually the privilege of not making principal repayments is granted for a short period, typically on construction loans, sometimes on loans obtained from sellers and on loans outstanding on financially troubled property where the problems are likely to be solved if a grace period on amortization is extended by the lender.

Investment The total value of a property, as opposed to an investor's investment, which is known as equity.

Investment Real Estate Property capable of meeting an investor's income, tax shelter, turnover and/or capital appreciation objectives.

Investor One motivated principally by anticipated financial rewards and interested principally in return on and of one's investment in a manner based upon one's investment objectives.

Junior Mortgage Loan A loan which is inferior in priority to another mortgage loan; also known as second mortgage, third mortgage, etc.

Land-to-Building Ratio An accounting allocation which assigns a percentage to land area and building area. For example, a 100,000 square foot land plot with a 20,000 square foot building on it would have a 5 to 1 land-to-building ratio; on the same plot of land a 40,000 square foot building would have a 2.5 to 1 ratio.

Land Residual Technique A method of estimating land value when a building's value can accurately be established through an estimate of its cost, economic life and return; the entire property's net income can then be allocated between the improvement and the land, and the residual net income to the land can be capitalized to estimate the land's value.

Layering A continuum of real estate objectives ranging from user motivations to investor motivations.

Lease A contract by which an owner (lessor) transfers the rights of occupancy and use to another party (lessee) in return for the payment of rent over a specified time period or periods.

Leasehold The rights to occupy and use real property under the terms of a lease.

Leasehold Financing A loan on a leasehold interest which can develop for a variety of reasons.

Leasehold Interest An interest or interests developed in a property by a lessee or a lessee's assignee under the terms of a lease.

Lessee One who has the rights to occupy or use a property under the terms of a lease; a tenant.

Lessor One who grants the rights to occupy or use a property to another party under the terms of a lease; a landlord.

Leverage The use of financing to extend an investor's means of controlling a property and increasing yield.

Liability Responsibility, particularly for something which exposes an investor to loss or damages.

Limited Partner A partner in a limited partnership who generally contributes capital; one whose losses can be limited to the amount of his or her capital contribution in return for giving up participation in management decisions.

Limited Partnership A partnership which has a general partner or partners who contribute skills, effort, time and, sometimes, capital and a limited partner or partners who contribute capital to accomplish a joint purpose; one which has the corporate characteristics of central management (vested in the general partners) and limited liability (vested in the limited partners), but lacks continuity and free transferability of interests.

Liquidity The quality of assets which are quickly convertible into cash.

Loan-to-Value Ratio A ratio, usually expressed as a percentage, which represents the amount a lender is willing to lend in relation to the value of a property; used to determine the amount of the loan. The amount remaining represents any cash equity required as a downpayment.

Locational Quotient A figure which indicates whether a local employment group is basic or nonbasic. For example, a comparative analysis showing a large percentage share of employment for a local group would indicate that it is probably one which exports goods or services to other economic units.

Long-Term Financing See Permanent Mortgage Loan.

Market Absorption Rate The annual rate for a given type of real estate at which people are buying or renting a unit of space; usually expressed in the number of square feet per year or the number of different kinds of apartments or house units.

Market Area Delineation The process of identifying the physical size and boundaries of an area affected by an activity level; also known as trade area delineation.

Market Data Approach to Value A method of estimating a property's value by seeking out recent comparable sales and offerings and applying confirmed prices to the subject property through a series of adjustments for any differences between the comparable properties and the subject property.

Market Value The sum of money an average well-informed buyer will pay for a property and an average well-informed seller will accept for a property, both knowing all the uses to which the property can be put and all material facts, with neither the buyer nor the seller acting under duress or because of any unusual circumstance; also known as fair market value.

Mix In residential real estate, mix describes the distribution of the types of dwelling units within a property, such as one-bedroom and two-bedroom apartments, generally stated as percentages; in retail real estate, mix describes tenant compatibility. A good mix will enhance a property's income stream.

Mortgage An instrument by which real property is pledged as security for the fulfillment of a debt.

Mortgage-Equity Band of Investment Technique A method of estimating a capitalization rate which utilizes current market terms of long-term mortgage financing as functions as well as an equity yield and recapture rate. Once a capitalization rate is estimated, it is used to process stabilized net income to arrive at an estimate of present value.

Mortgage Loan The amount lent by a lender against real property mortgaged by a borrower; colloquially called a mortgage.

Mortgagee The party to whom real property is pledged in order to obtain a loan; the lender.

Mortgagor The party who pledges real property as security in order to obtain a loan on the property; the borrower.

Net Income 1. The amount of income which will remain after provisions have been made for vacancy and collection losses and operating expenses, but before provision for debt service or depreciation for tax purposes. 2. The figure used after stabilization of gross income, effective gross income and operating expenses as one function in arriving at value using the income approach.

Net Lease A lease in which most or all operating expenses are paid by the lessee; designed to protect the lessor against erosion of income due to expense increases; coming to be known as a bond investment and, if it requires about as little management as a bond investment and, if properly designed, has few expenses for the investor. The critical question to examine regarding any net lease, whether called "net", "net-net", "net-net-net" or "bond net", is the degree of the lessor's exposure to expense increases.

Net Worth The amount by which assets exceed liabilities; wealth. Equity forms an addition to net worth. Thus, an increase in equity causes net worth or wealth to increase.

Non-Recourse A condition which prevents a lender from attaching personal assets in the event of a loan default; can be achieved by inserting an exculpatory clause in note and mortgage instruments, by incorporating or by becoming a limited partner.

Note An instrument creating and evidencing a debt and promising payment in accordance with its terms.

Objectives The basic requirement for any planning or negotiating process. In real estate, the four major objectives for investment are income, tax shelter, turnover and appreciation.

Overages An amount of rent due over a base minimum rent from a percentage of a lessee's gross sales in which the lessor has the right to participate.

Overimprovement An improvement in which too much capital is invested, with the result that the improvement takes a disproportionate share of the return.

Oversupply A condition in which the number of units available exceeds the number of units demanded.

Owner-Occupier One who simultaneously owns and uses a property; someone occupying the extreme user end of the layering spectrum, generally motivated principally by the amenity of ownership.

Participation A lender's requirement of a part of the equity interest to increase the lender's yield; effectively, a dilution of equity and/or an increase in debt service.

Partnership A group of people who agree to pool capital, abilities, effort or time, or a combination of these, for a stated purpose and to divide up the profits and losses or other results of the contributions to the partnership in a specified manner.

Percentage Clause A provision in a lease requiring a tenant to pay additional rent (overages) in the amount of a percentage of gross sales over a specified level of business; a protection for the owner against erosion of income from inflation.

Permanent Mortgage Loan A long-term loan against real property, usually for 15 or more years; also known as a take-out loan when it replaces a construction loan and, by providing the money to repay the construction lender, takes the construction lender out of the picture.

Points Payments made to a lender to obtain a loan; expressed as percentage points of the total original loan amount. Points either effectively raise a lender's yield and are then considered additional interest or are fees for services rendered.

Prepayment Penalty A payment exacted by a lender from a borrower if a mortgage loan is paid off before its term is up; levied as a percentage of the loan balance, usually a declining percentage as the mortgage matures; charged to allow a lender to realize some of the yield it anticipated when it wrote the loan.

Price The actual sum a seller accepts and a buyer pays under normal or special circumstances for a property. In most instances, price is the same as value; but price may exceed value if a buyer needs a property for a special reason; price may be less than value if a seller needs to sell for a special reason.

Prime Rate The short-term interest rate charged the most creditworthy corporations; the rate to which construction loan interest rates may be pegged.

Principal A sum of capital borrowed.

Principle of Balance A proper proportion of the four factors which produce value and profits: labor, investor/manager, improvements and land. When the four are in balance, the greatest net return to the land can be produced.

Principle of Change A condition whereby all property is subject to transformation from one state to another as a result of ongoing economic and social trends. Change can be sudden (revolutionary) or slow (evolutionary).

Principle of Conformity A condition of uses in harmony. The degrees of conformity can operate at great variance from place to place and time to time and are dictated by conditions in the market place. Conformity applies to social and economic characteristics, but not to such qualities as race, religion, color, ethnic origin, sex, age, et cetera.

Principle of Future Benefits The anticipation of beneficial results from the future financial performance of a property. Value is the present worth of the right to receive a property's future benefits.

Principle of Highest and Best Use The use or improvement which results in the greatest net return to the land over a certain period; the legal and probable use that will result in the highest land value.

Principle of Substitution Of two similar products on the market, the less expensive one will tend to drive out or drive down the price of the more expensive, given equality of circumstances.

Principle of Supply and Demand The relationship between the amount of a given kind of real estate product at a given price, including existing stock, conversions and construction in process, vacant land, and the amount of that real estate sought due to a desire for it and the ability to obtain it; more generally, the relationship between the availability of a commodity and the effective desire for it.

Property 1. The totality of rights or interests inherent in ownership of a property. 2. Ownership of real estate. 3. A particular parcel of land or real estate.

Purchase Money Mortgage A mortgage granted to a seller by a buyer to accomplish acquisition of a property. This form of mortgage allows title to a property to pass to the buyer.

Real Estate 1. Land, its above and below ground assets, and improvements. 2. Ownership of the above.

Refinancing Restructuring of financing with either a new loan or a modification of an existing loan, usually for a greater sum of money or to take advantage of better terms. Refinancing is used when an existing loan has been substantially paid off or when current loan terms are more attractive than those of the existing loan.

Reproduction Cost The sum it would take to duplicate exactly an existing improvement using the same materials and construction techniques, regardless of new techniques or materials developed since the improvement's actual construction and without regard to any inadequacies or overbuilding currently present in the improvement.

Residual The amount left at the end of a process, e.g., the value which returns to a lessor at the end of a lease.

Return On and Of 1. Return on equity is calculated by dividing annual net income by equity; also known as interim yield on equity. 2. Return of the investment is accomplished through the recapture of the amount invested over the period the property is owned in the form of a portion of net income or in the form of a portion of the disposition proceeds, or in the form of both.

Reverse Leverage The use of financing which results in an equity yield that is lower than the lender's yield; also known as negative leverage.

Reversion A return of rights to an owner after a period during which the owner has granted the rights away. A reversion occurs at the end of a lease when the rights return to the owner.

Risk A hazard of loss which largely determines yield requirements; rated in terms of the credit involved and/or the venture itself.

Sandwich Position   A leasehold interest between a fee interest and a sublessee.

Self-Amortized Mortgage Loan   See Definition 2 under Amortized Mortgage Loan; also known as a self-liquidating mortgage loan.

Shift-Share Analysis   A study identifying the employment groups which have positive or negative effects on an economic unit's growth and also the groups which are shifting into or out of the unit.

Short-Term Financing   A loan made for a short duration, usually one to three years. Short-term financing is typically used to meet construction, gap financing and working capital requirements.

Site Share   The amount of market absorption that a specific property can capture. In retail uses, this would be translated into sales volume; in housing, the number of units rented or sold, and in office and industrial uses, the number of square feet sold or leased.

Sole Proprietorship   An ownership form in which total operating and ownership control is vested in a single person who owns the property in question outright.

Stabilization   A process whereby the income and expenses of a subject property are compared to those of comparable properties to adjust the subject property's income and expenses to those normally accepted by or found in the market place.

Straight-Line Depreciation   The basic accounting procedure for writing down a wasting asset to reflect wear and tear over time; under this method, an equal amount of cost can be written off against income each year over an economic life which meets government requirements. Thus, a write-off of $4,000 would be permitted each year on a property worth $100,000 with a life of 25 years. See Appendix for an example.

Subordination   Placement of one lien or right ahead of another.

Sum-of-the-Years Digits   An accelerated depreciation method which allows an investor to write off a higher percentage of the cost of an improvement in the earlier years of ownership, e.g., with an economic life of 25 years, the factor allowed the first year would be 25/325 (the numerator is the number of years remaining; the denominator is the sum of the original number of years), which would allow a write-off of $7,692 the first year on a property worth $100,000; the next year the factor would be 24/325 and the write-off would be $7,385; in each subsequent year the write-off would decline; at some point it would fall below the write-off allowed under the straight-line method. See Appendix for an example.

Sweat Equity A substitution of time and effort for capital in order to achieve an increase in value and, thus, in the difference between value and debt or equity; an example would be renovation by an investor rather than by hired labor.

Tax Shelter A reduction in current taxes through deferral to a future period; the reduction, or tax savings, accomplished through real estate investment comes mainly from interest deductions, depreciation write-offs and/or the shifting of profits from periodic income taxed at a high rate to profits from a sale taxed at a lower capital gains rate.

Term 1. The specified duration of a loan. 2. The specified duration of a lease.

Terms 1. All conditions contained in a loan agreement; more narrowly, the downpayment requirement, the term of the loan and the cost of obtaining financing, which may include interest, points, fees and/or participation. 2. All conditions contained in a lease agreement. 3. All conditions contained in a sale agreement.

Total Return A total return on and of an investment incorporates a return on the capital invested in land and a return on and of the capital invested in improvements. At the end of the ownership period, the total return tells you what you made on the investment.

Underimprovement An improvement in which too little capital is invested.

Undersupply A condition in which the number of units available is less than the number of units demanded.

Unimproved Property Land which has not been developed.

Use Real Estate Property capable of meeting a user's need for amenities; especially property designed to allow an owner-occupier to fulfill amenity objectives. The user's objectives do not include the real estate investment objective of a financial return from the property itself. Use real estate can include factories, office buildings, homes, retail stores or any property which is owner-occupied.

User One whose returns generally come from non-real estate considerations; someone motivated principally by amenities capable of meeting utilitarian and/or emotional needs; a tenant or owner-occupier.

Variable Rate Mortgage Loan A loan with an interest rate which changes with the movement of specified money market interest rates.

Venturer An investor who takes relatively high risks in order to achieve higher rewards within a relatively short time frame; generally one most attracted to turnover projects. If this investor takes an active turnover role, he or she is a developer.

Wraparound Mortgage Loan A loan written by an institutional lender which allows a borrower to obtain financing above an existing first mortgage loan with a relatively low interest rate and a relatively long remaining term; accomplished by having the face amount of the wraparound include the first loan's balance and the new amount loaned, thus having the borrower pay interest and amortization on the total to the wraparound lender, which remits the first lender's payments to that lender. Because only a portion of the total amount is loaned by the wraparound lender, it can charge a lower overall interest rate than might be charged for a refinancing.

Yield 1. Interim yield is an annual return on cash equity; used with net income as a function in the income approach to estimating value. Yield is a function of risk, liquidity, management and size of an investment. 2. Total yield is the return on original equity which can be calculated only upon disposition of a property. It is a summation of interim yields adjusted at the time of disposition for any change in equity, including appreciation or depreciation from original cost.

APPENDIX: EXAMPLES OF SELECTED DEPRECIATION METHODS*
Straight-Line Depreciation

Year	Unrecovered Basis (Beginning of Year)	Annual Deduction	Accumulated Depreciation	Adjusted Basis (End of Year)
1	$100,000	$4,000	$4,000	$96,000
2	96,000	4,000	8,000	92,000
3	92,000	4,000	12,000	88,000
4	88,000	4,000	16,000	84,000
5	84,000	4,000	20,000	80,000
6	80,000	4,000	24,000	76,000
7	76,000	4,000	28,000	72,000
8	72,000	4,000	32,000	68,000
9	68,000	4,000	36,000	64,000
10	64,000	4,000	40,000	60,000
11	60,000	4,000	44,000	56,000
12	56,000	4,000	48,000	52,000
13	52,000	4,000	52,000	48,000
14	48,000	4,000	56,000	44,000
15	44,000	4,000	60,000	40,000
16	40,000	4,000	64,000	36,000
17	36,000	4,000	68,000	32,000
18	32,000	4,000	72,000	28,000
19	28,000	4,000	76,000	24,000
20	24,000	4,000	80,000	20,000
21	20,000	4,000	84,000	16,000
22	16,000	4,000	88,000	12,000
23	12,000	4,000	92,000	8,000
24	8,000	4,000	96,000	4,000
25	4,000	4,000	100,000	-0-

*Assumes an improvement cost of $100,000 and an economic life of 25 years.

Accelerated Depreciation: 200% (or Double) Declining Balance

Year	Unrecovered Basis (Beginning of Year)	Annual Deduction	Accumulated Depreciation	Adjusted Basis (End of Year)
1	$100,000	$8,000	$ 8,000	$92,000
2	92,000	7,360	15,360	84,640
3	84,640	6,771	22,131	77,869
4	77,869	6,230	28,361	71,639
5	71,639	5,731	34,092	65,908
6	65,908	5,273	39,365	60,635
7	60,635	4,851	44,216	55,784
8	55,784	4,463	48,679	51,321
9	51,321	4,106	52,785	47,215
10	47,215	3,777†	56,562	43,438
11	43,438	3,475	60,037	39,963
12	39,963	3,197	63,234	36,766
13	36,766	2,941	66,175	33,825
14	33,825	2,706	68,881	31,119
15	31,119	2,490	71,371	28,629
16	28,629	2,290	73,661	26,339
17	26,339	2,107	75,768	24,232
18	24,232	1,939	77,707	22,293
19	22,293	1,783	79,490	20,510
20	20,510	1,641	81,131	18,869
21	18,869	1,510	82,641	17,359
22	17,359	1,389	84,030	15,970
23	15,970	1,278	85,308	14,692
24	14,692	1,175	86,483	13,517
25	13,517	1,081	87,564	12,436

†Crossover point where the accelerated depreciation write-off is less than straight-line; most investors switch to straight-line at this point.

Accelerated Depreciation: Sum-of-the-Years Digits

Year	Unrecovered Basis (Beginning of Year)	Annual Deduction‡	Accumulated Depreciation	Adjusted Basis (End of Year)	Decimal Equivalent
1	$100,000	$7,690	$ 7,690	$92,310	.0769
2	92,310	7,380	15,070	84,930	.0738
3	84,930	7,080	22,150	77,850	.0708
4	77,850	6,770	28,920	71,080	.0677
5	71,080	6,460	35,380	64,620	.0646
6	64,620	6,150	41,530	58,470	.0615
7	58,470	5,850	47,380	52,620	.0585
8	52,620	5,540	52,920	47,080	.0554
9	47,080	5,230	58,150	41,850	.0523
10	41,850	4,920	63,070	36,930	.0492
11	36,930	4,620	67,690	32,310	.0462
12	32,310	4,310	72,000	28,000	.0431
13	28,000	4,000	76,000	24,000	.0400
14	24,000	3,690§	79,690	20,310	.0369
15	20,310	3,380	83,070	16,930	.0338
16	16,930	3,080	86,150	13,850	.0308
17	13,850	2,770	88,920	11,080	.0277
18	11,080	2,460	91,380	8,620	.0246
19	8,620	2,150	93,530	6,470	.0215
20	6,470	1,850	95,380	4,620	.0185
21	4,620	1,540	96,920	3,080	.0154
22	3,080	1,230	98,150	1,850	.0123
23	1,850	920	99,070	930	.0092
24	930	620	99,690	310	.0062
25	310	310	100,000	-0-	.0031

‡Rounded to nearest $10.

§Crossover point where the accelerated depreciation write-off is less than straight-line.

Index

Absorption rate, 68, 216, 219
Accelerated method of depreciation, 60, 61, 373, 392, 393
Access clause in leases, 358
Accountants, 65, 310, 364
    for financial analysis, 17
    to handle tax shelter, 63
    services of, in general, 135–138, 140–141
Activity (*see* Economic activity; Human activity)
Actual buyer, 212
Addition clause in leases, 345–346
Advertising professionals, 146
Advisors, 16, 17, 65, 135–137, 363–367
    accountants as (*see* Accountants)
    appraisers as, 135, 138, 141–142, 178
        (*See also* Market value, appraiser's approaches to)
    architects as, 135–138, 143
        landscape, 147
    choosing, specific, 138–139
    engineers as, 135–138, 143
        civil, 146
        site, soils or geological, and traffic, 147
    insurance brokers as, 135, 138, 145
    lawyers as (*see* Lawyers)
    real estate brokers as, 135, 136, 138, 143–145, 363–365
    worksheet to establish need for, 148–149
Aggregate demand, 296–297, 373
Aggregate supply, 297–298, 373
Alteration clause in leases, 345–346
American Bar Association, 146
American Institute of Architects, 143
American Institute of Certified Public Accountants, 141

American Institute of Real Estate Appraisers, 142
Amortization, 48, 231, 373
Amortized mortgage loans, 248–249, 373
    table, 250–251
    (*See also* Financing)
Antidiscrimination laws, 360
Apartment buildings, 98–100
    cooperative, 98
    financial feasibility analysis for, 310, 312–320
        worksheets for, 313, 315–317
    goals attainable with, 45
    immediate income and, 88–89
    liquidity of, 103–104
    protection against increasing operating expenses with, 53
    (*See also* Residential real estate)
Appraisers, 135, 138, 141–142, 178
    (*See also* Market value, appraiser's approaches to)
Appreciation (*see* Capital appreciation)
Appreciation equity, 80–82, 373
Architects, 135–138, 143
    landscape, 147
Assemblage, 65, 215–216, 373–374
Assignments in leases, 351–352
Association clause in leases, 356–357
Available capital:
    capital turnover and, 68
        (*See also* Capital turnover)
    and investments in small properties, 95
    and ownership choices, 121
    as parameter of investor profile, 13, 23–24
    in sole ownerships, 124

Average buyer, 212
Average seller, 212, 213

Balance, principle of, 181–182, 385
Balanced market, 164, 165
Balanced supply and demand, 167
Balloon mortgage loans, 257–258, 374
  with wraparound loans, 264
BOMA (Building Owners and
    Managers Association
    International), 96
Bond net lease, 54, 374
Borrowing:
  by corporations, 130
  realizing appreciated equity through,
      81–82
  (*See also* Financing; Loans; Mortgage
    loans)
Brokers (*see* Insurance brokers;
    Mortgage brokers; Real estate
    brokers)
Building codes, 136, 169, 187
Building Owners and Managers
    Association International
    (BOMA), 96
Building residual technique, 224, 374
Bulblets, 155, 159, 161, 374
Bundle of rights (bundle of sticks), 153,
    183–190, 374
Business type clause in leases, 352
Buyer, actual and average, 212

Capital:
  contributions of, in limited
      partnerships, 127, 128
  eroded by inflation, 14
    (*See also* Inflation)
  needed for acquiring partnership
      interest, 129
  reduction of need for, 366–367
  (*See also* Available capital; Capital
    appreciation; Capital gains;
    Capital turnover; Working
    capital)
Capital appreciation, 1, 28, 89, 374
  capitalization rate and increase in, 80
  financing and, 232
  as goal, 43–44, 68–82
    table, 82

Capital appreciation (*Cont.*):
  and investments in undeveloped
      land, 113
  long-term, 77–78
  prices and, 218
  with single family homes, 99
Capital gains, 61–64, 374–375
  of corporations, 130
  in general partnerships, 126
  from land investments, 113, 115
  and oversupply, 169
  in sole ownerships, 123
  taxation of, 77–79
    post-1976, 77
    reduced through installment sale,
      259
Capital turnover, 79, 90, 375
  actual buyers interested in, 212
  and existing structures, 92
  financial feasibility analysis for, 310
  as goal, 43, 44, 64–68
  profits from, 68
    at beginning of supply and demand
      cycle, 168–169
  undersupply and, 165
  with undeveloped land, 113,
    157–158, 216
Capitalization rate, 57–58, 224, 375
  in apartment building financial
      feasibility analysis, 317
  capital appreciation and increase in,
      80
  in income approach to value,
      224–225, 227
  in shopping center financial
      feasibility analysis, 326, 329
Cash equity, 48, 375
Cash flow, 49, 50, 375
  in apartment building financial
      feasibility analysis, 318
  cash flow statement worksheet,
      18–19
  constant and, 251–254
  in shopping center financial
      feasibility analysis, 331
Census of Retail Trade, 304
Change, principle of, 175–176, 181,
    385
Choices:
  relativity of, within parameters of
      investor profile, 14–15
  (*See also specific types of real estate*)

Cities:
building of, 154–159
effects of highway construction on, 161–162
Civil engineers, 146
Coercion, lack of, market value and concept of, 213–214
Collection losses, analysis of, in income approach to value, 221, 222
Commercial leases, cost-of-living clause in, 55
Commercial real estate:
depreciation write-offs on, 60
passing on increases in operating expenses with, 53–54
risk/yield of, compared with that of residential property, 87–88
at times of depression, 70
transformed into residential property, 174
type of, needed to generate immediate income, 89
(*See also* Retail real estate; Shopping centers)
Commissions:
of insurance brokers, 145
of real estate brokers, 144
(*See also* Fees)
Comparable sales, 218–219, 228, 375
Competition:
with existing structures, 92
substitution as, 173
supply and demand and, 166, 167, 169
Component depreciation, 375
depreciation recapture avoided with, 61–62
Condemnations, 175, 212
Condominiums, 98
Conformity, principle of, 176–177, 180, 385
Conservative investor profile, 36–37
worksheet to determine, 38
Constant, 248–255, 267, 375
application of, table, 250–251
debt service and, 249, 252
equity build up and, 249–252
table, 250–251
interest rate and, table, 253
and term of loan, table, 254
Construction:
costs of: new, 92
office buildings, 179

Construction (*Cont.*):
highway, 71–73, 160–162, 181, 205–209
new: costs of, 92
depreciation on, 61
Construction clause in leases, 345
Construction loans, 235–236, 376
interest rate on, 67, 266
leasehold financing, 265
short-term: for capital turnover, 67
interest-only payments as, 258
Contract rent, 221, 264, 322, 346, 376
Contract sales, 376
Control:
in corporations, 131
as feature of real estate investments, 2–4
in general partnerships, 125–126
in limited partnerships, 126–127
as parameter of investor profile, 14, 15, 30, 34–37
in sole ownerships, 122–123
(*See also* Management; Participation)
Cooperative apartment buildings, 98
Corporate owner-occupiers, 275–277
Corporations, 121, 129–131, 376
Cost approach to value, 218–221, 230, 376
Cost-of-living clause, 55, 70, 76, 349, 376
Costs:
construction: new, 92
office buildings, 179
conversions, 74
holding, 5
capital appreciation and, 75
on land, 115–116
on undeveloped land, 113
incorporation, 130–131
labor and materials: cost of new construction and, 92
supply and demand and, 170–171
professional, 137
(*See also* Commissions; Fees)
reproduction, 218–219, 386
Credit rating (*see* Financing; Tenant credit)
Crossover, 62, 249–251, 376

Date of leases, 344
Debt liability (*see* Personal debt liability)

Debt service, 50, 376
 in apartment building financial
  feasibility analysis, 318
 constant and, 249, 252
 coverage for, dangers of low
  coverage, 255, 257, 376–377
 effects of financing on, 236
 homeownership and, 280
 in income approach to value, 223
 loan terms and, 247–248
 participation requirements of lenders
  and, 235
 in shopping center financial
  feasibility analysis, 330–331
Declining balance method of
 accelerated depreciation, 377
 double (200%), 60, 392
 150%, 60
Deflation, 2, 69–71, 343
Demand:
 aggregate, 296–297, 373
 effective: at beginning of supply and
  demand cycle, 168
  conditions basic to, 165–166
  highest and best use and, 180
 market analysis with analysis of, 287
 shortcomings of excess, 166–167
 substitution and, 172, 174
 (*See also* Supply and demand)
Demographic description, market
 analysis with, 287, 293–296
Depreciation, 377
 component, 61–62, 375
  depreciation recapture avoided
   with, 61–62
 in cost approach to value, 220
 in income approach to value, 223
 land, 59–60, 90, 113
Depreciation recapture, 377
 ways of avoiding, 61–62
Depreciation write-offs, 46, 90
 in apartment building financial
  feasibility analysis, 319
 to establish real estate taxable
  income, 50
 in general partnerships, 126
 on new properties, 158
 in shopping center financial
  feasibility analysis, 331
 in sole ownerships, 123
 as tax shelter, 46, 59–62
 (*See also specific depreciation write-off
  methods*)

Depressions, 69–71, 108
 (*See also* Inflation)
Destruction of property clause in leases,
 357
Developer, 36, 64, 66, 377
Developer's equity, 48, 377
Developing real estate, management of,
 33–34, 68
Development:
 capital appreciation and, 71–73
 capital turnover and, 64–66, 68
 as form of change, 175
 and land investments, 90, 113–116
 risks attached to, 28–29, 158
Disclosure statements for private and
 public partnerships, 129
Disposition of property, actual yield
 determination at time of, 56,
 229–230, 371
Dividends, taxation of, 62, 130
Dodge Construction News (journal), 198
Dollars and Cents for Shopping Centers
 (journal), 198
Double (200%) declining balance
 method of accelerated
 depreciation, 60, 392
Downpayments, 247–249, 377
 constant and, 248, 249, 255
 table, 252
Durability of income (*see* Quality and
 durability of income)

Earned income, taxation on, 62
Easement, 188, 378
Economic activity:
 market analysis with identification of,
  287–291, 364
 and real estate trends, 154–157, 162
Economic base study, 294–295, 378
Economic life of property, 75, 223, 226
 duration of long-term loans and,
  236–237
Economic obsolescence, 52, 73,
 220–221, 378
Economic principles governing real
 estate, 163–183
 balance as, 181–182, 385
 change as, 175–176, 181, 385
 conformity as, 176–177, 180, 385
 future benefits as, 182–183, 385
 highest and best use as,177–182,385
 substitution as, 172–174, 385

Economic principles governing real
  estate (*Cont.*):
  supply and demand as (*see* Supply and
    demand)
Economic rent, 221, 264, 322, 346, 378
Economists, real estate, 147
Effective demand:
  at beginning of supply and demand
    cycle, 168
  conditions basic to, 165–166
  highest and best use and, 180
Effective gross income (effective gross
  rent), 49–50
  in income approach to value, 222
Eminent domain, 186–187, 357
Encyclopedia of Associations, 172
Engineers, 135–138, 143
  civil, 146
  traffic, site, and soils or geological,
    147
Engineers Joint Council, 143
Environmental protection statutes,
  94, 136, 169
Environmental scientists, 147
Equity, 47, 378
  appreciated, 80–82, 373
  capital appreciation and protection
    of, 71–72
  cash, 48, 375
  determination of, upon disposition of
    property, 56
  developer's, 48, 377
  downpayments and requirements in,
    247
  effects of highway construction on, 71
  effects of lender's participation
    requirements on, 235
  financing and, 232
    (*See also* Financing)
  homeownership and, 279
  in income approach to value,
    225–227
  inflation, 48
  and junior mortgages, 260, 262
  needed for large-scale properties, 94
  net worth and, 48, 80
  sweat, 124, 366, 388
Equity build up, 48, 378
  constant and, 249–252
    table, 250–251
Equity interest:
  for advisors, 137–138
  in limited partnerships, 128

Equity-to-value ratio, 247, 378
Escalation clause, 53–54, 105, 108,
  348–349, 379
Escape clause in leases, 360
Excess demand, shortcomings of,
  166–167, 370
Exchange value, 211
Exculpatory clause, 124, 126, 127, 237,
  379
Existing structures (*see* Older
  structures)
Expenses (*see* Operating expenses)
Experience as parameter of investor
  profile, 14, 15, 30, 32–35, 37
Export industries, 156–157, 379

Factories (*see* Industrial real estate)
Fee ownership, 184–189, 366–367,
  379
  mortgaging of fee, leasehold
    financing and, 265
Fees:
  of appraisers, 142
  of architects and engineers, 143
  of lawyers, 146
  of managers, 33–34
  to obtain new mortgage, 262
  organization, for limited
    partnerships, 127–128
  (*See also* Commissions)
Financial feasibility analysis, 17, 142,
  309–333, 372
  for apartment buildings, 310,
    312–320
    worksheets for, 313, 315–317
  for shopping centers, 310, 320–333
    worksheets for, 324, 326–328
    worksheets for, 334–337
Financial planners, 17
Financing, 1, 28, 231–268
  analyzing, in income approach to
    value, 225
  for capital turnover, 67, 68
  capitalization rate and, 80
    (*See also* Capitalization rate)
  effects of money supply on supply
    and demand, 170
  gap, 235–236, 379
  for industrial property, 112–113
  kinds of, 231, 235–236, 257–268
    level constant payment plan, table,
    269

Financing, kinds of (*Cont.*):
  tables, 261, 264
  (*See also specific kinds of financing*)
  for land investments, 116
  leverage in (*see* Leverage)
  for office buildings, 110
  position of lenders, 234–236
  for residential real estate, 103
  for retail real estate, 107
  for special purpose real estate, 90, 118
  terms of (*see* Constant;
      Downpayments)
  (*See also* Borrowing; Debt service;
      Interest deductions; Interest
      rates; Loans; Mortgage loans)
Forced sales, market value and,
    213–214
Frictional vacancy, 164
Functional obsolescence, 52, 91, 220,
    222–223, 379
Future benefits as economic principle,
    182–183, 385

Gains (*see* Capital gains)
Gap financing, 235–236, 379
General contractors, 147
General partnerships (and partners),
    125, 128, 379
Geographers, 147
Geological engineers, 147
Goals (*see* Objectives)
Government housing, 61, 90
Government programs, effects of, 170,
    194
Government regulation:
  and land investments, 114
  and large-scale properties, 94
Government rights, 186–187, 357
Gross income (rent roll), 49, 50, 222,
    223, 379
  effective: at beginning of supply and
      demand cycle, 168
    conditions basic to, 165–166
    highest and best use and, 180
  in income approach to value,
      221–222
  loan terms and, 247–248
  (*See also* Rent)
Gross sales, 55, 348, 379
Ground leases, 60, 76, 87, 115, 116, 278

Highest and best use, principle of,
    177–182, 385
Highway construction, 71–73,
    160–162, 181, 205–209
Holding costs, 5
  capital appreciation and, 75
  on land, 113, 115
Holding periods:
  average, 79
  capital turnover and, 67–68
Homeownership:
  debt service and, 280
  equity and, 279
  (*See also* Owner-occupied property;
      Single family homes)
Housing (*see* Residential real estate)
Human activity, real estate and, 2,
    191–210
  case studies, 199–208

Improved property, 47, 90, 379
  income streams from, 5–6, 59
  operating expenses on, 5–6
Improvement clause in leases,
    345–346
Improvements, 47, 380
  cost approach to value of,
      219–221
  highest and best use principle and,
      178–182
  overimprovement, 177–180, 182,
      384
  as protection against increased
      operating expenses, 54
  tax shelter and, 59
  underimprovement, 178, 181, 182,
      388
Income, 49, 380
  earned, 62
  as goal, 49–58
  interest, 62
  objectives and, 44, 274
  as parameter of investor profile, 13,
      16–19, 36
    cash flow statement, 18–19
    retirement, 252–253, 254
  (*See also* Cash flow; Dividends;
      Effective gross income; Gross
      income; Net income; Real estate
      taxable income)

Income analysis:
 in apartment building financial
  feasibility analysis, 313–314
 worksheet for, 313
 in shopping center financial
  feasibility analysis, 323
 worksheet for, 324, 334
Income approach to market value,
 221–229
Income production, 1
 actual buyers interested in, 212
 apartment buildings and immediate,
  88–89
 from existing structures, 91
 as goal, 43–46, 49–58, 64
  table, 53
 from homeownership, 280
 owner-occupier real estate and,
  278
 prices of income-producing
  property, 216–217
 from residential property, 88–89
  (*See also* Gross income)
 from single family homes, 99
 at times of inflation, 70–71
  (*See also* Quality and durability of
  income)
Income streams, 50, 380
 from apartment buildings, 45
 constant and, 252–253
 as dependent on supply and demand,
  165
 financeability and quality of, 67
 financial feasibility analysis to
  determine, 310
 from ground leases, 278
 from improved property, 5–6, 59
 risk/yield and, 55–57
Incorporation costs, 130–131
Individual control (*see* Control)
Industrial leases, 111
 cost-of-living clause in, 55
Industrial real estate:
 adaptability of, 52
 depreciation write-offs on, 60
 goals attainable with, 45
 passing on increases in operating
  expenses with, 53–54
 selecting, 87, 88, 90, 93, 110–113
Inflation, 1, 14
 benefits of financing and, 233–234

Inflation (*Cont.*):
 capital appreciation from, 69–72,
  79–80
 capital eroded by, 14
 effects of, on income, 55
 effects of, on interest rates, 234
 leases and, 342
Inflation equity, 48, 380
Information (and information sources),
 198–199
Inheritance, tax on capital gains and, 77
Inspectors, termite, 147
Installment sales, 259, 380
Insurance brokers, 135, 138, 145
Insurance clause in leases, 354
Insurance value, 211
Intangible rights (legal rights), 183–184
Interest, 47, 183–190, 380
 equity: for advisors, 65, 137–138, 366
  capital needed for acquiring, in
   partnerships, 129
  in limited partnerships, 128
 leasehold, 76–77, 187, 221, 264, 360,
  381
Interest deductions, 90, 233
 in apartment building financial
  feasibility analysis, 319
 to establish real estate taxable
  income, 50
 in general partnerships, 126
 with junior mortgages, 260, 262
 on new property, 158
 in sole ownerships, 123
 as tax shelter, 46, 58–59
Interest income, taxation on, 62
Interest-only mortgage loans, 258, 380
 purchase money loans as, 259
Interest rates:
 constant and, 248–251, 254
  table, 253
 on construction loans, 67, 266
 effects of inflation on, 234
 on junior mortgages, 260
 on leasehold financing, 266
 prime, 266, 385
 variable, 265–266
 on wraparound loans, 263
Intrinsic value of real property, 2, 69
Investment profile, 363–366
 clarity of, and choice of objectives, 45
  (*See also* Objectives)

Investment profile (*Cont.*):
ownership choices and, 121
(*See also* Ownership choices)
parameters of, 13–41
available capital as, 13, 23–24
(*See also* Available capital)
conservative profile, 36–38
worksheet for, 38
control as, 14, 15, 30, 34–37
(*See also* Control)
experience as, 14, 15, 30, 32–35, 37
income as, 13, 16–19, 36
cash flow statement, 18–19
(*See also* Income; Income
production; Income streams)
liquidity as, 13–16, 21–22, 36
(*See also* Liquidity)
management role as, 14, 15, 30,
33–34, 36, 37
(*See also* Management)
moderate profile, 36, 37
worksheet for, 40
net worth as, 19–21, 36
net worth statement, 20–21
(*See also* Net worth)
participation as, 14, 15, 30–32, 36,
37
(*See also* Participation)
risk/yield requirement as, 13–16,
26–29, 36
(*See also* Risk/yield; Risks; Yield)
security as, 13–16, 24–25, 36
(*See also* Security)
sensitivity to loss as, 13, 16, 22–23
(*See also* Losses)
term preference as, 13, 29–31,
36
venturous profile of, 36, 37
·worksheet, 39
worksheet of, 40
Investment real estate, 273–274, 381
motivation to acquire, 275–276
mixed motivation, 278–283
(*See also specific types of investment real
estate*)
Investments, 47, 380
real estate compared with other,
1–10
risk attached to all, 14
(*See also specific types of investments*)
Investors, 381

Investors (*Cont.*):
prices paid by, as opposed to users,
214–216
as productive force, 182

Junior mortgage loans (second
mortgage loans), 259–263, 366, 381
for land, 116
refinancing vs., 260–262
table, 261
as wraparounds, 263

Labor:
compensation of, 187
as productive force, 182
Labor costs:
and costs of new construction, 92
supply and demand and, 170–171
Land:
birth of, into real estate, 154
and capital appreciation, 75
capital gains from, 113, 115
cost approach to value, 218–219, 221
depreciation of, 59–60, 90, 113
development and, 90, 113–116
(*See also* Development)
effects of external change on, 71–73
existing structures and, 92
goals attainable with, 45
highest and best use of, 177–180, 182
inflation and, 70
leases for, 114
ground leases, 60, 76, 87, 115, 116,
278
market analysis of, 287
mortgage loans for, 59
purchase money loans, 259
undeveloped (*see* Undeveloped land)
Land planners, 147
Land residual technique, 219, 381
Land-to-building ratio, 60–61, 381
Land use, capital appreciation and
potential for, 89
Landmarks, renovation of, 61, 90
Landscape architects, 147
Large-scale property, advantages and
disadvantages of, 93–94
Laws:
antidiscrimination, 360

Laws (*Cont.*):
  building codes, 136, 169, 187
  environmental protection statutes,
    94, 136, 169
  (*See also* Zoning)
Lawyers, 65
  role of, when investing for tax shelter,
    63
  and selection of ownerships, 122, 128,
    129
  services of, in general, 135, 138,
    145–146
Layering of objectives, 273–275, 381
Leasehold, 339, 344–345, 381
Leasehold financing, 264–268, 381
Leasehold interest, 76–77, 187, 221,
  264, 360, 381
Leases, 339–361, 381
  in achievement of income goal, 49
  in apartment building financial
    feasibility analysis, 312
  changes that may affect, 341–342
  cost-of-living clause in, 55, 70, 76,
    349, 376
  escalation clause in, 53–54, 105,
    108, 348–349, 379
  industrial, 111
    cost-of-living clause in, 55
  land, 114
    ground leases, 60, 76, 87, 115, 116,
      278
  lawyers in drafting of, 137
  major clauses, 343–361
    access clause, 358
    alteration, addition, and/or
      improvement clauses,
      345–346
    assignments and subletting clause,
      351–352
    association clause, 356–357
    construction or renovation
      clauses, 345
    date of lease and parties, 344
    destruction of property clause, 357
    eminent domain, 357
    insurance clause, 354
    maintenance and repairs clause,
      354–355
    miscellaneous, 359–361
    notice clause, 357–358
    options clause, 350–351

Leases, major clauses (*Cont.*):
    property description, 344–345
    recordkeeping clause, 350
    remedies for default clause, 358
    rent clause, 348–349
    security deposits, 359
    signs clause, 355–356
    subordination clause, 358
    surrender clause, 359
    term, 346–348
    type of business clause, 352
    use of premises clause, 353
    utilities clause, 353–354
  office building, 108
  pre-leasing, 68
  rent increases with, to minimize
    increased operating expenses, 53
  residential real estate, 100–101
  retail real estate, 105
  in shopping center financial
    feasibility analysis, 321–323
  short-term, land, 114
  for special purpose real estate, 117
  (*See also* Net leases)
Leasing agents, 147
Legal counsel (*see* Lawyers)
Legal rights (intangible rights), 183–184
Lending officers, 147
Lessee, 339, 381
Lessor, 339, 381
Leverage, 231–234, 267, 381
  dangers of, 255–257
    table, 256
  table, 233
Liability, 381
  ownership choices and, 121
    corporations, 129
    partnerships, 127
    sole proprietorships, 123–124
  (*See also* Personal debt and
    operating liabilities)
Life cycle of real estate, 153–163, 175
Limited partnerships (and partners),
  125–128, 364, 382
  corporations compared with, 131
  liquidity through, 28
Liquidity, 4–5, 382
  of apartment buildings, 103–104
  development and, 29
  devices providing more, 28
  of industrial real estate, 113

Liquidity (*Cont.*):
  of land, 116
  of office buildings, 110
  as parameter of investor profile,
    13–16, 21–22, 36
  of residential real estate, 103–104
  of retail real estate, 107
  risk and, 27–28
  of special purpose real estate,
    118–119
Loan-to-value ratio, 59, 225–226, 255,
    382
  in income approach to market value,
    225
  on leaseholds, 265
  for special purpose real estate, 118
  for unimproved land, 67, 116
  (*See also* Capitalization rate)
Loans:
  construction (*see* Construction loans)
  effects of inflation and deflation on
    repayment of, 69, 70
  personal, 27, 237
  (*See also* Borrowing; Financing;
    Mortgage Loans)
Local taxes as restriction on supply,
    169
Location:
  as function of demand, 168
  of industrial real estate, 111–112
  of land, 115
  of office buildings, 108–109
  of older properties, 91–92
  of residential real estate, 102
  of retail real estate, 106
  of special purpose real estate,
    117–118
Locational quotient, 295, 382
Long-term appreciation, 77–78
Long-term financing (*see* Financing)
Long-term leases, cost-of-living clause
    in, 70, 76
Losses:
  analysis of collection, in income
    approach to value, 221–222
  in partnerships, 126–128
  sensitivity to, as parameter of investor
    profile, 13, 16, 22–23
  [*See also* Real estate taxable income
    (or losses)]
Low income (moderate income)
  government housing, 61, 90

MAI (Member of the American
    Institute; appraiser professional
    designation), 142
Maintenance:
  choices, 356–366
  need for regular, 4
  on small residential real estate, 99
Maintenance and repairs clause in
    leases, 354–355
Management:
  in corporations, 131
  development and, 29, 68
  in general partnerships, 125–126
  of industrial real estate, 112
  of land, 116
  in limited partnerships, 126
  with net leases, 28
  of office buildings, 109
  as parameter of investor profile, 14,
    15, 30, 33–34, 36, 37
  of residential real estate, 102–103
  of retail real estate, 106–107
  in sole ownerships, 122, 123
  of special purpose real estate, 118
  (*See also* Control; Participation)
Market:
  analyzed, 147, 287–307, 364–365, 372
    with activity identification,
      287–291, 364
    in apartment building financial
      feasibility analysis, 312
    with demand analysis, 287,
      296–297
    with demographic description, 287,
      293–296
    with market area delineation, 287,
      291–293, 382
    of residential real estate, 299–302
    of retail real estate, 302–307
    in shopping center financial
      feasibility analysis, 320–321
    with supply analysis, 287, 297–299
  balanced, 164, 165
  national, absence of, 5
Market area delineation, market
    analysis with, 287, 291–293, 382
Market data approach to value,
    218–219, 228–229, 382
Market value, 211–214, 382–383
  appraiser's approaches to, 218–230
    cost approach, 218–221, 229, 230,
      376

Market value, appraiser's approaches
to (*Cont.*):
income approach, 221–229
market data approach, 228–229,
382
price and, 214–218
effects of different prices on, table,
217
(*See also* Prices)
Marketability studies developed by
appraisers, 142
Material costs:
and costs of new construction,
92
supply and demand and, 170–171
Member of the American Institute
(MAI; appraiser professional
designation), 142
Mix, 142, 352, 383
Mobile home parks, goals attainable
with, 45
Mobile homes, 98
Moderate (low) income government
housing, 61, 90
Moderate investor profile, 36, 37
worksheet for, 40
Money supply, 170, 246
(*See also* Financing)
Mortgage, 237, 242–245, 383
Mortgage brokers, 147
Mortgage-equity band of investment
technique, 225, 383
Mortgage forms, 238–245
Mortgage loans, 383
amortized, 248–249, 373
table, 250–251
(*See also* Financing)
for land, 59
permanent, 236, 384
reduced payments on, at times of
depression, 70
in sole proprietorships, 123–124
(*See also* Borrowing; Debt service;
Interest deductions; Interest
rates; Payments)
Mortgagee, 237, 383
Mortgagor, 237, 383
Multi-Housing News (journal), 198

National Apartment Association, 96
National Association of Home Builders,
96

National Association of Insurance
Brokers, 145
National Association of Realtors, 142,
145
National market, absence of, 5
Net income, 49, 50, 383
in apartment building financial
feasibility analysis, 315
increase in, capital appreciation and,
80
loan terms and, 247–248
reduced by increased operating
expenses, 54
in shopping center financial
feasibility analysis, 325–326
stabilized, 223, 387
in income approach to value, 221,
223–224, 227–228
Net leases, 111, 383
bond, 54, 374
liquidity through, 28
as protection against increased
operating expenses, 54–55, 349
Net worth, 19, 383
effects of sales on, 79–81
equity and, 48, 80–81
increasing, with capital appreciation,
68
as parameter of investment profile,
13, 16, 19–21
net worth statement, 20–21
New construction:
costs of, 92
depreciation on, 61
New property:
advantages of, 158–159
existing property compared with,
90–92
residential, depreciation write-offs
on, 60
Non-real estate investments, real estate
investments compared with, 2–6
Non-recourse financing, 237, 246,
383–384
Note, 238–241, 384
Notice clause in leases, 357–358

Objectives, 43–85, 372, 384
capital appreciation as, 68–82
capital turnover as, 64–68
changing, 83–84

Objectives (*Cont.*):
  combining investment parameters
      with, 14
    (*See also* Investment profile,
        parameters of)
  income as, 43–46, 49–58, 64
    table, 53
    (*See also* Income; Income
        production)
  layering of, 273–275, 381
  and ownership choices, 121
    (*See also* Ownership choices)
  tax shelter as (*see* Tax shelter)
  worksheet for selection of, 85
Obsolescence, 220–223
  economic, 220–221, 378
  functional, 52, 220, 222–223, 379
Office buildings:
  adaptability of, 52
  construction costs for, 179
  depreciation write-offs on, 60
  goals attainable with, 45
  highest and best use principle applied
      to, 179
  passing on increases in operating
      expenses with, 54
  selecting, 87, 88, 90, 92–94
  substitution of, 174
Older structures (existing structures):
  cost approach to value of, 229
  depreciation on, 60–61
  new structures compared with,
      90–92
  selecting, 90–92
150% declining balance, 60
Operating expenses:
  and acquisitions for capital turnover,
      67
  analysis of, in income approach to
      value, 222–223
  in apartment building financial
      feasibility analysis, 315–316
    worksheet for, 316
  on improved property, 5–6
  with large-scale property, 93–94
  protection against increasing, 52–54
    table, 53
  reducing rents in proportion to, in
      deflationary periods, 70
  in shopping center financial
      feasibility analysis, 325
    worksheet for, 326, 335

Operating expenses (*Cont.*):
  tenant's responsibility for, 342–343
Operating liability (*see* Personal debt
    and operating liabilities)
Opportunities:
  identifying, 191–210, 364, 372
    case studies, 199–210
Options in leases, 350–351
Organization fees for limited
    partnerships, 127–128
Overages, 55, 105, 322, 348, 384
Overimprovement, 177–180, 182, 384
Oversupply, 164–169, 298, 384
  capital gains and, 169
  creation of, 166–167
  effects of, on effective demand, 165
Owner-managed property, productivity
    of, 34
Owner-occupied property:
  downpayments on, 247
  motivation to acquire, 274–283
    mixed motivation, 278–283
  (*See also* Homeownership; Users)
Ownership choices, 121–134
  corporations, 121, 129–131, 376
  partnerships, 35, 121, 124–129, 363,
      384
    general, 125, 128, 379
    limited, 125–128, 364, 382
      corporations compared with,
          131
      liquidity through, 28
  sole proprietorships, 121–124, 364,
      387
  worksheet for, 132–134

Parameters of investment profile (*see*
    Investment profile, parameters of)
Parking lots, 72, 75
Participation:
  control and, 34, 35
  as parameter of investment profile,
      14, 15, 30–32, 36, 37
Participation requirements of lenders,
    234–235, 384
Parties to a lease, 344
Partnerships, 35, 121, 124–129, 363, 384
  general, 125, 128, 379
  limited, 125–128, 364, 382
    corporations compared with, 131
    liquidity through, 28

Payments, mortgage:
  level constant payment plan, table, 269
  prepayment penalties, 262, 385
  reduced at times of depression, 70
Percentage clause, 55, 105, 322, 348, 384
Permanent mortgage loan, 236, 384
Personal debt and operating liabilities:
  in corporations, 130
  in general partnerships, 126
  in limited partnerships, 127
  in sole ownerships, 123
Personal loans, 27, 237
Physical rights (tangible rights), 183–184
Points, 234, 255, 262, 385
Pre-leasing, 68
Prepayment penalties, 262, 385
Prices, 214–218, 385
  effects of different, table, 217
  of owner-occupied property, 277, 279–280
Prime rate, 266, 385
Principal, 50, 248–249, 385
Private partnerships, 128–129
Productive forces:
  in real estate, 181–182
  (*See also* Improvements; Investors; Labor; Land)
Professional costs, 137
  (*See also* Commissions; Fees)
Professional publications, 198
Profits:
  with capital turnover, 68
    (*See also* Capital turnover)
  created by shopping centers, 160–161
  in general partnerships, 126
  in limited partnerships, 127–128
  net income vs., 50
    (*See also* Net income)
  in partnerships, 125
  in sole ownerships, 123
  supply and demand and, 166–169
    (*See also* Supply and demand)
  (*See also* Returns; Yield)
Property, 46–47, 386
  (*See also specific types of property*)
Property description:
  in apartment building financial feasibility analysis, 312
  in leases, 344–345

Property description (*Cont.*):
  in shopping center financial feasibility analysis, 320
Public partnerships, 128–129
Public relations specialists, 147
Purchase money mortgage, 258–260, 366, 386

Quality and durability of income:
  and ability to repay, 235
  from industrial real estate, 111
  from land, 115
  from office buildings, 108
  from residential real estate, 101–102
  from retail real estate, 105–106
  risk/yield and, 50–58
  from special purpose real estate, 117

Real estate, 153, 386
  human activity and, 2, 191–210
    case studies, 199–210
  intrinsic value of, 2, 69
Real estate brokers, 135, 136, 138, 143–145, 363–365
Real estate economists, 147
Real estate investments:
  advantages of, 1–4
  disadvantages of, 4–6
  key investment comparisons, table, 7–9
  putting together all elements of, 363–372
  (*See also specific types of real estate investments*)
Real estate taxable income (or losses), 49–50
  in apartment building financial feasibility analysis, 318–320
  in shopping center financial feasibility analysis, 331–333
Recapture of investment, 178, 223, 226, 229
  (*See also* Depreciation recapture)
Recessions (*see* Depressions; Inflation)
Recordkeeping clause in leases, 350
Redevelopment, 159–160
Refinancing, 81, 371, 386
  balloon payments met through, 258
  second mortgage vs., 260–262
    table, 261

Rehabilitation:
  depreciation and, 61
  (*See also* Renovation)
Remedies for default clause in leases,
  358
Renovation, 159, 174, 363–365
  capital turnover and, 66
  of historic landmarks, 61, 90
  (*See also* Improvements)
Renovation clause in leases, 345
Rent:
  contract, 221, 264, 322, 346, 376
  economic, 221, 264, 322, 346, 378
  in existing structures, 92
  tenant quality and, 94, 96
  (*See also* Gross income)
Rent clause in leases, 348–349
Rent controls, 99
Reproduction costs, 218–219, 386
Residential Member (RM; appraiser
  professional designation), 142
Residential real estate:
  commercial property transformed
    into, 174
  depreciation on, 60, 61
  in depressions, 70–71
  desirability of, 87–88
  goals attainable with, 45
  industrial property transformed into,
    65
  leases for, 100–101
  market analysis of, 299–302
  over the water, 168
  prices of, 279–280
  qualities required of, to generate
    immediate income, 88–89
  quality and durability of income
    from, 101–102
  range of substitution with, 172–174
  selecting, 87, 88, 90, 93–95, 97–104
  tax shelter with new, 158–159
  (*See also specific types of residential real
    estate*)
Residual, 75, 361, 386
  building residual technique,224,
    374
  land residual technique, 219, 381
Retail real estate:
  changes in functional utility of,
    52
  depreciation write-offs on, 60
  goals attainable with, 45

Retail real estate (*Cont.*):
  market analysis of, 302–307
  passing on increases in operating
    expenses with, 54
  selecting, 87, 88, 90, 104–107
  (*See also* Commercial real estate;
    Shopping centers)
Retirement communities, 157
Return on and of, 27, 56, 386
Returns:
  total, 388
  (*See also* Profits; Yield)
Reverse leverage, 255–257, 386
  table, 256
Reversion, 386
Rights:
  bundle of, 153, 183–190, 374
  governmental, 186–187, 357
  priorities of, 186–188, 225–226
Risk/yield:
  comparative, 87–88
  with improved real estate, 59
  and income streams, 55–57
  as parameter of investment profile,
    13–16, 26–29, 36
  and quality and durability of income,
    50–58
  (*See also* Risks; Yield)
Risks, 386
  in capital appreciation, 72, 73
  in capital turnover, 67–68
  of development, 28–29, 158
  insurance against major, to establish
    liquidity level, 22
  of investing for tax shelter, 63
  involved in all investments, 14
  in partnerships, 125
  in sole ownerships, 123–124
RM (Residential Member; appraiser
  professional designation), 142

Sale-leasebacks, 360–361
Sales, 5
  accelerated depreciation and, 61
  approach of oversupply as time to
    sell, 165
  comparable, 218–219, 228, 375
  contract, 376
  equity and, 48, 80–81
  forced, 213–214
  gross, 379

Sales (*Cont.*):
  home, 280
  installment, 259, 260, 380
Sandwich position, 265, 351, 366– 367, 387
Scrap value, 211
Second mortgage loans (*see* Junior mortgage loans)
Securing a loan, 237
Security:
  control and, 35
  need for, as parameter of investment profile, 13– 16, 24– 26, 36
Security deposits, 359
Selection, 87– 119, 299
  of industrial real estate, 87, 88, 90, 93, 110– 113
  of land, 113– 116
  of office buildings, 87, 88, 90, 92– 94, 107– 110
  of residential real estate, 87, 88, 90, 93– 95, 97– 104
  of retail real estate, 87, 88, 90, 104– 107
  selection worksheet, 119
  of special purpose real estate, 87, 90, 94, 116– 119
Sellers, actual and average, 212, 213
Senior Real Estate Analyst (SREA), 142
Senior Real Property Appraiser (SRPA), 142
Senior Residential Appraiser (SRA), 142
Shift-share analysis, 296, 387
Shopping Center Digest (journal), 198
Shopping Center World (journal), 198
Shopping centers, 208
  adaptability of, 52
  capital appreciation with, 79– 80
  effects of, on real estate trends, 160, 161
  financial feasibility analysis for, 310, 320– 333
  worksheets for, 324, 326– 328
  goals attainable with, 45
  profits created by, 160– 161
  selecting, 87, 92– 94, 105
Short-term construction loans:
  for capital turnover, 67
  interest-only payments as, 258
Short-term financing, 235, 387
  (*See also* Financing)

Short-term leases:
  on land, 114
  rent increases on, to minimize increased operating expenses, 53, 346– 347
  risks involved with, 28
Sign clause in leases, 355– 356
Single family homes, 98– 99
  financing and liquidity of, 103– 104
  market data approach to value of, 229
Site planners (and engineers), 147
Site share, 299, 306, 387
Size of property, 93– 95
  industrial, 110– 111
  land, 114
  office buildings, 108
  residential, 97– 100
  retail, 104– 105
  special purpose, 117
SMSA (Standard Metropolitan Statistical Area), 295
Society of Industrial Realtors, 145
Society of Real Estate Appraisers, 142
Soils engineers, 147
Sole proprietorships, 121– 124, 364, 387
Special purpose real estate
  approach to value of, 229
  financing, 90, 118
  functional obsolescence problem with, 52
  goals attainable with, 45
  limited adaptability of, 52
  risks attached to, 88
  selecting, 87, 90, 94, 116– 119
SRA (Senior Residential Appraiser), 142
SREA (Senior Real Estate Analyst), 142
SRPA (Senior Real Property Appraiser), 142
Stabilized net income, 223, 309, 387
  in income approach to value, 221, 223– 224, 227– 228
Standard Metropolitan Statistical Area (SMSA), 295
Stores (*see* Retail real estate; Shopping centers)
Straight-line method of depreciation, 60– 62, 387, 391
Subletting clause in leases, 351– 352
Subordination, 186– 187, 259– 260, 265, 387
Subordination clause in leases, 358

Substitution, principle of, 172–174, 181, 385
Sum-of-the-years digits method of accelerated depreciation, 60, 387–388, 393
Supply:
  money, 170, 246
  real estate: aggregate, 297–298, 373
    market analysis with analysis of, 287, 297–299
    substitution and creation of new, 173
Supply and demand, 164–172, 369–371, 385–386
  market value and, 213
  principle of, 164–172
  and test of highest and best use, 180
Surrender clause in leases, 359
Surveyors, 147
Sweat equity, 124, 366, 388

Tangible rights (physical rights), 183–184
Tax deferral, 63
Tax Reform Act (1976), 77
Tax shelter, 1, 43, 44, 46, 58–64, 90, 388
  actual buyers interested in, 212
  capital gains as, 62
  (*See also* Capital gains)
  depreciation write-offs as, 46, 59–62
  (*See also* Depreciation write-offs)
  homeownership and, 280
  interest deductions as, 46, 58–59
  (*See also* Interest deductions)
  new property and, 158–159
  single family homes and, 99
Taxable income, real estate, 49–50
  in apartment building financial feasibility analysis, 318–320
  in shopping center financial feasibility analysis, 331–333
Taxable value, 211
Taxation:
  of capital gains, 77–79
    post-1976, 77
    reduced with installment sales, 259, 260
  of corporations, 130
  dividend, 62, 130
  earned income, 62

Taxation (*Cont.*):
  of general partnerships, 126
  interest income, 62
  in limited partnerships, 128
  local, as restriction to supply, 169
  of sole proprietorships, 123
"Taxpayer," 75, 195
Technological changes:
  effects of, on supply and demand, 168
  utility changes and, 52
Tenant credit:
  financeability and, 90
  ground leases and, 115, 116
  liquidity of special purpose real estate and, 118
  relation between risk and, 27–29
  and rent on industrial property, 111
  table, 82
  tenants as credit risk, 50–51
Tenants, 283–284
  quality of: capital appreciation and, 75
    effects of, during depressions, 70–71
    rents and, 94, 96
    (*See also* Rent)
    turnover of, affecting quality of income, 101
Terminology, 373–389
  regional variations in, 46
Termite inspectors, 147
Terms, 388
  of financing (*see* Constant; Downpayments)
  of investments, 13, 29–31, 36
  of leases, 165, 346–348
Total return, 56, 371, 388
Traffic engineers, 147
Trends of real estate, life cycle and, 153–163, 175
Turnover of tenants affecting quality of income, 101
200% declining balance method of accelerated depreciation, 60, 392

Underimprovement, 178, 181–182, 388
Undersupply, 164, 298, 388
  and acquisitions for capital turnover, 165
  effects of, on effective demand, 165–166

Undeveloped land, 115, 116
  capital appreciation and, 113
  capital turnover and, 113, 157–158, 216
    development and, 65, 67
    and prices paid, 216
  holding expenses on, 5, 113, 115
Use:
  capital appreciation and multiplicity of, 73–75
  capital turnover and changes in, 65–66
  effects of economic obsolescence on, 220–221
  highest and best, 177–182, 385
  prices and, 214–215
  rights affecting, 188
Use of premises clause in leases, 353
Use real estate, 275–278, 388
Use value, 211
Users, 388
  developing user profile, 284–285
  prices paid by, as opposed to investors, 214–216
  (*See also* Owner-occupied property)
Utilities clause in leases, 353–354

Vacancies:
  in apartment building financial feasibility analysis, 314
  frictional, 164
  in income approach to value, 221, 222
  in shopping center financial feasibility analysis, 323, 325
Vacation homes, 88, 281–282
Value:
  in apartment building financial feasibility analysis, 318
  creation of: examples of, 57–58
    through financing, 232
  intrinsic, 2, 69
  (*See also* Market value)

Variable rate mortgage loans, 265–266, 389
Venturous investor profile, 36, 37, 389
  worksheet for, 39

Wealth:
  experience and, 95–96
  (*See also* Net worth)
Working capital:
  capital turnover and, 65, 67, 68
  in partnerships, 124–125
Wraparound mortgage loans, 262–264, 389
  table, 264

Yield, 27, 389
  actual determination of, at time of disposition, 56, 229–230, 371
  capital appreciation and, 79–80
  comparative, 50–58, 87–88
  constant and, 252, 254
  as dependent on supply and demand, 165
  effects of lender's participation requirements on, 235
  effects of leverage on, 231, 232
  importance of, 371
  in income approach to value, 224
  prices and, 214–215
  reverse leverage and, 256–257
  rights and, 187–189
  (*See also* Risk/yield)

Zoning, 187
  changes in, 72
    capital appreciation and, 75
    capital turnover and, 64–65
    land investments and, 115
  changes promoted by, 175
  conformity and, 176–177
  as restriction to supply, 169